The Best Things to Do in LOS ANGELES

1001 IDEAS

The Best Things to Do *in* LOS ANGELES

1001 IDEAS

By Joy Yoon

UNIVERSE PUBLISHING
A Division of
Rizzoli International Publications, Inc.

First published in the United States of America in 2013
by Universe Publishing,
A Division of Rizzoli International Publications, Inc.
300 Park Avenue South
New York, NY 10010
www.rizzoliusa.com

2013 2014 2015 2016 / 10 9 8 7 6 5 4 3 2 1

Distributed in the U.S. trade by Random House, New York

Printed in the United States of America

ISBN-13: 978-0-7893-2257-9

Library of Congress Catalog Control Number: 2013935347

DEDICATION

To my parents, who gave me my first taste of all the great things Los Angeles has to offer; my sisters and brothers, who continue to explore with me; my dearest friends and family, who trust my suggestions; Jeff Chang for all his guidance; Mason, Henry, Cassius, Lucea, Arto and Ella, the children who will continue to discover new and exciting things about this city as they grow older; and Simon, who is yet to see all the best things—but now we have a lifetime to share them together.

TABLE OF CONTENTS

ACKNOWLEDGMENTS

First thanks go to the people at Universe who trusted me with this book: Jacob Lehman and Charles Miers. A special thanks goes to Jacob, my editor, for helping me persevere through this wonderful but arduous project with patience and encouragement. I'd also like to thank the copyeditors and researchers for all their hard work.

I would especially like to thank my expert contributors—Michael "Flea" Balzary, Shaniqwa Jarvis, Albert Yeh, Gary Baseman, Paul Mittleman, Sasha Spielberg, Mike Sonksen, Grace Yoon, Ludo Lefebvre, Michael Leon, Jenni Tarma, and Kristen Burke—for their expertise, generosity, and enthusiasm when I contacted them (hunted them down while on tour, interrupted them mid-semester, distracted them between shows) about contributing to this book. And an extra thank you to Jason 71.

Thanks to those who visited and promised to visit—Fraser, Katherine, Celia, Daniel, Mai, Alex, Maya, Bradford and Kerry Ann. The fear of you coming without the best things ready for your arrival helped me work on this book that much harder.

Finally, I'd like to thank all of the people—friends, family members, acquaintances, and a few I've never met—who shared their personal lists of bests with me over the last three years. Your tips were invaluable, and through them I discovered many more wonderful things than I already knew about Los Angeles. There are too many to name, but you know who you are, and your suggestions can be found throughout this book. Enjoy.

INTRODUCTION

Los Angeles is more than just a city, it's the ultimate playground, a mishmash of neighborhoods, people, and different ways of life wedged in between an ocean, mountain ranges, rivers, lakes, and national parks. It is home to some of the world's best art and culture, it is America's capital of street food, and it is an international icon of glitz and glamour. Yes, there's plenty to do here—in fact, too much to do. And with so much happening across so many areas, it's no small feat trying to get your head around what's on offer and navigating your way around the city to find it all. Among all the possible things that one can do—including all the hidden treats to be found in the city's many nooks and crannies—there are, of course, some that will capture the imagination more than others. In *The Best Things to Do in Los Angeles*, I've done the hard part for you and plotted out the most brilliant points on this conceptual map of the city.

Writing a guidebook on the place I call home has been a genuine eye-opener. Identifying things to do was the easy part, but narrowing those down to the very best was the hard part. I was born and raised in Los Angeles, and I have long been aware of the riches this city holds—amazing museums, historic landmarks, glamorous avenues full of shopping havens, restaurants galore, and, of course, the very epicenter of cinema, Hollywood, just around the corner; and I have appreciated them as best I could. But despite it all, great treasures alone do not "best things" make. Like an incredible meal, it's the quality of the overall experience that propels something from merely "good" into the realm of the spectacularly unforgettable. In Los Angeles, there are plenty of the latter to be enjoyed, and more than many visitors or even Angelenos could have ever imagined. In this book, I have drawn from years of observation and participation (a lifetime of unintentional research) to present unique angles on the very best experiences the city has to offer. I also tried to be as open-minded as possible, which meant venturing outside of my comfort zone and not just including the obvious. Competition was stiff and certain things did not make the cut, regardless of their fame or reputation. Instead of just visiting the Walk of Fame, take a guided star tour. Why just go see a movie when, before you watch a film, you can size up your hand- and footprints against those of the stars that have graced the silver screen at Grauman's Chinese Theater?

Los Angeles is huge. The size of the city itself is undeniably intimidating, particularly to first-time visitors. I've spent over three decades exploring different parts, from fishing trips to Redondo Beach when I was just two years old to weekly trips to the Central Library; from eating at Clifton's Cafeteria to wandering around downtown with my father, perfecting my breaststroke at the pool of the famous Ambassador Hotel (sadly demolished), and casting my gaze over the city from the Griffith Park Observatory. Looking back, these things are still as special now as they were back then, if not more so. Then there were the things I've always wanted to do but never had the chance, things that writing this book allowed me to do. And my contributors—many of whom I'm fortunate to count among my friends—helped fuel my love for this city even more because of the breadth of their knowledge and enthusiasm. Their insight was a blessing and it encouraged me to continue to explore and hunt down even more treasured tidbits to add to what seemed like an endless list.

This project went from being a Sisyphus- to Sir Edmund Hillary–like experience. After hundreds of hours working to push this book up my insurmountable hill, I finally made it and reached the top. And though it would seem that I would be content with all that I have discovered after writing a book about Los Angeles, it has only reignited my love and passion for this city and I continue to search for secrets yet to be revealed. I hope you have as much fun as I did discovering the best things to do here—and find a few new ones of your very own.

HOW TO USE THIS BOOK

In the spirit of this book's east-coast cousin, this is intended to be both inspirational and informative. It's a guidebook, yes—but it's a guidebook that makes the pleasure of discovering and getting to know a wonderful city its priority, and just happens along the way to arm you with the know-how to do so. More than a regular guidebook, it's intended to cut through the obvious and leave the mundane behind, like so much dust in the trail of your car as you cruise down the Pacific Coast Highway. Instead it aims to open your eyes to the things that make Los Angeles such a truly spectacular and unique metropolis.

Where most guidebooks tackle a place one location or activity at a time, the approach of this book is different. In keeping with the diversity and breadth of such a large and cosmopolitan city, the book is organized by theme, and lists ideas for things to do within each theme in no particular order. Each entry may be numbered, but none is ranked—the objective here was not to raise one aspect of L.A. life over another, but rather to sift through the wealth of experiences on offer and make a catalogue of the very greatest.

There are "Classics" in the first chapter, which include trips to the city's icons and explorations of the legends that have made the city so famous around the world. There are heights to scale and vantage points to find in "Views and Sights," and treasures hidden in plain sight in "On the Street." There are within these pages the very best recommendations for exploring the city's staggering parks and surrounding landscapes; for shopping, eating, and drinking to your heart's, belly's, or wallet's content; and tips for improving your L.A. self, either with classes and spas or just through exposure to the city's amazing repertoire of cultural institutions. And there are some things that are just, well—L.A. Alongside your author's favorites, there are personal lists of great things about the city put together by some of its most expert and distinguished inhabitants.

And where most guidebooks are for visitors, and often for travelers who may have come from afar to see a place for the very first time, this book is intended to be as valuable to the lifelong local as to the excited tourist. On one level, your author's research for this book involved many months of scouring the streets for the best places to go, racking the minds of the city's experts in one thing or another, and canvasing friends, family, and old-fashioned popular opinion for the features and destinations that a book like this just had to include. But on another level, your author's research for this book has taken more than thirty years, and has involved the slow and intuitive development of the kind of intimate knowledge and affectionate curiosity for the city only a true Angeleno can have. She hopes you make the most of that knowledge, and acquire some affection for the place yourself.

And finally, a note on directions. As anybody will know who's ever been to Los Angeles—or read about it, or seen photographs of it, or watched it roll by as the scenery in a movie—it is a motorist's city. (See chapter 9 for the prime examples and finest exceptions to this notion.) Celebrated in pop art as the city of gas stations and freeways, and in cinema as the city of traffic and car chases, it is in reality an accessible and approachable city, with an efficient and often overlooked public transit system—and with more potential for walking and cycling than most people give it credit for. In this age of GPS and the Internet, I've opted to list each entry's address, plain and simple, and will trust the reader to do the necessary research online or by phone to figure out the best way to get there. While I encourage anyone in Los Angeles, whether newcomer or old-timer, to explore as much and as far on foot, or on bicycle, or by means of public transportation, I recommend that anybody intent on spending time here have access to a car. Perhaps the most useful tip an Angeleno can give is to say that it pays before any trip to be sure of the best route, and to understand what the parking situation will be when you get there.

CHAPTER 1

The Classics

Finding the best things to do in any city seems easy enough—just a simple Google search and off you go. But when you take a minute to define what really is "the best," it's a lot harder than you think. When it comes to a metropolis as big and expansive as Los Angeles, finding something to do isn't the issue, it's figuring out where to start.

Although we tend to focus on what's in front of us—celebrities, palm trees, and sunshine—Los Angeles is more than just something you've seen on TV or in a movie; it's full of character and has a life all of its own. From the big and the bold like the Hollywood Sign to the small and relatively unknown like HMS *Bounty*, true classics share top billing and are among L.A.'s greatest assets.

So many destinations in this city have an eclectic and rich history that has chronicled and shaped L.A.'s landscape. Bursting with untold secrets and treasured relics, the classics in this chapter are representations of not only the present, but also the past. Legendary haunts, locations of famous events, and some spots off the beaten path embody the very essence of L.A. Whether it's riding on a funicular railway that's been around since 1901, admiring a Craftsman-style home built with no nails, or walking along the same cobblestone streets as the city's first settlers, going to all these places is definitely worth the effort.

Unfortunately, some icons have had their swan songs, and the fat lady has exited stage left. Places like the Ambassador Hotel (a former haunt of the rich and famous and site of Robert F. Kennedy's assassination), The Brown Derby (the celebrity watering hole during the golden age of cinema), and others have made way for new developments and ceded their status to icons of a new generation. But the classics that survive to this day deserve an entry here—they are so much a part of the history of this city—alongside the places that continue to shape L.A.'s character and reputation today.

1. See Los Angeles's answer to the blue plaques of Europe at the **Hollywood Walk of Fame.**

The Walk of Fame's terrazzo and brass stars lure tourists and locals alike to Hollywood Boulevard, with all the power of the sirens in Homer's *Odyssey*. Every year approximately ten million visitors heed their call and come to see the stars, walk alongside them, and, like a rite of passage, seek out their favorite star among more than 2,400 that are spread out along 15 city blocks. The Walk of Fame was created in the early 1950s to capture the essence of Hollywood glamour; since then famous individuals have been awarded a star for their roles in any of five categories: radio, theater, film, television, and music (with some earning multiple honors). The only person to have attained all five was Gene Autry. In order to get a star of his or her own, a notable personality must first be nominated and agree to their nomination (Julia Roberts has declined several times). Once agreed, a simple fee of $30,000 and a mandatory appearance at the unveiling cements their place in Walk-of-Fame history. There have been some remarkable exceptions over the years: fictional stars like Donald Duck, the Simpsons, and Woody Woodpecker have received honors, and the astronauts of Apollo XI were commemorated not with stars but with four identical circular terrazzo and brass moons on the corner of Hollywood and Vine. Don't know where to begin? Head to Grauman's Chinese Theatre, say hello to Michael Jackson's star, and take it from there. ***HOLLYWOOD BOULEVARD FROM LA BREA AVENUE TO GOWER STREET, AND VINE STREET BETWEEN SUNSET BOULEVARD AND YUCCA STREET. 323-469-8311. Michael Jackson's star is located at 6927 Hollywood Boulevard, in front of Grauman's Chinese Theatre. www.hollywoodchamber.net. To help find your favorite star, an official Hollywood Walk of Fame iPhone app is available for download from the Apple store.***

→ ***DID YOU KNOW?*** *As an entertainment family, the Barrymores have the most stars on the Walk of Fame.*

2. Hooray for **Hollywoodland!**

Drive north along Beachwood Drive toward the hills and you'll soon notice two towering stone gates welcoming you to Hollywoodland—a place that no longer exists. If by chance you happen to miss those markers, you definitely won't miss the emblematic structure that resides above them—it's the Hollywood Sign on top of Mount Lee. Trying to imagine Los Angeles without it is as strange as picturing Paris without the Eiffel Tower, or New York without the Empire State Building. But in 2010 that nightmare almost became a reality when developers who had bought the land beneath the sign threatened to destroy it unless the city bought its protection for the tidy sum of $22 million. It was an ironic ransom, given that the Hollywood sign (which originally read "Hollywoodland") was erected in 1923 merely as a sales gimmick for a residential development project funded by the publisher of *The Los Angeles Times*, Harry Chandler. With each steel letter measuring 50 feet tall and 30 feet wide, the original sign ran more than 450 feet long and was lit with 4,000 light bulbs, before it, with the housing development, was abandoned. In the decades that followed the Hollywoodland failure, the sign fell into disrepair, but it was restored in 1949 by the Hollywood Chamber of Commerce. During those repairs the "land" part of the sign was omitted—and so an icon was born. More than sixty years later, a few days before the threatened demolition would begin, one of the city's most famous residents stepped in with a multi-million dollar offer and bought the land back, ensuring the sign's safety for our enjoyment today. That resident was none other than *Playboy* founder Hugh Hefner.

THE TOP OF NORTH BEACHWOOD DRIVE IN HOLLYWOOD. www.hollywoodsign.org

→ ***DID YOU KNOW?*** *Contrary to popular belief, you can't walk directly up to the sign—the land there is restricted, and trespassers can expect to come across a small fence, several security cameras with infrared detectors, a monitoring helicopter, a voice-activated warning system asking you to leave, and a fine of $283.*

---

3. Follow in a movie star's footsteps at **Grauman's Chinese Theatre**.

Where else but in L.A. do people flock to a movie theater, but not to see a movie? Sid Grauman, the consummate showman and creator of two other institutions of Los Angeles cinema—the Million Dollar and the Egyptian theaters—knew there was no better way to worship the gods and goddesses of the silver screen than by building the greatest motion picture temple of all time. More than 80 years since Grauman's opened its giant pagoda doors, it remains the Mecca of movie sites for cinephiles the world over. In 1968 it was declared a historic and cultural landmark, and it has undergone several restoration projects since. Although the commercial area built up around Grauman's is an architectural eyesore, once you step inside the forecourt this magical public space transports you to Hollywood's golden age. Here you can catch a glimpse of footprints and handprints from the likes of Harrison Ford, Rita Hayworth, Brad Pitt, and Charlie Chaplin, as well as nose-prints (Bob Hope), leg-prints (Betty Grable), and even hoof-prints (Trigger). You may never rival their fame or fortune, but at least you might boast a bigger shoe size.

6801 HOLLYWOOD BOULEVARD NEAR ORANGE DRIVE IN HOLLYWOOD. 323-461-3331. www.tclchinesetheatres.com

---

4. See where the hits were made at the **Capitol Records Building**.

Although its architect, Welton Becket, may not have intended it to resemble a stack of vinyl records on a turntable, the wide, curved awnings over the windows of each story

and the tall spike emerging from the top of the Capitol Records Building are fitting for the home of a famed music label—and one of Hollywood's most distinctive landmarks. It was here that Frank Sinatra, the Beach Boys, and David Axelrod, among countless others, recorded some of their best work. Just a glimpse of this building is enough to inspire dreams of going platinum. There are no public tours, but you can visit the lobby, see the gold records on display, and soak up a part of music history. If you're in need of additional musical nostalgia, you'll find George Harrison's, Ringo Starr's, and John Lennon's stars on the Hollywood Walk of Fame just outside.
1750 VINE STREET BETWEEN HOLLYWOOD BOULEVARD AND YUCCA STREET IN HOLLYWOOD. 323-462-6252.

→ ***DID YOU KNOW?*** *Impress your friends with your knowledge of outmoded communications by squinting at the building from a distance at night and deciphering its blinking light. In 1956, Capitol's then president Alan Livingston wanted to advertise Capitol's status as the first record company with a West Coast office by making the light atop the tower spell out "Hollywood" in Morse code. In 1992, the message was changed to read "Capitol 50" in honor of the label's fiftieth anniversary, but has since been changed back to "Hollywood."*

5. Head downtown and "check out" the **Central Library**.

Every library is a sanctuary for the written word, a monument to books, and a shrine to knowledge. But the Central Library in Downtown L.A. is much more than that. Once slated for demolition in the 1970s and nearly destroyed by arson a decade later, the home to more than two million titles and Los Angeles's most valuable rare book collections also houses an amazing selection of artwork and a surprising archive of local ephemera. Decorating its hallowed halls and eight-story atrium are depictions by Dean Cornwell of periods of California's history, a beautiful mural by Albert Herter from 1929, a frieze by Julian E. Garnsey and A.W. Parsons of Sir Walter Scott's *Ivanhoe*, and panel carvings of Robin Hood, Alice, Mother Goose, and other classic children's literary characters. While the exhibition spaces offer a rotating calendar of shows from artists and institutions as diverse as Richard Neutra, Jim Henson, and the Getty Institute, be sure to keep your eyes peeled as you explore the rest of the library so you don't miss out on the Globe Chandelier, a Golden Hand, the Sphinxes, and the Lanterns; all artworks hidden in plain sight in various locations. Often referred to as the "photo morgue," the Central Library also houses one of the largest archives of photography (somewhere in the millions) on the history of Los Angeles and Southern California. Whether you're a resident or just a visitor, you can stop in and sign up for a library card to browse, borrow books, and use the more extensive collection of databases on their website. And if you're longing for the good old days, ride the ele-

vators—designed by David Bunn—often referred to as "observation pods"—where they've recycled some of the library's seven million Dewey Decimal catalog cards in quite an original way…
630 WEST 5TH STREET BETWEEN FLOWER STREET AND GRAND AVENUE IN DOWNTOWN LOS ANGELES. 213-228-7000. www.lapl.org/branches/central-library

→ ***FACT:*** *The Central Library in Downtown L.A. is the largest public library west of the Mississippi and also is within walking distance of the tallest building west of the Mississippi—the U.S. Bank building, which is located just across the street.*

---

6. Visit the **Chateau Marmont** and see where homeless stars go to roost.

The Chateau is the most noteworthy hotel in Hollywood history. In its heyday, virtually everyone who was important in the film industry stayed or partied in this faux-French hideaway. Some stars, like John Lennon and Jim Morrison, even called it home. Conceived in the late 1920s as an expensive apartment complex, the Depression soon saw that plan unravel and the Chateau was converted into a hotel. For decades it wavered in and out of Hollywood fashion until it found salvation with its current owner, the famed hotelier André Balazs. While the hotel itself has survived everything from five major earthquakes to Led Zeppelin crashing their motorcycles into the lobby, many of its notable guests have been less fortunate… Jim Morrison nearly killed himself swinging in through the window of his room, John Belushi overdosed in Bungalow 2, and Helmut Newton died of a heart attack after a car crash in the forecourt. Today, Hollywood's elite still comes to find a little peace and quiet from the paparazzi within its walls—and so can you. Whether you're renting a room, grabbing a bite to eat, stopping by for a nightcap, or hoping "accidentally" to bump into your favorite actor, you'll get a real taste of Hollywood at the Chateau. If you find renting a room here a bit out of your price range, the Bar Marmont just down the hill offers a small taste of the Chateau lifestyle (beautiful people in a moody atmosphere) at a much cheaper price.
8221 SUNSET BOULEVARD NEAR NORTH CRESENT HEIGHTS BOULEVARD IN LOS ANGELES. 323-656-1010. www.chateaumarmont.com

---

7. Find a little hocus pocus at the **Magic Castle**.

With the help of some friends, the television writer Milt Larsen fulfilled his late father William Larsen Sr.'s dream of establishing a club for magicians, and in 1963—*poof*—the Magic Castle was conjured out of thin air. Once a private home, the private clubhouse for the Academy of Magical Arts now works to promote public interest in and recognition of magic and magicians. Located high above Franklin Avenue and hidden within the Castle's walls is a labyrinth of nooks and crannies filled with zany artifacts and secrets to many of magic's mysteries. But the real trick is figuring out how to get inside… If you know the right people and say the right words—*abracadabra!*—all will be revealed. (It's actually "open sesame.") Once inside, you can converse with the spirit of Harry Houdini in the private séance room, catch a magic show from one of the visiting academy members, or request a song from the ghostly piano spirit. Though the chances of knowing an actual member are slim, don't fret—gaining admittance to the Castle isn't as hard as you might think. Just the tug of an ear, the flick of a wrist, the swipe of a credit card, and a reservation at the Magic Hotel adjacent to the club can be yours—and voilá, the secrets of magic will be revealed in no time.

7001 FRANKLIN AVENUE NEAR NORTH ORANGE DRIVE IN LOS ANGELES. 323-851-3313. www.magiccastle.com

8. See the palace of puppets at the **Bob Baker Marionette Theater**.

Founded in 1963 by puppeteers Bob Baker and Alton Wood, the Bob Baker Marionette Theater is the oldest and the best children's theater company in Los Angeles—and reportedly the longest running in the country. Bob's passion for puppets began at the tender age of eight and continued throughout high school, when he started making his own toy marionettes. For more than 70 years he has been entertaining the children and adults of L.A. with his wonderful shows. This author's favorite is the Day of the Dead show, in which day-glo puppets fly apart and magically come back together again. Catching a show here is as essential as seeing *Punch and Judy* on the English coast and should not be missed—you can even buy your own puppet at the gift shop or online.

1345 WEST 1ST STREET NEAR GLENDALE BOULEVARD IN LOS ANGELES. 213-250-9995. www.bobbakermarionettes.com

Griffith Park

Griffith Park is the Central Park of Los Angeles—but with a lot more character and heart. Within its cracks and crevices lies a deep and rich history of the city (the park was once an ostrich farm). Had it gone up in flames in the most recent fire, which quickly consumed a vast number of its 4,210 acres (it nearly burnt down the Observatory), Los Angeles would have lost something truly great. Luckily the park still stands and with it, all the amazing things within it. Though referred to as a park, anyone who's ever been here knows it's much more. Not only is it a haven from the rush and crush of urban life, and a place to find your Zen; it's also filled with other escapes such as museums, a zoo, various trails and paths, a merry-go-round, train rides, and, to top it all off, the renovated Observatory complete with a new theater. Griffith Park is a classic many times over.

4730 CRYSTAL SPRINGS DRIVE, WEST OF GOLDEN STATE FREEWAY (I-5) BETWEEN LOS FELIZ BOULEVARD TO THE SOUTH AND VENTURA FREEWAY (SR 134) TO THE NORTH, IN LOS FELIZ. 323-913-4688. www.laparks.org

---

9. *Why walk to the top of Griffith Park when you can drive?* You don't have to break a sweat in this city to enjoy the sights. At Griffith Park, all you need to do is take a short drive up a winding hillside. Once at the top, take a deep breath and enjoy the scenic view. If you're in no rush to drive back down, take a walk along the Mount Hollywood Trail. It offers a great view of the Hollywood sign and a chance to stretch your legs.

2800 EAST OBSERVATORY ROAD IN LOS ANGELES. To take a moonlight drive, be sure to get to Griffith Park by 10:00 p.m. as entrance gates close promptly at 10:00 p.m.

---

10. *Gaze at the* real *stars from the Griffith Observatory.* The Observatory is an L.A. favorite. Closed for several years for remodeling, it reopened in 2006 with much of its celebrated Art Deco character intact. Look out into the great beyond with the public telescopes at the Samuel Oschin Planetarium, and gaze upon the astronomy exhibits. If that's not sci-fi enough, Mr. Spock from *Star Trek* has now made the Observatory his home—Trekkies can rejoice in the Leonard Nimoy Event Horizon Theater. The new 200-seat presentation theater shows films and hosts live programs and demonstrations, taking you where no man has gone before…

2800 EAST OBSERVATORY ROAD IN LOS ANGELES. 213-473-0800. www.griffithobs.org

---

11. *Chug-a-chug-a-chug into the past at the Travel Town Museum.* Operated by the Los Angeles Live Steamers, an organization devoted to letting Angelenos relive the good old days, the trains at Travel Town are a reminder of when the city's main form of transportation ran on tracks instead of asphalt. You can learn about railroad history or skip the lessons and just ride one of the three 16-inch gauge trains operating at the museum. All aboard!

5200 ZOO DRIVE IN LOS ANGELES. 323-662-5874. www.traveltown.org

---

12. *For a bigger ride, choo-choo-choose your favorite train at the Griffith Park & Southern Railroad.* No matter how old you get, there's nothing like riding on a miniature train (1/3 scale), and since 1948, people of all ages have enjoyed coming to the Griffith Park & Southern Railroad to ride their favorite. From an original Freedom Train to the Stanley Diamond to the Colonel Griffith, each of these 18.5-inch gauge trains, with tracks over a mile long, is a ride into history. For those who need more than just riding along the tracks, the SR2-V Simulator uses visuals, sounds, and hydraulic motors to give your riding experience a bit more of a kick.

4400 CRYSTAL SPRINGS DRIVE NEAR LOS FELIZ BOULEVARD IN LOS ANGELES. 323-664-6903. www.griffithparktrainrides.com

---

13. *Discover the entrance to the original Batcave at Bronson Canyon.* Bronson Canyon has been a favorite filming location for movies and television shows alike for decades. Situated in the southwest section of Griffith Park, it's known for its dramatic manmade caves, carved out of the rock in the early 1900s when the area was still a functioning quarry. Walk to the west portal and you'll find the original entrance to the den in the classic *Batman* television series. But be warned: the cave's tunnel is a lot shallower than you think—Adam West just made it look big.

3200 CANYON DRIVE IN LOS ANGELES. Park in the last parking lot on your right hand side. Once you park, take the trail on your right after leaving the parking lot. From there it's just a short hike to Bronson Canyon. 323-666-5046.

→ ***FACT:*** *The street that gave its name to Bronson Canyon also inspired the stage name of the actor Charles Bronson.*

---

14. *Hike under the glow of a full moon with the Sierra Club.* For nearly 50 years, the Sierra Club, a local crew of hikers, has been leading free evening and weekend conditioning hikes at Griffith Park every week. Meet your Sierra guide at the Merry-Go-Round and follow along as he or she takes you through the ins and outs of Griffith Park's various paths and trails. If you're feeling adventurous and ready to go out and explore, the park can become your own personal outdoor gym. Hikes usually last about two hours, and on trails with nicknames like Razor Back and Cardiac Hill, you'll definitely feel the burn. Be sure to check out the special moonlight hike that happens once a month—it's probably the most romantic test of your hiking mettle you'll ever endure. Just remember to bring a good pair of hiking shoes.

Meet at the merry-go-round: PARK CENTER, 2 miles within the park off LOS FELIZ BOULEVARD AND RIVERSIDE DRIVE. 213-387-4287. www.angeles.sierraclub.org/griffith/location.asp

15. ***Get back to nature with a meal at the Trails.*** Situated in a little log cabin on Fern Dell, the Trails is every hungry and tired park explorer's salvation. The food (vegan chili, avocado sandwiches, and fresh baked goods) is healthy and delicious, the scenery beautiful, and it's the perfect place to spend a relaxing afternoon with a friend or even solo after a trek through the park. Eating sprouts never seemed so appealing.

2333 FERN DELL DRIVE IN LOS ANGELES. 323-871-2102.
www.facebook.com/trailscafe

16. ***Go where nature and music meet at the Greek.*** Built to resemble a Greek amphitheater, and once used as barracks during the Second World War, the Greek Theater (or simply "the Greek," to locals) is the perfect place for watching concerts under the stars. During warm summer nights you can smell the trees as you listen to musicians perform under the nighttime sky. Voted the best small outdoor venue in the city several times over, the theater has been used for all manner of classical and pop concerts, a diverse program of stage shows—and even the high school graduation of your author.

2700 NORTH VERMONT AVENUE IN LOS ANGELES. 323-665-5857.
www.greektheatrela.com. If you plan on leaving anytime during the show, be sure to get there early and scope out parking on the streets near the theater or within moderate walking distance; once you're in theater parking, you're stuck there until the crowds depart.

17. ***Play Cowboys and Injuns at the Museum of the American West.*** Every child grows up watching Westerns, immersed in the idea of living in the Wild West with nothing but a trusty steed, a gun that shoots straight, and a good hat to shield your face from the hot sun. Gunslingers of all ages can relive the history of the open plains at the Museum of the American West, formerly the Autry Museum of Western Heritage, with its amazing collection of paintings, firearms, costumes, photographs, and more. Even if haven't ridden since the merry-go-round, coming here makes you wish you were, as Gene Autry sang, back in the saddle again.

4700 WESTERN HERITAGE WAY IN LOS ANGELES. 323-667-2000. www.theautry.org

18. ***Enjoy some private time at the L.A. Zoo.*** This city-owned zoo is home to more than a thousand animals from around the world, and is one of the most spacious urban zoos in the country. With habitats custom built to mimic the animals' natural environments, you'll find one of the largest troops of

chimpanzees in the U.S. at the Mahale Mountain (after the Mahale Mountains National Park in Africa), while playful orangutans swing through the bamboo of the Red Ape Rain Forest. If you're in the mood for a trip down under, the Australian section of the zoo is a paradise of eucalyptus that's home to koalas, kangaroos, and wallabies. The real treats for animal-loving Angelenos are the four days every year when the zoo allows members to explore the grounds before it opens to the public. These rare occasions are worth the membership price alone, because, strange as it sounds, there are few things as special as feeling like you're the only human in the zoo.
5333 ZOO DRIVE IN LOS ANGELES. 323-644-4200. www.lazoo.org

---

19. *Go round and round the merry-go-round.* This treasured attraction, located in Park Center, has been a go-to for families for generations. Built in 1926 by the Spillman Engineering Company and moved to Griffith Park in 1937, this merry-go-round boasts 68 finely carved horses with jewel-encrusted bridles and a Stinson Miltary Band Organ, which plays a selection of more than 1,500 marches and waltzes. No matter how old you are, you're never too old to go around.
PARK CENTER, 2 miles within the park off LOS FELIZ BOULEVARD AND RIVERSIDE DRIVE. 323-665-3051. www.laparks.org/dos/parks/griffithpk/mgr.htm

---

20. *It's always tee time on one of Griffith Park's four golf courses.* Griffith Park is so big that it encompasses not one but two 18-hole golf courses (the Harding and Wilson Municipal Golf Courses). If that's not enough, there's also a respectable 9-hole course (the Roosevelt Municipal Golf Course), and a special Par 3 (the Los Feliz Municipal Golf Course). Take that, Central Park! It's the perfect place for a quick round with friends when you don't feel like driving out of the city—and if you don't have time for a round, hit a few at the practice range to tide you over until you do.
Harding: 4730 CRYSTAL SPRINGS DRIVE IN LOS ANGELES. 323-663-2555
Wilson: 4730 CRYSTAL SPRINGS DRIVE IN LOS ANGELES. 323-663-2555. Roosevelt: 2650 NORTH VERMONT AVENUE IN LOS ANGELES. 323-665-2011. Los Feliz: 3207 LOS FELIZ BOULEVARD IN LOS ANGELES. 323-663-7758. To reserve a start time on the City golf courses, you must obtain a golf registration card, which you can acquire by calling 818-291-9980 or register at www.laparks.org/howto_tennis_golf.htm. Once you have your card you can reserve a start time 24 hours a day at www.laparks.org/golf/index.htm

→ ***FACT:*** *Colonel Griffith J. Griffith, a Welsh immigrant who made his fortune mining, donated the land for Griffith Park in 1896. In perfect Hollywood fashion, he subsequently served jail time in 1903 for getting drunk one night and shooting his wife, convinced she was conspiring with the Pope to murder him.*

21. Get a steak and a story at **Musso & Frank.**

Every Angeleno has his or her share of Hollywood stories when it comes to their favorite places. And being introduced to this classic by the actor Crispin Glover several years ago for a birthday dinner happens to be your author's. Opened in 1919, Musso & Frank, Hollywood's oldest eatery, is steeped in history like a French dip in *jus*. With its dark wood paneling and red leather booths, it's a veritable time machine. The first booth on the left as you enter from Hollywood Boulevard was Charlie Chaplin's favorite table. In its heyday, Musso's was a popular destination for movie stars, directors, producers, and some of America's greatest writers. F. Scott Fitzgerald, Charles Bukowski, William Faulkner, Raymond Chandler, and even Ernest Hemingway drank in the back room here during their screenwriting days. Saddle up to the bar and ask for Ruben, the longtime bartender, who's been here since 1967—he'll serve you one of his excellent martinis and tell you stories about Bukowski you never knew. Ruben even served Rock Hudson the week before the actor died. The East and West Rooms were a divider back in the day—studio honchos would stay in the East, while the creative rebels stayed well in the West—so choose your side wisely.

6667 HOLLYWOOD BOULEVARD NEAR CHEROKEE AVENUE IN LOS ANGELES. 323-467-7788. www.mussoandfrank.com

22. Go to play, but stay to listen, at **McCabe's Guitar Shop.**

With one of the largest collections of stringed instruments in Los Angeles, as well as thousands of books, scores, and recordings, McCabe's is a true musical treasure trove. Lessons and workshops are available, taught by a staff of dedicated and skilled instructors, and its relaxing atmosphere makes it a joy to visit. But it's what's hidden away in the back room that has people coming back time and time again: McCabe's tiny stage and the distinguished roster of those who have performed upon it secures the store a place as a definitive L.A. musical institution. McCabe's has been feeding our love of music and the written word since 1958, with intimate shows featuring the likes of Jeff Buckley, Allen Ginsberg, guitar god Les Paul, Etta James, Tom Waits, McCoy Tyner, Gil Scott-Heron, the Horace Tapscott Trio, and hundreds more. Truly one of L.A.'s last remaining music havens, let's hope McCabe's stays open as long as the city does. Check out their online events calendar for a list of upcoming performances and ticket prices.

3101 PICO BOULEVARD NEAR 31ST STREET IN SANTA MONICA. 310-828-4497. www.mccabes.com

---

23. Two wrongs make the perfect right at **Roscoe's House of Chicken and Waffles.**

The partnership may seem strange to some, but once you've had a taste of the crispy and buttery fried chicken and waffles at this unlikely culinary institution, you'll no longer question their compatibility. For more than 30 years, Roscoe's has been feeding the hungry masses—and occasionally the odd peckish superstar—in its many locations around the city. Sure, the menu has other things—but once you've tried their mainstay you won't want anything else.

1514 NORTH GOWER STREET NEAR SUNSET BOULEVARD IN LOS ANGELES. 323-466-7453 or 323-466-9329. (There are four other locations throughout the Los Angeles area.)

---

24. Boogie down at **World on Wheels.**

Before inline skating and razor scooters, before fixies and skateboards, there was roller-skating. Think hard enough and you'll remember what I'm talking about. World on Wheels, built in the 1970s, is a skating gem. Retro in feel, though seemingly unintentionally, this old-school rink—with its wooden floors, colorful murals, mood lighting, and impeccable music selection—makes you forget you're skating in a circle. It not only hosts monthly roller-skating themed parties, but for those 21 and over, there's a full bar (and Thursdays from 6:00 p.m. to 1:00 a.m. are for 25 years and older). If you're not in the mood to skate, but want to groove to the beat, there's an upstairs dance floor to enjoy—and those who want to keep their feet firmly planted on solid ground should be sure to bring a pocket full of quarters for the video game arcade. Folks who come to skate dress casually, though there are a few regulars who insist on only wearing threads from the 1970s to keep the vibe authentic. Check out their website for the weekly schedule.

4645 VENICE BOULEVARD NEAR SAN VICENTE BOULEVARD IN LOS ANGELES. 323-933-5170. www.amfworldonwheels.com

---

25. Pose with the greats at **Fox Studios.**

Off of Pico Boulevard in West Los Angeles you'll find the home of Fox Studios. Founded in 1925 by William Fox, this legendary lot was home to a star-studded cast of actors and actresses. From Shirley Temple to Betty Grable, Gregory Peck to Elizabeth Taylor, Fox's stars have long commanded the silver screen (and let's not forget its most famous star to date, the lovely Marilyn Monroe). Though Fox does not offer guided tours, one of Los Angeles's lesser-known tourist attractions is to stand in front of the studio and take

pictures with all the giant show posters they have plastered out front. Who's going to know the difference? A photo of you next to a giant *Simpsons*, *Glee*, or *New Girl* poster is all you really need to say, "Yeah, showbiz and me are like *that*."
10201 WEST PICO BOULEVARD AT MOTOR AVENUE IN CENTURY CITY. 310-369.1000. www.foxstudios.com

---

26. Find a taste of Greece at **Papa Cristo's**.

L.A.'s oldest Greek market and deli has been around for more than 60 years. This family operated storefront, more formally known as C&K Importing and run by Chrys Chrys (yes, that's his real name) after he purchased it from his father Sam in 1968, has been a hub for Los Angeles's food lovers since 1948. Short in stature but giant in heart, Chrys proudly continues his father's legacy and is something of a celebrity among local epicureans. Stocked with authentic Greek ingredients, from an array of different feta cheeses and spices to wines and olives, Papa Cristo's brings Athens to L.A. and is the perfect shopping destination for homesick Greeks, displaced Mediterraneans, and anybody with Hellenic tastes. Hungry from perusing the market shelves? Just turn a corner to the restaurant inside the shop and order from a menu bursting with Greek delicacies. Whether you indulge in a plate of Macaronia (Greek spaghetti) or feast upon some of the best lamb chops in town, always make sure you have room for their homemade Baklava; no meal is complete without it.
2771 WEST PICO BOULEVARD AT SOUTH NORMANDIE AVENUE IN LOS ANGELES. 323-737-2970. www.papacristos.com

---

27. Get lost in L.A.'s original **Farmer's Market**.

Long before the Farmer's Market on Fairfax and 3rd became a popular tourist destination, it was originally a humble dairy farm. After the farm closed, the space reopened in 1934 as a farmer's market complete with its own white wooden clock tower (the original is still standing). Today's farmer's market not only sells fresh produce but is also home to a colorful maze of food stands and kitschy stores. Among the surprising delicacies favored by the locals are a mountain of nachos with an *agua fresca* (fresh fruit water) at Loteria; Roti Paratha and Mee Goreng from Singapore's Banana Leaf; the myriad hot sauces that claim to "kick the crap" out of your insides at Light My Fire; and fresh beef jerky from Huntington Meats. Whether you're here to eat, read a book, relax, or people-watch (weekends are best for the last), there's always a seat available at one of the market's original green metal tables. If you can't seem find your way out of this labyrinth of stalls, don't worry—there are worse places to get lost in L.A.
6333 WEST 3RD STREET AT FAIRFAX AVENUE IN LOS ANGELES. 323-933-9211. www.farmersmarketla.com

Leimert Park

Leimert Park, dubbed "the black Greenwich Village" by film director and resident John Singleton, is a predominately African-American neighborhood known for its rich art heritage. The area roughly contained between Crenshaw Boulevard and Vernon Avenue, and 4th Avenue/Roxton Avenue and Rodeo Road, started out as an experiment in urban planning in 1928 when it was developed by Walter H. Leimert and designed by the Olmsted brothers to become a model community for upper- and middle-income families. After being "restricted to whites" in the 1960s, it became the home to many African Americans, such as noteworthy residents Ray Charles and Ella Fitzgerald. It became the center for a thriving arts scene in Los Angeles, and has remained strong ever since.

28. *Find your rhythm at the Leimert Park fountains.* The famed intersection of 43rd and Degnan at the south end of Leimert Park is home to the iconic steeple of the Vision Theatre, formerly the Leimert Theater (renamed in 1990 when purchased by actress Marla Gibbs), created by Walter H. Leimert and Howard Hughes. The theater, built in 1931, is a focal point of the park and an attraction in itself. But just across the street is a cascading fountain, a landmark centerpiece of the neighborhood, which is home to a drum circle that convenes every Sunday. Brave percussionists are welcome to join in and slap their skins; otherwise find a place to stretch out and let the sounds of the water and the drums carry you away.

3314 WEST 43RD STREET NEAR CRENSHAW BOULEVARD IN LOS ANGELES. 323-472-0607. www.leimertparkbeat.com

29. *Grab the mic and rhyme at Project Blowed.* Hosted by Kaos Network, and co-founded in 1994 by the rapper Aceyalone of the Freestyle Fellowship and friends, Blowed is the longest-running hip-hop open mic in the world. Held every Thursday night in an unassuming club space on Leimert Boulevard, Blowed invites MCs of all stripes and backgrounds to get up and rhyme over live beats from locally known independent DJs. Standards are generally too high for Project Blowed to fall into the hip-hop karaoke category—the founders and regular DJs are accomplished musicians, and the project has spawned successful albums highlighting fresh voices that have risen to prominence through the collective—so while all are encouraged to attend, only those confident enough to hold their own in such esteemed company should step up to the mic. Call or inquire online if you're interested in going, and once you're there remember the golden rule: no wack spitting.

4343 LEIMERT BOULEVARD BETWEEN 43RD PLACE AND LEIMERT BOULEVARD IN LOS ANGELES.323-373-8029/ 323-296-5717.

30. *Be more than a player on The World Stage.* In 1989, the late great jazz drummer Billy Higgins (who performed with Ornette Coleman) and the poet and community activist Kamau Daaood founded The World Stage. Quickly hailed as a "black cultural Mecca" by the *Los Angeles Times*, this storefront enclave evolved into a gallery, performance space, and education center that hosts creative workshops on jazz and literature and also screens films. From freestyle jazz jam sessions to specific workshops for pianists and drummers, the World Stage programs cater to those looking to expand their understanding of the art and hone their craft alongside the masters. Over the years, workshops here have been taught by such luminaries as Max Roach, Elvin Jones, and Pharoah Sanders, and the space has been home to the world renowned Anansi Writers Workshop. Whether you're coming just to watch and listen, or with your own instrument in tow to join the musicians on stage, you'll leave with your passion for creativity renewed—and a better understanding of the role music and culture has had in shaping Los Angeles. ***4344 DEGNAN BOULEVARD IN LOS ANGELES. 323-293-2451. www.theworldstage.org***

31. *Buy a book and get a story at Eso Won Bookstore.* For years, Eso Won (which takes its name from an African proverb meaning "water over rocks") has been directing the flow of literature into the African-American community of Leimert Park. Owned (and charismatically run) by James Fulgate and Thomas Hamilton, Eso Won carries an unparalleled selection of international fiction and non-fiction that documents and highlights African-American achievement. It also hosts many of the best-known African-American authors and academics in the country for readings and discussions about contemporary politics, culture, and literature. A neighborhood bookstore in every sense of the word, Eso Won draws readers of all ages and interests, and is worth going into for a conversation with the owners alone.
4327 DEGNAN BOULEVARD IN LOS ANGELES. 323-290-1048.
www.esowonbookstore.com

→ ***FACT:*** *In 1995, Eso Won hosted a book signing for a memoir written by a young activist named Barack Obama. Just over a decade later he became the first African American President of the United States.*

32. Raise a glass to Dionysus at the **San Antonio Winery**.

Though one naturally assumes that Napa Valley is the only home to California winemaking, the San Antonio Winery stands testament to Los Angeles's great past as the last remaining of more than 100 working wineries that once operated in the city. Founded by Santo Cambianca of the Riboli Family, who immigrated from Italy in the early 20th century, the winery began production in Lincoln Heights in 1917. When the industry shifted its focus to the north, Santo remained in Los Angeles but acquired prime vineyards elsewhere—so while all the vineyards in Los Angeles were built over in the name of industrialization, Santo's nearby outlying properties continued to provide enough grapes to produce handcrafted wines at the winery. Come for a visit, grab a bite, and be sure to pick up a souvenir bottle at the gift shop. After all, a trip to L.A.'s only winery is something worth toasting to.

737 LAMAR STREET IN DOWNTOWN LOS ANGELES. 323-221-7261.
www.sanantoniowinery.com

33. Wait in line for a hot dog at **Pink's**.

Founded by Paul Pink in 1939, Pink's originally started as a pushcart that sold chilidogs for a dime. More than 70 years later, its celebrity-lined walls and long winding lines are proof of Pink's enduring popularity. Although gourmet hot-dog aficionados might think they could do better elsewhere—the meat is decent but not extraordinary, and the experience is certainly more for fun than for your health—eating a Pink's is as much a rite of passage as tap-dancing on stars on the Walk of Fame. So get in line, order a stretch chili cheese, and as you sit down to devour your gut-busting grease dog, just look to the photos of celebrities smiling back at you from the wall and ask yourself: Have the Fonz and Darth Vader ever been wrong?

709 NORTH LA BREA AVENUE AT MELROSE AVENUE IN LOS ANGELES. 323-931-4223.
www.pinkshollywood.com

34. Forget it, Jake, it's **Chinatown**.

Located in downtown Los Angeles, our Chinatown is one of the first modern Chinatowns in the U.S.—and also one of the first malls. Since the 1930s, Central Plaza, the focal point of Chinatown, has been the location of a variety of different stores and restaurants, and the backdrop to a surprising number of films. With its quaint walkways, dangling red paper lanterns, and pagoda-style rooftops, Chinatown hasn't changed much over the years, and longtime staples like Hop Louie, the Grand Star Jazz Club, and the Phoenix Bakery still manage to draw crowds. In recent years Chinatown has seen an influx of young creatives and the opening of new retail and gallery spaces;

the harmonious mix of the new guard with the old keeps Chinatown alive and kicking. ***947 NORTH BROADWAY BETWEEN COLLEGE AND BERNARD STREET IN LOS ANGELES. Note: Chinatown occupies several city blocks along Broadway, so be sure to explore. www.chinatownla.com***

---

35. Discover that we're not alone at the **Mount Wilson Observatory**.

Griffith Park Observatory is a great place to see some stars, but it's no more than a pair of opera glasses compared to the Mount Wilson Observatory. Founded in 1904 by George Ellery Hale, the Mount Wilson Observatory has been a dominant fixture in the world of astronomy for more than a century, with numerous significant discoveries of distant galaxies and revelations about the sun's magnetic fields to its name. With its 60-inch Hale telescope—the largest in the world dedicated to the general public for viewings—this place not only offers every Angeleno the chance to fulfill his or her every galactic fantasy, but also an opportunity to ponder whether we really are the only ones out there...

SAN GABRIEL MOUNTAINS ABOVE PASADENA. Directions can be found on the Mount Wilson Observatory website: www.mtwilson.edu

---

36. Take a short ride to heaven on **Angel's Flight**.

For 25 cents each way, you can take a ride on this landmark funicular railway that has connected Hill Street to Bunker Hill since 1901. The railway cars rely on each other's gravitational pull to move up and down, so the cars travel in opposite directions while connected to the same haulage cable. Though the distance between Hill Street and Bunker Hill isn't that far, Angel's Flight is one of those necessary attractions every visitor has to experience. Take my advice and splurge—spend a full dollar and take a few rides, because one trip up and down just isn't enough.

350 SOUTH GRAND AVENUE THROUGH THE CALIFORNIA PLAZA WATERCOURT OR 351 SOUTH HILL STREET NEAR 3RD STREET IN DOWNTOWN LOS ANGELES ARE BOTH ENTRANCES. Tickets can be purchased at the Grand Avenue entrance. If you enter from Hill Street you can pay once you reach the top. Note: When you buy a round-trip ticket on Angel's Flight you walk away with the ultimate memento, a complimentary Angel's Flight souvenir ticket. It'll be the best 50 cents you ever spent. www.metronet/riding/maps/angels-flight/

---

37. See where kitsch and Mexicana collide at **El Coyote**.

Driving down Beverly Boulevard near Poinsettia Place, you can't help but notice a giant neon sign that silently screams, "Pull over and come to El Coyote!" With red leather booths, waitresses dressed in Mexican folk garb, and chintzy knick-knacks lining the walls, El Coyote Café's focus over its 75 years in service has clearly been less on décor and more on the important things in life—excellent guacamole and powerful margaritas. What better way to start your weekend than with some of the best salt-rimmed libations El Coyote has to offer?

7312 BEVERLY BOULEVARD BETWEEN POINSETTIA PLACE AND FULLER AVENUE IN LOS ANGELES. 323-939-2255. www.elcoyotecafe.com

---

38. Rock out at the **Troubador**.

The heavy hitters have been coming out to play on the Troubador's stage for a very long time. From the unknown to the very well known, this one-time coffee house originally on La Cienega Boulevard and now housed on Santa Monica Boulevard has seen its fair share of hit-makers like Elton John (he had his first live show in the U.S. here), Van Morrison, and Joni Mitchell grace its stage. Known primarily as a rock club (Guns 'N' Roses played their first show and were discovered here), it has been by turns a major hub for folk music, new wave and punk, and heavy metal. Its long-standing history is legendary among those who hope to perform here. And even to this day the Troubador's musical firepower has yet to diminish as musical heavyweights like Prince, Fiona Apple, and Radiohead still come to play upon its stage.

9081 SANTA MONICA BOULEVARD AT DOHENY DRIVE IN WEST HOLLYWOOD. 310-276-6168. www.troubadour.com

---

39. Breathe in the sea air aboard the **Queen Mary**.

The Queen Mary has seen its ups and downs over the years, and not just on the high seas. Between 1936 and 1967 this superliner sailed the Atlantic, before it was retired and docked in Long Beach—and although it is no longer seaworthy, you can still take a voyage aboard the Queen Mary (sans the sea-sickness). Converted into a functioning hotel, the liner is now a destination for those looking to discover the history and haunting mystery behind this famous ship—or just to enjoy a romantic getaway. Booking a room isn't strictly necessary for visitors who simply want to explore the ship or conduct their own investigation into the paranormal, but it doesn't hurt to add to the overall experience.

1126 QUEENS HIGHWAY IN LONG BEACH. Tickets for tours are available daily. 877-342-0738. www.queenmary.com

---

40. Pump iron at **Muscle Beach** in Venice.

Glistening, sweaty, hard bodies have been coming to Muscle Beach in Santa Monica to pump up in public for decades. In the 1930s acrobats, weight lifters, and gymnasts

from around the city started to congregate at a designated park area just south of the Santa Monica Pier to strut their stuff. After a media scandal rocked Santa Monica, the original location of Muscle Beach was unceremoniously bulldozed early one morning without warning, and Los Angeles's athletes soon turned to the "Weight Pen" in Venice to find their muscle-straining solace. Since its boom in 1951, Muscle Beach has been the place to get fit, lift some serious weights, and flex your pecs for the ladies. Though it's enclosed in a metal gate and only half the size of a basketball court, it still draws all types—those who work out and those who just watch. So what do you bench?
1800 OCEAN FRONT WALK IN VENICE. 310-399-2775. www.venicebeach.com

→ ***FACT:*** *Former Mr. Olympia winner Arnold Schwarzenegger and Machete himself, Danny Trejo, used to pump iron here on a regular basis.*

---

41. Catch the country's oldest football game at the **Rose Bowl**.

The first and most prestigious postseason college football game played every year is the Rose Bowl. A tradition since 1902, when the Rose Bowl was first played at Tournament Park Stadium, the game has grown into an institution for loyal Angelenos and a mecca for traveling college football fans. As the game grew in popularity, its audience outgrew its grounds at Tournament Park, and the architect Myron Hunt was commissioned to design a new stadium. Originally constructed in 1923 in the shape of a horseshoe, years of expansion saw the stadium turn slowly into a complete bowl. This National Historic Landmark, which seats more than 90,000 fans at capacity, is not only a great sports venue but also a notable one. It's hosted Olympic Events, FIFA World Cup Finals, and five Super Bowls, and was named the number one venue in college sports by *Sports Illustrated*. But the classic thing to do is to come out each year for the Rose Bowl, the "Grandaddy of them all"—the oldest bowl game in the country.
1001 ROSE BOWL DRIVE IN PASADENA. 626-577-3101. www.rosebowlstadium.com

---

42. Watch (or run!) the **Los Angeles Marathon**.

For nearly thirty years, the L.A. Marathon has stopped traffic—literally. Every year since 1986, more than 25,000 applicants have signed up to attempt the 26.2 grueling miles across Los Angeles's urban terrain, from Dodgers Stadium through Downtown L.A. to Koreatown and down toward the Santa Monica Pier. On a Sunday in mid-March, major streets are blocked off and filled with people running or walking to complete their marathon goal, all within the allotted timeframe of eight hours. First timers shouldn't worry—the L.A. Marathon is a popular place for novice runners to get their toes wet. Non-competing supporters can join your author in cheering from the sidelines, which is almost as dedicated a pastime as running itself and can afford newcomers and old

Angelenos alike an excuse to explore a new neighborhood along the route. On your marks, get set, GO!

The Los Angeles Marathon takes place mid-March every year in Los Angeles. 213-542-3000. www.lamarathon.com

---

43. Practice reading lips at the **Silent Movie Theater**.

This is the only cinema in the world strictly devoted to showing films from the silent era, with live organ accompaniments exactly as they were originally intended. Opened in 1942 by Dorothy and John E. Hampton as a place where they could share their personal collection of silent films, it soon became a cultural institution, devoted to showing a program of silent films that shed light on changes in style, manners, and American society. It was also a place of relief during war times and the Depression, where many could escape to a world of sheer fantasy—and that fantasy remains to this day. Silent films with live organ accompaniment are shown on the first Wednesday and one Sunday of every month.

611 NORTH FAIRFAX AVENUE NEAR MELROSE AVENUE IN LOS ANGELES. 323-655-2510. www.cinefamily.org

---

44. Stroll along the golden hallway in the **Millennium Biltmore Hotel**.

A long time ago, before Beverly Hills and its hotels cornered the market on glamour and luxury, the Los Angeles Biltmore was the finest and one of the largest hotels in the country. Opened in 1923, the Biltmore was an architectural gem, with a European influenced exterior designed by the New York firm Schultze and Weaver. But the beauty that lay within the hotel—carved marble fountains, imported tapestries, Austrian crystal chandeliers, bronze details, Spanish artwork, and hand-painted frescoed mural ceilings by Giovanni Smeraldi, the same Italian artist whose work decorates the Vatican and the White House—outshone everything else. Particularly breathtaking is the main hallway. With its beautiful golden hue and ornately decorated ceilings, you'll find yourself walking down the hallway at a tortoise's pace as you attempt to take in all its splendor.

506 SOUTH GRAND AVENUE AT 5TH STREET IN DOWNTOWN LOS ANGELES. 213-624-1011. www.millenniumhotels.com

→ ***DID YOU KNOW?*** *The Biltmore was home to the Academy Awards from 1931 till 1942.*

---

45. Walk around the oldest part of Downtown L.A. on **Olvera Street**.

Built by L.A.'s first settlers in 1781, Olvera Street is an authentic outdoor Mexican

marketplace complete with cobblestone-lined walkways, unchanged for centuries. Technically less a street than an alleyway, you'll find the sidewalk lined with handmade and hand-painted crafts, sombreros, traditional clothing, authentic Mexican kitchenware like tortilla presses and heavy stone mortars and pestles, and—best of all—places to eat. Visit one of the 27 historic buildings, watch folkloric dancing (on weekends), and bear witness to the birthplace of the City of Los Angeles. Go on a weekday to avoid the busier and more touristy crowds on weekends.
845 NORTH ALAMEDA STREET IN DOWNTOWN LOS ANGELES. 213-485-8372. www.olvera-street.com

Santa Monica Pier

Not many boardwalks have been around for more than a century and are still popular with millions of visitors. With an amusement park, a merry-go-round that's listed as a National Historic Landmark, and a Ferris wheel with a view of the ocean so stunning it's called the Pacific Wheel, Santa Monica Pier still has it what it takes to compete against much younger and more energetic rival attractions—even at its age.
200 SANTA MONICA PIER IN SANTA MONICA. 310-458-8901. www.santamonicapier.org

46. Housed within the Looff Hippodrome, Santa Monica's first landmarked building is a ***carousel*** built in 1922. Forty-four beautifully hand-carved horses go round and round to the tune of a calliope, a musical instrument similar to a giant whistle, offering each rider a unique glimpse into the past.
310-394-8042

47. *Ride a real roller coaster at Pacific Park.* Pacific Park's arrival to the pier in 1996 marked the arrival of a more modern sense of family fun to Santa Monica. Have a go on the stomach dropping Pacific Plunge, or take a spin on the West Coaster, the only oceanfront steel roller coaster on the West Coast—at the West Coast's only amusement park on a pier.
380 SANTA MONICA PIER IN SANTA MONICA. 310-260-8744. For parties: 310-260-8744 ext. 283. www.pacpark.com

48. *Whack a mole or two at Playland Arcade.* The arcade on the pier has been a family affair since the 1950s. Here games old and new reside alongside each other, from air hockey and whack-a-mole to this author's favorite, skee ball. And if you're looking to remember your visit to the pier with more than a cheap trinket, there are photo booths with real film ready to capture the memories.

350 SANTA MONICA PIER IN SANTA MONICA. 310-451-5133. www.playlandarcadesmpier.com

49. *Get hands on with the creatures of the sea at the Santa Monica Pier Aquarium.* More than 100 species of marine life can be found in the Santa Monica Bay and you'll find them all here at the Santa Monica Pier Aquarium—also known as Heal the Bay's Marine Science Center. Not only do you leave knowing more about the bay's diverse animal and plant life—from seahorses to sharks, from anemones to octopuses—you also leave knowing a little more about how you can help the ocean.

1600 OCEAN FRONT WALK IN SANTA MONICA. Under the carousel building at the Santa Monica Pier. 310-393-6149. www.healthebay.org/smpa

50. *Channel Neil Young and dance under a Harvest Moon at the Annual Twilight Dance Series.* From July to September, the pier is transformed into the perfect summertime music destination as acts from all over the world come to perform free concerts. Started in 1983 in response to the proposed destruction of the Santa Monica Pier, the Twilight Dance Series was a way to raise money to aid in the pier's repair. Since it began, artists such as Patti Smith, Joan Baez, Hugh Masekela, and Angelique Kidjo have all graced this annual event. So come and partake in a genuine Los Angeles summer ritual and sway to the music with the stars up above and the sea down below.

www.twilightseries.org

51. See how junk became art at the **Watts Towers**.

One of the greatest examples of "do-it-yourself" architecture in the United States, Watts Towers stands as a testament to one man's dream. Built between 1921 and 1954 in Sabato "Sam or Simon" Rodia's backyard, and made exclusively out of recycled materials, the towers have been an icon of the neighborhood since they first began to take shape. The buildings, a collection of seventeen interconnected structures and three main towers (two of which reach heights of over ninety-nine feet), are proof that the best cultural monuments Los Angeles has to offer aren't always a part of an institution. Now an official National Historic Landmark, the towers serve as a great excuse to visit the neighborhood of Watts and see parts of Los Angeles that might typically be avoided on the tourist trail.

1727 EAST 107TH STREET NEAR SOUTH WILMINGTON AVENUE IN LOS ANGELES. 213-847-4646. www.wattstowers.us

52. Catch a fly ball (and Vin Scully) at **Dodger Stadium.**

Home of the Dodgers since 1962, Dodger Stadium is the third oldest ballpark in Major League Baseball. So what that the Dodgers were originally from Brooklyn? They've made their home here in Los Angeles for more than 48 years and they're here to stay. Pair that with the "the voice of Los Angeles," Vin Scully, who knows more about baseball than Julia Child did about cooking—and you'll get a free trip down baseball's memory lane with every game. Eat a famous Dodger Dog or three, and partake in America's favorite pastime.

1000 ELYSIAN PARK AVENUE IN LOS ANGELES. 323-224-1507. losangeles.dodgers.mlb.com

> → **FACT:** *Vin Scully was the principal announcer for the Brooklyn Dodgers, and when the club moved out west to Los Angeles he came with them and has been there ever since.*

53. Make like Kristi Yamaguchi and go ice-skating in **Pershing Square.**

Los Angeles isn't famous for its seasons, but that doesn't stop us from getting into the holiday spirit when Christmas comes rolling around. One of the first annual traditions for Angelenos is lacing up their skating boots at Pershing Square's Downtown on Ice, the largest outdoor ice-skating rink in L.A. Alhough skating during the day allows you to work on your tan, nighttime skating under the glow of the moon and surrounded by the twinkling lights of downtown L.A. is really where it's at.

532 SOUTH OLIVE AVENUE BETWEEN 5TH AND 6TH STREETS IN DOWNTOWN LOS ANGELES. Open only during the winter holidays. 213-847-4968. www.laparks.org

54. Religion and art meet at the Cathedral of **Our Lady of the Angels.**

Built by the Pritzker Prize-winning architect Professor José Rafael Moneo, the Cathedral of Our Lady of the Angels is to Los Angeles what Notre Dame is to Paris, St. Paul's is to London, and St. Patrick's is to New York. With its labyrinthine mausoleum below, a campanile above, a water wall and pool by Lita Albuquerque, stained glass windows by the Judson studios, and the late artist Robert Graham's great bronze doors and statue of our lady of the angels, the cathedral is an unusual mix of religion and art. It can all be a little overwhelming for those who come simply to communicate with the big guy in the sky—but it's an awe-inspiring sight for anyone, no matter how devout.

555 WEST TEMPLE STREET BETWEEN GRAND AVENUE AND HILL STREET IN DOWNTOWN LOS ANGELES. 213-680-5200. www.olacathedral.org

55. Indulge your senses at the **Walt Disney Concert Hall**.

Thank goodness they fixed the glare off this thing—people were complaining about the increase in temperature in their condos and the cost of air-conditioning skyrocketing after Frank Gehry's unconventional glimmering masterpiece was revealed. More than just architectural eye-candy, the Disney Concert Hall has become one of downtown Los Angeles's most recognized landmarks since it opened in 2003, and a home for music and arts to live and flourish. Inside this entrancing building, you'll find an elegantly crafted performance space whose heavenly acoustics (designed by Yasuhisa Toyota) allow audiences to better appreciate the mix of classical and contemporary music that fills the hall. Drive by to marvel at its billowing steel shell—then check online for concert programs and schedules to find a reason to come back for a real visit.

135 NORTH GRAND AVENUE AT IN DOWNTOWN LOS ANGELES. 323-850-2000. www.laphil.com

→ ***DID YOU KNOW?*** *The large concert organ within the hall designed by Gehry is made up of 6,125 pipes.*

56. Pay your respects to the bygone greats at **Hollywood Forever Cemetery**.

John Huston, Cecil B. DeMille, Estelle Getty, Art Pepper, Dee Dee and Johnny Ramone... The list of our most-missed most-famous whose spirits are to be found at the Hollywood Forever Cemetery goes on and on. But before you begin the hunt for the final resting places of your favorite stars, head to the Library of Lives: Hollywood Forever's onsite digital database provides you with a history of famous funerals complete with photos, audio and video clips, and, most importantly, directions. Just don't expect any autographs...

6000 SANTA MONICA BOULEVARD AT GOWER STREET IN LOS ANGELES. 323-469-1181. www.hollywoodforever.com

57. Enjoy al fresco movies at the Hollywood Forever Cemetery during the **Cinespia**

summer-long outdoor film series. Here, the glamour of Hollywood past never fades—so long as the projector is working and the picture shot on the side of the mausoleum is in focus. As macabre as it may sound, the cemetery is a peaceful and beautiful setting for outdoor movies, where less superstitious Angelenos can lounge under palm trees with a picnic and a drink just a few yards away from some of Hollywood's departed greats. Douglas Fairbanks on the screen *and* just a few feet away? How very noir.

Cinespia: Gates open at 7:00 p.m./ movie at 8:30 p.m. www.cinespia.org

Famous Works of Los Angeles Architecture

Los Angeles is home to countless movie stars, but more often than not, it's the actual houses they live in that are truly famous. Designed by a who's who of star architects—a cast that includes Frank Lloyd Wright, Charles Lummis, Richard Neutra, Rudolph Schindler, and John Lautner among many other notable names—some of the world's finest examples of modernist architecture can be found here. Locals, visitors, and architectural buffs: for those of you eager to venture out and explore some of the city's architectural wonders, here's a list of some of our most notable structures. (Please note that most of these residences are private, and should not be disturbed.)

58. *See stellar architecture at the Chemosphere.* Credit goes to the American architect John Lautner for this innovative California Modern house, built in 1960. The Chemosphere, a single-story octagon-shaped living space, is perched atop a 30-ft concrete pole in the Hollywood Hills. Faced with a site on a 45-degree angled slope, Lautner came up with this space-aged solution to build on the unbuildable, creating what *Encyclopedia Britannica* once called "the most modern home built in the world." To the untrained eye it looks like a spaceship landed here—which Lautner simply welded down and called home—but it remains to this day one of the most renowned Modernist buildings in America.
7776 TORREYSON DRIVE IN LOS ANGELES.

59. *Visit the embodiment of a residential masterpiece at the Schindler House (The Kings Road House).* Los Angeles has no shortage of great works of residential architecture. But none are as accessible or nearly as vibrant as the Austrian architect Rudolph Schindler's minimalist home and studio, which he built for himself in 1921. After being sent to Los Angeles in 1920, while building this house Schindler managed to introduce a new design layout for a two-family workable domestic/work space. This is where California Modern began. (At one point Schindler and Richard Neutra both lived here together.) Truly a building ahead of its time, it now houses the MAK (Austria's Museum of Applied Arts) Center for Art and Architecture in the original garage space, hosting an innovative roster of lectures and events that provide, more than anything, a good excuse to extend your visit.
835 NORTH KINGS ROAD NEAR SWEETZER AVENUE IN WEST HOLLYWOOD. 323-651-1510. www.makcenter.org

60. ***Enter a world of fantasy within the Bradbury Building.*** "Never judge a book by its cover" is a phrase that comes to mind when describing the Bradbury building, the oldest remaining commercial building downtown. In 1893, the architect George Wyman claimed to have been influenced by Ouija boards and Edward Bellamy's utopian novel, *Looking Backward*, in creating the futuristic Bradbury Building. Whatever he found helped him construct a masterpiece of Victorian futurism, whose complex interior is distinguished by laced ironwork, birdcage elevators, beautiful woodwork, yellowish tiles, and massive skylights. And while this is after all "just an office building," this breathtaking spectacle—a kaleidoscopic mix of history and Hollywood—shows you how much more a building can be.
304 SOUTH BROADWAY AT 3RD STREET IN DOWNTOWN LOS ANGELES. 213-626-1893. www.laconservancy.org/tours/downtown/bradbury.php

→ ***DID YOU KNOW?*** *The Bradbury Building is the residence of toymaker J. F. Sebastian in "Blade Runner."*

61. ***Modern meets Mayan at the Ennis House.*** In 2010, mere mortals were given the opportunity to purchase what many considered to be the most impressive of the Frank Lloyd Wright residences. But the offer was only valid for those with a few spare millions lying around. Built in 1924, Wright used Mayan art and architecture as the dominant influence in this home, using textile blocks all over the interior and exterior of the house. Donated to the Trust for Preservation of Cultural Heritage at USC only after its last owner Augustus O. Brown drove the property into disrepair, the home is now on the market due to all the unforeseen costs of maintaining it. In 2011, the business magnate Ronald Burkle came to the rescue and purchased the hilltop mansion for a bargain at $4.5 million. The view alone is worth the price.
2607 GLENDOWER AVENUE IN LOS FELIZ. 323-660-0607. www.ennishouse.com

62. ***See where Richard Neutra "cemented" his career with the Lovell Health House (the Lovell House).*** What do a naturopathic physician and one of Modernism's most important architects have in common? The first steel-framed house in the U.S., of course. In 1929 Dr. Philip Lovell commissioned Neutra to design a Cubist house with health and fitness in mind—and he created a masterpiece. This gem of International Modernist architecture, with a suspended concrete pool, vast window expanses, and balconies hung from steel cables, was perfectly tailored for Lovell. Neutra,

known for getting to know his clients well and analyzing their individual needs, touched on Lovell's work as a naturopath and designed the building based on the idea that a person's health is not just a result of their physical and mental make-up, but a result of their living environment as well.
4616 DUNDEE DRIVE IN LOS ANGELES.

63. ***See where "life and work" reside at Case Study House No.8 (the Eames House).*** From the late 1940s until the 1960s, *Arts & Architecture Magazine* (started by John Entenza, an important figure in the growth of Modernism in American architecture) sponsored experiments on American residential architecture. Entenza commissioned major architects during that period, such as Richard Neutra, Pierre Koenig, Eero Saarinen, and J.R. Davidson, among others, to design and build inexpensive and efficient model homes for all the soldiers returning from the end of World War II, helping to spark a housing boom. Of the twenty-five Case Study houses built, not all designs saw mass construction; number 8 was considered the most successful among them. In fact, it was so successful as a structural living space that Ray and Charles Eames moved in, making it their home and studio for the rest of their lives. Proof enough that this remarkable building—now a National Historic Landmark that has wooed many an architecture lover to L.A. just to see it—worked. Make an advance appointment through the Eames Foundation to set up a visit.
203 NORTH CHAUTAUQUA BOULEVARD IN PACIFIC PALISADES. Reservations are required for a visit 48 hours in advance. 310-459-9663. www.eamesfoundation.org

64. ***The John Sowden House (aka the Jaws House) will take a bite out of your imagination.*** This house isn't just a piece of architectural history; it has Hollywood history as well. Designed and built by Lloyd Wright, the eldest son of Frank Lloyd Wright, the Sowden House—also known as the "Jaws House" because of the facade's eerie resemblance to the open mouth of a shark—is Lloyd Wright's most natural continuation of his father's work. Though the structure says "Frank" because of the use of textile ornamental blocks and Mayan themes, this is one of his son's most memorable works. Not only famous for its exterior, this house is also notorious for what may have happened inside: Dr. George Hodel, the prime suspect in the infamous Black Dahlia murder, resided here, and it's said that the murder may have taken place inside this home.
5121 FRANKLIN AVENUE AT NORTH NORMANDIE AVENUE IN LOS FELIZ. www.sowdenhouse.com

65. *Look ma, no nails! Gamble House* was built nail-free. When siblings Charles and Henry Greene built the Gamble House for David and Mary Gamble of Procter & Gamble, they waved farewell to the Victorian era and embraced instead the Arts and Crafts design movement. Marked by clean lines, intricate workmanship, and beautiful details, this historic landmark—the best known example of Craftsman-style homes in the country—has been painfully restored to its former glory. It now also serves as an architectural conservancy and museum, and if you're a USC architecture student, you're in luck—every year, a pair of fifth-year students are carefully chosen to live in the house full-time. Tours are available for the rest of us.
4 WESTMORELAND PLACE IN PASADENA. 626-793-3334. www.gamblehouse.org

66. *Be transported to ancient times at Getty Villa.* Los Angeles has a lot of museums to choose from, but this was one of your author's favorites growing up. As a child coming here on school trips, you felt as if you were being transported to another world. Driving down the Pacific Coast Highway, going up a tall winding road, only to step out to what seemed like the top of the world… Situated across 64 acres in Malibu, and purchased by J. Paul Getty in 1945, this Mediterranean villa houses some of the most priceless artifacts in the world. It opened to the public in 1954, but after years of wear and tear (being on the seaside can take its toll), the villa closed in 1997 to undergo serious renovations, which were completed in 2006. Now restored to its full splendor, and with an expanding collection of artwork, the Getty Villa is one of Los Angeles's true architectural and cultural gems.
17985 PACIFIC COAST HIGHWAY IN PACIFIC PALISADES. Admission is free but booking in advance is required. 310-440-7300. www.getty.edu

67. *Take a ride down memory lane at Union Station.* Back in 1939, an exciting thing to do would be to take a train to an unknown destination. In Los Angeles, almost 75 years later, that hasn't changed. Union Station, with its inlaid marble tile, soaring wooden ceiling, and mixture of Spanish Colonial, Art Deco, and Modernist architectural design, has remained a beloved fixture of the city's streetscape and an icon of Los Angeles architecture over the years. And though it remains the city's public transportation hub and last grand train terminal, you can still find tranquility within its grounds. Find the secret outdoor patio in back for a little peace and quiet. And if you ever want to get away for the weekend, just buy a ticket: the trains run up and down the coast. All aboard to a weekend away from the hustle and bustle—and a break from being stuck behind the wheel.

800 NORTH ALAMEDA STREET IN DOWNTOWN LOS ANGELES. 800-872-7245. www.amtrak.com

68. *Tour the Hollyhock House.* Yes, a visit to this house is a must. Architect Frank Lloyd Wright's work has been loved, admired, and studied the world over. And of the 500+ buildings he completed within his lifetime, the Hollyhock House is one of the earliest examples of his work. Built in 1923 for Aline Barnsdall, it was soon given to the city in 1927. Visitors can purchase tickets at the Municipal Art Gallery to tour the heritage home now located within Barnsdall Park of the man the American Institute of Architects refers to as "the greatest American architect of all time."
4800 HOLLYWOOD BOULEVARD NEAR NORTH BERENDO STREET IN LOS ANGELES. 323-644-6269. www.hollyhockhouse.net

69. Try not to make a mess while eating a French Dip at **Philippe's.**

There's nothing like biting into a French dip. Those tender slices of meat, the French roll softened with savory *jus* (hence the name), the sinus-clearing mustard... This Los Angeles invention, a truly unique culinary experience, is divine. And at Philippe's, one of the oldest restaurants in Los Angeles, with wooden stools and booths, sawdust on the floors, and even its own railroad museum, you know you're getting the real deal. I recommend getting a lamb sandwich, double dipped, homemade potato salad, a pickle, lemonade, and, to top it all off, a slice of their banana cream pie. Use the mustard sparingly—too much may cause your brain to explode.
1001 NORTH ALAMEDA STREET AT ORD STREET IN DOWNTOWN LOS ANGELES. 213-628-3781. www.philippes.com

70. Order off-menu at **In-N-Out.**

"Fresh" is the magic word at this world-renowned burger establishment, founded in Baldwin Park in 1948 by Harry Snyder—and you won't get your food any other way. Order some fries and you'll see the In-N-Out chefs prepping the potatoes for their famous hand-cut fries right before your eyes. With its palm tree emblazoned logo, hidden Bible references on the paper utensils, and delicious food (my favorite is the double double with cheese), In-N-Out is a favorite for locals and out-of-towners alike. Even the Dude, aka The Big Lebowski, would approve.
Various locations all over Los Angeles. www.in-n-out.com

→ ***DID YOU KNOW?*** *There's a secret menu that anyone can order from as long as you know the lingo. Animal style: messy with extra sauce. Protein style: the bun is* *replaced with lettuce. 4x4: four patties, four slices of cheese. But don't try and order larger than a 4x4, they've stopped making them any bigger.*

71. Get your hands (and mouth) around a pastrami sandwich at **Langers**.

A friend of mine from Mexico City has only been to L.A. once, but what he remembers most about his stay was eating at Langers. If I even mention the name, he shakes his head and wrings his hands together as if he were praying for one of their sandwiches to magically appear. I swear he almost cried once while trying to describe the fattiness of Langers' hot pastrami. A MacArthur Park staple for more than 60 years, Langers still makes sandwiches as big and juicy and legendary as ever. They even won a James Beard Award, the equivalent of a food Oscar, in 2001. With the same brown booths, large windows, and forever rotating mix of patrons, Langers serves up every delicious sandwich (I recommend the #19: Pastrami, Swiss cheese and cole slaw with Russian dressing) with a side of nostalgia. And if you're in a rush, Langers provides curbside pick-up—just make sure to phone your order in ahead of time.

704 SOUTH ALVARADO STREET AT 7TH STREET IN LOS ANGELES. Open Monday through Saturday 8:00 a.m. to 4:00 p.m. Closed Sundays. Subway: Metro Red Line, Westlake/ McArthur Park Station. 213-483-8050. www.langersdeli.com

72. Dine with Churchill's ghost at the **HMS Bounty**.

Surrounded by Los Angeles history (across the street was our dearly departed Ambassador Hotel and the Brown Derby next door), this place was once a favorite of Winston Churchill, who always ate here while staying at the Ambassador. Cheap drinks, decent food, and a great bar ambience are all housed in the reportedly haunted Gaylord Hotel (once one of the most elegant buildings in town). The bathrooms alone will require a stiff one or a loyal friend to escort you. (Trust me ladies, go to the bathroom with a friend. You'll thank me later.) It was even rumored that Sirhan Sirhan ate at the Bounty Restaurant before heading over to the Ambassador to shoot Robert Kennedy. With such a rich history of its own—the Gay Room (after Henry Gaylord Wilshire), the Secret Harbour, The Golden Anchor, and now the HMS Bounty—whatever you call it, we hope it won't be setting sail anytime soon.

***3357 WILSHIRE BOULEVARD NEAR ALEXANDRIA AVENUE IN KOREATOWN.
213-385-7275. www.thehmsbounty.com***

73. Grab a cookie at **Diddy Riese**.

Located in Westwood, close to the UCLA campus, Diddy Riese has served its fair share of UCLA Bruins for years. From chocolate chip to peanut butter, white chocolate chip with macadamia nuts and more, for less than $5 a dozen, this place is indeed a college student's dream come true. But it's not just that—it's the ice cream sandwiches they make with the cookies, their often neglected but equally delicious brownies, and it's the lines you wait in with your friends as you eagerly anticipate wrapping your hands around a paper bag stained with buttery goodness that make this place so great. The "Freshman 15" never tasted better.

926 BROXTON AVENUE NEAR LE CONTE AVENUE IN WESTWOOD. 310-208-0448. www.diddyriese.com

---

74. Try to leave hungry after a visit to the **Original Pantry Cafe**.

On the corner of 9th and Figueroa in downtown Los Angeles you'll find an old-school eatery that's been feeding Angelenos on and off since the 1920s. At the Original Pantry Cafe, locals don't just eat its hearty diner fare, they inhale it. And with such agreeable business hours (it's open 24 hours), it doesn't even have a lock on the door. Any time, day or night, a visit to the Pantry is always an adventure. If you're hungry, avoid the weekend breakfast time crush and nights when sporting events let out of the Staples Center.

877 SOUTH FIGUEROA STREET AT 9TH STREET IN LOS ANGELES. 213-972-9279. www.pantrycafe.com

---

75. For a meal in what's not the real deal, head over to the **Pacific Dining Car**.

If greasy spoons aren't the answer to your late-night cravings, then stop by the Pacific Dining Car. This 4-star steakhouse located in a re-created train car—no, this is not a real train car—serves up choice cuts of meat, great sides, and plenty of wine in a cozy and quaint setting. It can be expensive compared to a greasy spoon, but the experience and the food are worth it. Since it's open 24 hours, expect to see all types here—the Dining Car has possibly the most diverse 4-star clientele in the world.

1310 WEST 6TH STREET NEAR WITMER STREET IN DOWNTOWN LOS ANGELES. 213-483-6000. www.pacificdiningcar.com

---

76. Anytime is a good time to drop by **Mel's Drive-In**.

Shopping, sight-seeing, and partying on Sunset Boulevard all require copious amounts of energy. Thank goodness for Mel's. This golden piece of Americana provides the hungry and tired with a place to recharge and relax. Insomniacs, shift changers, and night owls alike come to order a Melburger and shake to either start or end their "day"—and tourists are advised to do the same.

8585 WEST SUNSET BOULEVARD IN HOLLYWOOD. 310-854-7201. www.melsdrive-in.com

77. It's not L.A. without a matzo ball at **Canter's Deli.**

Since 1948, Canters has been the epitome of the 24-hour Jewish deli in L.A. For starters, it's always packed with an eclectic and young crowd, so you'll invariably find yourself wedged in between a hipster and a yuppie. The menu is a mix of matzo ball soup, piled high sandwiches, and lots of drinks. The ambiance is enjoyable and with its ability to accommodate large groups of unruly friends, it's a good hang-out spot. More energetic visitors should pop into the Kibitz Room next door for some music and a dance or two. How else will you find a hot date if you don't get out there and work off all that matzo ball you just ate? Oy vey.

419 NORTH FAIRFAX AVENUE AT OAKWOOD AVENUE IN LOS ANGELES.
323-651-2030. www.cantersdeli.com

78. Feast your eyes on kitsch at **Clifton's Cafeteria.**

This multi-storied, 600+ seat restaurant has been serving up cheap and good food in a kitschy setting for almost 80 years. It is a true gem in the downtown dining scene, with a large old-school menu (it still serves Jell-O) and enduringly low prices. Now under new management for the first time in decades, the Clifton will re-open in early 2014, with changes that include a 24-hour menu, a lounge, and a bakery—none of which could possibly detract from the experience of trying to concentrate on your food while taking in all the kitsch paraphernalia that lines the dining room walls.

648 SOUTH BROADWAY NEAR 7TH STREET IN DOWNTOWN LOS ANGELES.
213-627-1673. www.cliftonscafeteria.com

79. Take a trolley ride to nowhere in the **Formosa Cafe.**

This Chinese-themed cafe, named for the original name of Taiwan, is more film noir than Chinatown. Originally built as a trolley car—an Interurban No. 913 Pacific Electric streetcar, to be exact—it became a restaurant in 1925 when the prizefighter Jimmy Bernstein bought the car to open a lunch counter. Back in the day it was frequented by the likes of Old Blue Eyes himself, Frank Sinatra, who by all accounts used to enjoy the chow mein. These days, most locals forego the food and focus on the drinks, like a good old Singapore Sling and the old-school Rat-Pack ambience that goes with it.

7156 SANTA MONICA BOULEVARD AT FORMOSA AVENUE IN WEST HOLLYWOOD.
323-850-9050

80. Grab a Shirley Temple after the beach at **Chez Jay**.

It's a little-known fact that one of the essential mementos of home the astronaut Alan Shepard took with him on his historic trip to the Moon was a Chez Jay peanut. For more than 50 years, this cheerful local staple, with its Christmas lights, sawdust floors, and longstanding original menu, has remained practically unchanged and continues to be a Hollywood favorite. The locals come here for familiar faces, good nuts, the classic jukebox, and the unparalleled Shirley Temples.

1657 OCEAN AVENUE BETWEEN COLORADO AVENUE AND PICO BOULEVARD IN SANTA MONICA. 310-395-1741. www.chezjays.com

81. Indulge in a short stack at the **Olympic Cafe House of Breakfast**.

For 40 years, the House of Breakfast has quietly been making the best homemade buttermilk pancakes in town. Opened in 1972 by Japanese American Mitsuo Yamamoto, this cafe on the corner of Olympic and 5th has since become a neighborhood institution. Without changing the name or diluting the odd King Arthur and the Knights of the Round Table-inspired décor, Yamamoto focused on creating a menu filled with his favorite foods. From chicken teriyaki to homemade sausage patties and eggs and golden-brown pancakes of fluffy goodness, the House of Breakfast is a testament to Mitsuo's passion for simple, homey, and delicious food. Mitsuo passed away in 2000, but his daughter Linda and long-time assistant Jose continue to execute his culinary legacy to a T. If you like a side of spice with your breakfast, ask for William's homemade salsa. It's a surprising treat alongside something sweet, but it'll knock your socks off, so use sparingly.

3728 WEST OLYMPIC BOULEVARD AT 5TH AVENUE IN LOS ANGELES. 323-731-5405.

82. Count the number of umbrellas in your coconut at **Tiki Ti**.

Tiki may sound a little tacky, but who doesn't love a tiki bar? Opened in 1961 by the bartender Ray Buhen, with a room capacity for about thirty patrons, the Tiki Ti is a Polynesian wonderland right here in Hollywood. The drinks are as authentic as can be—Ray was around during the start of the tropical drink craze and the recipes have been passed down to his son and grandson who now run the bar. If you're not sure what to get and are confused by the 90 different tropical drinks—all with names like "Skull & Bones" and "The Ugo Booga"—try your luck with the "Wheel of Tiki-Ti Drinks" and leave your decisions to the alcohol gods. But be sure to say a little prayer; it doesn't hurt having the gods on your side.

4427 WEST SUNSET BOULEVARD NEAR VIRGIL PLACE IN LOS ANGELES. Note: Be sure to check their calendar online to make sure the bar is open as the doors are closed when the Buhens go on vacation. 323-669-9381. www.tiki-ti.com

83. Go see Marty and Elayne and grab a Blood and Sand at **The Dresden Room**.

After 50 years, the Dresden Room hasn't changed at all. With salmon-colored walls, faux nouveau glass panels, and white wraparound booths, it still draws in patrons of all (legal drinking) ages. Come by, grab a drink—like their classic Blood and Sand, a mix of scotch, vermouth, cherry brandy, and orange juice—and sit in what feels like a movie set from long ago (it was the actual movie set for *Swingers*), all while enjoying the sounds of longtime lounge singers Marty and Elayne. After 30 years, they're still at it—and no, they haven't changed a bit either.

1760 VERMONT AVENUE AT KINGSWELL AVENUE IN LOS ANGELES. Marty and Elayne perform every Tuesday through Saturday starting at 9:00 p.m. 323-665-4294. www.thedresden.com

84. Have a classic L.A. burger at the **Apple Pan**.

As you go down Pico Boulevard toward West Los Angeles, you'll encounter what looks like an old cabin. And although you're not sure what you're in for as you walk up to the screen door, the moment you step inside and see the long wraparound counter tops, red swivel stools, and sodas served in paper cones, you'll realize that you're right where you should be. Since 1947 the Apple Pan has been dishing out delicious burgers to die-hard burger fans from all over and sticking to their motto of "Quality Forever." The burgers here are so good they inspired an urban legend, which claims that Johnny Rockets copied the sauce from the Apple Pan's Hickory Burger. Call yourself a burger aficionado? Why not grab a Hickory and a side of fries—extra crispy—and judge yourself.

10801 WEST PICO BOULEVARD AT GLENDON AVENUE IN WEST LOS ANGELES. 310-475-3585. www.applepan.com

85. Rock reigns supreme at the **Rainbow Bar and Grill**.

Aqua Net and Hair Metal is alive and kicking at this long time rock 'n' roll hang out. Before it was a staple to rockers on the Sunset Strip, who came to wet their whistle before and after their shows, the Rainbow Grill was the Villa Nova Restaurant owned by Vicente Minnelli, Judy "Over the Rainbow" Garland's husband. The exclusive club upstairs is even named after Garland's hit song. Popular with rockers and groupies back in the day, it remains true to its rock roots and no matter what age, fans still come to party. If you're a Motorhead fan, you need look no further. Frontman Lemmy Kilmister is often sighted hanging out at the bar, drinking Jack and Coke, and playing on the electric one-armed bandit.

9015 SUNSET BOULEVARD BETWEEN HAMMOND STREET AND DOHENY DRIVE IN WEST HOLLYWOOD. 310-278-4232. www.rainbowbarandgrill.com

→ ***DID YOU KNOW?*** *John Belushi ate his last meal here before overdosing at the Chateau Marmont. And during its Hollywood heyday, Joe DiMaggio met Marilyn Monroe here.*

---

86. Eat like Frank Sinatra and Dean Martin did at **Dan Tana's.**

This place has got Old School Rat Pack written all over it, and it should. The 1964 eatery has been the home to old Hollywood and now new Hollywood without missing a beat—and without changing its red and white checkered tablecloths, red booths, and *Goodfellas* vibe. For those who can get in and afford it, it's the perfect place to grab a drink and hang out. But more than just that, it's the perfect place to tuck into a juicy steak, the famous Cobb salad, and a bit of Old Hollywood nostalgia.

9071 SANTA MONICA BOULEVARD NEAR DOHENY DRIVE IN WEST HOLLYWOOD. 310-275-9444. www.dantanasrestaurant.com

---

87. Power lunch at **Nate 'n Al.**

In Beverly Hills, the Grill on the Alley isn't the only place to go to see a power lunch. At Nate 'n Al's, a Jewish delicatessen that's been around since 1945, they've been serving meals with a side of attitude courtesy of their tough waitresses to generations of power agents. After a few meals here, you'll find out where the agents really get their hardnosed negotiating skills—the waitresses.

414 NORTH BEVERLY DRIVE NEAR BRIGHTON WAY IN BEVERLY HILLS. 310-274-0101. www.natenal.com

---

88. Old school French food is a staple at **Taix.**

Taxi, Tax, Take, Tex: whatever you call it, the French restaurant in Echo Park is a classic. Originally opened in the long-lost French quarter of downtown L.A., Taix was started by a family of shepherds and bakers from southeastern France. In 1962, it moved to its current location on Sunset Boulevard, and has been serving a mix of eclectic diners ever since. Inside you'll probably find a well-dressed elderly couple dining on the duck à l'orange while hipsters chow down on steak frites in the next booth over. Whatever you order, wherever you sit (bar area or main dining room), Taix serves up good food, a good time, and a taste of France, L.A.-style.

1911 WEST SUNSET BOULEVARD AT PARK AVENUE IN LOS ANGELES. 213-484-1265. www.taixfrench.com

89. The beach is at your doorstep when you stay at **Casa Del Mar**.

You no longer have to be a member to enter this once exclusive beachfront resort, but you'll definitely feel like one once you enter through its doors. With its amazing detailing, four-poster beds, and marble baths, it's no wonder this hotel was once a favorite for the rich and famous. But the real draw, for tourists and wealthy locals alike, is its proximity to the surf and the sand.

1910 OCEAN WAY IN SANTA MONICA. 310-581-5533. www.lhw.com/casadelmar

90. Stay in a mansion for a fraction of the price at the **Bissell House**.

Once the home to Anna Bissell McCay, the daughter of (and you don't hear this title very often) the vacuum magnate Melville Bissell, this beautiful Victorian mansion located on Millionaire's Row in South Pasadena was converted to a bed and breakfast in 1995. Chintzy but quaint, this B&B is an ideal place for those seeking a bit of tranquility. It has a lovely outdoor garden, is located within reasonable distance to downtown L.A. (15 minutes without traffic), and provides you with a full afternoon tea. (I doubt you'll find that at the Chateau Marmont.) Focus on charm rather than perfection—and you'll discover a small slice of paradise. It's also a great place to stay if you're in town for the Rose Parade, but with only seven rooms, you better book in advance. Be sure to ask for the Garden Room; it's got a jacuzzi tub.

201 ORANGE GROVE AVENUE NEAR COLUMBIA STREET IN SOUTH PASADENA. 626-441-3535. www.bissellhouse.com

91. Step into old-school Hollywood glamour at the **Beverly Hills Hotel**.

With its white-and-green awning, its signature banana leaf wallpaper, and its oh-so-spacious rooms, the "Pink Palace" *is* Beverly Hills. Built in 1912 to lure residents to the area, the Beverly Hills Hotel was redesigned in 1949, with much of the original design still around today. In 1987, the Sultan of Brunei purchased the hotel for $200 million and poured in another $100 million to bring it back to life. And lo and behold, much like Lazarus returning from the dead, the hotel is now more glamorous than ever. If you can afford it, I suggest a stay in one of the hotel's 23 one-of-a-kind bungalows, like the Presidential "Ultra" Bungalow. Just saying that out loud makes me feel poorer.

9641 SUNSET BOULEVARD AT BEVERLY DRIVE IN BEVERLY HILLS. 310-276-2251. www.beverlyhillshotel.com.

→ ***DID YOU KNOW?*** *Elizabeth Taylor honeymooned with six out of eight husbands here.*

92. If the sky's the limit, the **Hotel Bel Air** is for you.

A hideaway for the rich and famous would be a good way to describe this luxury 5-star hotel. Another would be expensive. Yes, the Sultan of Brunei owns this hotel as well. Located on 12-acres of prime real estate, the hotel, originally built in 1922 as the planning offices for Bel Air's developer, Alphonzo Bell, it was changed into a Spanish mission-style mansion with 91 rooms, ready to cater to those with very deep pockets. With its woodsy surroundings, lush gardens, and its own "swan lake," it's the perfect place to hide and get away.

701 STONE CANYON ROAD IN LOS ANGELES. 310-472-1211. www.hotelbelair.com

93. Visit the **Sportsmen's Lodge**.

In operation since the 1880s, the Sportmen's Lodge is a San Fernando Valley/Studio City landmark. Located in the heart of the valley's once prominent studio district, it was a popular spot for Old Hollywood, especially the stars of the old Westerns. Republic Studio, the home of many western films, is close by, and old silver-screen cowboys still come by to attend the annual Golden Boot and Silver Spurs Awards held here. In its early history it was known as the Hollywood Trout Farm because of its manmade lakes of natural spring water filled with trout. People could come catch their own dinner here, and the lodge's restaurant would cook it for them. After the earthquake the water was diverted elsewhere and the trout farm was no more, but with all the history the Sportmen's Lodge embodies, this remains a true classic Los Angeles haunt.

12825 VENTURA BOULEVARD NEAR COLDWATER CANYON AVENUE IN STUDIO CITY. 818-769-4700. www.sportsmenlodge.com

94. Hang out at the pool at the **Hollywood Roosevelt Hotel**.

Built in 1927 with original investors and Hollywood hotshots such as Douglas Fairbanks Sr., Mary Pickford, and Louis B. Mayer, this hotel hosted the very first Academy Awards in 1929. Even after decades of fashionable revamps, this hotel remains a classic destination for many and a great place to hang out. If you have a taste for otherworldly Hollywood nostalgia, check out the hallway mirror that the glamorous and apparently still vain ghost of Marilyn Monroe reportedly haunts. Or hang out by the pool—you may see the handsome ghost of Montgomery Clift. But don't worry, plenty of the living frequent this hotel as well.

7000 HOLLYWOOD BOULEVARD AT ORANGE DRIVE IN HOLLYWOOD. 323-466-7000. www.thompsonhotels.com

95. Avoid the pretensions of Sunset Blvd by staying at the **Sunset Tower Hotel.**

You won't find bouncers in front of the Sunset Tower Hotel on the weekends, thank goodness. Leave that to the other sceney, congested hotels that dot the Sunset Strip. At this stunning 1920s Art Deco landmark, you'll find floor-to-ceiling windows, sweeping views of Hollywood, and, most importantly, some sanity. Converted from a former residential hotel and best known as The Argyle, the Sunset Tower is back to its original name after its recent renovations and is thankfully better than ever. A great place to stay, grab a late-night drink at the Tower Bar, have brunch on the weekends, or dig into a plate of eggs benedict as you enjoy the poolside view.

8358 WEST SUNSET BOULEVARD NEAR KINGS ROAD IN HOLLYWOOD. 323-654-7100. www.sunsettowerhotel.com

Los Angeles Kitsch Architecture

A hotdog stand in the shape of a hotdog and a donut shop with a donut-shaped drive-thru seem completely logical. After all, how would anyone know what you're selling if it isn't out there for all the world to see? Though many would argue that one person's prize kitsch is another man's eyesore, the disappearance of such icons of the city's kitsch landscape could mark the loss of an extraordinary phase in American architectural history—a movement that took root here in Southern California in the 1920s and 1930s and stands testament to the great American car culture. Originally built to be eyecatching enough to be noticed through a windshield a quarter-mile down the freeway, only a handful of these extraordinary buildings have survived. Take a ride around the city and explore the last remaining relics of Los Angeles's kitsch past.

96. *It's donuts or bust at Randy's Donuts.* It's not just a giant donut perched on top of a drive-thru in Inglewood; it's a landmark, a donut temple, and an icon of Los Angeles history. Originally built in 1952 as part of the now-defunct Big Donut Drive-In chain by Russell C. Wendell, this 22-ft concrete donut remained even after the franchise crumbled, and is now a beacon for sweet-toothed foodies from all over the world.

805 WEST MANCHESTER BOULEVARD AT SOUTH LA CIENEGA BOULEVARD IN INGLEWOOD. 310-645-4707. www.randys-donuts.com

97. *Take a drive through the Donut Hole.* I like to think that driving through the Donut Hole is like Alice falling down the rabbit hole to Wonderland—but

this trip is much shorter and much tastier. Located in La Puente, the Donut Hole features two dark brown, 26-ft diameter drive-thru fiberglass donuts on either side of a small bakery, and is the last of a chain of five stores. Delicious fresh donuts aside, just driving through one giant donut is worth the trip alone—but the promise of two seals the deal. It's a real hole in one ... or two.
15300 AMAR ROAD NEAR ELLIOT AVENUE IN LA PUENTE. 626-968-2912

---

98. ***Say "Ahoy" to the Coca Cola Building.*** You'll find a few buildings in Los Angeles that are boat themed, but nothing as seaworthy as this Streamline Moderne structure on the corner of Central Avenue in Downtown Los Angeles. Designed by Robert V. Derrah in 1939, this nautical building houses a Coca Cola bottling plant. Replete with portholes, a catwalk, cargo doors, and topped by a bridge, the building is still ship-shape after all these years.
1334 SOUTH CENTRAL AVENUE AT EAST 12TH STREET IN DOWNTOWN LOS ANGELES.

---

99. ***Get a glimpse of the final frontier at Encounter.*** Ever wondered what it'd feel like shooting through the middle of a building in a space-age elevator playing sci-fi music? Wonder no more. At Encounter, the 70-foot-high futuristic restaurant at LAX, you can have an out-of-this-world dining experience all your own. Formerly a coffee shop, the space was revamped by the Walt Disney Imagineering team to house a futuristic interior complete with iridescent bar, cratered walls that recall the moon, and a wraparound patio—the perfect place for plane watching. The attraction is more the building itself than the food, so it's best enjoyed as a place to grab a drink and take in the departing and arriving sights.
209 WORLD WAY AT LOS ANGELES INTERNATIONAL AIRPORT (LAX).
310-215-5151. www.encounterlax.com

---

100. ***Sit with the Beatles at Bob's Big Boy.*** Built in 1949 by the architect Wayne McAllister, the Bob's Big Boy in Burbank, a Googie-style coffee house fully restored to perfection, is the oldest surviving Big Boy in the United States—and also the most popular. This Bob's has carhop service on the weekends and a vintage hot-rod show on Friday nights in the parking lot (Jay Leno, renowned Hollywood car aficionado, likes to stop by once in a while with one of his many classic rides). It even has a plaque designating the booth where the Beatles sat during their visit in 1964, while on their first American tour. Be sure to take a picture with the signature Bob statue (which is bolted down to prevent theft) and indulge in a double-decker hamburger and thick milkshake, served appropriately enough in a silver goblet.
4211 WEST RIVERSIDE DRIVE IN BURBANK. 818-843-9334. www.bobs.net

101. ***Visit the world's oldest operating McDonald's, the "Speedee."*** Big Mac lovers the world over can be seen posing near the golden arches and the 60-ft tall neon "Speedee the Chef" sign before they head inside to get their McFix at the oldest operating McDonald's in the world. Once you're done eating your favorite value meal, head over to the museum of McDonald's memorabilia adjacent to the restaurant to see how all those infamous happy meal characters have evolved over the years.

10207 LAKEWOOD BOULEVARD AT FLORENCE AVENUE IN DOWNEY. 562-622-9248

102. ***Enter a time warp at Pann's Restaurant.*** While on the secret route to and from LAX, you're bound to notice Pann's on the corner of La Brea and La Tijera. This classic diner, designed by Armet and Davis in 1958, has been a longtime favorite both for its delicious food and Googie architecture. Not much has changed in Pann's during the last half a century—when you sit down it's as if you're seeing exactly what Marilyn Monroe did when she used to frequent this place (it was her favorite diner). Be sure to try the fried chicken: it's mouth-wateringly tasty with a good crunch and price that can't be beat.

6710 LA TIJERA BOULEVARD AT LA CIENEGA BOULEVARD IN LOS ANGELES. 310-670-1441. www.panns.com

103. ***Bring a bib to Carney's Deli.*** Smack in the middle of Sunset Boulevard is a bright yellow Amtrak passenger car from the 1920s, known as Carney's Deli. This family-owned casual burger spot is a favorite for tourists and locals alike. Their trademark burgers and hotdogs drenched in chili are a must—as well as paper towels, antacids, and the name of a good dry cleaner. I recommend wearing short sleeves, as chili can run down arms and into elbow nooks more easily and more often than you might think.

8351 WEST SUNSET BOULEVARD NEAR KINGS ROAD IN WEST HOLLYWOOD. 323-654-8300. www.carneytrain.com

Expert Contributor: Shaniqwa Jarvis

Shaniqwa Jarvis is a professional photographer who has been traveling to, and shooting in, Los Angeles regularly for many years.

MY FIVE FAVORITE WAYS TO FEEL AT HOME IN L.A.

Los Angeles is a great place to ***get and stay healthy***. You can take hikes through Malibu Canyon, rollerblade through Venice, snack at M Cafe, and drink fresh juices at Beverly Hills Juice Club. Whenever I'm not feeling my healthiest, I head to the ***Tonic Bar at Erewhon***—there are often a few special people lurking about at the bar, which makes the experience that much more fun.
7660 BEVERLY BOULEVARD IN LOS ANGELES. 323-937-0777. www.erewhonmarket.com

I don't know when I started the ***Taco Crawl***, but it feeds into my taco obsession. I try to do the crawl with friends and may stop off at random bars and shops in between, eating a taco at each place. The East Side crawl consists of a shrimp taco or shrimp ceviche from ***El 7 Mares***, fish and shrimp tacos from ***Best Fish Taco*** in Ensenada, and then hard-shell chicken tacos from ***Delta Tacos*** and ***Los Burritos***.
EL 7 MARES: 3131 WEST SUNSET BOULEVARD IN LOS ANGELES. 323-665-0865. BEST FISH TACO: 1650 HILLHURST AVENUE IN ENSENADA. 323-466-5552. DELTA TACOS: 3806 WEST SUNSET BOULEVARD IN LOS ANGELES. 323-664-2848. LOS BURRITOS: 4929 SUNSET BOULEVARD IN LOS ANGELES. 323-666-2161.

Being a photographer means I am constantly carrying very heavy equipment on shoulders that are already high due to stress. I find spending a day at the ***Olympic Spa*** to be the perfect way to decompress. It is not your typical day spa, as it functions more like a traditional Japanese *on-sen*. There are several baths, saunas, and exfoliating and massage treatments. When you are done you can feast at their Korean restaurant for a home-cooked meal.
3915 WEST OLYMPIC BOULEVARD IN LOS ANGELES. 323-857-0666. www.olympicspala.com

The first time I went to ***Slauson Swap Meet***, I was quite young and carried a 110 camera with me. I remember photographing the stalls and all of the jewelry. I find as an adult I'm still fascinated by this place. It is a fascinating place to photograph because there are very colorful people you don't normally see interacting with one another in Los Angeles. There are rows upon rows of women getting very detailed

manicures and pedicures, and many stalls that deal in jewelry—and if you're lucky some will show you their special dipping process.
Slauson Super Mall. 1600 WEST SLAUSON AVENUE IN LOS ANGELES. 323-778-6055.

I love ***riding my bicycle in Los Angeles***. With each year I see more and more cyclists out on the road, which makes me happy. There are certain roads I prefer to cycle on, but my favorite route is from Downtown, riding along until Larchmont. The visuals change dynamically every five or six streets. When you're downtown you may want to photograph Broadway, which runs north to south: at the northern end sits Chinatown, and all the old theaters are at the southern end. You can see most of Downtown LA's skyscrapers on this route as well. I always like to get off my bike at the highway crossing of the 110 and the 101 to photograph the traffic beneath me.

CHAPTER 2

Views and Sights

It's not only the destination but the journey that makes Los Angeles so unique, as every road traveled is replete with interesting sights to behold. From old to new, the forever-changing landscape of Los Angeles always offers a surprise. Don't blink or you'll miss the amazing architecture, the city's immense natural beauty, and some truly awe-inspiring views. Like the cliché about Hollywood itself, this chapter is all about looks.

Though the city's skyline is sometimes overcast and blanketed with haze, don't be fooled by the smog—it's key for certain scientific research. The weather gods shine down upon us almost all year-round, parting the skies and revealing the true beauty of this city. From mountaintops to rooftops, coastal shores to wooded hills, there are sights aplenty in fair L.A., and on clear days they can go on as far as the eye can see.

Getting yourself to higher ground is a fundamental part of any visit to L.A.'s Griffith Park Observatory, located in Griffith Park. This may be the city's signature vantage point—but each winding hillside road or canyon edge offers a different perspective that is breathtaking no matter where you are. And let's not forget the staggering vistas of the Pacific Ocean and its seemingly infinite reach, and its piers, beaches, islands, sunrises, and sunsets. For all that can be said about the concrete expanse of the motor megalopolis, in Los Angeles the freeways, meandering roads, and bridges offer some of the best ocean views around.

And some of the most enjoyable sights in this city aren't natural or man-made; sometimes it's the people who take center stage. Los Angeles's colorful locals are, in their own right, sights to behold. This city is one of America's greatest backdrops for diversity, and it is filled with unique characters. The occasional random celebrity sighting also makes L.A. a very special place.

Scenic Drives

Some may say that parts of L.A. have more potholes than the moon, but I say that it just makes for a more memorable ride. Road conditions here in L.A. vary from smooth to rugged, but the scene never changes; it's always sublime. When the roads are clear and the lights are glowing green, there's nothing like being behind the wheel of a car driving up hills and down canyons, left and right, zigging and zagging your way all over our fair city. Exploring this city can also lead to magical moments—like being surrounded by skyscrapers one minute, and staring out at the Pacific the next—just as the sun begins to dip below the horizon basking in its golden glow.

104. *Don't get caught* cruising *on Sunset Boulevard.* When you think of Sunset, the first thing that comes to mind is "the Strip," a two-mile stretch dotted with clubs, bars, and hotels that tourists and newcomers alike flock to in hopes of experiencing a "real taste" of Los Angeles. As any local will tell you, that "taste" is minimal and very fleeting—but if you can overcome the weekend traffic, the hordes of drunken revelers, and the tacky décor, you'll discover what Sunset is really about. For 22 miles, Sunset Boulevard runs from Downtown Los Angeles, through Silverlake, into Hollywood, past Beverly Hills and Pacific Palisades, and plants you smack dab right in front of the Pacific Ocean. The grit and hustle of the urban jungle soon fades and is replaced by lush foliage and towering trees, and suddenly you're surrounded by nature. Sure, the bleakness portrayed in Billy Wilder's film *Sunset Boulevard* still lingers, but the real discovery is how just one road lets you experience two totally different worlds. (Cruising on the Strip is not allowed, unless you want a real L.A. experience with a citation from the police.)

105. When you think canyon, the first thing that springs to mind is the Grand one. (Sorry, wrong state.) By anyone's geographical definition, a canyon is a deep ravine between cliffs often carved from the landscape by a river—not so for the famed canyons of this fair city. ***Topanga, Laurel, Coldwater, and Benedict*** are the fantastic four of Los Angeles's winding "canyon" roads, made famous by countless books and movies and uniquely beloved by Angelenos for providing the curious phenomenon of a beautiful, peaceful drive. My favorite time to take on the canyons is late at night, especially when it's moonless; it's like driving into the abyss. As you cruise along with your windows down, the cool wind whipping your face, and nothing to be heard but the sound of your own engine and possibly some suitable music blaring out of your stereo, it's as if you're the only person in the city, and this, your personal road to freedom.

106. *Go for a drive to the beach.* The use of the word "beach" in Los Angeles is as vague as "pasta" might be in Italy. There are plenty of choices to choose from, so when an Angeleno says "the beach" they're not necessarily referring to one in particular, but rather to their local or preferred stretch of the coastline. But as you drive along seventy-five miles of coast, what you'll discover is that one side of Los Angeles is literally just one giant beach. The beach can be the perfect place for a picnic, an after-lunch nap, a place to break a sweat playing volleyball or to cool off taking a dip, a place to catch a wave or even just the perfect place to meditate. From dawn to dusk, the beach is a beautiful place to be—but it's when the sun goes down that you realize that it's more than just sand and water. As much as the beach is pleasing to the eye, you'll discover that it's just as good for the ears and the nose as well. Just take a deep breath and a good listen and you'll know what I mean.

107. *Take a drive on "The Grand Concourse of Los Angeles"—also known as Wilshire Boulevard.* Named after Henry Gaylord Wilshire, this one-time barley field is now one of the main thoroughfares of Los Angeles, stretching from downtown's central business hub to the Pacific. While Sunset gives you a drastic change from the urban to the pastoral on a winding road, Wilshire gives you a longer look at the different neighborhoods in the city. On this 16-mile, somewhat pothole-riddled stretch (mostly between Western Avenue and La Cienega Boulevard), you'll discover pockets of people from the worker bees of downtown to the rich and famous of Rodeo Drive, from the college crowd of UCLA all the way to the surfer bums of Santa Monica. The people-watching this boulevard affords makes it one of my favorite drives to take.

108. *Cruise down Pacific Coast Highway (PCH) with the top down.* Driving in a convertible is the only way to enjoy PCH. Well, that's not exactly true, you can appreciate this legendary highway in anything that moves—but you should, at least once in your lifetime, drive down PCH in a convertible with the top down, the wind blowing through your hair, and a stellar playlist. With the top down you can enjoy unrestricted views of the Zuma, Santa Monica, and Venice boardwalks, piers, and million-dollar beachfront homes as you inhale the salty ocean air. And if you get hungry during your seaside cruise, you'll find plenty of places to stop for a bite. (Expect a lot of Surf 'n' Turf.)

109. ***Head for them thar Hills!*** The Hills, now known as the former home of that badly staged MTV reality show, is not what you'd imagine. Instead of bad break-ups, drama over exes, spray tans, creepy bad boys, and laughably large fake boobs, let's focus on the real reality: nature, sunshine, and—if you manage to get out of your car for a few well-spent hours—horseback riding and long walks. With all the glamour and action of the city beneath, not only tourists but longtime locals alike forget that away from the beaches there is a whole other world of peaceful countryside surrounding L.A. Driving up into the Hills is a scenic pleasure in itself, and finding a spot to get out of the car and stroll around in, with stunning views of the city and the sea around you, is easy. And if ever you get lost, just remember the Hills will always guide you in one direction: north. Working out what that means as far as getting back into town is concerned, is up to you to decipher.

110. Take a quick drive over the ***Vincent Thomas Bridge***. Okay, so it's not as epic at the seventy-five miles of coastal beauty you'd get along the beach, but please, don't scoff. Just a little over two miles, the Vincent Thomas Bridge, also known as "San Pedro's Golden Gate," is a stunner. As you drive across it you're dangling 185 feet above the main channel of L.A. Harbor. From here you get views all the way from Long Beach to Downtown L.A to the ports. If that's not enough, the bridge now glows at night with the help of solar powered blue LED lights, giving it an almost extraterrestrial appeal. Note: Before this bridge was built, Terminal Island was accessible by ferry for five cents. Some people were known to swim across to avoid paying the fare. Frankly, I'd rather drive.
430 NORTH SEASIDE AVENUE IN LOS ANGELES.

111. Behold the "Taj Mahal of Tiles" also known as the **Adamson House**.

In Malibu, the Adamson House—neither a structure with Mughal architectural influences nor a mausoleum—has garnered such a name purely because of its extraordinary reliance on tiling. This two-story, ten-room house, designed by Stiles O. Clements and completed in 1930, features everything you'd expect from a forward-looking building of its age—wrought ironwork, woodworking, hand-painted ceilings—but what this house is best known for is its use of local Malibu tile. There are tiles everywhere, from the beautiful ceramic wall clock to the floor-to-ceiling tiled bathroom walls, and even an imitation Persian carpet made of tiles. What's most astonishing is that throughout the house, no two tiles are alike.
23200 PACIFIC COAST HIGHWAY IN MALIBU. Cash only. 310-456-8432. www.adamsonhouse.org

112. Muster up some courage and go by the **Witch's House**.

The Spadena House, also known as the Witch's House, is one of the most interesting houses in Beverly Hills. Built in 1921 by the art director Harry C. Oliver, the curiously designed storybook house—originally built as a silent film set—was moved from Culver City to its current location in Beverly Hills to solve the frequent traffic problems its admirers caused in the streets nearby. Drive by the house's pointed and lopsided roof, its tiny windows, its garden, and its moat, and you'll see for yourself what the fuss is really all about. Just remember to be courteous; all names aside, this is still a private residence.

516 WALDEN DRIVE AT CARMELITA AVENUE IN BEVERLY HILLS.

113. Say hi to Kermit, perched on top of the **Jim Henson Company**.

On La Brea Avenue, high above eye-level on what was the entrance gate to the original Charlie Chaplin Studios, you'll find one of the most beloved amphibians of all time. Kermit the Frog, dressed as "the tramp" (Chaplin) himself, "oversees" what is now known as the Jim Henson Company. Tipping his hat and offering a smile, Kermit welcomes you to L.A. and to a piece of history.

1416 NORTH LA BREA AVENUE NEAR SUNSET BOULEVARD IN HOLLYWOOD. 323-802-1500. www.henson.com

114. See where Spanish and Egyptian ideas collide at the **Vista Theater**.

How fitting is it that the first two initials of the architect that built this theater spells L.A.? It must have been fate. In 1923, L.A. Smith began building a Spanish-style theater on Sunset Drive—but half-way through construction, an architectural detour was made. King Tut's tomb was discovered, and amidst the full-blown Egyptian craze that followed, Smith decided to switch on some Egyptian motifs—resulting in the strange visuals you see in the Vista today. With its carved serpents and Cleopatra sculptures overhead, this Vaudeville house, which housed the headquarters for Ed Wood Productions in its upstairs office, is the perfect example of mishmash Hollywood today.

4473 SUNSET DRIVE NEAR HILLHURST AVENUE IN LOS FELIZ. 323-660-6639. www.vintagecinemas.com

115. See a film in an Art Deco classic at the **Aero Theater**.

To claim that the Aero Theater has an interesting history is saying a lot, especially for a theater in this town, but it does. Originally built in 1939 specifically for workers of

Douglas Aircraft to see first-run-films during World War II, it soon transitioned to become a neighborhood favorite for residents in Santa Monica. The single screen movie house underwent a $1 million facelift, which restored much of its original Deco charm. Since then, non-profit American Cinematheque has used the Aero for various themed screenings, actors' retrospectives (Christian Bale and James Caan), and industry talks (a *TRON* panel), making the venue an important stop on the L.A. cine-circuit.

1328 MONTANA AVENUE IN SANTA MONICA. 310-260-1528. www.aerotheatre.com

---

116. Stroll around **Greystone Mansion** in Beverly Hills without getting arrested.

Unlike most homes in Beverly Hills with their around the clock security and "Do Not Trespass" signs, you'll find this grand home, or at least the land around it, wide open. Greystone Mansion is the largest home ever built in Beverly Hills with a whopping 55 rooms. Constructed by Edward L. Doheny for his son Edward Jr. in 1928 for a cool $4 million (that's almost $50 million today), it's surrounded by a sixteen-acre garden which is open today as a public park (the mansion itself is closed to the public).

905 LOMA VISTA DRIVE IN BEVERLY HILLS. Admission is free and complimentary parking can be found inside. 310-285-6830. www.greystonemansion.org

→ ***DID YOU KNOW?*** *Just like in a Hollywood crime thriller, Edward Sr.'s personal secretary murdered Edward Jr. when he was denied a raise, and then killed himself.*

---

117. Join in the grand tradition of photographing the **Hale House**, the "most photographed house in the city."

Unlike the homes of the fictional Brady Bunch or Norman Bates in *Psycho*, the Hale House has never been showcased on the big or little screen. Instead, this Queen Anne style Victorian built in 1885, with its elaborately decorated and highly colorful exterior, has only had the privilege of being captured on film—of the 35mm-camera variety (ring a bell?). The gingerbread-like house with its shingles and brick chimney, once located in Highland Park, is now located in the Heritage Square Museum (p. 104) in the Montecito Heights section of Los Angeles. It's not only a stunning example of Victorian architecture, but a fun one as well.

3800 HOMER STREET IN LOS ANGELES. 323-225-2700. www.heritagesquare.org/Hale_House

---

118. See the history of the California Water Wars at **Lake Hollywood Reservoir**.

If you've ever watched the movie *Chinatown* then you know that it was a fictional account of the California Water Wars, but the basic plot it was based on was actually factual. Let's just say back then, Los Angeles and the Owens River Valley folk didn't see eye to eye and a war erupted over diverted water turning farmland to desert. And one of the key players during that time was superintendent of the newly formed LADWP, William Mulholland (as in Mulholland Drive). But instead of delving into L.A.'s unsavory waterlogged past, let's focus on the Lake Hollywood Reservoir built in 1924 by Mulholland as part of the Owens River Aqueduct. A reservoir for drinking water (thus precluding swimming, boating, and dogs), it not only provides a great view, but a little noir as well, *Chinatown* style.

2600 LAKE HOLLYWOOD DRIVE IN HOLLYWOOD. 323-463-0830.
www.hike-la.com/hike_lake_hollywood_trail.html

---

119. Water and William Mulholland go hand and hand at the **William Mulholland Memorial Fountain.**

A passage from Samuel Taylor Coleridge's poem *The Rime of the Ancient Mariner* comes to mind whenever I see this giant fountain on the corner of Los Feliz and Riverside Drive. "Water, water, everywhere nor any drop to drink," is a fitting statement to describe Mulholland, a pivotal character in the California Water Wars that began in 1898. Mulholland, along with then mayor Frederick Eaton, diverted water from the Owens River into L.A., displacing hundreds of farmers and drying up the vegetation. You don't really get a sense of any of that when you look at this beautiful fountain, but I guess that's the point. A perfect place for photo shoots (weddings and quinceañeras) or indulging in a Fellini-esque *La Dolce Vita* moment à la Anita Ekberg (not legally), the fountain helps wash away memories of L.A.'s murky water history.

CORNER OF RIVERSIDE DRIVE AND LOS FELIZ BOULEVARD IN LOS ANGELES.

---

120. Venice, Italy, isn't the only **Venice** famous for its canals.

Yes, there's the Venetian in Las Vegas, but that's another book entirely. Here it's all about L.A., and if you've ever been to Venice, California, you should be familiar with the name Abbot Kinney. After all, it's the street name of Venice's main shopping and dining thoroughfare. But Abbot Kinney isn't just the name of a street; it's also the name of the developer behind "Venice of America," who created this beachtown resort. Back in 1905 he sought to re-create the look and feel of Venice, Italy, in Los Angeles by building a series of canals, complete with gondolas. Though initially quite popular, as the automobile industry grew, the canals were quickly viewed as outdated and were neglected for many years. But give the city credit. Instead of filling them in with cement and turning them into roads, they've been renovated, preserving that small taste of Italy at our doorsteps. The Venice Canals play host to the Holiday Boat Parade, which begins at Carroll and Grand Canal and is an annual neighborhood ritual. People get into the holiday spirit with costumes and more as they cruise the waterway.

CARROLL COURT AND EASTERN CANAL COURT IN VENICE. www.venicecanalsassociation.org

---

121. If you want another taste of Venice, go see the **Venice Columns**.

Architecturally, the Venice Columns are pretty much all that's left of Abbot Kinney's grand visions for "Venice of America." The logistics of a Venice in Southern California was apparently not the only thing to be considered impractical; the Venetian-themed architecture was eventually abandoned as well. Once it fell into disrepair, almost all was lost, except for the columns. Nothing mind-numbingly spectacular here—the tacky paint job certainly doesn't help, but it's a nice reminder of how Venice in L.A. almost came to be.

77 WINDWARD AVENUE AT PACIFIC AVENUE IN VENICE. www.veniceofamerica.org

---

122. Rub shoulders with John Travolta, Tom Cruise, and Will Smith at the **Château Èlysée**.

Okay, technically the rubbing shoulders part will probably never happen unless this particular chain of events happens to you. You arrive in Los Angeles, penniless. A day later, a hotshot director spots you begging for quarters on the corner of Wilshire and La Brea. He gives you the starring role in his next blockbuster film. You win numerous accolades including the Oscar, earn $20 million a film, and soon find yourself on Oprah's couch crying about your tragic past and win the hearts of millions. Suddenly L. Ron Hubbard visits you in a dream, riding in his spaceship alongside John Travolta and Tom Cruise, urging you to dedicate your life and your newly acquired fortune to Scientology. You wake up, call your agent and are instantly whisked away to the Chateau Elysee. A former hotel copied from a seventeenth-century French-Normandy castle, the Chateau, once home to the likes of Bette Davis, Errol Flynn, and Katherine Hepburn, is now your home. Did I mention it's now the Celebrity Center for the Church of Scientology? And since this particular chain of events may never happen, I suggest just enjoying the Chateau from afar, but don't stare too long; "you know who" may be staring right back at you.

5930 FRANKLIN AVENUE BETWEEN TAMARIND AND BRONSON AVENUE IN LOS ANGELES. 323-960-3100.

---

123. Go where the stars lived at the **Los Altos Apartments**.

It's easy to walk past the Los Altos Apartments and not know that you're walking past a piece of history. I've been doing it my whole life. It wasn't till I was in my early twenties and searching for an apartment to rent that I learned what this place was really all about.

From the outside, this plain white building with large signage on top doesn't hint at anything special. But once you walk inside and see its beautiful courtyard and fountain, the ballroom and fireplace, and interior details preserved since the time of old Hollywood, it makes you want to grab a pen and sign a lease. And although I didn't move in (the rent is a tad high), I was tempted. When you rent in L.A., you're not just paying for the roof over your head—you're also paying for the privilege to make statements like "Bette Davis once peed in my bathroom."

4121 WILSHIRE BOULEVARD AT BRONSON AVENUE IN KOREATOWN.

The Perfect Photo of the Hollywood Sign

After reading this book, I'm sure the occupants of Beachwood Drive won't be my biggest fans, but if you're writing a guidebook for the best places to take a picture of the Hollywood Sign, our city's cultural icon, a few sacrifices have to be made. (I guess apologies should be made to the residents of this idyllic neighborhood in advance for the influx of traffic—because I'm sure *everyone* will be reading this book.)

124. The first *real* view of the Hollywood Sign can be spotted just by driving up ***North Beachwood Drive.*** While there, remember to be courteous to the residents. If you decide to stop your car in the middle of the road to take a few snaps, use caution and common sense, or you may end up as road kill.

START AT BEACHWOOD DRIVE AND FRANKLIN AVENUE IN LOS ANGELES. HEAD NORTH.

125. While on Beachwood Drive, if you decide it might be better to see the Hollywood Sign from the back of a horse, head to the ***Sunset Ranch Hollywood.*** This horse ranch is located just under the Hollywood Sign; not many places can boast about a view like that. Not only will you get to see the sign, you'll also get a guided tour of Griffith Park as well as scenic views of L.A., the perfect package for the visually hungry.

3400 NORTH BEACHWOOD DRIVE IN HOLLYWOOD. 323-469-5450.
www.sunsetranchhollywood.com.

126. Go to ***Hollywood and Highland*** for a view. Filled with stores to shop from, carts to browse, and restaurants to dine in, the Hollywood and Highland complex provides you with a lot of options, but it also provides you with a view. Walk to the back of the plaza and take the elevator up to the viewing bridges up top and find yourself with a view of the Hollywood Sign most people don't even notice.

CORNER OF HOLLYWOOD BOULEVARD AND HIGHLAND AVENUE IN HOLLYWOOD.

127. Get an incredibly close view from ***Deronda Drive***. If you can flow with the directions on this slight windy course, you'll be rewarded with an amazing view. Just punch Deronda Drive and Rockcliff into your GPS, bring a camera, and you're set. If you go to your left, you'll find a gate. You can park and take your picture from here.

128. Get a behind-the-scenes view of the Hollywood Sign from the top of ***Mount Lee***. Mount Lee has always played back-up to the Hollywood Sign. Some people even refer to it as "the Hollywood Sign hill." But once you see the view of the sign from up top, you'll be singing a different tune. Follow the same directions provided for the Deronda Drive view listed above. At the gate you'll find a road you can hike up that will lead you up behind the Hollywood Sign.

129. The **I.Magnin Building** is hidden in plain sight.

Finding the I.Magnin building in Los Angeles is like finding Waldo. It's a bit tricky, and once you find it, you're a bit embarrassed; it's been in front of you the whole time. The ever-changing landscape of the L.A. real estate market has seen the rise and fall of many a building here, but this 1939 Art Deco gem still remains. Originally built as the home for department store I.Magnin by architects Myron Hunt and H.C. Chambers, the exterior relief of running deer hinted at the interior treasures. When I.Magnin relocated to Bullocks Wilshire, it was renamed the Wilshire Galleria and now houses a predominantly Korean upscale mini-mall. And although most people won't remember the building's history, walking through its Art Deco halls complete with beautiful chandeliers and golden hued interiors is a reminder of how things once were.

3240 WILSHIRE BOULEVARD AT NEW HAMPSHIRE AVENUE IN KOREATOWN. 213-381-3610.

130. Window displays became an art form at **Bullocks Wilshire**.

I'd like to think that all L.A. department stores took a note from Bullocks Wilshire back in its heyday. Designed by John and Donald Parkinson and completed in 1929, this Art Deco gem with its 241-foot tower sheathed in (now tarnished green) copper, was not only one of the first stores to have valet parking to cater to the city's burgeoning car culture, but it also turned its traditional window display out to face the street. Why? To be as distracting as possible and capture the attention of drivers passing by, luring them over to shop. Brilliant marketing strategy or a fender bender waiting to happen, either way Bullock's became the premiere shopping mecca in L.A. In the early nineties it suffered major damage from the 1992 riots and finally shuttered its doors in 1993,

but a year later its long-time neighbor Southwestern Law School acquired the building and restored it to its original glory.
3050 WILSHIRE BOULEVARD AT WESTMORELAND AVENUE IN KOREATOWN. 213-738-6700. www.swlaw.edu

---

131. Catch views as far as the eye can see at **Griffith Observatory**.

Not only is the Observatory the place to see real stars (p. 21), it's also a classic place to visit for a view of L.A.—but that's not the only thing you'll see here. Visit the Astronomers Monument, a tribute to the six greatest astronomers of all time. (I'll leave you to do the guesswork.) Walk the orbit of Venus in less than a minute on the scale model of the solar system carved out on the front sidewalk, or walk along the Gottlieb Transit Corridor and stand on one of the sunset or moonset radial lines that point out towards the horizon. But if it's a view of L.A. you seek, head toward the Observation Terraces. West points you toward the Pacific, while east gives you downtown L.A. Whichever you pick, you'll be given a panoramic view of our fair city. And with a few telescopes and benches scattered around, you can either take a closer look or take a minute to relax. After all, not only have you walked around the whole solar system in just a few minutes, you've just seen the whole of L.A. without breaking a sweat. The Observatory: there's definitely more than meets the eye.
2800 EAST OBSERVATORY AVENUE IN LOS ANGELES. 213-473-0800. www.griffithobs.org

---

132. Make the stars blush by stealing a few kisses under the night sky at the **Roof Observation Deck** at Griffith Observatory.

The Observatory has been mentioned several times already in this book, but there's a reason for it. It just fits so many criteria of what you want to find in this city—one of those perfect places. A perfect place to visit almost any time, you really haven't seen L.A. till you've seen it from here at night. Open till 10 p.m. almost every night, not only does the Roof Observation Deck provide a breathtaking view of the city with its twinkling lights, it's also the perfect excuse to leave your jacket in the car and cuddle in close on those cold nights. And if you're looking to impress someone with your knowledge of constellations, here are a few basics: the Big Dipper, due north, is most visible during the spring, and Polaris is the North Star. In autumn look for four stars that form a square, the top left star is part of Andromeda and the other three are part of Pegasus.
2800 EAST OBSERVATORY AVENUE IN LOS ANGELES. Entry gates into Griffith Park close at 10 p.m. so enter anytime beforehand if you're planning a night under the stars. 213-473-0800. www.griffithobs.org

133. See where Bono got his inspiration at the **Rosslyn Hotel**.

People think that the Rosslyn Hotel, with its giant heart-shaped neon sign, was the location of Irish super band U2's 1987 music video "Where the Streets Have No Name," but that's actually not the case. Although the original Rosslyn and its annex sister building (once the tallest building in L.A.) are just across the street from each other and offer absolutely amazing views of downtown from their rooftops, they didn't film there. Instead, U2 filmed two blocks over on the corner of Main and 7th, on top of a one-story liquor store (now a Mexican restaurant), with a miniature Hotel Rosslyn sign erected in the background—hence the mix-up. And if you're still not convinced it's not the Rosslyn Hotel they're on, take a closer look: the sign says "1100 New Million Dollar Hotel Rosslyn," its sister building. Another clue: the Hotel Cecil in the background is two blocks away from the Rosslyns. Though the rooftops are not open to the public, if you'd like to experience a piece of history, you can move in—the Rosslyns are now lofts. And the rooftops are available for filming, so feel free to come up for a nighttime visit when the giant heart-shaped signs light up the sky.

451 SOUTH MAIN STREET AT 5TH STREET IN DOWNTOWN L.A. 213-627-2786. 213-621-3166 for filming. www.rosslynlofts.net

134. Amodioa! Romantik! Romanticismo! Whatever language you speak, when it comes to romance, the end result is always the same when you **take a ride on Gondola Amore.** A cruise in a gondola—with heart-shaped seats, no less—around the Riviera at Redondo Beach provides the perfect setting for love, for new couples just starting out, or old-timers alike. And if the sea air, along with other distractions, gets your appetite going during your cruise, don't worry: appetizers are included with each ride.

RIVIERA IN REDONDO BEACH. 310-376-6977. gondolaamore.com

135. Get a glimpse of the "Riviera of America" on **Malibu Pier**.

Located in the heart of surf country, the Malibu Pier stands out as an historic landmark. With Surfrider Beach just adjacent to the pier attracting surfers from all over the world, the pier's atmosphere is the perfect complement to the coastal location and the area's rich history—and it's got a pretty good view as well.

23000 PACIFIC COAST HIGHWAY IN MALIBU. www.malibupiersportfishing.com

136. When you're done enjoying the pier, head over to **Neptune's Net** for the freshest catch of the day.

Around since 1958, "The Net" has become the perfect surfside dining hangout for locals, tourists, celebrities, and herds of motorcyclists on Harleys. They all come here for the fresh seafood, the delicious chowder, the laid-back atmosphere, and of course, to watch the perfect Malibu sunset.

42505 PACIFIC COAST HIGHWAY IN MALIBU. 310-457-3095. www.neptunesnet.com

137. Drive up or down the 101 near downtown and catch a glimpse of the **High School for the Visual and Performing Arts**.

At first sight, the strangely shaped building with the winding steel walkway leading to nowhere is confounding. What is it? Why is it there? As soon as you investigate further, you'll discover that's not the only strange thing going on here architecturally. The campus has not one but seven quirky buildings, each with their own unique design (their library is in the shape of a cone), devoted to music, dance, theater art, and visual art. Open to the community and seemingly functional, this high school is a prime example of the kind of innovation a tight school system budget can come up with.

450 NORTH GRAND BOULEVARD AND CESAR E. CHAVEZ AVENUE IN DOWNTOWN L.A. 213-217-8600. www.central-lausd-ca.schoolloop.com

Bridge and Tunnel

For much of America, bridges and tunnels are gateways to the past, reminders of the country we've conquered, and the priceless links between cities and suburbs. In L.A., where roads are everything and the car is king, bridges are as much a part of the city's fabric as the buildings themselves. But for all their irrefutable practicality, a few of these structures stand out as gemstones in the jewelry of the city's streetscapes. And as much as there is to experience out in the wide-open spaces of Los Angeles, a view from inside a somewhat confined space can be just as spectacular. Subways don't have the monopoly on tunnels in this town. Here, tunnels were carved and created for another use: the automobile. Whether to alleviate traffic or created as a destination marker, a ride through one of Los Angeles's famous tunnels can be a surprisingly picturesque diversion.

Bridges

138. ***Angeles Crest Highway.*** Yes, it doesn't say "bridge" in its title, but this highway, a segment of California State Route 2 known as the Angeles Crest Scenic Byway, has several concrete arch bridges along its 66-mile route going over canyons like La Canada, Woodwardia, and Slide. You may not even notice you're on or passing a bridge, but I can't blame you—you'll be too distracted by the view. Surrounded by the majestic ridges of the San Gabriel Mountains, you'll pass through the Angeles National Forest on the highest road in Southern California—and it's an awe-inspiring sight.
CA STATE ROUTE 2. Directions: SR-1 to US-101 to I-210 to Route 138.

139. With the ***Henry Ford Bridge*** and the ***Commodore Schuyler F. Heim Bridge***, you get two bridges for the price of one—they run parallel to one another! They used to link the mainland to Terminal Island; the Ford was the only railroad link, and the Heim was the largest vertical lift bridge on the West Coast. Both are amazing to behold, especially when the bridge has to be raised for an oncoming ship. And for those bridge buffs, Joseph B. Strauss, who later went on to engineer the Golden Gate, designed the original Ford Bridge.
CA-103 TOWARDS STATE ROUTE 47, TERMINAL ISLAND FREEWAY.

140. To be or not to be...a bridge, that is the question that many have about the ***Franklin Avenue Bridge*** also known as the ***Shakespeare Bridge***. If a bridge's span is this short, doth thou still call it a bridge? Others may doubt it, but have no fear, 'tis a bridge for sure. And with its Gothic arches, columns and turret towers, this charming structure would make the great playwright himself spout a sonnet or two.
FRANKLIN AVENUE AND ST. GEORGE STREET IN LOS FELIZ.

141. Cross over the ***Dell Street Bridge***. Of the four bridges (Linnie, Sherman, Dell, and Howland) that cross over the Venice Canals, I chose the Dell because it's the first I ever crossed, and therefore my favorite. But I'll leave it to you to decide which is yours. And as you stand there contemplating and examining your choices, be sure to take note of how beautiful the Venice Canals are, how lovely the houses that line the waterway—and whether it's sunset or moonlight or any time of day, how magical it all is.
DELL AVENUE AT CARROLL CANAL IN VENICE.

142. Question: What's long and red, and doesn't touch water? Answer: ***Echo Park Lake Bridge***. Constructed over 100 years ago, the Echo Park Lake Bridge in Echo Park is a great place to go to see lotus flowers that bloom here from June through September. Whether you're in the mood to stand on possibly the oldest bridge in Los Angeles, or just look out onto the lake where Jack Nicholson paddled around in *Chinatown*, there's plenty to see.
751 ECHO PARK AVENUE IN ECHO PARK.

143. Get a view or three from the ***North Broadway Bridge***. The North Broadway Bridge, with its cut outs, detailing, portico, and columns, is one of the better-looking bridges (out of twenty-seven) that cross the L.A. River. Not only do you get a great towering view of downtown L.A. from a distance, but also find yourself in view of the North Spring and North Main Bridges. Bring a few friends, a few cameras, and snap away—the end results will be a unique souvenir of your trip to the bridge.
NORTH BROADWAY OVER THE LOS ANGELES RIVER NEAR AVENUE 18 IN LOS ANGELES.

144. Take in the view from ***Colorado Blvd. Bridge (Colorado Street Bridge)*** just make sure it's a safe distance from the ledge. It's hard to believe that this beautiful bridge with its concrete Beaux Art arches, railing, and lovely lights could have such an unattractive nickname, but sometimes there's no getting around it. Built in 1913 by the Kansas City firm of Waddell & Harrington, the bridge became a popular destination for those down on their luck and in poor spirits during the Great Depression of the 1930s. After close to fifty despondent jumpers fell from its heights, the Colorado Blvd. Bridge became known as the "Suicide Bridge" and the name has stuck ever since. If you come to visit the bridge, please don't jump (they've installed a suicide prevention rail)—instead, take in the view of Pasadena and the Foothills, and enjoy a nice stroll. If you're lucky or unlucky, depending on how you look at it, you'll run into a ghost or two that are reported to haunt this bridge.

→ ***NOTE:*** *The Bridge provides a beautiful view, but the real beauty is the bridge itself.*

WEST COLORADO BOULEVARD NEAR ARROYO BOULEVARD IN PASADENA.

145. Meet "the handsome small sister of the Colorado Street Bridge," the ***La Loma Bridge***. At its opening over 90 years ago, La Loma was given the "small sister" nickname due to its aesthetic similarities to the Colorado Street Bridge.

With its open spandrel arch structure filled with Greek and Roman influences, it's a real beauty. The best way to enjoy La Loma is on the ground. The tree-lined pedestrian and equestrian walkways that pass under the bridge allow you several vantage points to the bridge that you wouldn't normally have with others. And when it's springtime and there's green all around, you feel transported to another place altogether.
LA LOMA ROAD AT ARROYO BOULEVARD IN PASADENA.

---

146. *Head to Glendale to get a taste of Belgian architecture.* On Geneva St., Glenoaks Blvd., and Kenilworth Avenue, you can find three prime examples of Vierandeel truss types. Don't worry; I don't know how to pronounce the name either. The Vierandeel truss bridges, designed by Belgian architect Arthur Vierandeel and rarely seen outside of Belgium, may be the oldest in the U.S. Built in 1937 as part of the Verdugo Flood Control Project, these bridges are unique in the country and are worth a visit just to see what Los Angeles might've looked like had this direction gathered steam and overcome the obstacles of cost three quarters of a century ago.
GENEVA STREET, GLENOAKS BOULEVARD AND KENILWORTH AVENUE NEAR GLENOAKS BOULEVARD OVER THE VERDUGO WASH.

---

147. *L.A. River Bridges,* the veins of Downtown L.A. From First to Seventh, the concrete spans that cross over the riverbed link downtown to various parts of the city. From modern to ornate, these bridges are a huge part of what L.A. means to its locals. They provide the best views of the L.A. River, and you'll find that even Angelenos who've lived here all their lives still slow down to look around as they drive over. Just watch out for dips in the road leading up to the bridges or your muffler might end up dragging behind you.
1ST TO 7TH STREETS AT MISSION ROAD IN LOS ANGELES.

Tunnels

---

148. *2nd Street Tunnel.* Music videos, car commercials, movie chase scenes—if you've ever seen one filmed in a 1,500 foot-long tunnel lined with shiny white tile that has the clinical appeal of a hospital bathroom, then you're visually familiar with the 2nd Street Tunnel in Downtown L.A. Originally built in 1924 to help alleviate traffic, the 2nd Street tunnel has become a popular destination for shoots due to how the light reflects off the tiles while driving through it, especially at night. In a car, on foot, or by bike (please use caution and be aware of traffic), this little piece of cinematic wonder gives you a real sense of "tunnel vision." The one thing you'll never see

on screen? The homeless people that sometimes hang out inside the tunnel's walkways.
2ND STREET AND HILL STREET TO FLOWER STREET IN DOWNTOWN L.A.

149. *McClure Tunnel.* If you're driving along the 10 Freeway heading west, there's really not much to see. But once you spot the dark, ivy-strewn McClure Tunnel, you know everything is about to change. This tunnel gives meaning to the phrase "light at the end of the tunnel" because once you resurface at the other end, you'll suddenly find yourself at the Pacific Ocean. You'll then coast along the Santa Monica beaches and soon join the Pacific Coast Highway. At night, you'll often be greeted by the lights from the Santa Monica Pier, the sounds of nighttime revelers, and, if you're lucky, a full moon.
I-10 FREEWAY WEST TO SANTA MONICA.

150. *Figueroa Street Tunnels.* My favorite tunnels in L.A. are located on the 110 North Freeway heading to Pasadena, where the ride is vastly improved because of these "holes in mountains." For one, because you have never seen any oncoming traffic for a stretch of it, and for another, from the freeway you can see quaint neighborhoods and houses that are distinctly not very L.A., and last but not least, you get to drive through four tunnels. What makes these four my favorite is not because they're beautiful or have any special significance, but for the sheer superstitious notion that if I hold my breath while driving through all of them, by the time I exit the last tunnel, whatever wish I made at the first tunnel will come true. Childish? Maybe. Dangerous? That's contingent on how bad traffic is. But I guess it all really depends on what you wished for.
110 FREEWAY NORTH FROM DOWNTOWN L.A. TO PASADENA.

151. Take the Catalina Express to . . . **Catalina Island.**

Just 22 miles heading southwest off the coast of Los Angeles, you'll find the island of Catalina, one of the Channel Islands. With a little over 4,000 inhabitants, you could hardly call Catalina a bustling metropolis, but what it lacks in size and population it makes up for with its rich varieties of flora and fauna, and a multitude of outdoor activities. But in order to partake, you'll need to get there first. Departing from Long Beach, San Pedro, or Dana Point by boat, you'll really get the wind in your hair, some sun, and a taste of ocean spray on your face. (If you're looking for a bit more comfort, there are different levels of seating available as well as different types of vessels to choose from.) Just remember to bring a comb and sun block or you might disembark from your ride resembling a red-faced tumbleweed.
800-481-3470. www.catalinaexpress.com

152. And while you're there, take a tour on a **glass bottom boat.**

Catalina has many wondrous views, particularly of its sea life. What better way to take advantage of its famous pristine waters than to ride on a glass bottom boat. It provides children and adults alike with the perfect combination of discovery and excitement, and you'll get to enjoy the sea without having to get wet. And if that's not enough, why not take a ride on the semi-sub, which takes you five feet under the sea for almost a full 360 of the ocean? You'll enjoy the reefs and trips to the Marine Preserve to see the colorful fish and kelp forests, but if you really want to make it memorable, take a nighttime voyage and see what nocturnal creatures are lurking below.

877-510-2888. www.catalinaadventuretours.com

153. Take a stroll on the **Parkway Promenade.**

For the residents of San Pedro, once a small fishing village, living on the Pacific Rim hasn't always been a day at the beach. Growing up in the shadow of the Port of Los Angeles, many rarely had a chance to venture to the water's edge with all the shipping activity blocking much of the access to the local beaches and the ocean itself. But now with the new waterfront renovation, the sea of container ships and cranes and trucks and trains has somewhat parted and in its place is a pedestrian friendly, waterfront parkway with a spectacular fountain complete with water shows. Finally giving the community its due, with a little Vegas flair thrown in for good measure.

110 FREEWAY SOUTH TO SAN PEDRO. www.sanpedrowaterfront.com

154. Go people-watching on **Will Rogers State Beach . . .**

Will Rogers will always be famous for two things: Pamela Anderson's breasts. For those die-hard *Baywatch* fans, coming here and wearing your red swimsuit while practicing your slow-mo beach run sequence is a must. Anywhere else would be an insult to the name Hasselhoff.

17700 PACIFIC COAST HIGHWAY IN SANTA MONICA. 310-305-9503. www.parks.ca.gov

155. . . . and go whale-watching on an **L.A. Harbor Breeze Cruise.**

Just sit right back and I'll tell you a tail—a whale's tail that is, while you're aboard this three-hour tour. Blue whales, the largest mammals on the planet, once hunted to the brink of extinction, are thankfully still around, and can be found in record numbers off of Santa Monica Bay. Never seen one of the most amazing creatures on the planet in the flesh? Well now's your chance to see them up close (safety for the animal and passengers will determine how close). And if you're lucky, you'll get to see it expel water from its blowhole, which can sometimes reach 30 feet or more. Sheer beauty and sheer power, the blue whale is a definite sight to see on the L.A. Harbor Breeze Cruises.

100 AQUARIUM WAY, DOCK #2 IN LONG BEACH. 562-432-4900. www.lawhalewatching.com

---

156. If you want a meal with a view that's out of this world, then visit the **Cosmic Café**.

Located in the San Gabriel Mountains at the Mount Wilson Observatory (p. 31), it's the perfect place to grab a bite and see Los Angeles. The fare is simple, fresh, and delicious. And considering it's a trek to the top (if you hike or bike), any food would be appreciated; kudos to them for making sure it is good. So find somewhere to sit down and enjoy the beautiful sights, and dig in.

RED BOX AT MOUNT WILSON ROAD IN MT. WILSON. www.mtwilson.edu/cafe.php

---

157. Even at over a hundred years old, **Castle Green** can still make a building "green" with envy.

This castle is imposing; at first glance you don't know what to make of the Moorish/Spanish-style building on the corner of Raymond and Green Street in Old Town Pasadena. With its many towers, domes, and arches, the architecture that makes up this seven-story behemoth truly makes it a sight to behold. Once a lavish resort as part of the Hotel Green, the complex was soon divided and the Castle separated into individually owned units. And although you can't visit the premises unless you're lucky enough to make it onto one of its semi-annual tours, book a lavish wedding in one of its charming rooms, or have the good fortune to live there, the exterior view may be all you really need.

99 SOUTH RAYMOND AVENUE BETWEEN GREEN STREET AND DAYTON STREET IN PASADENA. 626-385-7774. www.castlegreen.com

---

158. The **Huntington Gardens** provide you with an ever-changing extravaganza of colors.

I once heard someone say that there was nothing that could rival an English garden. Instead of remarking with a rebuttal as I often do, I just assumed that the person in question suffered the misfortune of never having visited the Huntington Gardens. I do hope that person has done so by now. Huntington boasts 150 acres of botanical wonders, with twelve specialized gardens. Of the twelve, the most notable are the Desert Garden, with the largest mature cacti garden (ouch) in the U.S.; the Japanese

Garden complete with its own bridge and furnished Japanese house; and, last but not least, the Rose Garden. The Rose Garden painstakingly details the history of the rose over the last 2,000 years. And for kids, there's the Helen and Peter Bing Children's Garden: a lovely playground where they can explore basic scientific principles hands-on—playing with magnetic sand, smelling their way around the Fragrance Garden, or crawling through a rainbow prism tunnel.

1151 OXFORD ROAD IN SAN MARINO. Two entrance gates: Oxford Road and Allen Avenue. 626-405-2100. www.huntington.org

---

159. Get a side of chicken and a taste of high-end contemporary architecture at the **KFC** on Western Avenue in Koreatown.

The one thing that most fast-food chains lack is imagination—especially when it comes to their buildings. Fast-food joints are usually just square boxes with windows, a drive thru, and a parking lot. But then you see the Kentucky Fried Chicken off of Western Avenue in Koreatown and you begin to wonder: maybe they do care. Built by Jeff Daniels in 1990, who once worked for the architect Frank Gehry, the building was created as an abstract interpretation of—you guessed it—a bucket of chicken. It's a pinch of futurism in a form one might not expect to find—and it's finger lickin' good.

340 NORTH WESTERN AVENUE AT OAKWOOD AVENUE IN LOS ANGELES. 323-467-7421. www.kfc.com

---

160. Find a sea of shining turquoise in the middle of the city at the **Eastern Colombia Building**.

If you look out your window while driving on the 10 Freeway, you're bound to notice a certain building. It's not because this building is taller than the others or weirder for that matter, though it does have a very large four-sided clock tower emblazoned with the word "Eastern" in neon. On the contrary, the Eastern Building is one of the loveliest and finest examples of Art Deco architecture in L.A. This 13-story building, encased as it is in turquoise terra cotta with deep blue and gold trim, is a splash of color in the Broadway Theater District. (Be sure to look out for the amazing blue and gold sunburst just above the building's main entrance.) And while you're there, don't forget to look down: the sidewalks surrounding the Broadway and Ninth Street sides of the building are multi-colored terrazzo (same material as the Stars on the Walk of Fame: p. 16) laid in zigzag and chevron patterns. Best of all, pedestrians can walk through the building; it's a retail arcade.

849 SOUTH BROADWAY IN DOWNTOWN L.A. 323-930-3742. www.easterncolumbialofts.com

161. Watch a ball game from the highest tier of **Dodger Stadium**.

Not only are you figuratively behind home plate, the best seat in the house—you also get a bird's-eye view of the whole stadium that makes you feel that the diamond is all yours.

1000 ELYSIAN PARK AVENUE IN LOS ANGELES. 323-224-1507. losangeles.dodgers.mlb.com

162. Learn to read palms on **Canon Drive**.

In Beverly Hills, you'll find yourself driving up a street lined with truly impressive-looking palm trees. As you look up at the towering trunks, you'll get a real sense of the L.A. you've only heard and read about, but now you've finally seen it. (Ironically, these palm trees that have become such an iconic symbol of Los Angeles are not actually native. While there are native palms too, the tall massive palms that line this street are not.)

START AT SANTA MONICA BOULEVARD AND CANON DRIVE AND HEAD NORTH.

163. Japan is in L.A. at **Yamashiro**.

For almost 90 years, Yamashiro has been a part of Hollywood history. Once a private estate that housed a priceless collection of Asian artifacts, it has since been transformed into a restaurant with a public garden. With a 600-year-old pagoda imported from Japan, a swimming pool, and tranquil inner garden, Yamashiro serves you Japanese cuisine with a heaping slice of eye candy. You wouldn't expect anything less from a place also known as "the Mountain Palace."

1999 NORTH SYCAMORE AVENUE IN HOLLYWOOD. 323-466-5125. www.yamashirorestaurant.com

164. Take a ride on the wheel of fortune at **Pacific Park**.

Walking along the Santa Monica Pier you'll see great views of the surrounding coastline, but if you want the best view, you've got to go up. Head over to Pacific Park, the amusement park located on the pier, and buy a ticket for the Ferris wheel. Though the line may be long and the ride shorter than you expect, if timed right, the sunset view from the top is the best around.

380 SANTA MONICA PIER IN SANTA MONICA. 310-260-8744. For parties: 310-260-8744 ext. 283. www.pacpark.com

165. Get a 360-degree view of Los Angeles on a **helicopter tour**.

Sure all the places mentioned in this chapter can give you glimpses here and there, but to really experience L.A. you'll have to take to the sky. Helicopter tours give you amazing views of the Hollywood Sign, Santa Monica, the Coastline, and souvenir photos very few can boast about taking themselves. Los Angeles Helicopter Tours operate out of the Van Nuys, Burbank, and the El Monte airport.

818-859-5500 or visit www.los-angeles-helicopter-tours.com

166. Find a taste of London with a view of L.A. at the **SoHo House** in West Hollywood.

This members-only clubhouse on the top two floors on Sunset is where British tourists and ex-pats converge upon when they long for a taste of home—the perfect place for elitists that like to hang out with other people with similar accents. I compare being a member to comedian Ricky Gervais's jokes about not wanting to ride ferries: "But that would mean mixing with the general public and I don't (insert grimace here)." Sound like your kind of place? You can fill out a form online and wait for approval to become a member, or wrangle up a guest visit with a friend that already has membership and decide for yourself if a bar, a sitting room, a roof top garden with a pleasant view and a retractable roof, as well as the chance to dine and mingle with the upper crust is worth the $1,800 membership fee. You might be better off parking up on a hill, drinking tea out of thermos, and listening to the BBC on the radio.

9200 WEST SUNSET BOULEVARD #817 IN WEST HOLLYWOOD. 310-432-9200. www.sohohousewh.com

Sights of Sanctuary

With millions of people residing in Los Angeles, to be alone in this city seems an improbable notion. To escape, to find a still place, a moment to yourself to relish in solitude, or even a private place to share with a friend, can be difficult to imagine as you sit in rush-hour traffic, walk along a crowded beach looking for an empty patch of sand to claim, or even go to the grocery store to buy a carton of milk. Don't despair: explore the right places and the city will reveal unto you a sanctuary of your very own.

167. *Take a break along Mulholland.* This mysterious road filled with twists and turns has the ability to transport you up and way from the city. Here you find freedom from freeways, a taste of the old and unchanged, and in one single glance, will find yourself helplessly in love with L.A. Along this road vantage points such as the Hollywood and Universal City overlooks provide you with sweeping views of the city, and at times, a sense of calm, especially at night, from a long day at work. And as you continue to drive along its winding path, hopefully you'll discover a few private spots of your own.
Hollywood Bowl Overlook: 7036 MULHOLLAND DRIVE IN HOLLYWOOD. Universal City Overlook: 7701 MULHOLLAND DRIVE IN HOLLYWOOD.

168. *Get a taste of the Cold War when you visit the San Vicente Mountain Park.* Off the well-traveled portion of Mulholland, along a rugged path, you'll find within hiking distance, an unusual park that offers a firsthand look at the Soviet Missile Crisis in the 1950s. You'll find yourself face-to-face with strange equipment that was used as a Nike Missile defense site here, as well as sixteen other locations, used to protect L.A. from any impending danger. But once the Cold War ended, they became obsolete, and the site was carefully preserved and turned into a park by the Santa Monica Mountain Conservancy to remind us of our not-too-distant past. Getting to the park usually requires a two-mile hike, but on occasion the gate is left open allowing you to drive all the way up.
17500 MULHOLLAND DRIVE IN ENCINO ALONG THE UNPAVED PORTION.
www.lamountains.com

169. *Stop alongside the Pacific Coast Highway for a breath of fresh air and a salt-tinged kiss or two.* The beach at night is my favorite place. Long gone are the sun-tanning crowds that line the shore on a hot summer's day. Long gone is all their chatter. After the sun has dipped its golden head below the ocean's dark horizon, the beach lies deserted, and ready for you and you alone. There you'll stand and feel as if you're the only person in the world as you stare out into black, as the waves wash away all the tensions of city life and leave you at peace. And if the solitude of the beach at night becomes too much, then come back when the moon is full with someone you love.

170. *Reap the fruits of your labor at Runyon Canyon.* Come to Runyon Canyon to work up a sweat; its steep steps and hilly trails ensure that. But once you get to the top of Runyon, you're quickly rewarded with a chance to rest in the form of a huge oversized bench. Depending on what you're in the mood for—a sunrise or a sunset—as you sit on your rustic throne, look out onto the city and let your feet dangle. Whether it's early or late, either way, be sure bring your sunglasses: you'll need them.

171. ***Get a million-dollar view of the Pacific for free at Getty Villa.*** High up in the Pacific Palisades resides a building inspired by the Villa of the Papyri, a home famously covered in ash by the eruption of Vesuvius and named after the discovery of a papyrus scroll library that was located within. The Getty Villa (p. 42), though most commonly lauded for the artworks inside, is also worth visiting for its outside alone—particularly the outer peristyle, a columned porch that makes me swoon, not only because of the beautifully manicured formal garden with a smattering of Roman sculptures thrown in for good measure, but because of the 220-foot-long reflecting pool and the amazing views of the Pacific. While wandering the grounds at certain times you feel as if you are alone in making this discovery that is the Getty Villa. And as you stand there, overlooking the ocean, you can only imagine how beautiful Ancient Rome must have been.

17985 PACIFIC COAST HIGHWAY IN PACIFIC PALISADES. Admission is free but booking in advance is required. 310-440-7300. www.getty.edu

172. ***Get another million-dollar view for free across town at the Getty Center.*** "One man, two visions," is how one might describe the J. Paul Getty museums. The more contemporary of the two, the Richard Meier-designed Center, is a modern marvel. The stark design is accentuated even more by the painstakingly designed flowering plant garden designed by Robert Irwin. And during your visit you'll be surprised to be treated with so many different incredible views. The tram ride there offers you an ascending view; the view from on top gives you a clear view of the L.A. Basin; from the Center you get a view of the gardens; and at night, you'll see the nighttime traffic on the 405 as the red and white lights twinkle past each other, like blood cells that flow through L.A.'s veins.

1200 GETTY CENTER DRIVE IN LOS ANGELES. 310-440-7300. www.getty.edu

173. ***Do a 360 at Baldwin Hills Scenic Overlook.*** It's more than just looking to get a work out as you walk or drive up a winding mile-long trail, or climb up the steep stone staircase at the Baldwin Hills Scenic Overlook. You also come to find an unobstructed full view of this city. And if you don't think being able to do a 360 from one point in L.A. isn't all that impressive, then consider the angle: this scenic overlook looks north while all the others look south.

6300 HETZLER ROAD IN CULVER CITY. www.parks.ca.gov

174. Owned by Larry Flynt, the **Flynt Building** is probably not what you might think.

In 1972, architect William Pereira designed a huge, modern oval building on the corner of Wilshire and La Cienega Blvd. with hints of modern Rococo design. In 1984, Larry Flynt, owner/creator of *Hustler*, bought it and made it the home of Flynt Publications. You'd expect a purchase from a man with a solid gold wheelchair who built an empire off of pornography to be a bit more ostentatious and gaudy, maybe a few boobs here and there—but this building is anything but. This oval-shaped building (one of the few remaining in existence), with its smoked glass and beautifully-designed lobby, screams class and classic. Maybe Flynt knew all along that this building and his magazine would go hand-in-hand; after all, *Hustler*'s been around for almost forty years too. I guess that makes it a classic in its own right.

8484 WILSHIRE BOULEVARD BETWEEN LA CIENEGA BOULEVARD AND HAMILTON DRIVE. 323-782-7877. www.flyntbuilding.com

175. You get two for the price of one at the **Wiltern Theater**.

On the corner of Wil(shire) and (Wes)tern there's no way to miss the Wiltern Theater. With its signature blue-green glazed terra-cotta tiles, the building pops out against the high-rise condos that face its corner. Though the theater looks like one giant building, it's actually two, the Wiltern Theater and the twelve-story Pellisier Building, also known as the Wiltern Center. The Wiltern is a theater used for events, while the Pellisier is an office building that once housed contemporary street artist Shepard Fairey's studio.

3790 WILSHIRE BOULEVARD AT WESTERN AVENUE IN KOREATOWN. 213-380-5005. www.livenation.com

176. Go see the twins at the **Wilshire Colonnade**.

Just down the street from the Wiltern Theater on Oxford are two identical, eleven-story Normandy-style towers. These two office buildings are beautiful to see, but it's what's in between and underneath their unusual arches that's the surprise. Trees, a concentric oval fountain, and an open airy marble-clad space gives you a place to slow down and relax. And if you'd like another view to take in from this place, get low. While lying on the ground, you'll get an optical illusion, as the two towers seem as if they're curving inward.

3701 WILSHIRE BOULEVARD AT SOUTH SERRANO AVENUE IN KOREATOWN. 213-381-3753.

177. You'll find a play date for you and your dog at the **Silverlake Dog Park**.

When I was in high school my biology teacher spent one entire class explaining his theory about men with cute dogs. Those with cute dogs usually dated more often than those without. He even put his theory to the test by buying a small dog. It proved quite effective and in turn, I was left feeling very sorry for the dog. Years later, I found myself at Silverlake Dog Park overcome with a sense of déjà vu. My teacher's theory was being played out right before my eyes. At this park, as well as at Runyon Canyon Dog Park, humans co-habit on this patch of dirt and grass with their pets as they enjoy the outdoors. And while dogs are out in the open about how they feel (a butt sniff and a hump is hard to miss), their owners are a little harder to decipher. But once you hear, "Do you prefer drip or French-pressed coffee?" you know that they're secretly wishing for their animal side to come out as freely as their dogs. Note: The dog park is separated into two sections, one for small dogs and one for others.

1873 SILVER LAKE BOULEVARD NEAR DUANE STREET IN SILVERLAKE.

People-Watching

Los Angeles is a giant fish bowl with the lenses of the world tightly in focus, snapping pics of celebrities and reality stars and even a few locals—it's the people here that make the city so interesting.

178. ***For Celebrities.*** See one of the Olsen twins or, if you're lucky, see two, at ***Barneys New York*** in Beverly Hills. Without fail, every time I step foot inside Barneys's luxury department store, I see a celebrity. If it's not an actress, it's a musician. If it's not a musician, then it's a reality star. And during a big sale, you're bound to bump into something or someone. Even stars appreciate a good bargain.

9570 WILSHIRE BOULEVARD AT SOUTH CAMDEN DRIVE IN BEVERLY HILLS.
310-276-4400. www.barneys.com

179. If you're on a budget and the pricey goods at Barneys are a bit too much, head over to ***Urth Caffé*** for a cup of coffee and a star sighting. Maybe it's the selection of fine teas that draws celebrities here in droves. I heard someone swear their allegiance to the green tea almond milk latte once. Or it could be the organic coffee. I personally think it's the two "f's" in Caffé instead of one that has them hooked, but what do I know, I'm not a celebrity. No matter the reason, they come here as do wannabes, posers, fashionistas and more, and wait in line for their Urth fix. Some even opt for a seat at one

of their tables to relax and enjoy their drinks before rushing off to their next audition. Urth Caffé has several outposts, but I suggest starting at the original on Melrose Avenue.
8565 MELROSE AVENUE AT WESTMOUNT DRIVE IN HOLLYWOOD. 310-659-0628. www.urthcaffe.com

180. *LA Mill* is no ordinary coffee shop. LA Mill provides the ultimate coffee experience for coffee lovers, with chemistry set-like contraptions erected at your table to give you an über caffeine jolt from their specially selected beans. And with this kind of set up, I guess you wouldn't be surprised by how many swoon-worthy actors come here to indulge their caffeine fix. Being situated in the hip Silverlake area (a mini celeb central) makes LA Mill the ideal place for stars and normal folks to intermingle and eat, drink, and stare. I'm not going to name names of who actually goes here because then they'll realize that I really am looking at them and not some imaginary person standing behind them. And unless someone actually famous is present, the real star of this place is always the coffee.
1636 SILVER LAKE BOULEVARD IN SILVER LAKE. 323-663-4441. www.lamillcoffee.com

181. *The Ivy on Robertson Boulevard* is a paparazzi favorite. The question that crosses my mind driving past The Ivy on Robertson Boulevard is "When isn't a slew of paparazzi camped outside this place?" If you've ever picked up a copy of *US Weekly*, *OK*, *Life & Style*, or *People*, or seen an episode of *TMZ* or *E!News*, you've heard of the Ivy and all the stars that come to eat here every single day. With its open patio and white picket fence, they can't help being drawn here like bees to nectar, or in many waning stars' circumstances, moths to a flashing camera bulb. And no matter how often you hear about celebrities dodging paparazzis seeking privacy, those that come here are all about the limelight. I guess having your name screamed at you by crazed camera-wielding creepy men is something you eventually begin to crave.
113 NORTH ROBERTSON BOULEVARD BETWEEN ALDEN DRIVE AND BEVERLY DRIVE IN LOS ANGELES. 310-274-8303. www.theivyrestaurant.com

182. You're guaranteed to see a celeb at a ***TV taping***. To go to the *Jimmy Kimmel Show*, *The Tonight Show*, or the *Ellen Show*, you have to call to reserve your tickets in advance. But once you have them, a celebrity sighting is a sure thing. ***Jimmy Kimmel Live*** tickets: 866-JIMMY TIX (Call weekdays 1:00 p.m.-4:00 p.m. PST). ***Tonight Show with Jay Leno*** tickets: 818-840-3537

(Also available the morning of the show at the NBC Studios in Burbank or at Universal Studios Hollywood ticket booth). The ***Ellen Show*** tickets: 818-260-5600. www.ellentv.com. ***The Price is Right***, a game show rite of passage is taped in L.A. as well. You won't see anyone famous, but you might get the opportunity to "Come on down" and try for your chance to spin the big wheel and win.

Call 1-855-447-7423 for tickets.

183. Stars can usually be found at their own ***Star Dedication Ceremony*** on the Hollywood Walk of Fame. When celebrities receive a star on the Hollywood Walk of Fame (p. 16), the ceremonies are open to the public. Good news. However, since the ceremonies are scheduled very sporadically, you'll have to keep up on when they're going to happen. Check the Hollywood Chamber's website www.walkoffame.com for events and updates, and follow @wofstargirl on Twitter. She's the VP of Media Relations for the Hollywood Walk of Fame ceremonies.

184. ***Line the Red Carpet for a Movie Premiere.*** Grauman's Chinese Theatre (p. 17) is the go-to place for hosting star-studded movie premieres. And why wouldn't it be; it is after all a movie palace. You don't have to camp out waiting for a premiere to happen; Grauman's lists them in advance on their website so you have a chance to clear your calendar in hopes of seeing that special someone's mega-watt million-dollar smile. Just make sure you get there early to stake out a good vantage point, and bring your camera.

6801 HOLLYWOOD BOULEVARD NEAR ORANGE DRIVE IN HOLLYWOOD. 323-464-3331. www.tclchinesetheatres.com

185. ***Attend an Awards Show.*** To sit in the bleachers at the Oscars (www.oscars.org), you need to register for a lottery six months in advance and chances are you might not get a seat. But don't fret, there are other award shows with tickets that are actually available to the public you can attend. ***People's Choice Awards***, second week of January at the Shrine Auditorium and Exposition Center. www.peopleschoice.com. The ***Writers Guild Awards*** honors achievements in writing for film and TV in February. Hyatt Regency Century Plaza. 323-951-4000. www.wga.org. ***IDA Documentary Awards Gala***, for distinguished documentary filmmakers, early December at the Directors Guild of America.

IDA: 1201 WEST 5TH STREET, SUITE M270, LOS ANGELES.

186. *For athletes:* Watch the stars and athletes get into shape at ***UCLA***. You can catch March Madness every spring and see some of the top college players go head to head at Pauley Pavilion. Nicole Kidman used to do laps in their outdoor pool. And the Chelsea football club from the Premiere League practices here during their off season. With guest appearances by Real Madrid and world famous footballers who come for International Exhibition Games. Enough said.
405 HILGARD AVENUE IN WESTWOOD. 310-825-4321. www.ucla.edu

187. Spin around at the **Bonaventure.**

This hotel boasts a revolving restaurant and bar on the top floor that provides you with an amazing view of downtown L.A. Is it worth the $35 valet parking? Between the revolving bar, the twinkling lights, and the nighttime view, I'd say it's pretty darn close.
404 SOUTH FIGUEROA STREET AT WEST 4TH STREET IN DOWNTOWN LOS ANGELES. 213-624-1000. www.starwoodhotels.com

188. Get a view of Beverly Hills from **Thompson Beverly Hills Hotel.**

In L.A., the view you usually crave is of one looking down. This time, you'll only look up. At the rooftop pool and bar of the Thompson Beverly Hills, you'll get a city view worthy of the real estate the property occupies.
9630 WILSHIRE BOULEVARD AT CRESCENT DRIVE IN BEVERLY HILLS. Open only to hotel guests and Thompson Hotel Members. 310-273-1400. www.thompsonhotels.com

Drive-in Movies

Los Angeles is the land of automobiles AND movies, so wouldn't it make sense to have drive-in movies all over the place? I'm sure at one time, moviegoers with a license had their choice of theaters to drive up to, but as land prices rose, tearing down the drive-ins and erecting buildings in their place was more economical. So we cling to the last remaining drive-in we have (the Vineland), and rejoice at the mini-versions that spring up all over the city—and hope that the combination of car and film will continue to linger on forever.

189. *For a drive-in worth the drive, catch a flick at The Full Moon Drive-In.* I know what you're thinking: driving all the way down to San Diego to watch a movie is a bit much. But if you're a big fan of the classics, the trip is more than worthwhile. An old-school idea with a modern twist, Full Moon is the first drive-in in the U.S. to take classic films and transform them into state-of-the-art digital projections. Just think about it: some of your favorite old flicks on the big screen like you've never seen them before. With its 1950s ambiance, a vintage feel inspired by their special ads and grand old marquee, a classic concession stand, and live entertainment, the Full Moon is the perfect way for film lovers to awaken their old-Hollywood nostalgia.
1500 FELSPAR STREET IN SAN DIEGO (NEXT TO THE PACIFIC BEACH COMMUNITY PARK). 888-211-0404. www.fullmoondrivein.com

190. *Visit the last real Drive-In at Vineland Drive-In.* If you're expecting spic and span and HD, you're in the wrong place. The Vineland Drive-In in the City of Industry is the last Drive-In left in Los Angeles. So expect run down, expect sketchy bathrooms and mediocre snacks, and expect to have an experience people rarely have: a cheap movie from the comforts of your car. And if you're going to stay for a double feature, be sure to stretch between films; it's amazing how difficult it is to drive home with a numb butt. For parents who can't find a babysitter but still want to watch a movie, this might be your saving grace. Bring your kids—they can't embarrass you too much from the confines of your car.
443 NORTH VINELAND AVENUE IN CITY OF INDUSTRY. 626-961-9262. www.vinelanddriveintheater.com

191. *No movie watching setting is as fun as the Annual Brand X Santa Monica Drive-In at the Pier.* Every Friday in June, free screenings take place on the Pier Parking Deck of the Santa Monica Pier. Mostly ocean themed and geared for an audience of all ages, the screenings are more about spending time with friends and family than the film itself. Screenings start at 8:30 p.m. but if you show up early, don't worry; booths, giveaways, and fun start at 7:30 p.m. Bring your own beach chairs and blankets. Chairs available for rent. No alcohol permitted.
200 SANTA MONICA PIER IN SANTA MONICA.

192. Want to see a movie even closer to the water? Then ***try the Venice Canals Hot Summer Row-In Movie Nights*** in August. For two Saturdays in August, it's free. Whether you pull up a chair or drop anchor don't forget to bring a few movie watching necessities: a pillow, popcorn, a drink, Junior Mints, and a life vest.

DELL STREET BRIDGE OVER CARROLL CANAL IN VENICE.

www.venicecanalsassociation.org. Or contact@venicecanalsassociation.org for more info.

Expert Contributor: Jenni Tarma

Jenni Tarma is a Finnish musician, who has lived in the Echo Park neighborhood of Los Angeles for six years and splits her time between touring and not touring.

MY FIVE FAVORITE VIEWS IN L.A.

Fireworks in Elysian Park on Dodger game nights. For residents of Echo Park, Dodger games have their downsides—not least of which for me is the very real possibility that the resulting traffic will prevent me from crossing the street back to my house for a good twenty minutes. Your best bet is to take an after-dark hike to the top of Elysian Park, seat yourself and your friends on a bench, and watch the post-game fireworks exploding over the Downtown Los Angeles skyline.
www.laparks.org

From the window of Asia de Cuba at the Mondrian Hotel. Irrespective of the swanky Hollywood atmosphere at this hotel, there's no denying the view from the patio of the restaurant, designed by Philippe Starck—in fact, it'll probably make your bill more palatable at the end of dinner. The restaurant boasts one of the most stunning, sparkling views of the city imaginable; combined with the classy white-on-white interior and insane celebrity-spotting potential, it's a 360-degree panoramic feast for the eyes.
8440 SUNSET BOULEVARD IN WEST HOLLYWOOD. 323-650-8999. www.mondrianhotel.com

From the Pacific Coast Highway in Malibu. Kerouac's vision of the "groaning continent" stretching out to the east never feels more fitting or powerful than when looking out over the ocean in Malibu. The view from anywhere along the Pacific Coast Highway is simply so overwhelming in its scale that my mind always ends up spinning, trying to assimilate the sheer size of the landmass behind me as I stand on its tiny, razor-sharp edge. Try looking out from the very edge of the continent at nighttime (maybe after a couple of cocktails) to get the maximum impact of the quintessential Los Angeles sight: fancy houses, sand, palm trees, and the glorious ocean.

From the garden cafe of the Norton Simon Museum. This small museum is a fantastic semi-secret Los Angeles haunt, and invariably the ace up my sleeve when it comes to entertaining visiting relatives. It feels wonderfully off the beaten path, and the garden in particular is an absolute gem—and a great opportunity to take in the remarkable collection of sculptures, including work by the likes of Constantin Brancusi, Barbara Hepworth, and Henry Moore. You can either enjoy the combination of beautifully landscaped rare, tropical trees and the finest work of twentieth-century sculptors from your vantage point, over coffee and a pastry on the patio of the tiny outdoor cafe, or take a gander through the footpaths, where there's a bronze statue cleverly integrated into the shrubbery at every turn. Either way, you completely get the sense of having stumbled upon a magical, secret garden tucked away into a quiet corner of Pasadena.

411 WEST COLORADO BOULEVARD IN PASADENA. 626-449-6840. www.nortonsimon.org

From a booth at the 101 Coffee Shop. The 101 Coffee Shop is one of the classic late-night Los Angeles hangouts. Correction: it's one of the classic late-night, brunch-hour, or simply general snack-time hangouts. Get settled in one of the comfy booths, take in the killer retro-yet-modern interior design, and get ready to observe one of the most diverse and visually intriguing cross-sections of Hollywood humanity visible at any time of day or night. You're likely to see musicians grabbing post-show food, actors who just wrapped up a long day on set having a beer, and hipsters making a pit stop to refuel after a night out on the town. It's open 24 hours a day, so things tend to get even more interesting right after everywhere else's closing time, when the place is suddenly rammed with ravenous masses pouring in from the streets of Hollywood. The people-watching potential here is truly off the charts.

6145 FRANKLIN AVENUE IN HOLLYWOOD. 323-467-1175.

Expert Contributor: Sasha Spielberg

Sasha Spielberg was born and raised in Los Angeles. She is an actress and singer in a band called Wardell. Sasha also makes music in Just Friends, part of Nicolas Jaar's label, Clown and Sunset.

MY FIVE FAVORITE PLACES TO "HANG"— OR GO ON A BLIND DATE

Sushi Kimagure Ike. This was once in Hollywood, then moved to Pasadena. You must sit at the bar, and Ike will feed you, and you will like it. In terms of a hot spot for a blind date: if conversation fails, there is always the master, Ike.
220 SOUTH RAYMOND AVENUE IN PASADENA. 626-535-0880.

I always love going to the ***Aero Cinema*** on Montana. They choose their movies wisely there, and if you're up for it (or you're afraid of conversation), see a double feature! (The previous sentence applies to a blind-date disaster.)
1328 MONTANA AVENUE IN SANTA MONICA. 310-260-1528. www.americancinematheque.com

Try a date at the 24-hour ***Wi Korean Spa.*** Go there late, after dinner at a nice restaurant, and get a full body scrub after a sauna in the "jade room." For two weeks after my last visit, I couldn't stop stroking my inner arm. People stared, and I was okay with it.
2700 WILSHIRE BOULEVARD IN LOS ANGELES. 213-487-2700. www.wispausa.com

CT Nails III for airbrush nail design (a pre-blind-date spot). If you're terrible at making decisions, avoid coming here—there are hundreds of nail designs to choose from. Or, come here knowing exactly what you want after doing major research, and just turn away from the big board of nail art. You will get distracted. Don't do it. Stick with your gut instinct. This trip is not a joke, and the manicures last a while—so let's hope the blind date's worth it.
7854 SANTA MONICA BOULEVARD IN WEST HOLLYWOOD. 323-654-9385.

Hollywood Cemetery is always fun during the summer. Pick up Pizzeria Mozza, especially the chopped salad, and bring blankets. This is also a good blind-date spot because you literally can redefine the term "blind date" by not looking once at your date, as you will inevitably be distracted by the abundance of people-watching.
6000 SANTA MONICA BOULEVARD IN LOS ANGELES. 323-469-6349. www.hollywoodforever.com

CHAPTER 3

On the Street

This chapter is dedicated to one of the most underappreciated and overlooked things about Los Angeles: its streets. Though L.A. isn't renowned for its walkability, there are so many things one misses when not on foot. To pedestrians, this city offers more than just a world the rest of us zoom past every day; it offers the chance to explore a street culture that's vibrant and unique.

While most people think that walking in L.A. has gone the way of the payphone, in fact it's something that is secretly cherished by many Angelenos. With time to explore you'll find bustling blocks, secret gardens, paths, and places only accessible on foot. So give yourself the opportunity to discover how fun and inspiring pounding the pavement can be. You can get lost among thousands of books and meet a few of your favorite authors at the Los Angeles Times Festival of Books or do some cardio while soaking up the culture during monthly neighborhood art walks. And let's not forget the best part about wandering around: discovering delicious street food.

More than any other chapter in the book, this one encourages you to leave your car at home and go out, explore, and slow down. You'll find plenty of things worth seeking out—street festivals, food festivals, top-notch farmers' markets, parades, flea markets, record fairs, and tours of famous movie locations. But more than that, you'll get to experience the city in an entirely new way. You'll discover details in things you've driven past dozens or even hundreds of times, things you never noticed until you approached them from a different vantage point, and you might learn that on the streets of L.A. there is definitely more than initially meets the eye.

Parades

193. ***Eat a fried feast at the L.A. County Fair.*** Every year as summer draws to a close, you feel a shiver in your stomach that runs down to your toes. When that happens, it's a sure sign to pack everyone in the car and head out to the Fairplex in Pomona to partake in the L.A. County Fair. Here you'll find attractions, rides, booths, shows, horse races, parades, and competitions galore. But the real reason to go is for the fair food. At the County Fair, the motto seems to be: If it can be fried, it will be caked in batter and dropped into boiling hot oil. Underneath the batter, you'll find: deep-fried Spam, avocadoes, Twinkies, Oreos, Krispy Kreme donuts, and even frogs' legs, which I recommend you try at your own discretion. Taking it easy on the oil? There's a healthy selection of chocolate-covered bacon, and turkey legs the size of small babies. Thankfully, everything is so spread out on the large fair grounds that overfed fairgoers can use the opportunity to walk off some of the grease and build up an appetite once more before digging in for the nth time. So bring a comfortable pair of shoes, your game face, a bottle of antacids, and some friends to revel in all the fun.

1101 WEST MCKINLEY AVENUE, POMONA. 909-623-3111. www.lacountyfair.com

194. ***Try not to get tangled up at The Annual Festival of the Kites and Yo-yo Competition.*** Every mid-March, spectators and competitors alike journey to Redondo Beach for Los Angeles's longest running (38 years and counting) kite festival. For one glorious afternoon, the skyline is filled with colorful kites as they soar above the Pacific; their strings tugged by kite enthusiasts of all ages along the shore. If you don't know how to fly a kite, how about "walking the dog"? At the Yo-yo Jam contest, you can join a nostalgic crowd and watch as yo-yoers amaze you with tricks you've never seen before—not to mention all the tricks you've seen but could never master back in the day. With everything that's going on you'll easily be distracted, so be careful or you'll get tangled up in more than you bargained for. With live music and the annual Craig's Hot Dog on a Stick eating contest to keep you busy between flights, this annual festival will soon become your annual festival.

www.pierkites.com. www.redondopier.com

195. ***Go see "America's Best Parade," the Doo Dah Parade.*** Since its origins in Old Town Pasadena in 1978, this most extraordinary of Los Angeles's street parades has gained national notoriety for the eccentricity of its lineup. Zombies of Debt, BBQ & Hibachi Marching Grill Team, Men of

Leisure, Fabulous Sons of Ed Wood, the Bastard Sons of Lee Marvin, Dead Robert Palmer Girls (two of my favorites), and lots more march down the streets of Pasadena all in the name of good clean fun. The parade also raises money for charity from its pancake breakfast, T-shirts, and after-party. Eccentric or not, their hearts are in the right place. Originally held around Thanksgiving before that other big Pasadena event, the Rose Parade, the Doo Dah is now held in April/May and has moved to East Pasadena for the first time in 33 years. Check out their website for information on date, time, and starting place.

www.pasadenadoodahparade.info

---

196. ***Start off the New Year in flip-flops rather than snowshoes at The Rose Parade.*** While New York can boast better pizza and a more user-friendly public transportation system (a mere technicality), we can lay claim to many things—one in particular being better winter weather. The Rose Parade, also known as the Tournament of Roses, actually started out as a snub toward New York—while the haughty East Coasters suffered through freezing cold winters, our biggest and brightest New Year's parade heralded great weather and flowers in full bloom. Since the parade began more than 100 years ago, it has grown bigger each year with the addition of marching bands, motorized floats, equestrian units, and more. Whether you live in L.A. or are just visiting from out of town, it's a rite of passage to catch a glimpse of this parade in person. You can either buy a seat in the stands, or, if you're more adventurous, camp out on the sidewalk a day or two in advance for a free space.

www.tournamentofroses.com/theroseparade.aspx

---

197. Or if you can't make it to the actual parade, ***get closer to the floats at the Rose Parade experience.*** Camping out on the street or trying to buy tickets in the grandstand for the Rose Parade is tough, and sometimes waking up early on New Year's Day to watch the parade on TV is even tougher. But those of us who find we have more time before the actual event now have a chance to enjoy the parade in a different way altogether. Before the Rose Parade, you can head over to one of three float-decorating areas to get a sneak peek at what will be debuting on New Year's Day. Here you'll see magical creatures and creations of all kinds as they enter the final stages of decorating. After the parade, head over to Sierra Madre and Washington boulevards for your chance to see all the completed floats up close and personal. You can't touch them, but you can get close enough to enjoy the beauty and sheer size of these painstakingly detailed creations. Don't forget

your camera! The Post-Parade viewing is on January 2nd and 3rd. Come bright and early for the best views.
www.tournamentofroses.com/theroseparade.aspx

198. *Show tolerance, love, and pride at the Gay Pride Parade.* Since the early 1970s, the Gay Pride Parade has made its home in Los Angeles. It was here where the world's first LGBT (Lesbian, Gay, Bisexual, Transgender) Pride Parade was held, and it remains a major focus for the LGBT community in Los Angeles. Over half a million people show up each year to support this fun, equality promoting, tolerance-inducing event.
www.lapride.org

199. *Share in Dr. Martin Luther King Jr.'s dream at The Kingdom Day Parade.* Every January in Los Angeles, generally on the officially recognized Martin Luther King Jr. holiday (the third Monday in January), a parade is held in his honor to celebrate his life and legacy. The parade, founded by Larry E. Grant, showcases bands, floats, community groups, celebrities, and a diverse group of supporters and attendees. The parade begins at Martin Luther King Boulevard and Western Avenue, and ends at Leimert Park with a festival full of music, food, and fun. The details change each year—as does the lineup of entertainment along the way—so check online to make sure you don't miss anything. It's rare to find a public event that is as enjoyable as it is meaningful.
www.kingdomdayparadecore-ca.org

200. Reenact my favorite scene from *The Wizard of Oz* at the **Antelope Valley California Poppy Reserve (AVCPR).**

In Antelope Valley, you'll see hundreds upon hundreds of poppies when they bloom in the spring. It's here that I get to act out one of my favorite cinematic scenes: As I walk through the fields, I make sure the coast is clear before I say aloud, in my best Wicked Witch of the West voice, "Poppies. Poppies. Poppies will put them to sleep. Sleep. Now they'll sleep..." It's the little things in life that keep me happy. The AVCPR is a wonderful place to bring friends and family, get out of the city, see the flowers, marvel at the wildlife, and have a picnic. The website is updated every couple of days during bloom season, which usually starts in March, so you'll know exactly when everything's looking its best. And be prepared when you come: sunscreen, a jacket, and allergy medicine (pollen and wind can be a dangerous combination) are definitely a must.
15101 LANCASTER ROAD, LANCASTER, LOS ANGELES. www.parks.ca.gov

201. Call the flower hotline at the **Payne Foundation.**

Want to see more flowers? The Theodore Payne Foundation, a nonprofit founded in 1960 dedicated to promoting and preserving California's native flora, has a hotline you can call to find out where flowers are blooming across the city. It's updated every Thursday from March through May and has information on more than 90 wildflower sites, from the Grotto Trails and Circle X Ranch in the Santa Monica Mountains to the Pacific Crest Trail above Anza Borrego Desert State Park. They also have a nursery that's open to the public year round in Sun Valley, with a huge selection of local plants—visit their website to see their current inventory.

Wildflower Hotline (March to May): 818-768-3533. Theodore Payne Foundation: 10459 TUXFORD STREET, SUN VALLEY. (818) 768-1802. www.theodorepayne.org

202. Become an architect of sand castles at the **Long Beach International Sea Festival.**

Every summer from June through August (three months should keep you plenty busy), the Long Beach Sea Festival offers visitors a staggering range of oceanic and beach-themed events. Everything from the USA Swimming Open Water National Championships to the Urban Ocean Festival at the Aquarium of the Pacific and around 100 more scattered in between. From castle building to moonlight movies at the beach and boat racing along the shore, you're sure to find an event for landlubbers and water babies alike.

www.longbeachseafestival.com

203. Get your yearly Moz fix at **The Smiths/Morrissey Convention.**

Every June since 1997, more than 1,000 Smiths and Morrissey fans, doppelgangers, and die-hard loyalists have congregated at Hollywood's Music Box Theater for this eccentric yearly convention. For seven full hours, acolytes of the gloomy Mancunians listen to their favorite music, watch videos, and dance while competing for prizes throughout the night by answering some pretty tricky trivia questions. The one question I've always wanted to know the answer to is: "What shampoo does Morrissey use?" Because not only does he have a great voice—he's got a great head of hair as well.

www.musicconventions.com

204. Leave your Kindle plugged in at home and turn the pages of a real book at the ***L.A. Times* Festival of Books.**

Hurray for the tangible! In April at the *L.A. Times* Festival of Books, one of my most favorite weekend events in Los Angeles, you'll find yourself rubbing elbows with famous

authors from all over the world. You'll see a few, get their autographs (if you buy their books), and hear them speak on a few panels. But the real stars of this event are the books themselves. More than 400 different titles make their way to the festival each year, along with more than 100,000 people. And with the festival's recent move from UCLA to USC (as if the rivalry wasn't big enough already) the central location and parking situation should make for an even bigger event. Book lovers rejoice!
For information and updates, follow the **L.A. Times** ***Festival of Books on Twitter at (@latimesfob).***
events.latimes.com/festivalofbooks

Halloween Haunts Los Angeles

205. *Watch West Hollywood's population expand exponentially for one night only at the West Hollywood Halloween Carnaval.* For more than 20 years, West Hollywood (or WeHo, as we locals call it) has played host to the Halloween Costume Carnaval. On Halloween, the 39,000-person population of this city grows to nearly half a million, second only to the Rose Parade audience in sheer size. You'll find tons of free and fun things to do in the week leading up the Carnaval: youth carnivals, pumpkin carving contests, costume contests for pets, "drag races" where men are brutally forced to run in heels, and other such contests serve to build anticipation for Halloween and the amazing parade. Whether you dress up or just go as a spectator, the WeHo Carnaval is more fun than fright and a definite must. Carpooling, early arrival, and taxis are highly recommended.
www.westhollywoodhalloween.com

206. *Visit the undead during Halloween Horror Nights at Universal Studios.* This is not for the faint of heart (i.e., your author), but if you love a good scare, this is the perfect place to celebrate Halloween. For several nights in September and October, Universal Studios is transformed into your worst nightmare: the undead come to life, and spooky mazes are overrun with murderers and monsters on the loose. Wear comfortable shoes because between the long lines and the likelihood that you'll be chased by a psycho killer with a chainsaw, you'll need the extra support. And unless you like being up all night dealing with little ones' nightmares, I'd leave the kids at home. (Before you dust off your zombie outfit for this outing, take note: costumes and make-up are not allowed for visitors.)
www.halloweenhorrornights.com

207. It's kid friendly during the day, and adult friendly at night at ***Knott's Scary Farm Halloween Haunt and Camp Spooky.*** Before any other theme park did it, Knott's Berry Farm's annual Halloween Haunt was *the* original Halloween event in Southern California. An annual tradition (and your author's very first Halloween theme park experience), Knott's provides something for kids and adults alike. Fun activities such as costume parties, trick-or-treating, and mazes keep youngsters occupied during the day, and after dark vampires and werewolves come out to keep the grown-ups on their toes. And though Knott's Farm might not seem that scary—after all, Snoopy lives here—believe me, I have a scar to remind me of my encounter with the undead, and I've never run so fast in my life.
www.knotts.com

208. On the ground or in the air, ***make your heart race at Fright Fest.*** If you want to add some extra chills to the high you'll get from riding some of Six Flags Magic Mountain's super-fast coasters, then the Fright Fest event is for you. The high-speed, stomach-dropping rides in the dark will seem like a walk in the park compared to the ghoul-filled mazes and the slew of demented-looking zombie clowns that are waiting for you to get off your ride. Even some of the bravest Angelenos have been known to sleep with the lights on after a night here.
www.sixflags.com/national/index.aspx

209. ***Party with the spirits at The Queen Mary Dark Harbor Halloween Terror Fest.*** The name alone is a mouthful—but try repeating it while you're being chased by a real ghost. Okay, there aren't that many stories about people actually being chased by ghosts on this ocean liner, but according to legend, a few ghosts do roam about. Throw in a few absolutely confusing mazes, a dance party, a live band, and the fact that it's Halloween—and the person you were dancing with a second ago may just vanish into thin air.
1126 QUEENS HIGHWAY IN LONG BEACH. 562-499-1771.
www.queenmary.com/Dark-Harbor

210. ***For a REAL scare, head to the Old Town Haunt in Old Town Pasadena.*** Located in Pasadena's oldest standing building, the history of this building and the ground beneath it is a bit too scary to imagine. With reports stemming for decades about a mysterious and twisted history, missing people, strange noises, crazed captives, and the discovery of dozens of human and animal remains, this is not a place I would visit, ever. But if you're a thrill seeker, and I'm talking a boatload of thrills, then take your chances in the catacombs under the Union Savings Bank building, and pray that whatever you discover down there doesn't come home with you.

20 NORTH RAYMOND AT COLORADO BOULEVARD IN PASADENA. 626-248-7652. Parking: 90 minutes free parking in parking garage before 10 p.m., one block south of Haunt on Raymond, west side of street. www.oldtownhaunt.com

211. *Scream and sneeze at the same time on the Los Angeles Haunted Hayride.* Leave it to Los Angeles to take the pleasant, somewhat romantic East-Coast tradition of a simple hayride and twist it into a farmer's worst nightmare. The Los Angeles Haunted Hayride in the Old Zoo in Griffith Park (p. 225) is not your run-of-the-mill Halloween haunting. The story of the Old Zoo is strange and mysterious, with a past shrouded in missing animals, patrons, and a church fire that killed dozens. If you can brave the hoard of zombies , a hay-maze with clowns, and other ungodly terrors, you will be rewarded with a glimpse at an incredible old-American abandoned zoo—just suck it up, and keep your eyes partially shut during the bumpy ride.

Griffith Park (Old Zoo), 4730 CRYSTAL SPRINGS AVENUE IN LOS ANGELES. 310-993-8289. www.losangeleshauntedhayride.com

212. *For a taste of the macabre, take The Haunted Hollywood Tour.* Departing from Grauman's Chinese Theater (p. 17) in Hollywood, this nighttime tour takes you on a drive around town to sites of reported Hollywood hauntings and murders in a spooky classic white stretch car. You'll visit the ghost of Marilyn Monroe at the Roosevelt, drive by the very spot where Sharon Tate's body was discovered, and pay your respects at the Hollywood Forever Cemetery. Only in Los Angeles can you spend a night with your favorite deceased stars.

213. *Tie on a blindfold and be spanked by the very Devil himself at The Ghostly Equestrian Ball.* This *adults only* Halloween event, presented by Hollywood Bondage Ball and Bar Sinister, is exactly what you'd imagine it to be. Filled with latex and leather with a lot of whips, gags, and yep, you guessed it, bondage, it's the perfect place to let out your inner kink. Just remember to have a safety word.

www.bondageball.com

214. *Dance the night away on Halloween at Monster Massive.* Touted as the largest Halloween event in the world, tens of thousands of costumed dance music lovers head to the L.A. Sports Arena and its surrounding area for

a huge dance fest. Let yourself go and dance all night long as top DJs from all over the world keep the music spinning, the beats pumping, and your adrenaline rushing. (Recent years have been hosted by the likes of John Digweed, Judge Jules, Carl Cox, Moby, and Felix Da Housecat). Monster Massive is from 7 p.m.–4 a.m.
www.monstermassive.com

215. Discover the L.A. art scene on foot at **The Downtown Art Walk.**

The second Tuesday of each month, art lovers make their way to downtown L.A. to explore one of America's leading contemporary art scenes on foot. Guide yourself around this free event and discover a flourishing art scene. While the Art Walk focuses mostly on Spring and Main streets, where the majority of L.A.'s galleries are located, it also provides a destination for art loving fashionistas with Fashion Gallery Block—bring a fellow art lover/clothes horse and have fun. And with the Pershing Square Metro Stop just two blocks away, you can avoid the headache of finding parking and focus your energy on absorbing some culture. Start your journey at the art walk lounge, where you'll find maps, a bike valet service, and free refreshments.
434 SOUTH SPRING STREET IN DOWNTOWN LOS ANGELES. 213-617-4929.
www.downtownartwalk.org

216. Downtown L.A. too far? Then head over to the annual **Artwalk Culver City.**

Instead of once every month like Downtown, the Artwalk Culver City opens the doors to the area's top galleries and exhibition spaces just once a year, keeping us in a state of heightened suspense for months at a time. With a cluster of galleries near Washington and La Cienega Boulevards, and shows that feature new and distinguished artists, the Artwalk is a great place to see some quality work. It's free, self-guided, and you get to wander through 37 local art galleries and spaces at your leisure. If you plan on driving here, be sure to read all street signs, as parking in residential areas can be quite tricky. It's best to carpool or park in the available parking structures.
For more information, call the Culver City Cultural Affairs Hotline at 310-253-5716.
www.culvercity.org

217. Jump for joy, just not off the bridge, for the Celebration of the **Colorado Street Bridge.**

It's one of the few if only events in Los Angeles that an actual working bridge is shut down for. The Colorado Street Bridge (p. 71), one of L.A.'s most beautiful and certainly its most haunted, closes down each July in celebration of, well, itself. Full of live music,

dancing, and amazing antique cars, the celebration gives you a chance to relax, enjoy the splendor of the bridge, and not worry about oncoming traffic. After all, how many people can say they partied on a bridge?
***COLORADO BOULEVARD AT SOUTH ARROYO BOULEVARD IN PASADENA*.**

218. Get down and dirty at the **L.A. Street Food Fest**.

Founders Shawna Dawson and Sonja Rasula give you a good reason to dig deep and dig in—more than 60 vendors come together for this event, and once you've had a chance to sample their wares, you'll start to see food carts in a whole new light. This fest is all about having a great, deliciously feel-good time: supporting independent small business owners, creating a sense of community, all while stuffing your face with incredible homemade treats. Gourmet to lowbrow, old school carts to tricked out trucks, the famous to the infamous—find it here, from innovative hamburgers and overloaded hot dogs to frozen desserts and vegan snacks. To top off the feel-good vibes, proceeds from each event are donated to at least one local charity, and business and marketing advice is offered to new vendors. I'll eat to that.
www.lastreetfoodfest.wordpress.com

Cultural Street Fairs

Los Angeles is a city rich in diversity, attracting people from around the world. And to celebrate their heritage, they share their foods and culture for the benefit of all of us, with festivals that pop up year-round across the city.

219. *Celebrate New Year's Thai-style at the Thai New Year Songkran Festival.* Everyone knows that New Year's Day falls on January 1, but for a large part of the Asian community in Los Angeles (one of the largest in the world outside of Asia), the official date falls on a different day every year according to the Chinese lunisolar calendar, and is followed by a two-week-long celebration period. Join in on the fun as the huge Thai community in Los Angeles rings in the New Year with three events around the city filled with dance, music, and of course, mouthwatering Thai food. There's the Street Fair, the biggest of the three, that hosts the annual crowning of Miss Thai New Year and the delicious International Curry Festival where you can sample curries from around the world—not only Thai, but also Indian, Indonesian, Japanese, African and Caribbean varieties. There's also Songkran New Year at the Pacific Asia Museum presenting classical Thai music, dance, and art in the museum's beautiful courtyard, and the Songkran Festival at the Wat Thai Buddhist Temple in North Hollywood, which has an outdoor market with traditional Thai handicrafts, foods, and live dance and musical performances. Each provides a unique Thai New Year experience, but one thing's for sure—you'll start your year with a new sense of what that really means, on a global scale.

Info for the Street Fair: announcements are made each year at www.thainewyear.com.
Info for the Pacific Asia Museum: 626-449-2742, www.pacificasiamuseum.org.
Info for Wat Thai Buddhist Temple: 8225 COLDWATER CANYON AVENUE IN NORTH HOLLYWOOD. Free shuttle from Kaiser Permanente Hospital parking. 818-780-4200, ext 601 or 609. www.watthaiusa.org/contact.htm

---

220. ***Celebrar Cinco de Mayo at Fiesta Broadway. Cinco de Mayo is one of my favorite "holidays."*** Not only do I get to indulge in one of my favorite cuisines, but I also get to partake in the celebration and commemoration of Mexico's victory over the French Army at the Battle of Puebla. Though I doubt many come knowing too much about the history, they do come knowing that they'll have a good time. An entire mile-long stretch of downtown L.A. from Broadway to 1st and Olympic is shut down for the Fiesta, which depending on when the fifth actually is, falls on the Sunday before, after, or sometimes on the day of. Drawing more than half a million revelers downtown to celebrate with music, games, food, and live entertainment, Fiesta is the largest Cinco de Mayo festival in the world.

BROADWAY FROM 1ST TO OLYMPIC, DOWNTOWN LOS ANGELES.
www.fiestabroadway.la

---

221. ***Smack a piñata on Olvera Street.*** At the famed Mexican Marketplace, Cinco de Mayo is celebrated with traditional mariachi music, folklorico dancers, and piñatas (who can say no to a piñata?). With its old-world feel and historic surrounds, El Pueblo de Los Angeles Historic Site is the perfect place to celebrate this most festive of holidays.

845 NORTH ALAMEDA STREET IN DOWNTOWN LOS ANGELES. 213-485-8372.
www.olvera-street.com/html/fiestas.html

---

222. ***Celebrate French Independence Day with a good old-fashioned game of Petanque on Bastille Day.*** Just because Mexico defeated France doesn't mean the French don't have their own reasons to celebrate, too. Bastille Day in Los Angeles, technically July 14th, isn't on the same scale as Cinco de Mayo but does have its own, how you say, flair? The Bastille Day Celebration takes place annually in Elysian Park at the Monticello Old Lodge next to Dodgers Stadium, and is loaded with fun and fromage. Get your Fran-

cophile fix by entering a Petanque tournament (the traditional French take on lawn bowling), watching the Parisian Waiter Race (exactly what you'd imagine it'd be), and being dazzled by performers, a few berets—and tasty French treats from the sweet (macaroons and cookies) to the savory (crêpes and merguez). Bastille Day, in a phrase, is très bien.
www.bastilledaylosangeles.com

223. ***Discover a taste of Turkey at the Anatolian Cultures & Food Festival.*** In May, the Orange County Great Park is transformed into the Anatolian Peninsula. The area once known as Asia Minor, the Anatolian Peninsula is rich in history, culture, and food. Here at the annual festival you'll really get to experience Anatolia as you wander through artfully constructed sets and under the arches of places such as Troy, Lydia, the Roman Empire, Ottoman Empire, and the Turkish Republic. The festival also has a wide variety of different foods, a children's activity area, a marketplace for shopping, and a performance from the Whirling Dervishes. And if you've seen all you can on land, why not step into one of Orange County Great Park's Giant Helium Balloons for an aerial view from high up above?
When: in May (please check website for dates). The Orange County Great Park in Irvine (http://www.ocgp.org). www.anatolianfestival.org

224. ***Don kilts at the Queen Mary Scottish Festival.*** Every year in February, the Scottish Clans of Southern California gather in Long Beach in front of the Queen Mary (p. 32), Scotland's most famous ship and an icon of Scottish craftsmanship built on the River Clyde. Scottish clans? We're not on par with *Braveheart*, but Southern California is home to quite a few. This festival celebrates that legacy with music, dance, and my favorite, historical reenactments. Spend the weekend enjoying the parade of clans, listen to the various bag piping competitions, explore the different whisky regions with a Scotch master in a whisky tasting, or just relax. While you're here, be sure to sit back to watch the Highland games. Careful observation will show that it may take a man to throw a hammer, but it takes a real man to throw one in a kilt.
Long Beach in Los Angeles. www.queenmary.com/scotsfest

225. Where else could they announce that "Murphys Get in Free" as a gimmick that actually works but at the ***L.A. County Irish Fair***? Every March, the Celts come together to celebrate everything Irish at the L.A. County Fairgrounds in Pomona (home of the L.A. County Fair). Irish dancing and music, storytelling, sheepherding demonstrations à la *Babe*, period costumes, archery, your fill of Irish food (think shepherd's pie and Guinness) and prod-

ucts, and various performances on one of their many stages—makes this a great event to visit. But be forewarned, Irish dancing has a hypnotic effect among certain spectators. So don't be surprised if you find yourself between two slightly inebriated men who claim to be "Lord of the Dance."
1101 WEST MCKINLEY AVENUE, POMONA. www.la-irishfair.com

226. *The monarchy reigns supreme for six weekends at The Original Renaissance Pleasure Faire.* Though the word "pleasure" could make your mind wander off in all the wrong directions, rest assured that this Faire is for all ages. At the Santa Fe Dam Recreational Area, you'll be taken back to merry old England during the time of Shakespeare, Sir Francis Drake, Queen Elizabeth I (whom you'll see walking around with her ladies in waiting), and other distinguished Brits. Theater, dance, and comedy are performed on eight stages; there's a carousel; an archery area to live out your Robin Hood fantasies; a jousting area; and the ever-present giant turkey leg. To have the full Renaissance experience, period costumes are available for rent, so come and enjoy ye self.
15501 EAST ARROW HIGHWAY IN IRWINDALE at the intersection of the 605 and 210 freeways, Irwindale exit off the 605. www.renfair.com/socal

227. *Find a little taste of New York at L.A.'s incarnation of the Feast of San Gennaro.* For more than 80 years in Little Italy, New Yorkers have celebrated the Feast of San Gennaro on Mulberry Street. This ten-day festival dedicated to the Catholic Saint Gennaro is beloved by many (mostly those who love fried funnel cake), and slightly despised by the neighbors. In 2002, New York Italian transplants missing a taste of home decided to re-create the feast here. The Feast of San Gennaro in Los Angeles, only four days in duration, still has plenty to offer in Italian music, food, and culture. Kids can make their own pizzas, adults can eat a cannoli or five, and in traditional Italian-American style, everyone can spend time with their family and friends. So very authentic. *Mangia!*
1651 NORTH HIGHLAND AVENUE IN HOLLYWOOD. www.feastofla.org/index.html

228. Get ready, get set, go! at the **Venice Canal Races.**

The Venice Canals (p. 63) are a great place to walk around—you'll get a taste of the original Venice as you stroll along the canals, and a dose of L.A.'s past (the canals were originally developed back in 1905). It's peaceful here most of the time, but when there's activity brewing on the water, it's a whole other story: the Venice Canal annual races and festivities are bizarre, hilarious, and always so much fun. There's the 4th of July

Rubber Ducky Race and Downwind Regatta (motorized boats are banned), the spook-tacular Canalloween for trick-or-treating, and the Holiday Boat Parade in December when the canal is filled with homemade and wonderfully decorated water rafts vying for a prize and your applause. So make your way down to the Canals and cheer on the remnants of Venice's past.

www.venicecanalsassociation.org

---

229. Heritage Square Museum is home to eight historic houses in Montecito Heights, all constructed during the Victorian Era. As you stroll through the site, you'll get an up close and personal history of Southern California's development through its amazing and innovative architecture. From the Longfellow-Hasting Octagon House (one of only five hundred octagonal buildings remaining in the U.S.) to the John J. Ford House (decorated and crafted by hand), and of course the Hale House (p. 62)—the Heritage Square Museum truly transports you to a whole new world of historical wonders.

3800 HOMER STREET IN LOS ANGELES. 323-225-2700. www.heritagesquare.org

---

230. Stand at the Crossroads of the World, Los Angeles's first outdoor mall. Located on Sunset Boulevard at Las Palmas, Crossroads of the World is hard to miss. Just look for a 60-foot tall tower with a revolving neon globe that says "Crossroads of the World," and you're there. This block-long center—built in 1936 and designed by Robert V. Derrah, the master of Streamline Moderne (the Coca-Cola building, p. 53)—was created with two themes in mind. One was based off of a tugboat design, complete with decks and portholes that became the center's focal point. And the second was a European village, with influences ranging from Cape Cod all the way to Asia. Both tugboat and European village in one? Sounds odd, but together it makes for some great architecture, especially when you walk toward the Selma Avenue side of the mall, where you'll find a lighthouse and a Cape Cod-style village. In total, there are nine buildings with varying architecture styles and themes. In the 1970s, Morton La Kretz and his daughter Margaret saved Crossroads from the wrecking ball, thereby saving a piece of L.A. history for us all. And once you visit Crossroads, you'll discover why La Kretz and his daughter have continued to dedicate themselves to the restoration and upkeep of such a special architectural oasis.

6671 SUNSET BOULEVARD IN HOLLYWOOD. 323-463-5611. www.crossroadshollywood.com

→ ***FACT:*** *The U.S. Postmaster declared the mall its own street, allowing all incoming mail to be addressed simply to "Crossroads of the World."*

231. Watch the cherry blossoms bloom at the **Descanso Gardens.**

Cherry blossom season, which heralds the start of spring, is one of best times to visit Japan, but since a round-trip ticket can cost you upwards of a $1000—not to mention transportation and hotels, and the fact that you don't speak a lick of Japanese—you might be better off staying at home for the time being. But don't fret, you can find a preview of Japan right in your own backyard: Descanso Garden's Cherry Blossom Festival highlights all things Japanese. From a traditional Japanese tea ceremony to bento boxes for a relaxing lunch on the lawn—it's like having the best of both worlds. When you finish your guided tour through the different cherry trees, you can stop to buy a tree and take a little part of Japan home with you. (*Descanso* is Spanish for "rest," so why not grab a ride on the Garden's "**green tram**," where you can sit back and listen to a narrated tour of the surrounding flora. And since it's a zero-emission electric tram, you won't feel so bad not hoofing it the whole day.) And while you're here, visit the **Boddy House**. Built for E. Manchester Boddy, the man who founded Descanso Gardens, this 22-room mansion is absolutely stunning and provides a panoramic view of the San Gabriel Mountains. Boddy, publisher and owner of the former *Los Angeles Daily News*, knew what he was doing when he hired architect James E. Dolena to build the perfect home for him and his family. The best part is, not only can you rent the home for a special event or a wedding, but you can also get a docent-guided tour here on the weekends for free with your Descanso Gardens admission ticket.

418 DESCANSO DRIVE IN LA CAÑADA FLINTRIDGE. Call ahead to make sure the Boddy House is open to visit. 818-949-4290. Tickets for the tram tour of the gardens can be purchased at the Visitor Center. (Call the Visitor Center ahead of time to make sure it's running.) 818-949-4200. www.descansogardens.org

232. Work your way into local government and explore **L.A.'s Underground Tunnels!**

The next time you're walking around Spring Street and 1st, take a minute to contemplate just how many people are walking beneath your feet. Though not well known for its underground, long before the Red Line Subway made its debut, Los Angeles was already pioneering subterranean transport. From Spring and Temple Streets to 1st Street and Grand Avenue, a complex network of pedestrian tunnels exists just a few yards below the asphalt surface. The surviving passageways run under a group of government buildings—the Clara Shortridge Foltz Criminal Justice Center, the Hall of Justice, the Kenneth Hahn Hall of Administration, the Hall of Records (designed by Richard Neutra), and the Stanley Mosk Courthouse. In the past, the tunnels were used to transport a multitude of things, most notably billions of dollars in cash between governmental departments. To reach these tunnels all one had to do was find the county

archives, which resided below the Hall of Records at 222 North Hill Street. There was even a hidden entrance located beneath the Hall of Records with an elevator that took you down to the bottom floor. Unfortunately, due to heightened security in the aftermath of the last decade, the tunnels have been closed. Now the only people with access are government employees with golf carts zipping back and forth from building to building—and really, what better reason is there to get into politics?
SPRING STREET AND 1ST STREET IN LOS ANGELES.

---

233. Go back in time at **Angelino Heights**.

If you find yourself east of Echo Park Lake, north of the 101, and nostalgic for Victorian architecture, then stop—you've found it. The center of Echo Park known as Angelino Heights is a unique and beautifully preserved section of Victorian-era L.A., famous for its mix of architectural styles. You'll find homes ranging from the modest to the grand, from the simplicity of Craftsman to the quirky and ubiquitous Streamline Moderne. The ups and downs of the L.A. real estate boom are to thank for the cornucopia of interesting houses, which adds to the appeal of an otherwise quiet off-the-radar neighborhood. And at the heart of it is a section of more than 50 Victorian houses on Carroll Avenue called "the hill" by some locals; walk along its historic sidewalks to get an idea of what 1880 Los Angeles really looked like.
ANGELINO HEIGHTS AT ECHO PARK IN LOS ANGELES.

---

234. For Craftsman lovers, a stroll down **Lake Avenue in Pasadena** will feel as if you've died and gone to **Bungalow Heaven**.

So named by one-time City Historic Preservation staff member John Merritt, Bungalow Heaven has the largest concentration of Craftsman bungalows in one area. Here you'll find more than 800 Craftsman bungalows built in 1900–1930, many of them professionally or via a kit from the Ready-Cut Bungalow—which reportedly shipped more than 40,000 kits to the L.A. area alone. Those that remain are a strong reminder that at one time, the Arts and Crafts movement was our architectural ideal. Annual historic home tours are conducted, including a visit to the ultimate bungalow, the Gamble House (p. 42). And if you'd like to commemorate your trip, there are B.H. souvenirs readily available for purchase.
LAKE AVENUE (BETWEEN ORANGE GROVE AND WASHINGTON BOULEVARDS) IN PASADENA.
www.bungalowheaven.org

---

235. Mansions, mansions, and more mansions line **Millionaire's Row**.

I know what you're thinking—but before you conclude that the row I'm talking about is

located anywhere near Beverly Hills, you're wrong. Millionaire's Row, also known as Orange Grove Boulevard, is in Pasadena. This street has been home to the rich and famous since the early twentieth century, attracting heavy financial hitters like William Wrigley Jr. of Wrigley Chewing Gum, David Gamble of Procter & Gamble, Adolphus Busch, the co-founder of Anheuser Busch, and many other highfalutin millionaires. Just a quick gander at the sheer size of the homes that line this row and you'll see exactly what I mean.
ORANGE GROVE BOULEVARD IN PASADENA.

---

236. While on Millionaire's Row, stop by and visit the **Tournament House (Wrigley House).**

How much chewing gum would you have to sell to buy an absolutely stunning, beautifully crafted, white Italian Renaissance-style mansion built by architect G. Lawrence Stimson, on Millionaire's Row? A lot. In 1914, Wrigley bought this home for himself and his wife for $170,000 and paid an additional $25,000 for the adjoining property to make way for a garden. When his wife passed away, he offered the home to the city of Pasadena under the condition it become the permanent headquarters for the Tournament of Roses, as she loved watching the parade from the front yard. The city accepted (why wouldn't they?), and it became the Tournament House and Wrigley Gardens. It remains the headquarters for the Pasadena Tournament of Roses Association till this day. Note: In 1914, this mansion was considered modest compared to other mansions on the block, which is quite a shock once you see it for yourself.
391 SOUTH ORANGE GROVE BOULEVARD IN PASADENA. 646-449-4100.
www.tournamentofroses.com/pasadenatournamentofroses/thehouse/toursofthehouse.aspx

---

237. See the true beauty of L.A. around **Windsor Square.**

A lot of Angelenos themselves, let alone tourists, confuse Windsor Square for Hancock Park. Windsor Square occupies the area between Wilshire Boulevard and Beverly Boulevard, and from Van Ness Avenue to Arden Boulevard, and distinguished by incredibly wide streets and a bounty of lush, towering trees. It's one of the oldest and most well-preserved neighborhoods in Los Angeles, and simply driving, riding, biking, or walking around its streets is enough to remind you of the iconoclastic beauty of the city.
WINDSOR SQUARE IN WILSHIRE, LOS ANGELES.

→ ***FACT:*** *In the 2012 Oscar winning silent film,* The Artist *the homes of both George Valentin (104 Fremont Place) and Peppy Miller (56 Fremont Place, former home of silent film star Mary Pickford) are located here. Silent film superstar Charlie Chaplin filmed his movie* The Kid *just behind George Valentin's pretend home.*

238. Marvel (discreetly) at the **House of Davids**.

Forget the Playboy Mansion—Youngwood Court, also known as the House of Davids, is where the real action is. Many years ago Norwood Young, the longtime owner of Youngwood, lined his semi-circular driveway with 21 three-foot-high replicas of Michelangelo's "David," a monument to the perfect male form, on columned pedestals. Although the Hancock Park Homeowners Association has repeatedly voiced its disdain for the house of homage, it's become something of a cult favorite among Angelenos in the know, who will drive out of their way to roll by whenever they can. Be sure to see the house during Christmastime, when the Davids are decadently decorated with a mixture of classical and kitsch. As Nat King Cole, the former owner of the residence, might say: Mr. Youngwood has taken the liberty to make the home simply "unforgettable."

CORNER OF MUIRFIELD ROAD AND 3RD STREET IN LOS ANGELES.

239. Take a break from driving at **Larchmont Village**.

Hidden within Windsor Village is Larchmont, a quaint street that's unusual for L.A. in that it's best enjoyed on foot. Larchmont is lined with shops and restaurants, and hosts a weekly farmer's market that is the focal point for this small community as well as a popular gathering place for locals and visitors alike. Grab a bite, sit on a bench, have a cup of coffee, and take a minute to recharge before you continue your exploration of the surrounding areas.

LARCHMONT AVENUE BETWEEN 1ST STREET AND BEVERLY BOULEVARD IN LOS ANGELES.

240. Pique your interest in real estate at **Hancock Park**.

Like a lot of things in this town, Hancock Park was named after someone influential in its development. Case in point: the philanthropist and property developer George Allan Hancock, who once lived in a house that occupied what is now the La Brea Tar Pits (p. 130), took the 440 acres he inherited from his father and subdivided them into residential lots, creating what we now know as Hancock Park. Located west of Windsor Square, the homes here are each designed by celebrated architects such as Paul Williams and A.C. Chisholm, and have a history of housing the crème de la crème of Los Angeles—Doheny, Chandler, Huntington, Crocker, and Van de Kamp among them. Take a turn around the streets and you'll soon be wishing you lived here too.

HANCOCK PARK, BETWEEN VAN NESS AVENUE, MELROSE AVENUE, LA BREA AVENUE, AND WILSHIRE BOULEVARD IN LOS ANGELES.

241. Have bargains, will travel–to the **Rose Bowl Flea Market.**

Sometimes it doesn't hurt to stay home on a Saturday night and go to bed early, say around 9 p.m. Because those who rise early the next day—especially if it's the 2nd Sunday of the month—will be rewarded with treasures beyond their wildest dreams! Okay, I might be exaggerating a little, but there are plenty of treasures to uncover at the Rose Bowl Flea Market, Los Angeles's (and, some believe, America's) ultimate bazaar. Here more than a thousand vendors come to hawk goods that range from the lust worthy to the downright confusing all around the grounds of this historic stadium. With everything including the kitchen sink for sale at the Rose Bowl Flea Market, you won't come away empty-handed.

ROSE BOWL, 1001 ROSE BOWL DRIVE IN PASADENA. 323 560 7469. www.rgcshows.com/RoseBowl.aspx

242. The perfect alternative to the Rose Bowl Flea is the **Pasadena City College (PCC) Flea Market.**

On the first Sunday of each month, Pasadena City College's parking lot is transformed into a bustling market, where you get to explore the wonders of bargain hunting on a smaller but well-edited scale. Some locals say this is as good as the Rose Bowl Flea, if not better—it's certainly more variable, so depending on when you go it might just be. (Plus, entrance to this flea market is free.) But since they are on consecutive Sundays you can see for yourself which one you like better.

1570 EAST COLORADO BOULEVARD. Parking can be difficult so come early. 626-585-7906. www.pasadena.edu/themarket

243. Alleviate the guilt of your retail therapy at **Melrose Trading Post,** also known as the **Fairfax High School Flea Market.**

Every Sunday nearly 200 eclectic vendors come to sell their wares in the parking lot of Fairfax High School. Overseen by the Greenway Art Alliance and run by the Greenway Friends of Fairfax, which is right next door to the high school, it is the most successful ongoing fundraising event in the history of the LAUSD. While you're here, hang out in the food court, listen to the jazz band, or stumble upon something amazing that will undoubtedly turn your friends pea green with envy. An added bonus is the off chance that you'll run into a celebrity or two—only the most die-hard of L.A.'s rich and famous are savvy enough for this flea.

7850 MELROSE AVENUE. www.melrosetradingpost.org

244. Redecorate your house in the fashion of *Dangerous Liaisons* at the **Santa Monica Airport Outdoor Antique & Collectible Market.**

One of the best flea markets in the L.A. area, the Santa Monica market is where L.A.'s best-versed antique lovers come to buy anything from high-end collectibles to eccentric odds and ends. You'll find vendors here on the first and last Sunday of every month, come rain or shine, selling everything from Victorian to mid-century era antiques, clothing, and jewelry.

AIRPORT AVENUE OFF OF BUNDY IN SANTA MONICA. 323-933-2511.

245. Pick up a treasure at the **Long Beach Antique Market.**

A grid layout is so much easier to navigate, and if you're looking to shop the whole day without getting lost, then the 3rd Sunday of every month down at the Long Beach Veterans Stadium is the perfect place for you. And versus other flea markets that can leave you feeling claustrophobic, there's plenty of elbowroom here.

4901 EAST CONANT STREET IN LONG BEACH. 323-655-5703.
www.longbeachantiquemarket.com

246. Hunt down that rare *objet* at the **Roadium Open-Air Market,**

which is open seven days a week, 365 days a year. You don't run across many open-air markets that are open daily, but the Roadium has been operating on the same premises for more than 60 years. People come here to buy a variety of new merchandise at reduced prices, but the vendors also have a constantly changing selection of antiques, collectibles, and second-hand goods. On an average weekday you'll find close to 500 sellers at what is one of California's oldest markets. So if you're a buyer looking for a deal on new or old goods, or a seller who just doesn't want to settle down with a shop of your own, this is the place for you.

2500 REDONDO BEACH BOULEVARD IN TORRANCE. 323-321-3709 or 800- 833-0304.
www.roadium.com

Literary Los Angeles

Los Angeles's landscape is littered with literature. (Say that five times fast.) The shadow of the silver screen over Los Angeles is such that writing in this city tends to bring to mind scripts and screenplays, but L.A. has an incredibly rich history of local authors and locally-inspired works that have made it one of the most literary cities in America—from Nathanael West and Raymond Chandler to Charles Bukowski, John Fante, Ray Bradbury, and James Ellroy. These writers captured the ambience and mood of this unique city, and though the ever-changing landscape of Los Angeles is always on the verge of losing something, some parts of it still remain. What's great about Los Angeles is that much of its geography is unchanged, so even now you can retrace the steps of seminal characters—and the minds that created them.

Where would the modern notion of a private detective be without ***Raymond Chandler***? Forget about it, kid. Born in Chicago, Chandler made his way to Los Angeles after a stint in the UK as a civil servant. In L.A. he taught himself how to write pulp fiction and began to cement his career as a writer. Often credited with inventing Los Angeles's literary landscape, Chandler wrote brilliant noir crime stories that shaped the modern image of the private eye, chiefly modeled on his unforgettable protagonist Philip Marlowe, and perfectly conveyed the mood of Los Angeles in the 1930s and 40s. Even now, characters in fiction that are, like Marlowe, tough yet complex, are defined as "Chandleresque." His influence can also be found in American film noir, both in the numerous treatments of his stories on celluloid to his own screenwriting adaptations for *The Big Sleep* (co-written with William Faulkner) and *Double Indemnity* (co-written with Billy Wilder from a book by fellow L.A. author, James M. Cain).

247. Picture yourself in *The Big Sleep* and head to Raymond Chandler Square on the corner of Hollywood and Cahuenga Boulevards to visit the supposed location of Philip Marlowe's office.

248. Drive by Bullocks Wilshire (p. 66), which was mentioned in the twisted murder mystery, *The Lady in the Lake*.
3050 WILSHIRE BOULEVARD IN LOS ANGELES.

249. Reenact the search for Orrin Quest in *The Little Sister*, and find the Hotel Barclay (formerly the Van Nuys building) in downtown L.A. on the corner of 4th and Main, the site of the gruesome ice pick murder . . .

Oh how I love ***Bukowski***, let me count the ways. One beer, two vodkas, three bottles of wine, four pints of whiskey . . . ***Henry Charles Bukowski*** (born Heinrich Karl Bukowski) was a German-American poet, novelist, short story writer, and one tough son of a bitch. Why do I love him so? It might have to do with the fact that we both went to the same high school, but I think it's really because I love his writing. Los Angeles's answer to Allen Ginsberg, and often referred to as the "Poet Laureate of Skid Row," Bukowski wove his own version of Los Angeles into every fiber of his expansive body of work. Heavily influenced by all things L.A., his writing focused on the ordinary lives of poor Americans, and revolved around the seemingly primal daily acts of writing, drinking, womanizing, working, and horse racing.

250. Go see Bukowski's (and Ray Bradbury's, and this author's) former alma mater, ***Los Angeles High School*** on the corner of Olympic and Rimpau Boulevards. The outside of the school is now a popular destination for weekend skateboarders, and while it's no Père Lachaise, if you look around closely you'll find evidence of prior visits from Bukoswki devotees.
4650 WEST OLYMPIC BOULEVARD IN LOS ANGELES.

251. Relive Hank's finest days at the campus of ***Los Angeles City College***. Once the original location for UCLA, Bukowski attended classes here for two years and took courses in literature and art before leaving without a diploma.
855 NORTH VERMONT AVENUE IN LOS ANGELES. 323-953-4000.

252. Even writers have day jobs, and Bukowski had his at the ***Terminal Annex***. During the 1960s he spent his days there as a clerk filing letters, a position he held for over a decade and which allowed him to gather necessary material (and bile) for his first novel, *Post Office*. True to the novel, Bukowski even resorted to having a letter-filing system set up in his apartment so he could practice at home. Nowadays the Terminal Annex on Alameda is no longer a functioning mail-processing facility—but its customer service windows remain open, and its influence on literary American legacy remains unassailable.
1055 NORTH VIGNES STREET IN DOWNTOWN LOS ANGELES. 213-617-4405. www.usps.com

253. Once you're done admiring the Mission and Spanish Colonial Revival design of the Terminal Annex, head across the street to grab a French Dip at

Philippe's (p. 43), just like Hank used to do. (He wasn't always starving in the name of art and alcohol, you know.)
1001 NORTH ALAMEDA STREET IN LOS ANGELES. 213-628-3781.

---

254. ***The Pink Elephant Liquor Store*** in East Hollywood was one of Bukowski's favorite haunts.
1836 NORTH WESTERN AVENUE BETWEEN HOLLYWOOD BOULEVARD AND FRANKLIN AVENUE IN LOS ANGELES. 323-462-0060. www.pinkelephantsliquor.com

---

255. Grab a drink or several at ***Frank 'N' Hank's*** bar in Koreatown, which is seen briefly in the opening credits of the Bukowski biopic, *Barfly*, starring Mickey Rourke in a role he was born to play.
518 SOUTH WESTERN AVENUE NEAR 6TH STREET IN KOREATOWN. 213-383-2087.

---

256. Hear real-life stories about Hank from Ruben at ***Musso & Frank's*** (p. 25). Not only can the bartenders there mix the perfect martini, but they can also tell you a tale or two about their famous old customer as well...
6667 HOLLYWOOD BOULEVARD IN HOLLYWOOD. 323-467-7788.

---

257. ***Bukowski's Bungalow*** can still be found at 5124 De Longpre Avenue in Los Angeles and is now listed as a Los Angeles Historic-Cultural Monument—and, in a move that would've tickled Hank to no end, has been renamed Bukowski Court.
5124 DE LONGPRE AVENUE IN LOS ANGELES.

Chandler was British, Bukowski German, and ***John Fante*** was Italian. Over the course of sixty years, John Fante, an Italian-American immigrant and one of the most treasured voices of immigrant American literature, wrote five novels, four of which are now referred to as the Saga of Arturo Bandini. In his work, Fante used recurring themes that focused on poverty, family, the Catholic religion, being Italian American, and the life of a writer—themes that are quite similar to Bukowski's.

In 1938, Fante unleashed his literary alter ego Arturo Bandini onto the world with the publication of his first novel *Wait Until Spring, Bandini*. The story continued with the semi-autobiographical novel, *Ask the Dust* (considered by some to be the greatest novel ever written about Los Angeles). Bandini's saga is a picture of a dystopic Los Angeles groaning and suffering during the Great Depression. *Dreams of Bunker Hill*, dictated to his wife Joyce late in his career, was completed before his death, and *The Road to Los Angeles* was published posthumously. Bukowski considered Fante his "god," and was heavily influenced by his work—so much so that early in his career he was known to go around shouting "I am Arturo Bandini!" and dedicate poems in Fante's honor at readings. He was instrumental in getting Fante's books republished in the late 1970s, before his death.

Unfortunately, Bandini's Bunker Hill is long gone, but a few pieces of his past still remain, such as Clifton's Cafeteria (p. 46), the Downtown Central Library (p. 18), and the Terminal Annex. (p. 112)

258. The newest Fante landmark is ***John Fante Square***, which can be found on the corner of Fifth Street and Grand Avenue just outside the Downtown Central Library. The library was not only a place often frequented by Fante, but also where Bukowski first discovered *Ask the Dust*.

259. For fans of L.A. authors who aren't so keen on driving or self-guided tours, ***Esotouric Tours*** takes on the responsibility of uncovering the city's compelling literary history. Richard Schave and Kim Cooper take visitors on an exploration of the city that even Charles Bukowski would be proud of. They go from authors' former residences to old haunts and real locations mentioned in the books, focusing on what was and what is, and safeguarding the author's visions. Tours currently offered include the Los Angeles of Charles Bukowski, Tom Waits, Raymond Chandler, John Fante, and *The Black Dahlia*.
www.esotouric.com

260. Explore the urban landscape in a totally new way by taking part in the **L.A. Scavenger Hunts.**

Scavenger hunts alone are always fun and exciting—but combining the traditional hunt with the feel-good factor of raising goods for the Union Rescue Mission and the L.A. Food Bank make it even more so. These daylong scavenger hunts have participants running all over L.A., all in the name of helping others. Teams of anywhere from two to five go on the prowl to gather goods from a list of 100 things for charities—and in the process have a good time, learn a lot they didn't know before about the city and leave with a lot of good karma. The team that finds the most stuff and earns the most points wins a grand prize. Bring a camera, a map of L.A., a backpack, some gumption, and, last but not least, a badass team name.
www.lascavengerhunt.com

261. Go to The Grove's **Annual Tree Lighting Ceremony.**

Since the ramp up to the holidays always seem to start months in advance, it's no surprise that before Thanksgiving in November, a tree lighting ceremony is held in The Grove, an outdoor shopping center located next to the Fairfax Farmer's Market. There are celebrity hosts, special musical performances, fireworks, and the big man himself, Santa Claus ready to help ring in some Christmas cheer, way too soon.

189 THE GROVE DRIVE IN LOS ANGELES. 323-900-8080. www.thegrovela.com

262. Before the Cathedral of Our Lady of the Angels there was the **Cathedral of Saint Vibiana** in downtown L.A., which opened in 1876.

Formerly the official cathedral of the Roman Catholic Archdiocese of Los Angeles, the original St. Vibiana's building is now a performing arts and event venue. The cathedral building is staggering, and a stroll around its four walls will be enough for you to understand why it's such a common subject of art students' sketches (you're bound to see some easels outside). But it's also a great place for weddings and private parties (for those lucky enough to afford it), and very occasionally is rented out for more public events.

214 SOUTH MAIN STREET IN DOWNTOWN LOS ANGELES. 213-626-1507. www.vibianala.com

263. Remember Robert F. Kennedy at **Inspiration Park.**

Located just outside the former Ambassador Hotel (now the New World Academy) is a park dedicated to the memory of Robert F. Kennedy—a great politician and the late brother of former President John F. Kennedy. The park does not mark the spot where Kennedy was killed—that location was dismantled and moved to a warehouse by LAUSD without the L.A. Conservatory's permission. Instead, the park—with two talking benches narrating local historical facts, and walls engraved with some of Kennedy's most memorable quotes—has become a place to reflect on the importance of social justice, as well as a place to enjoy a quiet moment of contemplation, play chess, or simply enjoy your lunch outdoors.

3400 WILSHIRE BOULEVARD IN LOS ANGELES.

264. See the White House of the West at the **Century Plaza Hotel.**

This landmark 19-story hotel located on the Avenue of the Stars in Century City is an architectural treasure. Built in 1966 by the famed Japanese-American architect Minoru Yamasaki, the designer of the World Trade Center Towers, the building was designed to be the centerpiece of an area which was to become "a city within a city." He created an arc-shaped luxury hotel with 726 rooms on the former back-lot of Century Fox

Studios, which soon became the home of many high-profile events. President Ronald Reagan was one of its first guests and was such a frequent guest that not only was the penthouse renamed for him, but the hotel was soon referred to as the "Western White House." In 2008 we heard whispers that the hotel would be demolished, but that was put to an end when conservation efforts had the Century Plaza Hotel added to the National Trust for Historic Preservation's list of the eleven most endangered historic places in America. A move that saved the hotel and had us all breathing a sigh of relief. ***2025 AVENUE OF THE STARS IN CENTURY CITY. 310-228-1234. www.centuryplaza.hyatt.com***

---

265. Get yourself tied up in a **Friendship Knot**.

In Little Tokyo, at the entrance of Onizuka Street, you'll find a sculpture of a giant knot. Known as the Friendship Knot, and presented to the City of Los Angeles by the Friends of Little Tokyo Arts (FOLTA) as a bicentennial gift on August 5th, 1981, this piece traveled from the Japanese artist Shinkishi Tajiri's home in the Netherlands to finally reach its current residence. ***SAN PEDRO AND SECOND STREET IN LOS ANGELES.***

---

266. You'll find a model of the **Space Shuttle Challenger** at the end of Onizuka Street,

which was named after Ellison S. Onizuka, the first Japanese-American astronaut. His first flight into space was on the Space Shuttle Discovery; it was on his second and final mission on the Space Shuttle Challenger that Onizuka lost his life. The model of the craft stands as a tribute to his achievements and legacy.

---

267. Follow the bright lights of **Broadway's Historic Theater and Commercial District.**

The Broadway Theater and Commercial District in Downtown Los Angeles is the first and largest historic theater district listed on the National Register of Historic Places. Along with its twelve movie theaters built between 1910 to 1931, it was also home to nearly two-dozen major department and clothing stores like the May Co. Department Store, the Broadway Department Store, and the Walter P. Story Building. Those businesses have all closed, but the buildings that housed them still remain. This is the only such concentration of movie palaces this large left in the country. Once awash with neon and filled with thousands of moviegoers, the former movie capital of the world has seen better days. But while many of the theaters have been converted into retail spaces, some—Broadway Theater and the Million Dollar Theater—have been wonderfully refurbished. For now, the lights on Broadway still burn bright, and the memory of the old movie palaces lives on intact. ***BROADWAY, FROM 3RD TO 9TH STREETS, LOS ANGELES.***

268. Before there was the Egyptian or the Chinese, there was the **Million Dollar Theater.**

In 1918, theater man Sid Grauman had Albert C. Martin design this 2,345-seat theater, one of the largest in the country. And if you know Sid, you know his theaters had to be as good looking on the inside as out, and the Million Dollar Theater was no exception. Decorated in Spanish Colonial Revival and Churrigueresque, a Spanish stucco style from the late seventeenth century, the exterior is covered with a mix of statues, bison heads, and other detailed sculpted natural features. The interior, designed by William Woollett, follows in the same vein, characterized beautifully by unusually ornate Spanish Baroque design. Closed in 2006, the theater reopened in 2008 for performances and special events after a yearlong refurbishment. The Million Dollar Theater is directly across the street from another downtown landmark, the Bradbury Building.

307 SOUTH BROADWAY AT 3RD STREET IN DOWNTOWN LOS ANGELES. 213-617-3600.

269. L is for Lavish and for the **Los Angeles Theatre.**

The last of the great movie palaces built on Broadway, the Los Angeles Theatre was estimated to cost over a million dollars in 1931. That's several million in current day standings. Lavish in design, lavish in décor, this S. Charles Lee-designed building with its five stories, towering columns, French Baroque decorations, murals, gilded mirrors, and attention to "detail, detail, detail," is spectacular. And with its grand central staircase that descends to a breathtaking tiered fountain, even King Louis XIV would agree that this theater is fit for movie royalty. The women's restroom here is one of the most beautiful I have ever seen; the mirrors and gilding alone are worth making up an excuse to go visit the powder room.

615 SOUTH BROADWAY AT 6TH STREET IN DOWNTOWN LOS ANGELES. 213-629-2939. www.losangelestheatre.com

270. Help save a part of L.A. with an **L.A. Conservancy Tour.**

The Los Angeles Conservancy was formed in 1978 out of necessity by a small group of concerned citizens to prevent the demolition of the Central Downtown Library. Now 6,000 members strong, the largest local preservation group in the U.S. provides tours of historic neighborhoods (Angeleno Heights) and buildings (Broadway Theaters) to help raise awareness and make sure our classic buildings remain intact for future generations to enjoy. A nonprofit membership organization that works to educate and help preserve the historic architectural and cultural resources of Los Angeles, it's tasked with no easy feat: under their watchful eye, many landmarks have been saved from the wrecking ball and when you go on a tour with them, they'll show you which ones,

and you'll see for yourself why they fought so hard to save them. Not only should you take a tour with the L.A. Conservancy, I urge everyone who thinks the past is worth saving to join as a member, and to donate, generously.
www.laconservancy.org/tours

Eat on the Street!

Los Angeles's food carts are dotted around the city like celebrities, and unlike other cities, where mobile kitchens still might represent a preference for economy over gastronomy, L.A.'s trucks count among the very best and most authentic vendors of local ethnic cuisine in America. The best way to find out which particular trucks are your favorites is, very simply, to try as many as you can. So keep your eyes peeled and take recommendations from friends and Angelinos alike—with a little help from these guidelines below.

271. *Tacos.* In L.A., the taco is king. From carts to trucks to pop-up stands that only appear in the shadow of night or on the weekend, tacos are an inescapable and delicious part of the L.A. street food scene. I recommend the suadero (brisket) and a healthy dollop of salsa verde.

272. *Death dogs/ Dirty dogs.* Our answer to the New York City hot dog, but way better. They're wrapped in bacon, cooked till slightly crispy, and served on a hot bun smeared with mayonnaise and topped with sautéed onion, bell peppers, and a whole roasted jalapeno. I'll have another, please.

273. *Churros.* A dense donut-like Mexican pastry in the shape of a stick covered in cinnamon sugar. There are newer stuffed versions with cream or fruit filling, but the original is still my favorite. Best enjoyed while hot.

274. *Fresh fruit vendors.* A medley of tropical fruits, peeled, sliced, and served in a plastic bag with some lime and chili salt is my idea of heaven. And for less than $5, it's a steal of a deal to boot. A great and tasty way to satisfy your USDA Food Pyramid fruit quota for the day.

275. *Ice cream trucks.* They take something normal like Flaming Hot Cheetos and then drench them in scorching nacho cheese and top them with spicy jalapeños. Is that legal? I think so. And once you're done, go back for an ice cream to extinguish its fiery flames.

276. *Mexican paletas.* When you hear the tinkle of their bells or the honk of their horns, you know you're in for a frozen treat. These small carts that wander through the streets of Los Angeles are filled with your regular run-of-the-mill ice cream, but sandwiched in between are fresh fruit delights. The fruit bars—made with real tamarind, horchata, strawberry, mango, and watermelon—are a welcome contrast to their cream-based counterparts and offer you a refreshing taste of Mexico. If you're a fan, try the coconut; it's deliciously creamy with real coconut flakes.

277. *Kogi's Spicy Korean BBQ tacos.* Check the name on the truck and make sure it says 'Kogi' because if it doesn't, you're not getting the real deal in Korean BBQ-To-Go. Chef Roy Choi jump-started the mobile food truck (a.k.a. the roach coach) craze back in 2009 by bringing together Korean and Mexican flavors and creating spicy pork tacos and kimchi (fermented spicy cabbage) quesadillas. Their ability to create massive buzz using social media not only led to Kogi-mania but also led *Newsweek* to proclaim Kogi as "America's first viral eatery." It brought the flavors of L.A. street culture back to its streets, all for a reasonable price. Its popularity caused an immediate influx of knock-off Kogi-inspired trucks that quickly followed suit. But remember, trust the originator, not the imitators. Follow Kogi on Twitter at (@KOGIBBQ)

278. *Elotes.* Corn on the cob, smeared with butter and mayonnaise, sprinkled with Mexican cotija cheese and chili with a squeeze of lime. All usually for $1.50. And now with a "Corn in a Cup" option, it's even easier to dig in and enjoy.

279. *Cart for a Cause.* A rotating line-up of stellar chefs, bargain fare at just $10, and the fact that all proceeds go to charity—make eating on the street and off a cart even more appealing. Check their Twitter and Facebook feeds for information and locations.
http://www.facebook.com/CartForACause

Expert contributor: Gary Baseman

Gary Baseman crosses many lines of art as a painter, illustrator, video and performance artist, animator, TV/movie producer, curator, and toy designer. His work has been published in *The New Yorker, The Atlantic Monthly, Time,* and *Rolling Stone,* and he designed the best-selling game "Cranium." His fine art has been displayed in galleries and museums in Brazil, Germany, Israel, Italy, Russia, and all over the United States.

Toby is Baseman's alter ego. First introduced in the "For the Love of Toby" exhibition in L.A. in 2005, he represents the blurring between fine art and toy culture. Toby's first travel photo was when Baseman snuck him into the Sistine Chapel in Rome to meet Michelangelo. The same day the photo was taken, the pope dropped dead. Then and there, Baseman knew Toby was special.

Baseman never travels without his trusty Toby. Here, Gary and Toby offer a few suggestions on the best places to take a photo in Los Angeles and capture its essence.

CAPTURING LOS ANGELES

The ceiling of Canter's Restaurant. Even though Canter's is described as a New York–style Jewish deli, to me it is the heart of the Fairfax district, which to me is the heart of L.A. My mom worked there for thirty-five years in the bakery. It is open twenty-four hours. Come get chicken soup and a potato knish and stare at the wild beautiful ceiling. You will find the meaning of life or the meaning of potato latkes.
419 NORTH FAIRFAX AVENUE IN WEST HOLLYWOOD. 323-651-2030. www.cantersdeli.com

The top of Runyon Canyon. First, it's a great hike on which to take your dog (or your invisible dog). It is great to people-watch and overhear everyone's conversations about their movie deals and agents. And once you get on top you can see a 180-degree view of the city.
2000 NORTH FULLER AVENUE IN HOLLYWOOD. www.laparks.org

Chris Burden's Urban Light installation at LACMA. It has become an instant landmark. Everyone is taking wedding photos there. I love to drive past it every day.
5905 WILSHIRE BOULEVARD IN LOS ANGELES. 323-857-6000. www.lacma.org

The lounge of Chateau Marmont. Such a beautiful 1920s building that captures the magic of Hollywood, and the tragedy of John Belushi's death. Get a drink and sneak a

photo. (Photos are not allowed ... sneak one anyway.) If you are too much of a coward, go to Musso & Frank and get a martini. That captures old Hollywood too.
8221 SUNSET BOULEVARD IN WEST HOLLYWOOD. 323-656-1010. www.chateaumarmont.com

The Witch's House (otherwise known as Spadena House). This is where I used to run when I was training for Fairfax High Track. It was originally in Culver City on a movie lot, but it moved to Beverly Hills in the 1930s or 1940s. It is a beautiful home, something out of *Hansel and Gretel*. A wonderful photo op, and the place to go to trick or treat.
516 WALDEN DRIVE IN BEVERLY HILLS. (Please note: The house is a private property, so be respectful and know that you can't go inside except on the rare occasion it's open to the public.)

Expert Contributor: Grace Yoon

Grace Yoon is a native Angeleno and walks everywhere.

THE FIVE BEST THINGS TO DISCOVER ON THE STREETS OF LOS ANGELES

It's best to go to the **Rose Bowl Flea Market** with a somewhat clear idea of what you're looking for as the sheer size of the market will have you searching among all the goodies for hours. I've found that the ring of merchants around the Bowl itself tends to sell new or handmade items and the vintage goldmine lies outside the main gate in the open lot. For those of you who like comic books and comic book memorabilia, venture into the Bowl itself ... you won't be disappointed.
1001 ROSE BOWL DRIVE IN PASADENA. 626-577-3100.

I stumbled upon **Heritage Square Museum** one day in the car with a friend of mine, who did location scouting for movies. While driving in Montecito Heights, we came upon a time warp: the museum consists of eight beautiful (and tour-able) Victorian-style homes, showcasing the development of Southern California through architecture. Heritage Square has a beautiful, otherworldly quality about it that made me want to speak in a whisper and had me expecting ghostly appearances around every elegant corner.
3800 HOMER STREET IN LOS ANGELES. 323-225-2700. www.heritagesquare.org

For all the public transportation I take, I had never seen the inside of ***Union Station*** until I was invited to a happy hour at Traxx Bar. Built in 1939 in the Mission style, Union Station is the central station for L.A.'s light rail system, and is one of the most remarkable buildings in the city. It joins the underground metro rail line with the Gold Line, which takes you on a comfortable, scenic trip from Downtown Los Angeles through Pasadena and back again—and in this instance, the station is as beautiful as the journey.
800 NORTH ALAMEDA STREET IN LOS ANGELES.

I've loved the ***Los Angeles Central Library*** since the first day I stepped inside its gorgeous interior. My favorite thing to do here is to head up to the Children's Literature section on the second level of the Goodhue Building. Here you can find an atrium with a huge four-part mural by Dean Cornwell depicting the different stages of the history of California, and a chandelier shaped like a golden globe adorned with the twelve astrological symbols.
630 WEST 5TH STREET IN LOS ANGELES. 213-228-7000. www.lapl.org

Grilled Cheese Invitational

Created by Tim Walker in 2003 as a competition between friends in an artist's loft in Downtown Los Angeles, the Grilled Cheese Invitational has grown into a national movement with regional competitions held across the country. Hundreds of would-be short-order chefs compete in four categories to create the best and most unique grilled cheese sandwiches imaginable: American Style (classic white bread, butter, and orange cheese); the Missionary (any type of bread, butter, and cheese); Kama Sutra (savory with any ingredients you choose); and the Honey Pot (a dessert-type sandwich with at least 60 percent cheese). For $12 you can gain entrance into this amazing event, and for a little extra you can have the honor of being a judge. If you're a cheese lover like I am, you may end up walking away with a grilled-cheese baby in your belly. And since I tasted about forty or so different sandwiches, I'm still not quite sure who the father is.
www.grilledcheeseinvitational.com

CHAPTER 4

Arts and Culture

From opera to theater, music, literature, dance, and, of course, film, Los Angeles is a far cry from its superficial stereotype. Instead it's a multifaceted outpost that gives space, energy, and support to every aspect of contemporary culture. From Ed Ruscha to Charles Bukowski, from Roman Polanski's *Chinatown* to Ariel Pink and even Rage Against the Machine, this city—long filled to the brim with creative intellectuals who ooze a certain *je ne sais quoi* that is uniquely Los Angeles—has become a hub for originality and innovation. Older institutions like the MOCA and Whisky A Go-Go stand strong alongside new icons such as the Walt Disney Concert Hall and the Getty Museum, which contribute to the city's continually evolving artistic scene.

Reflections of this city's enterprising creativity can be found everywhere, from graffiti running along the L.A. River to iconic murals that have become visual landmarks and art exhibits that showcase the work of established artists alongside burgeoning talent. From the surprising number of influential art patrons who call Los Angeles their home to experts in their respected fields who enrich our lives through their work, L.A. is a city that inspires self-expression. It's not just clubs, parties, and openings—it's retrospectives, performances, and lectures. It's lessons in a variety of artistic disciplines at no cost, public forums for discussion, book readings by respected authors and intellectuals, music and poetry improvisation, and a history of surprising venues that continue to survive well into the changing digital era.

And although the lights may have dimmed many moons ago on our version of Broadway—a strip of million-dollar theaters in Downtown Los Angeles—the structures and the history remain, and the cultural evolution of the city shows that their lights still shine bright in many other ways.

Philanthropists

A patron, a donor, a giver, a bestower, a humanitarian, a benefactor—no matter how you slice it, a philanthropist is someone who gives in order to improve the well-being of others either directly or indirectly. They are altruists whose concern for humankind has motivated them to make things better by donating. These individuals, who have made Los Angeles their home, have been among the guiding forces nurturing the city's developing and maturing artscape for many decades, and their contribution to the city's cultural reputation is tangible, whether or not their names are visible on buildings.

280. *Norton Simon.* He was not only successful at diversifying his businesses and stock portfolio, which made him a billionaire—he also applied this same notion to his art collection. This Portland, Oregon, native enrolled at the University of California, Berkeley, to study pre-law but left shortly after to go into the sheet-metal business. From there, he went on to invest in a bottling company, which he expanded and sold to Hunt's Foods while retaining a controlling interest. He expanded on the unfamiliar notion of food marketing and made Hunt's a household name. He also began diversifying his stock portfolio by buying up a number of businesses, such as McCall's Publishing, Canada Dry Corporation, Max Factor cosmetics, and Avis Car Rental, making him extremely wealthy. As a philanthropist, he was a trustee of the Los Angeles County Museum of History, Science and Art and supported the development of the Los Angeles County Museum of Art (LACMA). Simon generously lent his collection to museums all around the world, becoming an early adopter of the museum-without-walls concept developed by André Malraux. With more than 4,000 art objects in his private collection (one the world's most noteworthy), he soon sought out a location to display it all and found one—the Norton Simon Museum (previously the Pasadena Art Museum).

281. *Eli Broad.* Although most notable of the L.A. philanthropists, billionaire Eli Broad toes the line between altruism and egoism with his donations and "a desire to be respected," putting him on par with the Cleveland philanthropist and businessman Peter Lewis. Both men run a type of "venture philanthropy"—running philanthropic foundations less like charities and more like businesses, with their investments yielding returns. Originally from Detroit, Broad made his fortune founding Kaufman and Broad Home Corporation, the first home-builder company to be sold on the New York Stock

Exchange. He also took a small, family-owned insurance company Sun Life Insurance, and turned it into multibillion-dollar SunAmerica, which he sold to AIG for $18 billion in 1999. Angelenos since 1963, Eli and his wife, Edythe, started collecting in 1972—their first purchase was a Van Gogh for $95,000—and became huge names in the art scene when Broad donated $1 million to aid his friend Marcia Simon Weisman in the construction of the Museum of Contemporary Art (MOCA). He became its founding chairman from 1979 to 1984 and remains a trustee for life. Eli and Edythe founded the Broad Foundation and the Broad Art Foundation in 1984, the latter of which focuses on education, science, and arts, as well as public initiatives, and has been instrumental in shaping the art landscape in this city. In 1996, Broad led the fundraising campaign to build the Walt Disney Concert Hall. In 2000, he donated $23.2 million toward the Broad Art Center at UCLA, and three years later, he gave LACMA a donation of $60 million for its renovation and the creation of the Broad Contemporary Art Museum designed by Renzo Piano. In 2008, the foundation contributed $10 million to Santa Monica College as a programming endowment for their performing-arts center, the Eli and Edythe Broad Stage, and a performance space, The Edye, and he challenged MOCA in 2008 to remain independent and rebuild its endowment by giving them $30 million, contingent upon MOCA not merging with LACMA. He brought Jeffrey Deitch from New York on board to aid in its rebuilding. Broad and Deitch are now focused on the Broad Museum (opening in 2014), set to be built next to the Disney Concert Hall to house his $1.6 billion art collection—part of his vision to make Grand Avenue the arts mecca of downtown Los Angeles (perhaps soon to be known as *Broad* Angeles).

282. *Taft Schreiber.* Former Music Corporation of America (MCA) executive and director, Taft Schreiber was a top talent agent to the likes of Jack Benny, George Burns, Alfred Hitchcock, and a young Ronald Reagan. (Yes, *that* Ronald Reagan.) Through his dealings with MCA in the 1940s, Reagan amassed a large personal fortune, although how it was amassed was under suspicion and hinted at organized crime. During this time, MCA became a powerhouse moneymaker, benefiting from Reagan's position as SAG president in 1947 where he served seven additional one-year terms, which in turn made Schreiber a very rich man. An avid art collector, Schreiber used his money to build a pristine and edited collection of thirty-five masterworks that ranged from Pollock to Mondrian. He is also credited for getting Eli Broad interested in art collecting in the early 1970s. Eighteen pieces of Schreiber's collection were bequeathed to MOCA by his wife Rita, and are said to be worth around $60 million.

283. *Armand Hammer.* Although many do, don't confuse Armand Hammer, the man, for Arm & Hammer, the baking soda. Originally from New York City, Armand got his name from the arm-and-hammer symbol of the Socialist Labor Party of America, of which his father was a member. He made his money from Occidental Petroleum, a California-based oil and gas company, which he ran for decades as president and CEO. A nominee for the Nobel Peace Prize multiple times, Hammer had close ties to the Soviet Union and was watched by the FBI for the majority of his life. As an art collector, he filled the core of his collection with impressionist and postimpressionist paintings, and it is now part of the permanent collection of the UCLA Hammer Museum.

284. *Howard F. Ahmanson Sr.* The founder and financier of H. F. Ahmanson & Co., Howard F. Ahmanson Sr. made his fortune during the Great Depression selling insurance. Ahmanson also bought real estate, invested in oil, purchased Home Building and Loan, later known as Home Savings, and took advantage of the home-construction and real estate boom around Los Angeles. During the mid-1950s, Ahmanson took on a major role in the cultural development of Los Angeles. He served on the board of the Museum of Science and Industry, donated two million dollars to help fund the construction of LACMA, and created the organization that supported the Los Angeles County Art Institute. He also provided funding for his alma mater, the University of Southern California, which houses the Ahmanson Center, and he donated a major gift to support construction of the downtown music center known as the Ahmanson Theatre.

285. *Helen and Peter Bing.* Long before the name *Bing* became synonymous with tabloid fodder (lawsuits involving Steve Bing vs. Elizabeth Hurley and Steve Bing vs. Kirk Kerkorian), it was a name you grew up with that was associated with educational children's and artistic programming on PBS/KCET. For years, Dr. Peter Bing—public-health expert during the Johnson administration and heir to a real estate fortune amassed by his father, Leo Bing—and his wife, Helen, have been longtime patrons of the arts. Using his inheritance, he has donated to the Los Angeles County Museum of Art, founding the Leo S. Bing Theater, and created the Helen and Peter Bing Children's Garden at the Huntington Library. The Bings have also offered their continued support for PBS and various children's and arts programming throughout the city.

286. *Max Palevsky.* With a background in mathematics and electronics and a bit of business savvy, Max Palevsky went from working at Northrop and

Packard Bell to founding SDS, which later became Intel. He sold Intel to Xerox, earning $100 million in the process. An avid art collector, Palevsky donated millions to support visual arts, built an Arts and Crafts collection at LACMA, and gave one million dollars alongside Eli Broad to establish MOCA. He also funded the American Cinematheque's renovation of the Aero Theater in Santa Monica; the newly reopened space bears his name.

---

287. *George C. Page.* George C. Page's journey from Nebraska to California all started with an orange that was given to him when he was twelve years old. He was so enamored with the beauty of the fruit that he made it a goal to visit its place of origin. Four years later he made his way to California with only $2.30 to start his new life. One Christmas, as he filled a beautifully decorated box full of carefully packaged fruit to send home to his family in Nebraska, the other roomers at his boardinghouse took notice and offered him money to do the same for them, and his business was born. With his savings Page bought a vacant store and set up his own distribution company, Mission Pak, which shipped fruits such as oranges that grew year-round in California's temperate climates to cold-weather customers back East. With the success of his shipping business booming, Page soon moved into sports car manufacturing, real estate development, and more. As his fortune grew, Page gave back to the city. He and his wife Julliete financed the construction of the George C. Page Building at the Children's Hospital in Los Angeles and the George C. Page Stadium at Loyola Marymount University, and made donations for arts and scholarship programs and buildings at the University of Southern California and Pepperdine. But the most famous of his contributions to the L.A. landscape is his eponymous museum at the La Brea Tar Pits, which opened to the public in 1977. The Page Museum not only allowed the fossils at the tar pits that had captured his young imagination to remain close by, but also became a place that made fossils works of art in themselves.

---

288. *David Geffen.* This Brooklyn, New York, native made his fortune by hitting all the right notes. David Geffen started in the mailroom at the William Morris Agency and soon became *the* record executive when he created the Asylum Records branch under Atlantic Records and signed Joni Mitchell, Bob Dylan, Tom Waits, and more. When he left and started Geffen Records in 1980, the first person he signed was Donna Summer. He cofounded the movie studio DreamWorks SKG with Steven Spielberg and Jeffrey Katzenberg in 1994. As a philanthropist, Geffen has donated to medical research, the arts, and the theater. He bestowed $5 million to the Westwood Playhouse at UCLA, which was renamed the Geffen Playhouse, and in 1996, he donated

$5 million to the endowment drive for MOCA in Little Tokyo, which was dubbed the Geffen Contemporary.

289. *Frederick and Marcia Simon Weisman.* A successful businessman from Minnesota became even more successful when he married the daughter of Myer Simon, owner of the Val Vita Cannery and father of the philanthropist Norton Simon. Weisman diversified after a successful spell at Val Vita, made a fortune, and began to amass a huge art collection with his wife in the late 1940s, which established the duo as international figures in the art world. With their contrasting passions and fields of expertise in the arts, they made a formidable team, soon becoming top collectors of modern and contemporary art. Weisman's father, also a philanthropist, had instilled Frederick with a sense of corporate duty; Frederick utilized his reputation and fortune to make contributions and had his art collection available for public viewing. When the Weismans divorced in 1981, they split their extensive art collection. Marcia donated some of her half to the LACMA, while Frederick donated a majority of his portion to two museums, one at Pepperdine University in Malibu and the other to the University of Minnesota, which were named for him. Marcia Weisman went on to be a hugely influential force in the art world in Los Angeles. She became the driving force behind the city's initiative for a contemporary art museum, after her brother's merger of his collection with the Pasadena Art Museum saw the closure of the only contemporary museum between San Francisco and La Jolla. And as the cofounder of MOCA, Mrs. Weisman not only managed to secure the land to build the museum from her friend, the mayor Tom Bradley, but was also instrumental in galvanizing support for the construction by collecting one million dollars each from Eli Broad, Max Palevsky, and the Atlantic Richfield Company. She also started a program that resulted in the contribution of more than 8,000 works of art by hundred of donors to the Cedars-Sinai Medical Center Art Fund. Weisman donated more than one hundred prized works from her collection, like Jasper Johns's *Map*, to MOCA. David Hockney's iconic painting *American Collectors* captures Frederick and Marcia Weisman in their element, in their garden among sculptures by such artists as Henry Moore and William Turnbull.

290. A museum isn't always a museum at the **Museum of Jurassic Technology**.

At this "educational institution dedicated to the advancement of knowledge of the Lower Jurassic," nothing is what you'd expect. The name may be a bit puzzling, since the Lower Jurassic period, which this museum claims to have a "specialized repository of relics and artifacts" from, ended more than 150 million years before the appearance of hominoids and before anything could even be remotely be called technology, but who's going to notice? Their collections are obscure to say the least and mostly unclassifiable at best. With exhibits that range from the horn of Mary Davis of Saughall to the decaying dice of magician Ricky Jay, their cabinets of curiosities strain the notions of credibility and make this place that much more special. Art or not, treasures or trash, the Museum of Jurassic Technology lets us reevaluate our notions of what a museum is and should be, and it allows us to have a laugh or two. Once you're done, head to the Tula Tea Room, a miniature reconstruction of the study of Czar Nicolas II's Winter Palace in St. Petersburg, Russia, and over a cup of tea and a plate of cookies, ponder how Pope John Paul II's image was carved from a single human hair and placed within the eye of a needle. Long after you've forgotten what's his name's show at another institution, you'll definitely remember the Jurassic.

9341 VENICE BOULEVARD AT BAGLEY AVENUE, VENICE. 310-836-6131. www.mjt.org

---

291. See what develops after a visit to **The Getty Center**.

Overlooking Los Angeles is a gem: the Getty Center houses J. Paul Getty's vast collection of Western art, spanning from the Middle Ages to the present. But what's best about the Getty Center is its extensive collection of photography. From Edward Weston to Dorothy Norman, and Walker Evans to William Eggleston, the photographs that come through the center's Richard Meier–designed halls are some of the most beautiful I've ever seen—whether from the permanent collection or on loan. Be sure to check on the Getty Center's website for upcoming exhibitions and acquisitions, as there are many.

1200 GETTY CENTER DRIVE, LOS ANGELES. 310-440-7300. www.getty.edu

---

292. Study some photos up close at the **Getty Research Institute** (GRI), located at the Getty Center.

The Photo Study Collection, which is housed in the Getty Research Institute Library—home to an impressive 900,000 volumes of books, periodicals, and auction catalogs—has approximately two million study photos. There's nothing like having that many photographs on art and architecture from ancient to modern times available for closer inspection to make your photo journey to the Getty even more special. The library does not circulate its collection, but it does extend library privileges to any visitor. Check online to see the library guidelines on book access; you must fill out the forms indicated online and must have valid ID.

www.getty.edu/research

293. Celebrities aren't the only ones in Los Angeles who get a little work done; museums like the **Los Angeles County Museum of Art** (LACMA) do as well.

Everything needs a little lift now and again, and with the huge monetary injection provided by super patron of the arts Eli Broad, LACMA has been undergoing a ten-year face-lift, also known as the Transformation. Designed by the Renzo Piano Building Workshop, the first phase of the project, the BP Grand Entrance open-air pavilion filled with lampposts and visible from Wilshire Boulevard, as well as the three-story, 60,000-square-foot Broad Contemporary Art Museum (BCAM), opened in early 2008. The BCAM's inaugural installation featured works by Richard Serra, John Baldessari, Ed Ruscha, Robert Rauschenberg, Jasper Johns, Jeff Koons (one of Broad's favorites), and many more. Be sure to take some time and see the LACMA's impressive collections of Asian and Islamic art, as they are amongst the most significant in the world. If you're in the mood for different art forms, come enjoy the live jazz during summer months or take in a movie or two at the Bing Theater.

5905 WILSHIRE BOULEVARD BETWEEN FAIRFAX AND CURSON AVENUES. 323-857-6000. www.lacma.org

→ ***NOTE:*** *With more than 100,000 art objects dating from ancient times to the present day and located on twenty acres in a complex comprised of seven buildings, the LACMA is the largest museum in the western United States.*

294. Avoid getting stuck in the **La Brea Tar Pits**.

There are more than a hundred tar pits located in Hancock Park at the site of Rancho La Brea, now known as the La Brea Tar Pits. (*Brea* is Spanish for *tar.*) It has become one of the world's most recognizable fossil locations, with one of the largest and most diverse collections of extinct Ice Age plants and animals (mammoths, mastodons, sloths, bears, and the sabre-toothed cat—the state fossil of California) in the world. Every summer, the collection grows as new fossils are discovered in pit 91 (one of the few pits still being excavated). The Page Museum, financed by philanthropist George C. Page, was built next to the tar pits over half a century after Page first noticed in his teens that fossils had to be moved seven miles before being properly treated. He created the perfect home for fossils, a burial-mound structure designed by Willis E. Fagan and Franklin W. Thornton that was half underground to conserve energy and preserve the park's green landscape. It proved to be ideal for visitors to see life-size replicas of extinct mammals found in or around the tar pits. And once you're done exploring the grounds, head inside and watch through the Page Museum Fishbowl Laboratory windows as bones are cleaned and repaired.

5801 WILSHIRE BOULEVARD AT CURSON AVENUE, LOS ANGELES (next door to LACMA). www.tarpits.org

→ **NOTE:** *Wonder why tar bubbles? Hardy forms of bacteria embedded in the natural asphalt eat away at the petroleum in the tar. The end result is methane gas, which causes the tar to bubble.*

---

295. Get your motor running at the **Petersen Automotive Museum.**

In 1994, Robert E. Petersen, founder of *Hot Rod* and *Motor Trend* magazines, opened one of the world's largest automotive museums. Housed in a historic 1960s department-store building, the Petersen has more than one hundred vehicles on display. The ground floor of the four-story building contains the *Streetscape* exhibit, which gives you a virtual history of the automobile, while the second floor houses rotating exhibitions about the evolution of the automobile that range from race cars to classic cars to auto design and technology. For the future car lover in your family, the 6,500-square-foot May Family Discovery Center on the third floor of the Petersen Museum provides an interactive exhibit for kids to learn about cars through science. The interactive hands-on learning center teaches kids the basics of scientific principles through simple tutorials on fundamental car functions. And it wouldn't be an automotive museum in Los Angeles without a Hollywood gallery, featuring famous cars from TV shows and films, like Herbie the Love Bug and the General Lee. Green Hornet fans get a chance to see the 1966 Imperial known as Black Beauty and driven by Bruce Lee in the original TV series. But please don't try to reenact any of Lee's famous stunts from the show—the staff doesn't look too kindly on high-flying kicks.

***6060 WILSHIRE BOULEVARD AT FAIRFAX AVENUE, LOS ANGELES. 323-930-2277.
www.petersen.org***

→ **NOTE:** *Petersen Automotive Museum has an infamous place in contemporary culture as the last place rapper The Notorious B.I.G. was seen alive before he was gunned down fifty yards away after leaving the museum.*

---

296. Visit a hand-built museum at **El Alisal.**

Once the home of the man who made the Southwest aesthetic popular in Los Angeles, El Alisal is now a museum. Although it doesn't have any notable artworks inside, it's the actual structure that people come to see. Its builder, Charles Lummis, walked from Ohio to California and coined the phrase "See America First." On that journey, Lummis gained knowledge of the Southwest and a vast appreciation for Native American culture. His home is a rugged castle-like structure and an example of the Arts and Crafts philosophy that was influenced by mission architecture as well as the homes of Pueblo Indians he encountered. Built entirely by hand from found materials, including telephone poles from the Santa Fe Railroad, this museum stands as a testament to Lummis's vision and life.

200 EAST AVENUE 43 AT CARLATA AVENUE, LOS ANGELES. 323-222-0546.

→ ***NOTE:*** *Be sure to pay attention to the fireplace, which was carved by the creator of Mount Rushmore, Gutzon Borglum.*

---

297. Trace the history of Jewish life in America at the **Skirball Museum**...

Established in 1972, the Skirball works to educate people of and explore the connections between Jewish and American history through various exhibits like "Masters of Illusion: Jewish Magicians of the Golden Age" or "Visions and Values: Jewish Life from Antiquity to America." "Visions and Values," the museum's main exhibition, follows the history of Jews for more than 4,000 years and features alternating displays of works from the museum's vast collec6tion of more than 30,000 Jewish artifacts. Multimedia installations, archaeological and biblical artifacts, historical documents, photos, ceremonial objects, and more are housed and displayed in a modern and environmentally sensitive structure located in the Santa Monica Mountains and designed by Israeli-born architect Moshe Safdie. A visit here reminds us that there is more to Jewish history than meets the eye, and that it is relatable to various cultures on many levels.

---

298. ... and while you're here, help load the animals onto **Noah's Ark** two by two.

It's a story you've heard at least once: for forty days and forty nights, God flooded the Earth and wiped out everything except for Noah and his ark filled with animals. And at the Skirball, you can experience ark life firsthand—minus the seasickness. Permanently on display, this attraction, designed by Olson Sundberg Kundig Allen Architects of Seattle, offers everyone the opportunity to climb aboard a gigantic wooden ark, crawl around, and explore. Filled will hundreds of handcrafted life-size animals, like elephants, giraffes, and flamingos, many of them puppets operated by the ark's staff, this interactive indoor/outdoor exhibit allows you to experience the ark's voyage from dismal and dreary to hopeful and bright, with a rainbow-mist installation waiting for you as part of the outdoor experience.

2701 NORTH SEPULVEDA BOULEVARD, LOS ANGELES. 310-440-4500. www.skirball.org

---

299. Myth comes to life at **The Getty Villa**.

While the Getty Center focuses on Western art, the villa houses works of ancient times. Greek, Roman, and Etruscan antiquities make their home in Jorge Silvetti's architectural vision. A simple walk through the villa's many galleries becomes a journey into mythical times, as it is the only museum in the United States devoted exclusively to the art of the ancient Mediterranean. Arranged by themes such as gods and goddesses, the Trojan War, and gems and jewels, the villas treasures will have you spouting Homer in no time. Be sure to visit their collection of notable classic statuary on display. There is even a special climate-controlled room featuring the statue of the *Victorious Youth*, also known as the Getty Bronze, one of the few life-size Greek bronzes to have survived to modern times.

17985 PACIFIC COAST HIGHWAY, PACIFIC PALISADES. 310-440-7300. www.getty.edu

---

300. Before there was Eli Broad and the Broad Museum, there was the **Norton Simon**.

As an early supporter of the development of LACMA, Norton Simon (see Philanthropists, above) helped pioneer the concept of museums without walls by actively lending his collection to museums all over the world. But by the 1970s, with his collection exceeding 4,000 objects, Simon sought a permanent location for his art. That's when the Pasadena Art Museum came into play. It was the only modern museum at the time, built by Ladd and Kelsey in 1968 and renovated by architect Frank Gehry in 1995. Rather than Simon building a museum himself, in 1974 the Pasadena Art Museum, struggling with debt, came to an agreement with him. He would take on the responsibility of their debt, collections, and expansion, and in return, the museum would be renamed. His art collection, a rich hodgepodge from all over the world including South Asian art, impressionist art, old masters, modern art, and more, made it one of the finest in the world and a premiere destination for art lovers. Two of my favorite exhibits are the Blue Four Galka Scheyer Collection (which includes works by Paul Klee, Lyonel Feininger, Alexei Jawlensky, and Wassily Kandinsky) and the collection of Japanese wood-block prints, the majority of which were once owned by Frank Lloyd Wright. Be sure to take a stroll and visit the garden and pond, which takes its inspiration from Monet's Giverny.

411 WEST COLORADO BOULEVARD, PASADENA. 626-449-6840. www.nortonsimon.org

---

301. Get in touch with the Pacific Rim at the **Pacific Asia Museum**.

Containing a Peking-style imperial palace courtyard, bronze and copper work imported from China, and an exact copy of an arched entrance from a Buddhist library in Beijing—including its upturned roofline, stone carvings, and Oriental decor—it was only fitting that the Grace Nicholson Treasure House of Oriental Art, built in 1925, would become the Pacific Asia Museum half a century later. One of the country's leading museums, with more than 15,000 art objects, it is recognized for its importance in the education of people about Asian art. Its vast collection includes pieces like rare ukiyo-e works by Utagawa Hiroshige and Katsushika Hokusai from the Edo period,

posters by Japan's foremost graphic designer, Tanaka Ikko (art director for household goods company Muji), more than 1,000 works of ceramic art, and prize examples of imperial Chinese silk robes. The museum's library, with 9,000-plus volumes, is also the only library in the region dedicated to Asian and Pacific Island art and history; it is open to the public by appointment only.
46 NORTH LOS ROBLES AVENUE AT UNION STREET, PASADENA. 626-449-2742. www.pacificasiamuseum.org

---

302. Visit one of the three exhibition spaces of the **Museum of Contemporary Art** (MOCA)...

A Los Angeles cornerstone, MOCA, the only museum in L.A. devoted exclusively to contemporary art, has supported and exhibited contemporary art from around the world since its beginnings. Spearheaded by philanthropist Marcia Simon Weisman back in 1979, her initiative got one-million-dollar contributions from philanthropists Eli Broad and Max Palevsky to help fund construction for a new museum. Designed by renowned Japanese architect Arata Isozaki, the Grand Avenue location is the heart of MOCA's three spaces (which include the Geffen Contemporary at MOCA and the MOCA Pacific Design Center). The museum hosts exhibitions focused around its permanent collection of almost 6,000 modern and contemporary pieces, many of which came from several major private collectors. Eighteen pieces of art were donated by Rita and Taft Schreiber and included paintings by Mondrian and Gorky as well as Jackson Pollock's *Number 1, 1949*. Eighty pieces of abstract expressionism and pop art were purchased from Italian art collector Giuseppe Panza in 1984 for eleven million dollars (he donated seventy items to the MOCA in 1994); these became the foundation for its permanent collection.
250 SOUTH GRAND AVENUE NEAR WEST 3RD STREET, DOWNTOWN LOS ANGELES. 213-626-6222. www.moca.org

---

303. ... and let **Leonard Nimoy** teach you about some of MOCA's key artworks.

Visit MOCA's collection of audio tours and videos online to learn more about abstract expressionism and minimalism. Just click on Postwar Direction, a selection of works from MOCA's permanent collection, and sit back as actor Leonard Nimoy (Spock in *Star Trek*) explains Pollock's *Number 1*, Willem de Kooning's *Two Women with Still Life*, Mark Rothko's *No. 301 (Reds and Violet over Red/Red and Blue over Red)*, and Jasper Johns's *Map*, proving yet again that Vulcans do, in fact, know everything.
www.moca.org/audio

304. The temporary is now permanent at the **Geffen Contemporary** at MOCA.

In 1983, as ground broke on MOCA, a provisional exhibition space was opened downtown and referred to as the Temporary Contemporary. The place was leased from the city for five years at one dollar a year. Once a Union Hardware building from 1947, it subsequently became a city warehouse and then a police garage before a renovation led by architect Frank Gehry changed it into the perfect public space. Gehry built a shaded plaza out of steel trusses and chain-link fencing while leaving the exteriors intact, highlighted the large gallery spaces with industrial wire-glass skylights, and left steel beams exposed to lend a functional and visual effect. It soon became a popular destination, lauded as one of the great museum spaces, and MOCA, in turn, extended the lease for fifty years. The largest of the three MOCA spaces, the Geffen has some of the biggest and most stunning shows in town—however, it is also known for its frequent closures.

152 NORTH CENTRAL AVENUE, LOS ANGELES. 213-621-1741. www.moca.org/museum/moca_geffen.php

305. See a New York museum in Los Angeles at **The Paley Center for Media**, formerly the Museum of Television and Radio.

Originally in NYC, the MTR opened a West Coast branch in 1996, and with it came a Pandora's box of more than 140,000 radio and TV programs that you can watch in the console room. (I prefer radio to TV and enjoy listening to programs like Orson Welles's infamous *War of the Worlds* broadcast from 1938.) You also get the chance to see your favorite TV stars up close through the center's public program, which hosts discussions and screenings with journalists, writers, directors, and actors.

465 NORTH BEVERLY DRIVE IN BEVERLY HILLS. 310-786-1000. www.paleycenter.org

306. Listen and learn about music at the **Grammy Museum**.

Regardless of which genre you like, the Grammy Museum is the perfect place for any music lover. This three-story interactive space is a musical time capsule that highlights the true essence of music. Including galleries filled with instruments, clothing, and other personal memorabilia of famous artists, special exhibitions like John Lennon and his handwritten lyrics, and an exploration of the cultural odyssey that is hip-hop, the museum shows that music is alive and well. Be sure to check out the museum's interview concert series in the Clive Davis Theater; the intimate space makes you feel as if you're attending your own private performance.

800 WEST OLYMPIC BOULEVARD IN LOS ANGELES. 213-765-6800. www.grammymuseum.org

307. Juxtapose the old and the new at the **Hammer Museum.**

Armand Hammer, former CEO of Occidental Petroleum, pulled a fast one on LACMA when he decided to build his own museum to house his extensive art collection, which he had originally promised to them. Instead, he built the Hammer adjacent to Occidental's headquarters in Westwood for sixty million dollars and put all his artwork there. Known both for its impressive collection of Daumiers (7,500 works, the largest collection outside of Paris), Van Goghs, and old masters, as well as for its reputation for showing unknown and emerging artists and cutting-edge exhibitions, the Hammer is an important museum that straddles the past and present. Be sure to check out their dialogue series, *Hammer Conversations*, which features conversations with filmmakers, authors, comedians, and even a magician or two.

10899 WILSHIRE BOULEVARD AT WESTWOOD BOULEVARD, LOS ANGELES. hammer.ucla.edu

308. Explore a bountiful private collection at the **Frederick R. Weisman Art Foundation.**

When Fred Weisman died, he left behind a significant art legacy, with a personal collection of more than four hundred pieces of twentieth-century art. Instead of it being locked away in Weisman's former residence, never to be seen, the Frederick R. Weisman Art Foundation allows public viewing of the collection, which is comprised of artists such as Cezanne, Picasso, Kandinsky, Ernst, Miró, Magritte, Giacometti, Noguchi, Calder, Rothko, Goode, and more.

265 NORTH CAROLWOOD DRIVE IN LOS ANGELES. 310-277-5321. www.weismanfoundation.org

Look for Hidden Art

In addition to museums, galleries, and open-air public art, Los Angeles has some wonderful masterpieces tucked away in less obvious places. Pieces from corporate art collections, bas-reliefs, murals commissioned for building lobbies, and sculptures in plazas are all on permanent display in Los Angeles—if you know where to look. Accessing these semipublic works can be tricky, because many of them are located in offices, banks, and government buildings that do not have specific visiting hours. But rest assured that visiting them—even if you have no other business there—is perfectly legal. That's why they're there. Here are some of my favorites:

309. *7th and Figueroa.* The southwest corner of these two streets in downtown Los Angeles is the perfect illustration of the evolution of public

art in a corporate space. Originally, the developer agreed to allocate one percent of the construction costs to public art, and artists like Mark di Suvero, Walter Dusenberg, and David Hockney got involved. But that idea was scrapped in lieu of an overall artistic experience through discovery. Instead you'll find art on a human scale, with more intimate works and collaborations between artists and poets like George Herms and Charles Simic, James Surls and Robert Creeley, and Joe Fay and Gary Soto, to name only a few. The space is also known as Poet's Walk. Be sure to visit the *Corporate Head*, by Terry Allen and the poet Philip Levine. It'll show you how to really get a head for business.
725 SOUTH FIGUEROA STREET IN LOS ANGELES.

---

310. *HSBC Building (formerly Home Savings of America).* Howard Ahmanson incorporated a unique tradition into his business by installing public art in his branch offices. Although Home Savings no longer exists (it's now an HSBC), the artwork remains. The exterior murals of Italian glass, *Gardens of Villandry* and *Gardens of Chenonceaux*, are by Joyce Kozloff. Inside, you'll find the works of L.A. artists Tony Berlant and Carlos Almaraz, and a panorama mural by Richard Haas just under the sky lobby.
SOUTH FIGUEROA STREET AT 7TH STREET IN LOS ANGELES.

---

311. *Harbor Freeway Overture murals.* In 1993, muralist Kent Twitchell painted these three eight-story, 11,000-square-foot fresco murals on the Citicorp Plaza parking structures that stand as guardians to drivers heading north on the 110 Freeway. The people depicted are violinist Julie Gigante, various members of the L.A. Chamber Orchestra, including Tachi Kiuchi, the sponsor of the mural, and lead violinist and concertmaster Ralph Morrison.
LOCATED AT THE PARKING STRUCTURES ADJACENT TO 7TH STREET MARKETPLACE ON 7TH AND FIGUEROA, 110 FREEWAY NORTH.

---

312. *Lee Lawrie's friezes covering the outside of Central Library Downtown.* Once you take a good look at the exterior of the Central Library, you'll be surprised by how much you actually see—the pieces are hidden in plain sight. Lee Lawrie, one of the leading sculptors in America (he created the freestanding *Atlas* in Rockefeller Center), left his mark all over this Bertram Goodhue building. From sculptural figures of Herodotus (representing history), Leonardo da Vinci (arts), and Socrates (philosophy) that face Hope Street, to the figures over the Flower Street entryway, and from the image of light carved over the west entrance, to bas-reliefs and carvings facing 5th Street, Lawrie's handwork is what makes the Central

Library so special. Inside you can find the original torch of knowledge, which once graced the top of the library, as well as the Lotus Shaft Fountain in the Children's Court. Be sure to keep an eye out for the Globe Chandelier; it's a part of a model of the solar system, which can be found on the chains from which the globe is suspended.
630 WEST 5TH STREET IN LOS ANGELES.

313. ***Dean Cornwell murals, Lodwrick M. Cook Rotunda, second floor, Central Library Downtown.*** It's fitting that Dean Cornwell, who illustrated the works of authors such as Pearl S. Buck, Ernest Hemingway, and W. Somerset Maugham, managed to have his work featured alongside theirs in a building devoted to preserving their craft. Cornwell's massive murals depict four great eras of California's history and are truly a breathtaking sight.
630 WEST 5TH STREET IN LOS ANGELES.

314. Site, Memory, Reflection ***(bronze star medallion embedded into the street), 550 South Hope Street.*** If you're ever entered into the Central Library via Hope Street, then chances are you've walked over a piece of art every time without even knowing. The bronze star medallion, part of the *Site, Memory, Reflection* public artworks commissioned by Obayashi American Corporation and the Koll Company from artist Lita Albuquerque, is right under your feet. Want to get a better idea of what it really looks like? Climb up the stairs toward the library, and look down; you'll see the star pattern immediately.
550 SOUTH HOPE STREET IN LOS ANGELES.

315. Hey Day ***(star walk, bench with postcards, and fault line), Pershing Square at 5th Street between Olive and Hill.*** Artist Barbara McCarren gives you a taste of old Los Angeles with her *Hey Day* project. There are several elements that make up the artworks, but these three are my favorite: a fault line made of various broken pieces of stone which reminds you of L.A.'s shaky geological history; the terrazzo star constellations, which are composed of the same material used for the stars on the Hollywood Walk of Fame, playing on the idea of movie stars and stargazing; and last but not least, vintage porcelain postcards embedded into public benches that will make you long for old L.A.
532 SOUTH OLIVE STREET AT PERSHING SQUARE IN LOS ANGELES.

316. The Bike Stops Here *project.* They don't look much like bike racks, but they are. These works of art, commissioned by the Community Redevelopment Agency, were a way to encourage bike riding in downtown Los Angeles. They provided secure places to lock up a bike in important public areas. The racks might be difficult to spot, as they vary in appearance, taking the shape of old machinery, freestanding welded poles, and even a pig sculpture.
Various locations in Los Angeles; www.bicyclela.org/parking

317. Molecule Man, *Edward Roybal Building, 255 East Temple Street.* When I look at Jonathan Borofsky's four giant figures attached together to make up *Molecule Man*, I can't help but wonder if Molecule Man knows Particle Man, Triangle Man, Universe Man, and Person Man. Originally traced from a *Sports Illustrated* cover depicting two basketball players congratulating each other after winning the NBA Invitation finals, these four giant 30-foot-tall aluminum plates, riddled with holes and connected at the arms to form one structure, are representative of the idea that all of us are made from the same molecular structure. The sculpture suggests a commonality between everyone who sees it. And though tempting, don't climb *Molecule Man*—especially not with police headquarters so close by.
PLAZA OF 255 EAST TEMPLE STREET AT JUDGE JOHN ANDO IN LOS ANGELES.

318. Triforium, *Los Angeles Mall.* This is one of Los Angeles's most recognizable, most beloved, and most despised landmarks. A focal point and the symbol of the mall, L.A.'s Times Square, the *Triforium*, created by Joseph Young, was the first public sculpture to integrate light and sound by use of a computer. With its colored hand-blown glass prisms with lights located inside, this was to be an art piece the likes of which this city had never seen. Unfortunately, it didn't work out as planned due to monetary and technical difficulties and the fact that the art community thought it was ugly. Still, this remains one of the few public art pieces that uses modern technology in an attempt to make public art more than just something to look at.
LOS ANGELES MALL AT TEMPLE STREET IN LOS ANGELES.

319. *Noguchi Plaza,* To the Issei, *Japanese American Cultural and Community Center.* Make your way to the Japanese American Cultural and Community Center, and you'll find yourself face-to-face with Los Angeles native Isamu Noguchi's *To the Issei*, a monumental sculpture in honor of the first generation of Japanese who immigrated to America. These two twelve-

foot-long basalt rocks (commonly used in his works) are reminiscent of traditional Japanese rock arrangements. *To the Issei* is Noguchi's first and only public installation in Los Angeles. To appreciate the art and space he created, go in the early evenings on a weekday when the plaza is fairly, if not completely, empty.
244 SOUTH SAN PEDRO, LITTLE TOKYO, LOS ANGELES.

320. William Blake lovers, head over to the **Huntington Library Art Collections.**

I first visited the Huntington Library when I was in third grade to see Thomas Gainsborough's painting *Blue Boy* in person. Since then, Henry E. Huntington's private estate, which was converted into an educational institution in 1919 and is one of L.A.'s greatest cultural treasures, has remained one of my favorite places to visit. The library is of course home to a rich collection of rare books and manuscripts, including a Johannes Gutenberg's Bible, the first big book printed using movable type; the double elephant folio edition of Audubon's *Birds of America* (even Taschen can't boast that); and an unsurpassed collection of early editions of Shakespeare's works, including the first folio edition of his collected plays on display. But beyond its books and manuscripts, the library is also home to an amazing collection of American and European paintings. In particular, the prints and drawings collection houses one of the most extensive assemblages of the material of poet, painter, and printmaker William Blake in the world. It also has works by Winslow Homer, John Constable, Edward Lear, Albrecht Dürer, and many more. And if you're interested in seeing *Blue Boy*, it's on display in the Erburu Gallery.
1151 OXFORD ROAD IN SAN MARINO. 626-405-2100. www.huntington.org

321. Discover more than meets the eye at the **Fowler Museum** at UCLA.

You wouldn't guess it at first glance, but this quiet building at UCLA provides those who enter its doors with a rich look into unique cultures and customs from Asia, Africa, the Pacific Islands, and the Americas. It also boasts one of the largest collections of African artifacts. The Fowler's refreshing and innovative programming challenges the norms of society and shows some of the best contemporary and historical art from all over.
405 HILGARD AVENUE NEAR UCLA, WESTWOOD. 310-825-4361. www.fowler.ucla.edu

322. Party with a T. rex at the **Natural History Museum...**

One of Los Angeles's best-loved museums, the Natural History Museum is the largest natural and cultural history museum on the West Coast and the second oldest in L.A. Located near the University of Southern California (USC), the museum features an all-new, state-of-the-art 14,000-square-foot dinosaur hall, complete with the world's only Tyrannosaurus rex growth series, a never-before-displayed triceratops, dioramas of prehistoric animals, a gem and mineral hall, and a live insect zoo where you can see a white-eyed assassin bug or even a velvet ant! The museum's research center also has more than 35 million specimens and artifacts. If the amazing exhibits aren't enough, the museum hosts a live music series called First Fridays on the first Friday of each month from January to June with special musical performances.

900 EXPOSITION BOULEVARD, LOS ANGELES. 213-763-DINO. www.nhm.org

323. . . . and don't forget to bring your sleeping bag for one of their **Overnight Adventures.**

The Natural History Museum gives you and your family the opportunity to spend a night in the museum as part of their Overnight Adventures program. Designed for groups of 10 or more (smaller groups can participate in the family overnight), the programs give you a chance to learn about the exhibits at night. Who knows, maybe they'll let you sleep next to the dinosaurs if you're lucky. The Natural History Museum works in conjunction with the Page Museum at the La Brea Tar Pits for sleepovers, and it also has a Halloween-themed event (Camp Boo and Goo), where you can get close to fossils of animals long deceased.

FOR GROUP AND FAMILY OVERNIGHTS, CALL 213-763-3536.
www.nhm.org/site/activities-programs

324. Get three in one when you visit the **Autry National Center.**

When you come to visit the center, you get three museums for the price of one. Why? Because in 2003, the Southwest Museum of the American Indian (the oldest museum in Los Angeles), the Museum of the American West (formerly the Autry), and Women of the West Museum merged to become an intercultural history center. While the three share their collections, allowing for a comprehensive look at Western life in America, they also retain their separateness as individual entities providing unique niche experiences. The Southwest Museum of the American Indian houses one of the finest collections of Native American material in existence.

The Autry. 4700 WESTERN HERITAGE WAY, LOS ANGELES. 323-667-2000; Southwest Museum. 234 MUSEUM DRIVE, LOS ANGELES. 323-221-2164. www.theautry.org

325. Get closer to God at the **Holyland Bible Knowledge Society** (also known as the Holyland Exhibition) in Silverlake.

Founded in 1924, the Holyland Exhibition is not widely known but is filled with a rich and impressive collection of biblical-inspired objects. Founded by Antonio F. Futterer, a real-life Indiana Jones (he embarked on an expedition for the lost Ark of the Covenant), Holyland is filled with artifacts from the Middle East and treasures such as tapestries, jewelry, 5,000-year-old oil lamps, a mummy casket that dates to six hundred years before the birth of Christ, and more than three hundred glass slides depicting scenes from the Bible. Futterer even developed and copyrighted the Eye-O-Graphic Bible, a Cliffs Notes for the Old Testament, which includes simplified text, maps, slides, pictures, and genealogical charts, making Bible learning easy. A great place to visit during Lent or before Christmas, you must call for an appointment to set up a visit. Tours are only conducted in groups and last for two hours. A small fee covers a tour and refreshments.

2215 LAKE VIEW AVENUE, LOS ANGELES. 323-664-3162.

326. You'll die for the **Museum of Death** in Hollywood.

It contains the world's largest collection of serial murderer artwork, photos of the Charles Manson crime scenes, severed heads, morgue photos, and a coffin collection. If any of the above items interest you, then the Museum of Death is your kind of place. Take a self-guided tour and get a real education in death; if you can stomach it, stay longer and enjoy the death movies playing in back. People—mostly men—have been known to faint, so be warned. As the website states, there's "much, much more!"

6031 HOLLYWOOD BOULEVARD, HOLLYWOOD. No age limit, but recommended for mature audiences. www.museumofdeath.net

327. Hop on over to **The Bunny Museum**, the "Hoppiest Place on Earth."

The private residence of Candace Frazee and Steve Lubanski in Pasadena houses the largest collection of rabbit memorabilia in the world, with more than 20,000 items—even the *Guinness Book of World Records* agrees. So if you love bunnies and want to go see 28,012 of them (that's the number at the time this book was written), then hop on over. Note: The museum asks that visitors do not discard their pet rabbits there.

1933 JEFFERSON DRIVE BETWEEN WASHINGTON AND ALLEN, PASADENA. Open 365 days a year by appointment. Open house is held every holiday, when no appointment is necessary. 626-798-8848. www.thebunnymuseum.com

328. Develop a taste for urban planning at the Architecture and Design Museum (aka the A+D), where the future of architecture and design in Los Angeles is always on display. Los Angeles is known for its rich architectural and design past, but the A+D, founded in 2001, works to bring awareness to its future. This is the perfect place for those looking forward to seeing this city's changing urban landscape.
5900 WILSHIRE BOULEVARD, LOS ANGELES (across from LACMA). 323-932-9393. www.aplusd.org

329. Discover folk art at the Craft and Folk Art Museum.

Located across the street from LACMA (p. 130), the museum used to be a café known as The Egg and The Eye, which served more than fifty varieties of omelets and sold international folk art. It soon became a museum dedicated to indigenous craft and folk art that showcased the works of various cultures all over the world. Including textiles, ceramics, and basket weaving, the CAFAM is a place built on the idea of exploring and championing cultures through their crafts.
5814 WILSHIRE BOULEVARD, LOS ANGELES. 323-937-4230. www.cafam.org

330. Indulge your love for classic cars at The Nethercutt Collection.

J. B. Nethercutt and his wife Dorothy loved to collect a lot of things: dolls, musical instruments, and antique furniture among them. But it's their extensive collection of more than 250 American and European cars, dating from 1898 to 1997, all maintained and drivable, that'll make you put the pedal to the metal to see for yourselves. The Nethercutt Collection opened in 1971 to fulfill the collectors' desire to share these beautiful masterpieces with others. It occupies four levels on the top of the Merle Norman Cosmetics Factory and has been free to the public since the day it opened. In addition to the cars, be sure to take in Nethercutt's vast collection of automated mechanical instruments (music boxes, grand pianos, and a 5,000-pipe Mighty Wurlitzer Theatre Organ), as well as the remarkable vintage locomotives outside. And any budding Angelenos out there, who want to know more about the cars than what they look like, should visit the Nethercutt Automotive Research Library and Archives in the museum—it's one of the top automotive research facilities in the world.
15200 BLEDSOE STREET IN SAN FERNANDO VALLEY. 818-364-6464. www.Nethercuttcollection.org

331. Broaden your horizons at the **California African American Museum.**

For thirty years, this museum has been a leading institution for collecting, preserving, and exhibiting the history and culture of African-Americans, with collections of contemporary African-American art, art of the African diaspora, and traditional art. While it traces African-American history, the CAAM strongly focuses on African-American lives in California through photos, artworks, and more. The library of more than 20,000 books is available to the public and offers a unique opportunity to learn about the community.

600 STATE DRIVE IN EXPOSITION PARK, LOS ANGELES. 213-744-7432. www.caamuseum.org

332. See a different side of Japan at the **Japanese American National Museum.**

You won't find samurai armor on display or stories of feudal warlords here. The museum was originally housed in a remodeled Buddhist temple and is now in a pavilion space just a few yards away, next door to the Geffen Contemporary (p. 135). View photographs, personal possessions, and art and artifacts reflecting more than 130 years of Japanese immigration and assimilation into American culture as well their somewhat forgotten time spent in World War II internment camps.

100 NORTH CENTRAL AVENUE IN LOS ANGELES. 213-625-0414. www.janm.org

333. Learn about the biz at the **Hollywood Museum.**

At the "official" museum of Hollywood, you'll find all the glitz and glamour you expect and more. With the most extensive collection of memorabilia in the world, you'll see your share of showbiz treasures. Costumes, props, and thousands upon thousands of photos are housed in what is also a Hollywood treasure—the historic Max Factor Building. It's a place where many of the silver screen gods and goddesses came to get their hair and makeup done. Just stepping into the pink-hued art deco gem of a lobby will make you want to do your best Ginger Rogers impression. And for Marilyn Monroe fans, they've got an all-embracing collection ready for you to ogle.

1660 NORTH HIGHLAND AVENUE, HOLLYWOOD. 323-464-7776. www.thehollywoodmuseum.com

334. Do your best not to cry at the **Museum of Tolerance**.

The history of injustice is long and brutal, and here, they don't hide just how brutal it was. A trip to the museum is needed in order to learn about and, above all, never forget, events from the Holocaust to present-day discrimination.

9786 WEST PICO BOULEVARD, LOS ANGELES. 310-553-8403. www.museumoftolerance.com

335. Sit and learn at the **California Science Center**.

Learning is fun; learning about science is even more fun. And while you could walk through the museum to learn about bugs and animals, why not sit down and watch a movie instead? At IMAX Features, you can choose from several films that focus on science-related topics ranging from bugs in the jungle to monkeys in the wild to traveling in space. And since it's all in 3-D, it would have been just like walking around in the museum...but without breaking a sweat.

700 EXPOSITION PARK DRIVE, LOS ANGELES. 323-724-3623. www.californiasciencecenter.org

336. If they build the **Broad Museum**, will you come?

Eli and Edythe Broad's $130 million art mecca, due to open in 2014, will become a focal point in the "new" Grand Avenue in downtown Los Angeles. And as their Diller Scofidio + Renfro–designed "wraparound bonnet of interconnecting concrete trapezoids"—also referred to as The Veil—begins construction, you'll get to see it for yourself, from start to finish.

337. Choose a real piece of history instead of a museum, and go see the **Mission San Gabriel Arcángel**.

California has a rich colonial history, and nothing has remained as steadfast a reminder of it than the missions that were built during the Spanish colonization in the eighteenth century. In that time, twenty-one missions were built, stretching from San Diego to San Francisco. The San Gabriel Arcángel, founded in 1771 and named after the archangel Gabriel, was the fourth built and is still a fully functioning Roman Catholic mission with a church, museum, café, and school. Designed by Father Antonio Cruzado, the mission is famous for its Spanish and Moorish influences brought from Cruzado's home of Córdoba, Spain. It's also home to the historic Mission Cemetery, which contains around 6,000 graves and is the final resting place for Cruzado himself.

428 SOUTH MISSION DRIVE, SAN GABRIEL. sangabrielmissionchurch.org

338. See what's new at **Photo L.A.**

International photographers and galleries from all over converge upon Los Angeles for the photography fair Photo L.A., already in its twenty-first year. More than 10,000 photo newbies and aficionados come together to learn about, admire, or buy works on display. The exhibition also features multimedia installations, workshops, lectures on specific subject matter, like the correlation between jazz and hip-hop, with photographers Herman Leonard and B+ and book signings. Bring a Sharpie for some autographs, and don't forget your camera.

7354 BEVERLY BOULEVARD, LOS ANGELES. 323-965-1000. www.photola.com

339. Leave your mark on the **L.A. Riverbed**.

For years, the riverbed has been the canvas for street artists, and boy, what a canvas it is. The riverbed's fifty-one miles of wide-open concrete has been attracting graffiti since it was first built. Although not legally a designated graffiti spot, it's become the breeding ground for up-and-coming graffiti artists and, inadvertently, a tourist attraction. And while the city is currently undergoing river revitalization, leaving the fate of this outdoor art arena up in the air, one wonders when L.A. will finally acknowledge the greatest tradition of outdoor art and build an art park. I guess they haven't read the writing on the walls. (Free Revok!)

340. Peek into **Bonhams**.

Don't worry if your nickname isn't Moneybags; you can still see what's for sale by visiting their showroom before the goods hit the auction floor. Check out a preview of a unique Charlie Chaplin film or glimpse a Modigliani, and still leave with your savings account intact.

7601 WEST SUNSET BOULEVARD IN LOS ANGELES. 323-850-7500. www.bonhams.com

341. Go full circle at the **Velaslavasay Panorama** in the Union Theater.

At the panorama, they like to keep things old-school. There's nothing fancy, just drawings from the history of panorama paintings of the eighteenth and nineteenth centuries—anything that provides a 360-degree experience. In the panorama's exhibition hall, you'll find a painting/display that uses lighting and sounds which hark back to the days before motion pictures. This place has real charm and character, and that's as good a reason as any to come for a visit.

1122 WEST 24TH STREET AND HOOVER, LOS ANGELES. 213-746-2166. www.panoramaonview.com

342. Play among the artwork at **Franklin D. Murphy Sculpture Garden.**

UCLA's North Campus houses more than seventy sculptures on five acres. With works by William Turnbull, Alexander Calder, Auguste Rodin, Henry Moore, Henri Matisse, and David Smith, this is one of the top sculpture collections in the country.

CHARLES E. YOUNG DRIVE EAST IN WESTWOOD. (Check website for driving directions from the UCLA Hammer campus.) To schedule a tour, fill out an online tour request form or call the education department at 310-443-7041. Requests must be received one month prior to the date of the tour. hammer.ucla.edu

343. Enjoy Los Angeles's outdoor museum in **Elysian Park.**

Elysian Park is L.A.'s oldest park and with a little less than six hundred acres, it's also the second largest. Home to numerous historic sites, including the Los Angeles Police Academy, as well as miles of **walking trails** (p. 223), the park has become home to the Elysian Park Museum of Art (EPMoA). More of a renegade museum with no walls, the EPMoA proposes to reassess the park as a museum space. By using peer-to-peer curating, it hopes to get more people involved in the museum. Whether there's something you'd like to see in the park, someone you'd like to see in the park, or something noteworthy you'd like to document in the park, as long as it has something to do with the park, contact EPMoA. Just remember, since all exhibitions are in the park, which is a public space, anything can happen.

www.epmoa.org

344. See photos and only photos at the **Annenberg Space for Photography.**

Print or digital, as long as it's a photo, you'll find it in the Annenberg Space for Photography. This intimate yet state-of-the-art environment showcases the works of both world-renowned and emerging photographic talents and is the first solely photographic destination in Los Angeles. A must visit for any shutterbug.

2000 AVENUE OF THE STARS, LOS ANGELES. 213-403-3000.

www.annenbergspaceforphotography.org

Galleries

For those seeking a fresh point of view of what's happening in the art world today that is less board-room-driven, forego the typical museum visit and head over to a gallery. Intimate and abundant, galleries in Los Angeles showcase the unknown with the barely mainstream in the hopes of breaking in art's next best thing or just displaying what they love. And while each gallery and owner may not have the quantity you'd hope for, as space is limited unless you're Larry Gagosian, expect to see interesting choices that will leave you questioning what art really is.

345. *New Image Art.* Marsea Goldberg has a discerning eye for art and it shows. Since she founded New Image in 1994, she's helped launch the careers of several artists, such as Shepard Fairey, Ed Templeton, Chris Johanson, Retna, Richard Colman, Rebecca Westcott, Neck Face, Cleon Peterson, Faile, Tauba Auerbach, and Judith Supine. Maybe you've heard of some of them? Goldberg continues to show works of established and upcoming artists, so be sure to check with the gallery to see who'll be exhibited next. You never know, you might get a chance to see or buy artwork from the next big thing—or even meet the artist.
7920 SANTA MONICA BOULEVARD IN WEST HOLLYWOOD. 323-654-2192.
www.newimageartgallery.com

346. *PRISM.* Founded by 23-year-old artist PC Valmorbida, the gallery could have been just a flash in the pan. After all, he's 23, and galleries pop up in Los Angeles all the time. But since its impressive debut show, PRISM has continued to electrify the art community. Showing national and international artists ranging from Barry McGee to Andy Warhol, Clare Rojas, and Nobuyoshi Araki, the gallery serves to bridge the gap between high and low art. And although the spacious metallic gallery designed by Pattern Architecture may scream "younger and edgier," on opening nights, you'll be surprised to find hipsters hanging out with those who need new hips—art lovers come in all ages.
8746 WEST SUNSET BOULEVARD, WEST HOLLYWOOD. 310-289-1301.
www.prismla.com

347. *La Luz de Jesus Gallery.* You have contemporary art, you have modern art, you even have fine art, but what most galleries don't have is the ability to show a little more pop. Thank goodness for Billy Shire. His mission

to make underground artists and counterculture pieces like folk, outsider, or religious art accessible to the general public is what makes La Luz so special. The gallery's philosophy is that art should be by the people and for the people. Hear, hear!
4633 HOLLYWOOD BOULEVARD, LOS ANGELES. 323-666-7667. www.laluzdejesus.com

348. *Martha Otero Gallery.* Having honed her skills during stints at Regen, Jack Hanley, and Gagosian before starting up her own gallery in 2008, Otero now works on taking advantage of the natural light that streams through her A-framed building as well as fostering her art world connections so she can showcase works by Miguel Calderón, Jacob Hashimoto, and Jen Stark.
820 NORTH FAIRFAX AVENUE, LOS ANGELES. 323-951-1068. www.marthaotero.com

349. *Merry Karnowsky Gallery.* You'll find a champion not only for emerging artists but also for those who've been around the block at Merry Karnowsky Gallery. The gallery, founded in 1997, exhibits great contemporary works and showcases what the gallery refers to as "lowbrow" art: works of pop surrealism and Street Art that are diverse, innovative, and relevant. Karnowsky's roster of artists includes Audrey Kawasaki, FriendsWithYou, Pete Stern, Nicola Verlato, Mel Kadel, Vonn Sumner, Mercedes Helnwein, James Marshall (Dalek), and Miss Van.
170 SOUTH LA BREA AVENUE, LOS ANGELES. 323.933.4408. www.mkgallery.com

350. *Blum and Poe.* If you're wondering what caused that big art-gallery boom in Culver City, you can thank Blum and Poe. For a young gallery, they've been responsible for a number of firsts in Los Angeles. They were the first to represent Takashi Murakami and Yoshitomo Nara and the first gallery to take up residence in Culver City—for more firsts, come and see for yourself.
2727 SOUTH LA CIENEGA BOULEVARD, LOS ANGELES. 310-836-2062. www.blumandpoe.com

351. *Eighth Veil.* Founded in 2008 by Kane Austin and Nicole Katz, Eighth Veil, a contemporary art exhibition and publishing house, holds shows and offers artist residencies in their 1,000-square-foot space that also houses a printing press and bookbindery. They work with exhibiting artists as well as individuals to produce their own books on-site.
7174 WEST SUNSET BOULEVARD, LOS ANGELES. 323-645-6639. www.eighthveil.org

352. *Fahey/Klein Gallery.* A long-standing Los Angeles institution, Fahey/Klein shows some of the best vintage and fine art photography out there from well-known names such as Henri Cartier-Bresson, Man Ray, and Edward Weston, as well as contemporary photographers such as William Claxton and Herman Leonard.
148 NORTH LA BREA, LOS ANGELES. 323-934-2250. www.faheykleingallery.com

353. *Gagosian Gallery.* Who doesn't know the name Gagosian? Possibly the most powerful player on the global art circuit, Larry Gagosian has lured some of the most established artists from their longtime dealers with the promise of fame and celebrity. He also consults for the rich and richer (Eli Broad relies upon him)—he's basically the Simon Cowell of the art world. If you're looking to make it big in Los Angeles, you can't get any better than Gagosian. Showing here, in Hollywood terms, is a blockbuster.
456 NORTH CAMDEN DRIVE, BEVERLY HILLS. 310-271-9400. www.gagosian.com

354. *Honor Fraser.* All it took was a former model with a little Scottish aristocratic blood to kick the contemporary art gallery scene up a notch. Since she opened her gallery, Fraser has enjoyed early success that's stuck. Showing contemporary works that range from Tomoo Gokita to KAWS to Roy Lichtenstein, she enjoys mixing it up. From the art to the artist to the space to Fraser herself, everything here is very easy on the eyes.
2622 SOUTH LA CIENEGA BOULEVARD, LOS ANGELES. 310-837-0191. www.honorfraser.com

355. *LA><ART.* X marks the spot for the LA><ART space. Not only do you get to see emerging art and design, but it also has an amazing public programming schedule. From lectures and exhibitions to magic shows involving sawing a woman in half, the spontaneity of this place is what makes it a must-see.
2640 SOUTH LA CIENEGA BOULEVARD, LOS ANGELES. 310-559-0166. www.laxart.org

356. *Michael Kohn Gallery.* Owner and former *Flash Art* magazine critic Michael Kohn has a knack for the quirky. After all, he opened his gallery doors to East Village graffiti more than twenty years ago. Given that he has an artist roster that includes Bruce Conner, Walton Ford, and Mark Ryden, the only question I have to ask is why haven't you been here already?
8071 BEVERLY BOULEVARD AT CRESCENT HEIGHTS, LOS ANGELES. 323-658-8088. www.kohngallery.com

357. *Regen Projects.* Elizabeth Peyton, Catherine Opie, Raymond Pettibon, Wolfgang Tillmans, Matthew Barney, John Currin, Anish Kapoor, and Richard Prince. Enough said.
6750 SANTA MONICA BOULEVARD, LOS ANGELES. 310.276.5424. www.regenprojects.com

358. Go to **The World Stage** for some jazz.

Cofounded by legendary jazz drummer Billy Higgins, the World Stage continues his legacy for music and presents live music performances or jazz jam sessions every Friday and Saturday night. Come listen, support, and keep the music flowing. Each of these evenings presents two sets, at 8:30 p.m. and 10:15 p.m. A donation of $10 is appreciated, except for special engagements. Check the calendar for future performances.
4344 DEGNAN BOULEVARD IN LOS ANGELES. 323-293-2451. www.theworldstage.org

359. Come visit the "Carnegie Hall of the West"–the **Ambassador Auditorium**.

This place sings inside and out. For twenty seasons, the Ambassador hosted the world's best musicians and performers and achieved a reputation as one of the finest performance halls in the world. But when its doors closed in 1995, the only future this great music hall saw was a wrecking ball. It's been saved, though, and slowly restored to its former glory; music once again fills its halls. Come see where greats such as Yo-Yo Ma, Vladimir Horowitz, Luciano Pavarotti, and Pearl Bailey once performed.
131 SOUTH ST. JOHN AVENUE, PASADENA. 626-354-6407. theambassadorauditorium.org

360. See . . . well, *anything* at **UCLA Live** in Royce Hall.

In all my times attending UCLA Live in Royce Hall I have never seen a bad show. Renowned for its acoustic excellence and tremendous sight lines, Royce Hall offers a kaleidoscope of dance and musical artists from world-class chamber orchestras and hip hop dancers to fado singers and living legends. A fusion of everything that is global is celebrated here and it is stellar.
340 ROYCE DRIVE, LOS ANGELES. 310-825-4401. cap.ucla.edu

361. Feel the beat at the **Annual International Laureates Music Festival.**

For two weeks in July, the acclaimed iPalpiti (Italian for *heartbeats*) Orchestral Ensemble of International Laureates performs at various venues in Los Angeles. This ensemble of internationally lauded performers, all of whom are winners of prestigious international awards and represent twenty countries worldwide, have sold out concerts all over the world. Since iPalpiti began, it has grown to international recognition, and due to its popularity, a summer residency was established in Beverly Hills. When they're in town, expect to hear some amazing performances—especially their finale, when they perform at the Walt Disney Concert Hall.

1900 AVENUE OF THE STARS, SUITE 1880, LOS ANGELES. 310-205-0511. www.ipalpiti.org

---

362. Support the **Silverlake Conservatory of Music.**

We tend to forget how important some things are until they're gone. And at the rate the Los Angeles Unified School District is going, music in schools will definitely be something we'll miss. Thank goodness for Michael Balzary (Flea from the Red Hot Chili Peppers) and Keith Barry. In 2001, they set up the Silverlake Conservatory of Music, a nonprofit organization that focuses on fostering music education. The conservatory is lauded for its charitable programming that provides scholarships, which allow for free music lessons and instrument rentals for those who qualify. They put on recitals and perform as part of public events to showcase their budding musicians and singers as well as a yearly Hullabaloo Fundraiser to help raise money for the Conservatory's music education efforts.

3920 WEST SUNSET BOULEVARD IN LOS ANGELES. 323-665-3363. www.silverlakeconservatory.com

---

363. Hear a few twangs at the **Topanga Banjo-Fiddle Contest and Folk Festival.**

What do you get when you combine twenty-six five-string banjo pickers, five fiddlers, four judges, and more than five hundred eager fans? The beginnings of Southern California's favorite bluegrass, old-time, and folk music festival. Originally a way to raise money for the Santa Monica Friends Meeting House, the event grew into an annual Topanga Banjo and Fiddle Contest that has been going strong for more than fifty years and has seen performances from Jackson Browne, Taj Mahal, and banjo enthusiast (and actor) Steve Martin on their stages. At the Paramount Ranch near Agoura Hills in the Santa Monica Mountains, more than one hundred musicians come to compete and have fun. If you're not up for hitting the stage but still want to folk your heart out, go enjoy the art booths, folk performances, random jam sessions, and a dance barn.

May; check online for directions to each year's event. 818-382-4819. www.topangabanjofiddle.org

364. Go hear the **Gay Men's Chorus of Los Angeles** at the Alex Theatre.

For more than eighty years, Glendale's Alex Theatre has been a source of pride to the city's arts and culture enthusiasts. It boasts a diverse schedule of roughly 250 events ranging from music concerts to film screenings, live theater, and stand-up comedy. Its "atmospherium" design creates the feeling of being enclosed in an ancient garden; the open-air illusion is enhanced by the stage-set wall encircling the auditorium, giving it a very special feel. Here, you can come listen to one of the country's largest men's choral ensembles perform. The internationally known chorus puts on one heck of a show. Resident companies at the Alex also include the L.A. chamber orchestra, the Musical Theatre Guild, and the Glendale Youth Orchestra.

216 NORTH BRAND BOULEVARD, GLENDALE. 818-243-2539. www.alextheatre.org

365. Watch shows close up at **The Broad Stage.**

What do you say when the man who played Tootsie is the artistic chair of the new performing arts center at Santa Monica College? You say, "Where do I sign up?" This intimate space with 499 seats presents theater, dance, film, operas, musicals, and more, with events ranging from the Guthrie Festival to performances of *All That Jazz*. The Broad Stage's Arts Insights program offers free or low-cost educational opportunities by providing accessible programming to people from all walks of life. They also offer unique initiatives, like matinee shows for L.A. school students, master classes to learn from the finest in the field, and open rehearsals, which reveal the creative process.

1310 11TH STREET, SANTA MONICA. 310-434-3200. www.thebroadstage.com

366. Go to the Hollywood Bowl for the **Playboy Jazz Festival.**

As well as offering the city some of its best outdoor concert experiences, the Bowl is home to this annual event. With a roster that reads like a Who's Who, the Playboy Jazz Festival is a must for any jazz lover. Founded by Hugh Hefner, this two-day event features a full day of music each day and highlights both established and up-and-coming musicians. Past performers have included Ella Fitzgerald, Louis Armstrong, Wayne Shorter, Sonny Rollins, Benny Goodman, Dizzy Gillespie, and Nina Simone. Esperanza Spalding, who performed at the festival in 2009, won the Grammy for Best New Artist in 2011.

June. 310-450-1173. www.playboyjazzfestival.com

→ ***NOTE:*** *Bill Cosby has been the emcee for the festival almost every year since it began.*

367. Take in the cultural crème de la crème at the **Los Angeles Music Center**,

the West Coast equivalent to New York City's Lincoln Center. Made up of four halls—the Dorothy Chandler Pavilion (one of the three largest performing arts centers in the United States), the Mark Taper Forum, Ahmanson Theatre, and Walt Disney Concert Hall (just across the street from the original three halls)—it is the premier cultural destination in Los Angeles. Home to the Los Angeles Philharmonic, the Los Angeles Opera, the Los Angeles Master Chorale, and Glorya Kaufman Presents Dance at the Music Center, the venue hosts performances, free dance lessons, classes, and events of all kinds year round. Since 1964, a Christmas Eve tradition for the Dorothy Chandler Pavilion has been the annual free holiday celebration funded by Los Angeles County. It is six hours, from 3:00 p.m. to 9:00 p.m., of music and dance by groups from all around Los Angeles County, with the performances broadcast on the public television station KCET.

135 NORTH GRAND AVENUE IN LOS ANGELES. 213-972-7211. www.musiccenter.org

368. Enjoy the sounds of the **Los Angeles Philharmonic**.

Walt Disney Concert Hall is now home to the Los Angeles Philharmonic, which was established as the city's first permanent symphony orchestra in 1919 by founder William Andrews Clark Jr. Walt Disney Concert Hall is the fourth building in the Music Center of Los Angeles performing arts complex and is one of the most acoustically advanced music halls in the world. Out of the ten renowned conductors who have led the philharmonic, only Esa-Pekka Salonen and Gustavo Dudamel have been able to test the acoustic excellence. The philharmonic also provides free concerts throughout the year.

WALT DISNEY CONCERT HALL, 111 SOUTH GRAND AVENUE IN LOS ANGELES. 323-850-2000. www.laphil.com

369. Listen to soaring arias at the **L.A. Opera**.

In as little as two decades, the Los Angeles Opera, under the leadership of überpatrons Eli and Edythe Broad's general director, the famed operatic tenor Plácido Domingo, now stands out as a force in American opera. It has become the fourth largest opera company in the United States. From time to time, Domingo returns to his rightful place on stage as a featured performer: he starred in the world premiere of *Il Postino* as Pablo Neruda. The 2010 season saw Wagner's *Der Ring des Nibelungen* (the Ring cycle) presented here for the first time by the company.

DOROTHY CHANDLER PAVILION, 135 NORTH GRAND AVENUE IN LOS ANGELES. 213-972-8001. www.laopera.com

370. Hear a symphony performed by the **L.A. Chamber Orchestra** (LACO).

Founded in 1968 by cellist James Arkatov as an artistic outlet for the film and record studios' most gifted musicians, the orchestra was conceived as an ensemble that would allow these conservatory-trained players to balance studio work and teaching. Renowned pianist and conductor Jeffrey Kahane has led the group since 1997 and has continued the standard of excellence. The orchestra performs pieces ranging from baroque masterpieces to newly commissioned works and is recognized for championing young musicians. LACO performs fourteen orchestral series concerts a season.

350 SOUTH FIGUEROA STREET, SUITE 183, IN LOS ANGELES. 213-622-7001. www.laco.org

371. Get into the rhythm at **Glorya Kaufman Presents Dance** at the Music Center.

The music center has become the stage for world-class performances thanks to dance lover and philanthropist Glorya Kaufman, widow of Kaufman and Broad cofounder Donald Kaufman. Here, you'll see the art form of dance in various expressions performed by some of the biggest and most celebrated dance companies in the world, like the Ballet Nacional de Cuba, the American Ballet Theatre, the Joffrey Ballet, the Bolshoi Ballet, and the Music Center's dance theater residents.

135 NORTH GRAND AVENUE IN LOS ANGELES. 213-972-7211. www.musiccenter.org

372. See a new kind of theater at **REDCAT** (the Roy and Edna Disney/CalArts Theater).

Located in the underbelly of the Walt Disney Concert Hall, REDCAT challenges your idea of performance and theater art with its experimental and innovative approach to programming. In this CalArts-operated space, the aim is to provide an intellectual arena for the community, and this has made it ground zero for inventive and provocative performances, art, and music.

631 WEST 2ND STREET, LOS ANGELES. 213-237-2800. www.redcat.org

373. Practice your plie with the **L.A. Ballet**.

A young company founded in 2006, the ballet has made leaps and bounds in its programming under former New York City Ballet dancers and artistic directors Thordal Christensen and Colleen Neary. Neary has the distinction of being a *répétiteur* for the George Balanchine Trust, a designation that allows her to stage Balanchine ballets for professional companies. The Los Angeles Ballet performs from December through May at assorted venues throughout the area.

11755 EXPOSITION BOULEVARD IN LOS ANGELES. 310-477-7411. www.losangelesballet.org

374. See where it all began for some celebrities at the **Pasadena Playhouse**.

In 2010, the Pasadena Playhouse was under Chapter 11 bankruptcy protection and about to close. In 2011, the playhouse helped put together two musicals that were nominated for Tony Awards. It's been a roller coaster of a ride for this nonprofit playhouse, which was founded in 1917. Housed in a Spanish Colonial building designated the state theater of California, it has helped launch the careers of Raymond Burr, Robert Stack, Dustin Hoffman, Gene Hackman, and Sally Struthers. In recent years, the playhouse has become instrumental in launching new works and landmark revivals for the American theater.

39 SOUTH EL MOLINO AVENUE, PASADENA. 626-356-7529. www.pasadenaplayhouse.org

375. Get a bit of Broadway in Los Angeles at the **Pantages Theatre**.

This art deco gem and Hollywood landmark, formerly the RKO Theatre, has seen more handoffs than some football games. Its ownership has bounced from Pantages to Fox West to Howard Hughes to Pacific Theatres. It closed as a movie theater and reopened for stage productions, and since then, it has become one of Los Angeles's leading venues for live theater. See a Broadway musical here, as many—such as Disney's *The Lion King* or the Tony Award–winning *Wicked*—find their way to the Pantages stage.

6233 HOLLYWOOD BOULEVARD, LOS ANGELES. 323-468-1770. www.broadwayla.org

376. Catch a show at the **Geffen Playhouse**.

There are Pulitzer Prize–winning playwrights, Tony Award–winning directors, world premieres, and West Coast premieres, and that's barely scratching the surface of a typical Geffen Playhouse season. Housed in a Masonic lodge (one of the first twelve structures built in Westwood Village), the playhouse offers five plays per season on the main stage and three to four on its smaller Skirball-Kenis stage. Offering a high-caliber selection of musicals and plays, the playhouse often features well-known film and TV actors in productions, like Martin Sheen, Carrie Fisher, Jason Alexander, and Martin Short.

10886 LE CONTE AVENUE, LOS ANGELES. 310-208-5454. www.geffenplayhouse.com

377. On weekends, kids can get the inside scoop at **Saturday Scene**.

Does your child have a love for theater as well as for journalism? He or she can combine both passions at the Saturday Scene. The weekend production for kids at the Geffen Playhouse offers them the chance to be a kid reporter. Not only do they get a chance to go behind the scenes, meet a member of the cast or artistic team, and get to ask questions, but they also get a T-shirt, special press pass, and their article printed in the following Saturday Scene playbill. Their first published work before even hitting puberty? Now that's newsworthy.

E-mail education@geffenplayhouse.com and check online for necessary information. www.geffenplayhouse.com

---

378. Capture your kids' attention with **Storybook Theatre**.

For the finicky 3- to 9-year-old set, Theatre West has the solution for your theatergoing needs. The Storybook Theatre is the best children's theater in Los Angeles. As part of Theatre West, the oldest continually running theater company in L.A., Storybook upholds the standard of excellent theater (they've been honored by the U.S. Senate and House of Representatives and the L.A. City Council), even for those audience members who are still potty training. They put on three productions a year that focus mostly on nonthreatening fairy tales. What does that mean? They cut out anything that could be construed as scary but leave in enough energy and action to still make it fun. Another great thing about coming to a show here is the interactive experience: kids are invited on the spot to join actors on stage, with the outcome sometimes involving a good old food fight. Its performers are from the Actors' Equity Association, and Storybook has one of the only two union children's theater companies working in Los Angeles.

3333 CAHUENGA BOULEVARD WEST, LOS ANGELES. 323-851-4839. www.theatrewest.org

---

379. Check out the classics at **L.A. Theatre Works** at the Skirball Cultural Center.

For twenty-five years, they've been spreading the word—literally. From stage performances to radio shows to recordings, classic and contemporary plays have made their way all over the world thanks to L.A. Theatre Works. Works by playwrights such as Arthur Miller, Oscar Wilde, David Mamet, and Tom Stoppard have been performed by famous actors, like John Lithgow, Annette Bening, Hilary Swank, Jon Hamm, and Laurence Fishburne. Catch them performing some of your favorite playwrights' best work at the James Bridges Theater. In addition, the L.A. Theatre Works Audio Theatre Collection has more than four hundred recorded plays and is the largest library of its kind in the world.

Melnitz Hall: 235 CHARLES E. YOUNG DRIVE, LOS ANGELES. 310-827-0889. www.latw.org

380. See Shakespeare outdoors at the **Will Geer Theatricum Botanicum.**

From June through October, you can attend the annual summer season of Shakespeare and the classics in this rustic, outdoor amphitheater. The Theatricum Botanicum, located in a natural ravine in Topanga, started out as a protest against the victimization of the McCarthy era, when actor Will Geer was blacklisted. He opened a theater for blacklisted actors and folk singers on his property and found ways to keep it afloat. Now a nonprofit and home to characters like Richard III, Queen Elizabeth, King Oberon, Queen Titania, and Puck, it's where you go to see the works of Shakespeare come to life.

1419 NORTH TOPANGA CANYON BOULEVARD, TOPANGA CANYON. 310-455-2322. www.theatricum.com

381. Experience a play written by a Native American with **Native Voices** at the Autry.

Native Voices is a unique theater program devoted to developing and producing new works for the stage by Native American playwrights. Established in 1999, it provides a collaborative setting for Native American playwrights and actors from across the country and Canada to develop their work and see it fully realized on stage. Native Voices has held more than seventy workshops and staged public readings of new plays. All plays are appropriate for ages 14 and older.

WELLS FARGO THEATER, 4700 WESTERN HERITAGE WAY, LOS ANGELES. 323-667-2000. www.theautry.org

382. Take in a movie under the **Cinerama Dome** at the ArcLight.

Built in 1963, the Cinerama Dome has hosted premieres and blockbuster films for more than four decades. The first and largest theater of its kind, its geodesic dome is composed of 316 hexagons, making it one of the most recognizable theaters in L.A. But it's what's inside that makes watching a film here worth the ticket price ($16). With more than eight hundred seats, loge seating, a Kinoton projector that allows for 70mm films to be screened, Cinerama projectors that play three-strip Cinerama with stereophonic sound, an upgraded sound system with forty-four speakers, and a curved 126-degree screen that's eighty-six feet wide, this theater almost guarantees that even a bad movie will look and sound good.

6360 SUNSET BOULEVARD IN HOLLYWOOD. 323-464-1478. www.arclightcinemas.com

→ ***FACT:*** *In 2009, James Cameron's* Avatar *was the first film shown here using XPAND 3-D technology.*

383. See some of the best films screened one after another by **Cinefamily** at the Silent Movie Theatre.

The Cinefamily, a group of cinema lovers, has put together a screening schedule that will have you crying uncle just because everything is so good. A screening of *Noriko's Dinner Table* followed by a discussion with Sion Sono (*Suicide Club*) is too gruesome to pass up; you might also catch *Battleship Potemkin*, a Charlie Chaplin film, or even a few after-school specials—the hits just keep coming.

611 NORTH FAIRFAX AVENUE, LOS ANGELES. 323-655-2510. www.cinefamily.org

384. Buy a ticket and grab one of the **Last Remaining Seats**.

Launched in 1987 to draw attention to Broadway's neglected movie palaces, the annual Last Remaining Seats film series entertains thousands a year by showcasing classic films and a classic space. Hosted by special guests, like acclaimed film critic Leonard Maltin or stars of the film, the Last Remaining Seats experience is about more than just the film. The moment you enter one of the last remaining movie theaters on Broadway, you'll find it difficult to pull your eyes away from the architecture and design long enough to actually watch what's on the screen.

All eight screenings will take place in the movie palaces of downtown L.A.'s Broadway Historic Theatre District. www.laconservancy.org/remaining/index.php

385. Rent a rare film from **Vidiots** or **Cinefile**.

If you're a fan of obscure films no one's really heard of, the kind of films that make you sound like a real cinephile, then look no further. At Vidiots and Cinefile, you can find all the eclectic films you love. Both places carry a wide range of DVDs and good old VHS tapes and have a knowledgeable and helpful staff. You'll find what you're looking for and a few surprises as well. Just try to ask for something like Alejandro Jodorowsky's *The Holy Mountain* instead of *Sex and the City*.

VIDIOTS, 302 PICO BOULEVARD, SANTA MONICA. 310-392-8508. www.vidiotsvideo.com; CINEFILE, 11280 SANTA MONICA BOULEVARD, LOS ANGELES. 310-312-8836. www.cinefilevideo.com

386. Join your fellow movie buffs at the **American Cinematheque** at the Aero Theatre.

With all the special programming featuring actors and directors that the American Cinematheque has every year, it's no surprise that movie buffs love coming here to celebrate the world of cinema. My favorite time to partake in the cinematic glory is

Valentine's Day weekend, when it's all about romancing the screen: heartthrobs featured include Omar Sharif in *Doctor Zhivago*, Ryan Gosling in *The Notebook*, George Peppard in *Breakfast at Tiffany's*, Humphrey Bogart in *Casablanca*, and Cary Elwes in *The Princess Bride*. It's inconceivable that you won't find yourself sighing and swooning all over the place. But don't worry, you'll be in good company—I'll bring a box of Kleenex; you bring the chocolates.
1328 MONTANA AVENUE AT 14TH STREET, SANTA MONICA. 323-466-FILM.
www.americancinematheque.com

---

387. Catch a flick at the **Billy Wilder Theater** at the Hammer Museum.

My most memorable screening here was when I came to see legendary documentary filmmaker Albert Maysles screen his film *Meet Marlon Brando*. The hot pink–hued theater was packed, and as the lights dimmed and the movie began, the sound did not. For what seemed like an eternity (probably only a few minutes), the sound and picture were out of sync. And soon, the only thing you could hear was Maysles yelling out, "What the hell is going on? Is someone going to fix that?" Watching a film he directed while listening to him complain about the sound was one of those amazing cinematic experiences I'll never forget. And while the Wilder doesn't make a habit of having technical difficulties like this one, they do make sure their audiences have a great time.
10899 WILSHIRE BOULEVARD, LOS ANGELES. 310-443-7000.
hammer.ucla.edu/about/billy_wilder_theater.html

---

388. See a short film at the **Echo Park Film Center** (EPFC).

Microcinema is just as small and niche as it sounds, but it's even cooler and cuter than you can imagine. The EPFC is a nonprofit space where you can go see a microcinema screening of features, shorts, and documentaries that are locally and independently produced. It's no frills but lots of fun; you plunk down in a seat or on the floor and watch films being projected onto a pull-down screen, à la high school science class, making this experience totally old-school. Inspired from your visit? The EPFC provides filmmaking workshops and classes and has a small retail shop specializing in the Super 8 format. Who knows, maybe the next film you'll be watching here will be your own.
1200 NORTH ALVARADO STREET NEAR SUNSET BOULEVARD, LOS ANGELES. 213-484-8846.
www.echoparkfilmcenter.org

---

389. Get animated watching cartoons at the **Alex Film Society**.

You hardly get a chance to see things the way that they were originally presented, but at the Alex Film Society at the Alex Theatre, with their program of classic films,

cartoons, and extras, you get to enjoy it all in the manner it was intended. Nothing could be better than classic cartoons on the big screen.
216 NORTH BRAND BOULEVARD, GLENDALE. 818-243-2539. www.alexfilmsociety.org

---

390. Catch something off the beaten path at the **Landmark Nuart Theatre.**

For Angelenos, the Nuart has become a prime destination for cinephiles seeking films that weren't rolled out by the Hollywood machine. Since opening in 1974, it has specialized in revival, foreign, and art-house films and hosts frequent auteur lectures and film festivals. A bonus? *The Rocky Horror Picture Show* and its devotees take over the theater at midnight every Saturday in a "Time Warp."
11272 SANTA MONICA BOULEVARD, LOS ANGELES. 310-473-8530.
www.landmarktheatres.com

Film Festivals

Los Angeles hosts more film festivals than anywhere else in the world, and why wouldn't it? It's the home of Hollywood. These festivals focus on every aspect of society and culture. Check out those that show new and international films or fit your favorite genre.

391. *AFI Fest.* One of the film festivals started by the American Film Institute created by the National Endowment for the Arts in 1967, AFI Fest is the longest-running film festival in Los Angeles and shows more than one hundred films from all over the world for ten days each November. Many have gone on to win Oscars. It's the only film festival in the U.S. to hold FIAPF (Fédération Internationale des Associations de Producteurs de Films) accreditation, and they offer free tickets to all screenings. AFI members have early access to tickets once they become available.
2021 NORTH WESTERN AVENUE, LOS ANGELES. 323-467-4578. www.afi.com.

392. *Los Angeles Film Festival.* Held annually in June, the LAFF showcases the best in American and international cinema. The eleven-day festival includes panels, seminars, music-video showcases, free outdoor screenings, and much more.
Film Independent, 9911 WEST PICO BOULEVARD, LOS ANGELES. 866-345-6337.
www.lafilmfest.com

393. *Docuweek.* This annual showcase not only features some of the year's most promising documentary films, it also helps qualify you for Academy

Award consideration. And once you've been nominated, go to DocuDay, an all-day screening of the year's Oscar-nominated documentary films.
1201 WEST 5TH STREET, SUITE M270, LOS ANGELES. 213-534-3600. www.documentary.org

394. *L.A. Comedy Shorts Film Festival.* This four-day event in April is the largest comedy film festival in the U.S. and a gut buster. Come celebrate the films that make you laugh and the people who make them.
251 SOUTH MAIN STREET, LOS ANGELES. www.lacomedyshorts.com

395. *City of Lights, City of Angels French Film Festival.* Indulge your inner Francophile with a week of French movie premieres at COLCOA, one of the largest French film festivals in the world. Don't worry if your français isn't up to par—all films come with English subtitles. Très bien!
April. The Directors Guild Theater Complex, 7920 SUNSET BOULEVARD, LOS ANGELES. www.colcoa.org

396. *The Los Angeles Asian Pacific Film Festival.* Since this festival began, it's shown more than 3,000 films and videos by Asian artists. The premier showcase for film and video works by Asian-Pacific-American and Asian-Pacific international film artists, this festival coincides with Asian-Pacific Heritage Month. It also includes panels, workshops, and artists' awards.
May. Various locations. asianfilmfestla.org

397. *Dance Camera West Film Festival Los Angeles.* Devoted to promoting the vibrant and diverse art of dance by capturing it on film, the festival puts dance and its beauty on the big screen as experimental shorts, documentaries, and features.
May. www.dancecamerawest.org

398. *OUTFEST, The Los Angeles Gay and Lesbian Film Festival.* Outfest Los Angeles is the largest film festival in Southern California with almost two hundred films from twenty-five countries shown in seven different venues across Los Angeles.
July. www.outfest.org

399. *Los Angeles International Short Film Festival.* This is the largest short film festival in the world, with more than four hundred shorts.
September. www.lashortsfest.com

400. *The Feel Good Film Festival.* A festival devoted to films that have happy endings? Coming here, you know exactly what you're in for.
August. www.fgff.org

401. *Cinecon Classic Film Festival.* Celebrate the rare and remarkable movies from the silent and early sound era that have been forgotten over time. In five days, see more than thirty classic films screened in 35mm. Silent films include live piano accompaniment.
September. www.cinecon.org

402. *The Other Venice Film Festival (OVFF).* You won't arrive by gondola, but you will see a great variety of features, shorts, and docs, experimental films, political films, and youth- and women-directed films. The festival also includes filmmaker discussions, featured artists, music, and more.
October. othervenicefilmfestival.com

403. *Hollywood Film Festival.* A weeklong international film festival with a star-studded awards ceremony and a pre-Oscar showcase, this festival was created to bridge the gap between movie stars and the rest of the world.
October. www.hollywoodfilmfestival.com

404. *Los Angeles International Children's Film Festival.* For two weekends in October, the Los Angeles International Children's Film Festival screens more than 150 short films from around the world made for kids and teens. All films are free, so it's the perfect excuse for a family outing to the movies.
October. www.lachildrensfilm.org

405. *Annual Artivist Film Festival.* Get in touch with your inner activist at the Artivist Film Festival. This festival screens around seventy films for filmmakers and other creatives who use their work to create awareness about environmental issues, animal rights, human rights, and children's advocacy.
November. www.artivist.com

Expert Contributor: James Bewley

James Bewley is a program officer at the Andy Warhol Foundation for the Visual Arts. Prior to moving to New York, Bewley produced hundreds of events per year in his position as director of Public Programs at the UCLA Hammer Museum.

MY TEN FAVORITE CULTURAL DISTRACTIONS IN L.A.

The façade at ***LAXART***. Subtle, beautiful, always changing. It teases the great work on view inside.
2640 SOUTH LA CIENEGA BOULEVARD IN LOS ANGELES. 310-559-0166. www.laxart.org

The decaying dice from Ricky Jay's collection at the ***Museum of Jurassic Technology***. The fracturing, crystallizing cellulose nitrate, which were once radiant and potentially flammable, are fading now into tiny piles of sparkling dust, like broken dreams on Hollywood Boulevard.
9341 VENICE BOULEVARD IN LOS ANGELES. 310-836-6131. www.mjt.org

UCB Theatre. This black box across from the Scientology Center on Franklin Avenue supports an entire strata of comedic artistry. It functions as an atelier for young comedians and offers masters of the craft a space to hone new material. There's one in New York, too, but the intimacy of the L.A. space allows for a different kind of experience. I once sat next to a lady and her chair collapsed. I mean, I felt bad. But mostly I was glad it wasn't me.
5919 FRANKLIN AVENUE IN LOS ANGELES. 323-908-8702. www.losangeles.ucbtheatre.com

The George C. Page Museum. The tar pits are a bit of a disappointment once you realize those mammoths aren't real, but the Page Museum redeems an otherwise dull afternoon of asphalt bubbles and hot sun. The glassed-in Laboratory where the archeologists work with dental tools and toothpicks to identify dinosaur bones and clean dust off tiny things should be a part of every natural history museum as far as I'm concerned.
5801 WILSHIRE BOULEVARD IN LOS ANGELES. 323-934-7243. www.tarpits.org

Effulgence of the North, at the Velaslavasay Panorama. Few other spiral staircases in L.A. can deposit you so firmly in the middle of an Arctic ice floe. This installation is cool, nerdy, and transcendent, reaching at least three social sub-categories in Los Angeles. Plus they have a carnivorous garden out back. In a gazebo.
1122 WEST 24TH STREET IN LOS ANGELES. www.panoramaonview.org

LACMA Film Series. Where watching David Lynch's *Inland Empire* in a seat next to Ed Ruscha was no big deal. Really.
5905 WILSHIRE BOULEVARD IN LOS ANGELES. 323-857-6000. www.lacam.org

826 L.A.'s Time Travel Mart. A convenience store for the harried time traveler? And a tutoring center for young writers? Best. Idea. Ever. All right, kids, now let's get a decent time-travel story that doesn't hurt my head.
1714 WEST SUNSET BOULEVARD IN LOS ANGELES. 213-413-3388. www.826la.org

The Santa Monica Museum of Art. Their Al Taylor and Alberto Burri shows were stellar. Benefitting from keen curatorial editing and abundant natural light, works look fantastic, almost otherworldly, in that space.
2525 MICHIGAN AVENUE IN SANTA MONICA. 310-586-6488. www.smmoa.org

The Hammer Museum. I spent a lot of time there. More than a person should probably, but when you agree to a 24-hour apocalypse movie marathon, you get what you sign up for. Highlights include the reinstalled permanent collection, which now seems to vibrate at the same intensity as the rest of the work on display; the light-speed effect of the pre-show at the Billy Wilder Theater; and the public engagement projects being taken up by artists. Machine Project leading dream seminars and turning the coat checkroom into a tiny concert hall were strokes of genius that I hope continue with each radical rethinking of the audience experience.
10899 WILSHIRE BOULEVARD IN LOS ANGELES. 310-443-7000. www.hammer.ucla.edu

The peculiar artistry of ***downtown film shoots.*** To this day I get excited identifying the corner of my building at Fourth and Main when it pops up in the background of every commercial that involves either a bank robbery or a person thinking about car insurance. It's quite a thing to just spend a day changing a very noticeable L.A. into vaguely generic New York City: the sign-making wizards that transform loft-leasing agencies into porn palaces; riggers focusing blinding lights capable of turning night into day; and the massive coordination required for one fifteen-second shot of someone talking on a phone. It is absurd, beautiful choreography that never ceases to amaze and frustrate in equal measure.

CHAPTER 5

Eating and Drinking

Los Angeles is a food paradise. Chock-a-block with great restaurants and bars, you'd be hard pressed not to find a fantastic meal here or discover a great drink or a new style of cooking. Thanks to a diverse population, talented chefs with infinite vision, and a wealth of farm-fresh produce—combined with a dining community with an uninhibited palate—vittles in this city are a gastronomic delight. It's a city that overflows with eating and drinking pleasures, from the gourmet to the exotic and the casual. The variety can be overwhelming (and very filling). Get to know the full range of what's here and you can indulge any taste, whether it's lunch from a greasy barbecue truck or a late-night snack with an oenophile sushi master.

From the simple kimchi taco that ignited the food truck craze to the raw foods movement, food has always played a big role in the L.A. scene. Even the word "organic" doesn't ring truer than in this city. And where would sushi be without L.A.? The raw fish craze originated here during the 1980s with the power lunch/diet trend and gave birth to the California Roll. Although the roll may not be traditional, it's a marker of how far and how important the roles of different cuisines are in the city.

Like all great things, what makes the following entries the best are that they are memorable for all the right reasons. I looked beyond just tasty meals and famous menus, and found the most distinctive offerings, welcoming atmospheres, fun decor, and good service—things that, along with food and drink, put the following places in a league of their own. These are establishments where you will have a wholly satisfying experience.

Sample the Local Cuisine from a Famous Los Angeles Chef

What chefs don't have food empires nowadays? With Emmy-winning cable TV shows, multiple restaurants, specialty food lines and even a range of cookware available for purchase on HSN or QVC, celebrity chefs are ubiquitous. Some still cook in the same kitchens where they started, while others have branched out with new dining ventures, which means more time on the road and less in front of a stove. And while Los Angeles's diners have a reputation for their fickleness, these chefs and their restaurants seem to hold their interest and continue to tempt their palates as they spread across the city's culinary landscape. But just because they have multiple restaurants, it isn't any easier to sample their goods. These chefs' places are always full.

406. *Wolfgang Puck.* When you think of food in Los Angeles, the first name that comes to mind is Wolfgang Puck. This Emmy Award–winning celebrity chef, restaurateur, author, and businessman not only exemplifies the lifestyle in this city (he occasionally acts, too), but its food. Born in Austria, Puck learned to cook, as many children do, from this mother. He trained in Provence, Monaco, and Paris before making his way stateside to L.A. to become chef and co-owner of Ma Maison (closed) in 1975. Puck left six years later and opened Spago on the Sunset Strip (closed) in 1982. A year later he opened the still popular Chinois on Main, the first example of an Asian-fusion menu incorporating Chinese, American, and French influences. Fifteen years later, he opened ***Spago*** (p. 176) in Beverly Hills, which has remained the location of his flagship award-winning restaurant for the past fifteen years. Widely recognized as the crown jewel in Puck's culinary crown, Spago, under the watchful eye of Puck and his right-hand man, managing partner and James Beard Award–winning executive chef Lee Hefter, has been recognized as one of the top restaurants in the United States for over a decade. The menu features inventive and seasonal dishes that showcase the cream of the crop of California's abundant produce. On top of that distinction, Puck owns dozens of restaurants (fine and casual) from Singapore to London; a premiere catering service; and a line of kitchenware, appliances, cookbooks, and pre-packaged foods—and shows no intention of slowing down. In addition, he is the official caterer for the Academy Awards Governors Ball. But when it comes to the Academy Awards, don't expect to find Puck in the kitchen—that would be the wrong place to look. Instead, you'll find him on the red carpet mingling with stars, hand-feeding his signature smoked salmon and caviar pizzas to Oscar winners and nominees, and giving interviews, signing off with his signature motto, "Live, Love, Eat!"

Spago Restaurant: 176 NORTH CANON DRIVE IN BEVERLY HILLS. 310-385-0880.

Chinois (on Main): 2709 MAIN STREET IN SANTA MONICA. 310-392-9025.

CUT: Beverly Wilshire Hotel, 9500 WILSHIRE BOULEVARD IN BEVERLY HILLS. 310-276-8500.

WP24 by Wolfgang Puck: The Ritz-Carlton, 900 WEST OLYMPIC BOULEVARD IN LOS ANGELES. 213-743-8824.

Wolfgang Puck Bar & Grill: L.A. LIVE Complex, 800 WEST OLYMPIC BOULEVARD IN LOS ANGELES. 213-748-9700.

Red|Seven: Pacific Design Center, 700 NORTH SAN VICENTE BOULEVARD IN WEST HOLLYWOOD. 310-289-1587.

Wolfgang Puck Bistro: Universal Citywalk, 1000 UNIVERSAL CITY PLAZA #152 IN LOS ANGELES. 818-985-9653.

www.wolfgangpuck.com

---

407. *Joachim Splichal.* The yin to Wolfgang Puck's yang, Splichal is the only other chef/restaurateur that is on par with Puck in terms of sheer presence in Los Angeles. This German native, who came to Los Angeles in 1981, made a name for himself when he opened Patina in 1989. Fast forward twenty-four years and, with approximately sixty locations run by his company, Patina Restaurant Group, it's clear that Splichal's name is engrained into the city's food psyche. You'll find a majority of his food operations at arts centers and institutions, the perfect pairing of art and his art form—making delicious California French cuisine for the people.

Patina: 141 SOUTH GRAND AVENUE IN DOWNTOWN LOS ANGELES. 213-972-3331.

Concert Hall Café: Walt Disney Concert Hall, 111 SOUTH GRAND AVENUE IN DOWNTOWN LOS ANGELES. 213-972-3550.

Café Pinot: 700 WEST 5TH STREET IN DOWNTOWN LOS ANGELES. 213-239-6500.

Kendall's Brasserie and Bar: L.A. Music Center, 135 NORTH GRAND AVENUE IN LOS ANGELES. 213-972-7322.

Spotlight Café and 'Tina Tacos: The Music Center, 135 NORTH GRAND AVENUE IN LOS ANGELES. 213-972-7525.

Pinot Grill: 135 NORTH GRAND AVENUE IN LOS ANGELES. 213-842-0048.

Market Café at AT&T Center: 1150 SOUTH OLIVE STREET, GARDEN LEVEL, IN LOS ANGELES. 213-536-4090.

Market Café and Atrium Café at Wells Fargo Center: 330 SOUTH HOPE STREET IN DOWNTOWN LOS ANGELES. 213-680-7387.

Nick & Stef's Steakhouse: 330 SOUTH HOPE STREET IN DOWNTOWN LOS ANGELES. 213-680-0330.

Café Descanso at Descanso Gardens: 1418 DESCANSO DRIVE (PAST ENTRANCE TO THE GARDENS) IN LA CAÑADA FLINTRIDGE. 818-790-3663.
Hollywood Bowl: 2301 NORTH HIGHLAND BOULEVARD IN LOS ANGELES. 323-850-1885.
Norton Simon Café at Norton Simon Museum: 411 WEST COLORADO BOULEVARD IN PASADENA. 626-844-6970
Plaza Café, and Ray's and Stark Bar at LACMA: 5905 WILSHIRE BOULEVARD IN LOS ANGELES. Plaza Café: 323-857-6197, Ray's and Stark Bar: 323-857-6180.
www.patinagroup.com

---

408. *Nancy Silverton and Mark Peel.* When people get divorced, a good lawyer is instrumental in helping to divide the assets. But what happens when two well-known, award-winning chefs who are behind one of Los Angeles's most famous restaurants/bakeries, decide to split? What happens to their loyal customers? Do we have to pick sides? That seemed to be the case when former restaurant power couple Nancy Silverton and Mark Peel parted ways several years ago. They started La Brea Bakery, Nancy's baking empire, which sold for $55 million in 2001, and Campanile in 1989. Both places were housed next to each other in Charlie Chaplin's old office building and became cherished by the culinary set of L.A. Nancy made La Brea Bakery *the* destination in L.A. for fresh-baked artisan bread, and as Campanile's head pastry chef (formerly she was the head pastry chef at Spago), she made it worth going there for the desserts alone. Mark Peel brought his commendable culinary skills—honed during an apprenticeship at Ma Maison and later at two Michelin three-star restaurants (La Tour d'Argent in Paris and Moulin de Mougins in Cannes), as sous chef at Michael's (where he met Nancy), as former Chef de Cuisine at Spago, and after a stint at famed Chez Panisse—to Campanile's kitchen. He created a menu that focused on simple, fresh ingredients while touching on French and Italian influences. Both Nancy and Mark won many accolades in the food world. So what happened after the split? Nancy opened up her own Italian eatery, Pizzeria Mozza, with the orange-Crocs-wearing food superstar Mario Batali in 2006 and opened Osteria Mozza a year later. And after twenty-three years, Mark shuttered Campanile's doors in 2012 after losing his month-to-month lease. But fear not, Campanile will reopen in LAX at Terminal 4 (American Airlines) in May.
Osteria Mozza: 6602 MELROSE AVENUE IN LOS ANGELES. 323-297-0100.
Pizzeria Mozza: 641 NORTH HIGHLAND AVENUE IN LOS ANGELES. 323- 297-0101.
Mozza 2Go: 6610 MELROSE AVENUE IN LOS ANGELES. 323-297-1130.
www.mozzarestaurantgroup.com

---

409. *Nobu Matsuhisa.* New York may boast about having Nobu, but this chef's heart has been firmly planted in Los Angeles since 1977. Nobuyuki

"Nobu" Matsuhisa began his career apprenticing in Tokyo for seven years before moving to Peru to open a restaurant. Nobu, unable to find the ingredients readily found in Tokyo, developed his unique style of South American/Japanese cuisine through improvisation. He later moved to Alaska and, after a failed business attempt there, settled in Los Angeles. A decade later he opened up his first restaurant, ***Matsuhisa*** (p. 180). Extremely popular and often frequented by celebrities, it was here that Robert De Niro approached Nobu about setting up shop in Tribeca. Soon afterwards, Matsuhisa and De Niro, now partners, opened Nobu in New York City in 1993, and from there, meteoric fame. With his restaurant empire stretching all over the world, it's no wonder Nobu only catches up on sleep when he's on private jets flying from one location to another. But you'll find him at one time or another at Matsuhisa, where the menu is as thick as a short novel and everything on it is delicious. Ask him how he feels about New York and L.A., and he'll admit, "I like Los Angeles more."

Nobu Malibu: 22706 PACIFIC COAST HIGHWAY IN MALIBU. 310- 317-9140. Nobu: 903 NORTH LA CIENEGA BOULEVARD IN WEST HOLLYWOOD. 310-657-5711. www.noburestaurants.com; Matsuhisa: 129 NORTH LA CIENEGA BOULEVARD IN BEVERLY HILLS. 310-659-9639, www.nobumatsuhisa.com

410. *Suzanne Goin.* Suzanne Goin is L.A.'s food sweetheart. Every restaurant she owns not only delights and thrives, but also requires an advance reservation. Bringing the perfect blend of California Mediterranean to our plates with complete ease, it's not hard to imagine why Goin, a nine-time James Beard Award nominee and winner (California's Best Chef in 2006), who trained and worked at places such as Chez Panisse, Alain Passard's three-star L'Arpège, Didier Oudill's two-star Pain, and Campanile, is so well-versed in the art of simple food. It was during her stint at Campanile, where she became executive chef, that she met her future business partner Caroline Styne. She left after two years and they opened ***Lucques*** (p. 198) and A.O.C. (which started the tapas craze in L.A.). With her husband, chef David Lentz, she owns The Hungry Cat (no fuss seafood and delicious burgers) where they co-helm the kitchen. Her most recent venture, and the biggest and most ambitious restaurant in the Goin/Styne trifecta, is Tavern. It has its own bakery, take-out counter, and mini "larder," aka a gourmet shop (see Larder at Tavern, p. 191).

AOC: 8700 WEST 3RD STREET, LOS ANGELES. 310-859-9859. www.aocwinebar.com
Lucques: 8474 MELROSE AVENUE IN WEST HOLLYWOOD. 323-655-6277. www.lucques.com
The Hungry Cat: 1535 VINE STREET IN HOLLYWOOD. 323-462-2155. www.thehungrycat.com

Tavern: 11648 WEST SAN VICENTE BOULEVARD IN LOS ANGELES. 310-806-6464. www.tavernla.com
The Larder at Tavern: 11648 WEST SAN VICENTE BOULEVARD IN LOS ANGELES. 310-806-6464. tavernla.com/larder.html
The Larder at Maple Drive: 345 NORTH MAPLE DRIVE IN BEVERLY HILLS. 310-248-3779. www.thelarderattavern.com

411. *Mary Sue Milliken and Susan Feniger.* The Two Hot Tamales trailblazed their way through the L.A. culinary landscape when they opened their first restaurant, City Café (closed) in 1981. While everyone was focusing on Asian or European cuisine, Mary Sue Milliken and Susan Feniger took it to the next level incorporating new-world influences like Mexican, Thai, Indian, and more. They opened the critically acclaimed Border Grill in 1985, and the Latin-influenced Ciudad (closed) in 1998. For over thirty years, Mary Sue and Susan have set the standard and have become the superlative authorities of authentic Mexican cuisine. But their roles aren't just in the kitchen: Mary Sue and Susan are also active members of the community and various charities. Mary Sue is one of the founding members of Women Chefs & Restaurateurs and a national board member on Share Our Strength, and Susan is a founding board member of The Scleroderma Research Foundation. And in 2009, Susan opened up her first solo venture, Street, bringing L.A. a taste of street food from all over the world.
Border Grill Santa Monica: 1445 4TH STREET IN SANTA MONICA. 310-451-1655.
Border Grill Downtown L.A.: 445 SOUTH FIGUEROA STREET. 213-486-5171. www.bordergrill.com
Susan Feniger's STREET: 742 NORTH HIGHLAND AVENUE IN LOS ANGELES. 323-203-0500. www.eatatstreet.com

412. *Ludo Lefebvre.* For a man with no restaurant, Ludo Lefebvre sure knows how to start a food revolution. Once the award-winning chef of L'Orangerie and Bastide, it turns out that all Ludo needed was some foie gras, kimchi, complete free range, and no walls to be heralded as "The Chef of the Future" by *TIME* magazine. Lefebvre, now the "Pop-Up King," is a gourmet nomad who goes from stove to stove whipping up imaginative dishes for those fans who are lucky enough to be able to secure a reservation for his coveted LudoBites. When word gets out that LudoBites is on the move, be sure to mark your calendars and call till you break through the busy signal on the other end. It'll be time well spent.
www.ludolefebvre.com/ludobites

413. *Sang Yoon.* Sang Yoon has a résumé that reads like a Who's Who of food. He's worked with Joël Robuchon, Alain Ducasse, Michael McCarty, and Wolfgang Puck—and now he makes burgers. What happened?! Yoon bought ***Father's Office*** (p. 181) in Santa Monica in 2000, revamped it into a gastropub, added a slew of international beers on tap (making beer drinking an art form) and remade the burger (gourmet with no substitutions). With the constant press, patrons and cash flow, don't count on seeing Sang Yoon slow down any time soon. A second Father's Office location opened in 2008 and Lukshon, an Asian-themed restaurant opened in 2011, means that Yoon is always busy.
Lukshon: 3239 HELMS AVENUE IN CULVER CITY. 310-202-6808. www.lukshon.com
Father's Office: 3229 HELMS AVENUE IN CULVER CITY. 310-736-2224. www.fathersoffice.com
Father's Office Santa Monica: 1018 MONTANA AVENUE IN SANTA MONICA. 310-736-2224. www.fathersoffice.com

414. *Vinny Dotolo and Jon Shook.* Long before they were known as the "Food Dudes" or the "Animal Guys," Vinny and Jon were two students who met at the Art Institute of Fort Lauderdale while studying the culinary arts. From there they tag-teamed their way across America and in the late '90s landed smack dab in L.A. Since their arrival they've worked at Ben Ford and Govind Armstrong's Chadwick (closed), started their own catering company, starred in their own food show, made their mark with ***Animal***, their meat restaurant known for comfort food appeal and its bountiful use of bacon (Benedikt Taschen from Taschen Books is a partner), and ventured into seafood with ***Son of a Gun*** (p. 174). The boys have been very busy, but when it comes to food their rules haven't changed: they think outside the box and make sure it's consistently good.
Animal: 435 NORTH FAIRFAX AVENUE IN LOS ANGELES. 323-782-9225. www.animalrestaurant.com
Son of a Gun: 8370 WEST 3RD STREET IN LOS ANGELES. 323-782-9033. www.sonofagunrestaurant.com

415. Attempt to share your caramel corn at **ArcLight Cinemas**.

The lights go down, the movie starts and as you reach for your tub of deliciously sweet, crunchy and salty caramel popcorn, your hands touch. You turn to see whose hand it is, and as your eyes meet, the music in the theater seems to swell with anticipation. This is your moment, so you take it and tenderly whisper, "Get your own," and pull your caramel corn in for a passionate embrace.

Several locations. www.arclightcinemas.com

416. Try Korean Short-Rib Tacos from the **Kogi BBQ Truck**.

There once was a boy named Roy, who found cooking more than a joy. He loved to cook, but needed a hook, and created something not found in a book. He'd drive a truck all over town, and feed to the masses the new and unfound. In his tacos he would use ingredients that would amaze and amuse. He put Korean BBQ with kimchi in a tortilla; one taste of these and L.A. replied, "I feel ya." Now Kogi is all over the place, and best of all, really delicious to taste.

Check website for locations, www.kogibbq.com

417. Order a few lobster rolls from **Son of a Gun**.

One lobster roll from Son of a Gun will leave you unsatisfied, so it's best to order more—several more. At Son of Gun, you won't be able to get your hands on one of their lobster rolls made from sweet Maine lobster mixed with celery and lemon aioli, stuffed into a buttered roll and topped with a sprinkling of potato chips fast enough. And once you do, that moment of anticipated excitement is over far too soon as you've managed to devour the whole thing in a single bite. To prolong your lobster roll enjoyment, it's best to order a few.

8370 WEST 3RD STREET IN LOS ANGELES. 323-782-9033. www.sonofagunrestaurant.com

418. Taste the carne asada fries at **My Taco**.

The specialty here may be the barbacoa, a mouthwatering stew of lamb cooked on a hot griddle till crispy, but it's the carne asada fries you're really after. Not offering your average nachos, this Highland Park eatery located in a mini-mall serves up heaps of guacamole, melted cheese, and grilled carne asada on a mountain of French fries. It's everything you want in a mouthful: delicious, hot, spicy ooziness with a slight potato crunch. And if you get a bit carried away at the salsa bar with their delicious chipotle sauces and must-try spicy guacamoles, wash it all down with a glass of homemade watermelon agua fresca.

6300 YORK BOULEVARD #4 IN HIGHLAND PARK. 323-256-2698. www.my-taco.com

419. Have a crab Louie at **The Grill on the Alley**.

Steps from Rodeo Drive in the heart of Beverly Hills, you'll find the Grill. A favorite for those who love good food, enjoy first-class service, and appreciate a restaurant with an air of distinction, the Grill is also a must for crab Louie lovers. Order it for lunch or dinner and when your old-school waiter asks if you want your sauce on the side, depending on your penchant for dressing, you might want to ask for it heavy and a little extra on the side just in case.

9560 DAYTON WAY IN BEVERLY HILLS. 310-276-0615. www.thegrill.com

420. Order a guava tart from **Café Tropical**, and try not to eat the whole thing.

Who knew guava and cream cheese baked in a puff pastry shell could be so yummy. On any trip to Café Tropical you are sure to leave with a tart gently cradled in your arms, that, in all likelihood, will be devoured the moment you get home. Can't wait that long to indulge? Sit in at the café and enjoy your tart with a cup of café con leche. Be sure to cut your tart into several pieces; it'll make it a little less obvious to everyone else that you've eaten it all yourself.

2900 WEST SUNSET BOULEVARD IN LOS ANGELES. 323-661-8391. www.cafetropicalla.com

421. See how many soup dumplings you can eat at **Din Tai Fung**.

When director Ang Lee needed a hand double to create the perfect dumpling for a food scene in *Eat Drink Man Woman*, the hands he employed were none other than Yang Chi-hua, owner of the famous soup dumpling restaurant Din Tai Fung. It is renowned for its juicy pork dumplings: just one taste of the luscious pork and rich fatty juices concealed in each perfectly formed dumpling and you'll be hooked.

1108 SOUTH BALDWIN AVENUE IN ARCADIA. 626-574-7068. www.dintaifungusa.com

422. And when you're done, head down the street for a unique dessert soup at the **Shanghai Gourmet** (formerly known as Shanghai Bamboo House).

Soup is not something one thinks of as a dessert—especially one that's hot. But Shanghai Bamboo House makes a special dessert soup of rice balls filled with red beans in a hot and sweet broth. It's so good, you'll wish you hadn't eaten so many dumplings. Be sure to come by and try some of their delicious and unique savory options as well.

933 WEST DUARTE ROAD IN MONROVIA. 626-574-5960.

423. Give thanks to Grandma Elvira before eating your lasagna verde at **Angelini Osteria**.

Chef Gino Angelini's version—homemade spinach pasta layered with beef and veal ragù, and topped with creamy béchamel sauce and fried spinach leaves—is justly famous. This dish, an homage to his grandmother Elvira, is one they can both be proud of.

7313 BEVERLY BOULEVARD IN LOS ANGELES. 323-297-0070. www.angeliniosteria.com

424. Eat a dessert fit for royalty from the **Flan King**.

This classic flan, with a hint of coconut and vanilla, is so smooth and creamy that no other flan can compare. If any subjects attempt to derail the reign of this king, it's off with their heads.

Echo Park Farmer's Market (Fridays): 1125 LOGAN STREET IN ECHO PARK; Larchmont Village Farmers' Market (Sundays): 205 SOUTH LARCHMONT BOULEVARD IN LOS ANGELES. 323-960-0770. www.flan-king.com

Splurge on an Incredible Meal

Long gone are the days of Chef Masa Takayama and his famous Ginza Sushiko. Once offering the most expensive meal in Los Angeles, he closed up shop to move to New York to charge the most expensive meal there. But for those who still have an expense account they can openly abuse, or who are overcome with the desire to burn gaping holes into their wallets, fear not: the incredible splurge-worthy meal still exists in Los Angeles. The checks you'll receive at the end of the meal may be a small fortune, but for the quality, the service, the food, and the unique experience alone, they're worth every penny.

425. *Spago.* The flagship of Wolfgang Puck's culinary empire, this elegant restaurant, artistically decorated by his business partner and ex-wife, interior designer Barbara Lazaroff, continues to cater to its clientele of wheelers and dealers and A-list celebs. What to order? Just leave it to Executive Chef Lee Hefter. One of his artfully composed tasting menus will take you on an epicurean exploration that's worth its weight in gold.

176 NORTH CANON DRIVE IN BEVERLY HILLS. 310-385-0880. www.wolfgangpuck.com

426. *Urasawa.* If there was anyone in L.A. worthy of taking over the old Ginza Sushiko and its reputation as the most expensive restaurant in L.A., it's

Hiroyuki Urasawa, Masa Takayama's former apprentice. Here you'll indulge in a feast of fresh fish dishes created at the hands of a true sushi master. Sushi purists swear by him, and those who wish to worship at his counter save up for the opportunity. And the lucky few who have journeyed down this culinary rite of passage guarantee it's worth every penny.
218 NORTH RODEO DRIVE (SECOND FLOOR) IN BEVERLY HILLS. 310-247-8939.

→ **FACT:** *Hiroyuki Urasawa is one of the few chefs in the U.S. licensed to serve authentic blowfish.*

---

427. *CUT.* Wolfgang Puck's slick Richard Meier–designed steakhouse inside the Beverly Wilshire boasts some of the most expensive cuts of beef in the city, but it's the Wagyu that'll make you want to break the bank. The six-ounce Wagyu (Kobe-style) rib eye will set you back $130 (for you non-math majors, that's over $20 an ounce). With its fatty marbling and unbelievably rich and buttery texture you are guaranteed a meat-induced euphoria that'll have you asking yourself, is there such a thing as too rich?
Beverly Wilshire Hotel, 9500 WILSHIRE BOULEVARD IN BEVERLY HILLS. 310-276-8500. www.wolfgangpuck.com

---

428. *Kaluga Caviar at Petrossian.* There's caviar and then there's *caviar*. If you enjoy the latter and have deep pockets, then a trip to Petrossian in West Hollywood is just what the doctor ordered. For a mere $481 you can get 50 grams of Kaluga, not Beluga, caviar from the Huso Dauricus sturgeon; it is mellow, rich, and buttery in flavor. But if you're feeling exceedingly generous, go for the Petrossian Special Reserve Ossetra caviar. All you need is one look at its gray-gold hue to know that each grain is bursting with flavor imbued by the sea. This rare caviar is a tad bit more at $1,523 for 135 grams. But dare I say it's worth it.
321 NORTH ROBERTSON BOULEVARD IN WEST HOLLYWOOD. 310-271-6300. www.petrossian.com

---

429. *Saam.* Three days a week (Thursdays to Saturdays), tucked behind a nondescript door inside Chef José Andrés's The Bazaar, diners can partake in an epic twenty-course meal in the chef's secluded tasting room. Each mini "course"—one inventive surprise after the next—is so tantalizing that you won't flinch when you get the bill.
SLS Hotel at Beverly Hills, 465 SOUTH LA CIENEGA BOULEVARD IN LOS ANGELES. 310-246-5545. www.thebazaar.com/beverly-hills-saam

430. *Totoraku Teriyaki House Pico.* If you can manage to get your foot in the door, what awaits you inside Chef Kaz Oyama's restaurant is a new level of barbecue. The ultimate yakiniku experience includes everything from beef throat sashimi to mouthwatering steak tartare and rib eye prepared on a tabletop charcoal grill. Though the reservation is the hardest part of this experience (you'll need to go with a friend who has already been or get a referral), once you're there and come to terms with the $200 per person price, everything else is easy to swallow.
10610 WEST PICO BOULEVARD IN LOS ANGELES. 310-838-9881.

431. *Providence.* For the seafood lover in you, Chef Michael Cimarusti's two-Michelin-star restaurant is the perfect place to indulge. For years diners have heeded the siren calls from his kitchen and relished in his creations. With seafood so fresh and expertly prepared, it wouldn't be surprising if Cimarusti turned out to be part merman.
5955 MELROSE AVENUE IN LOS ANGELES. 323-460-4170. www.providencela.com

432. *Hatfield's.* Within this coolly austere restaurant, you'll find Chef Quinn Hatfield, a quiet and dedicated chef. While Hatfield's lacks the decorative embellishment of others, the delightfully simple market-driven California French cuisine is delicious, flavorful, and easily one of the best meals in town.
6703 MELROSE AVENUE IN LOS ANGELES.323-935-2977. hatfieldsrestaurant.com

433. *Il Ristorante di Giorgio Baldi.* If you have gold-lined pockets and an appreciation for fine ingredients, spoil yourself with an order of shaved truffles. Your meal will inherit a richness of flavor that will leave you delighted even as your dollars are discarded. If you're the type to throw caution to the wind, be prepared: this princely meal could leave you a pauper.
114 WEST CHANNEL ROAD IN SANTA MONICA. 310-573-1660 www.giorgiobaldi.us

434. Enjoy s'mores without roughing it at **Luna Park**.

No need to pack up the car and head out into the wilderness to enjoy your favorite campfire dessert. At Luna Park you can get all of the ingredients prepped and ready to go: a basket of homemade graham crackers, bittersweet chocolate sauce, and a fluffy cloud of toasted marshmallow heated in a mini ramekin. All you need to do is assemble and enjoy. One bite and you might have to restrain yourself from singing "Kumbaya" at the table.
672 SOUTH LA BREA AVENUE IN LOS ANGELES. 323-934-2110. www.lunaparkla.com

435. Float away on a custard puff from **Stan's Donuts.**

For decades this old-school doughnut shop owned by Stan Berman has been serving up some of the best fried dough in town, like their famous "Huell," filled with peanut butter and topped with chocolate frosting and chocolate chips. But if you're looking for another reason to venture all the way to Westwood for a visit, look no further than the "custard puff." One bite into the silky vanilla-tinged custard encased between two clouds of soft and fluffy dough and you'll think you've died and gone to heaven.

10948 WEYBURN AVENUE IN LOS ANGELES. 310-208-8660. stansdoughnuts.com

436. Dive into a bowl of roasted duck noodle soup at **Pa Ord Noodle.**

You won't be able to get enough of this rich and delicious soup filled with roasted duck, vegetables and your choice of noodles. And from the looks of it, no one else in the restaurant can either.

5301 SUNSET BOULEVARD IN LOS ANGELES. 323-461-3945.

437. **Sapp Coffee Shop** brings boat noodle soup onto friendlier shores.

Finding a good boat noodle soup outside of the bustling floating markets in Thailand can be tricky. It's hard to find the right mix of ingredients in order to achieve that full-bodied broth, and so few do it right. Thank goodness for Sapp! The soup, filled with different types of beef in a rich, delicious broth thickened with beef blood, is always hot, and each spoonful is packed with flavor powerful enough to transport you to Thailand. And if you're feeling adventurous, get "the works," which includes liver and tripe.

5183 HOLLYWOOD BOULEVARD IN LOS ANGELES. 323-665-1035. sapp.menutoeat.com

438. Enjoy raw fish Italian style at **Il Grano Restaurant.**

It looks familiar, it smells familiar, but when you start eating the crudo prepared by chef Salvatore Marino, it won't be like anything you've ever tasted. At Il Grano, the crudo, the Italian version of sashimi, is fresh, salty, sour and tasty—all the things you look for in a new favorite dish.

11359 SANTA MONICA BOULEVARD IN WEST LOS ANGELES. 310-477-7886. www.ilgrano.com

439. Get surf and turf done right at **Taylor's Steak House.**

At this old-school steak house, you'll find the perfect combination of meat and seafood all in one dish, the Filet Oscar. Lumps of crabmeat, asparagus and béarnaise sauce stacked atop a succulent piece of filet mignon will make you push the vegetables off

your plate. Who needs them! One bite and you'll only have eyes for Oscar.
3361 WEST 8TH STREET IN KOREATOWN IN LOS ANGELES. 213-382-8449. www.taylorssteakhouse.com

---

440. At **Crustacean Beverly Hills**, go for the obvious choice and get the garlic noodles.

The people who run this restaurant are known for their ability to keep a secret: if you've ever wondered how they make their mouthwatering garlic noodles, don't ask because they won't tell. But don't let that stop you from ordering this dish time and again. Just tell everyone it's for research purposes, as each dish you devour will be used in future attempts to crack the Crustacean Garlic Noodle Code.
9646 LITTLE SANTA MONICA BOULEVARD IN BEVERLY HILLS. 310-205-8990. www.anfamily.com

---

441. Grab a taste of Cuba at **El Rincon Criollo**.

The Cuban sandwich here is big. That already makes it a winner in this book. But include creamy melted cheese, salty slices of ham and pork, and a good sour pickle pressed between warm toasted bread and you'll be rendered speechless while you devour this sandwich.
4361 SEPULVEDA BOULEVARD IN CULVER CITY. 310-391-4478.

---

442. Order the original black cod with miso at **Matsuhisa**.

The love affair with this dish started here, and no other restaurant does it better.
129 NORTH LA CIENEGA BOULEVARD IN BEVERLY HILLS. 310-659-9639. www.nobumatsuhisa.com

---

443. Have a bowl of handmade udon at **Kotohira Restaurant**.

Once you've indulged in a bowl of udon at Kotohira, you'll keep coming back for more. The hard part: keeping those thick white noodles from slipping out of your chopsticks.
1747 WEST REDONDO BEACH BOULEVARD IN GARDENA. 310-323-3966.

Engage in a Legendary Los Angeles Food War

Who knew our favorite foods and restaurants could incite such deep-seated rivalry? From sandwiches to burgers, pies, sushi, and pizza, your pick could lead to a "conversation" with opposing Angelenos that rages for years.

FRENCH DIP. The French Dip is easy enough to make. Take thin slices of hot beef, place on a French roll or baguette, serve *au jus*, and voilà. Simple, right? But when it comes to who made it first or who makes it best in Los Angeles, the answer is cloudier than the *au jus* these icons are dipped in.

444. *Cole's vs. Philippe's.* Los Angeles welcomed the arrival of Cole's Pacific Electric Buffet and Philippe The Original in 1908. In that same year, both restaurants gave birth to the French Dip, which marked the beginning of an epic food-custody battle that's lasted for more than a hundred years. Its origins, unknown; the creator, shrouded in mystery. The controversy has yet to be resolved and the French Dip battle continues.
Cole's: 118 EAST 6TH STREET IN DOWNTOWN LOS ANGELES. 213-622-4090. 213nightlife.com/colesfrenchdip; Philippe's; 1001 NORTH ALAMEDA STREET (NEAR CHINATOWN) IN DOWNTOWN LOS ANGELES. 213-628-3781. www.philippes.com

HAMBURGERS. New York may boast some of the most expensive burgers in the country, but Los Angeles has some of the best tasting. L.A. burger culture is on overdrive and the options are endless. Your only dilemma is choosing just one.

445. *Father's Office vs. Umami.* The customer is not always right and at these establishments they don't mind letting you know. Here, chef knows best; all you have to decide is which chef is right for you. The Office Burger, for which Sang Yoon was once crowned "The True Burger King" by *Esquire* magazine, is the only burger they serve at Father's Office. It's a fresh-ground dry-aged rib-eye patty with arugula, caramelized onion–bacon compote, Gruyère, and Maytag blue cheese on a baguette. No substitutions are permitted, and it can sometimes come with a free side of attitude from the waitstaff. Umami Burger's Adam Fleischman has carefully reimagined the burger by adding a touch of Japanese creativity to an American classic. Umami, known as the fifth sense, after sweet, sour, bitter, and salty, is the added bonus to Fleischman's burgers. Also referred to by many as MSG, whatever it is that he puts in his secret sauces had *GQ* magazine declaring it "Burger of the Year." It's time to put all of your taste senses to work and decide for yourself.

Father's Office:1018 MONTANA AVENUE IN SANTA MONICA. 310-736-2224. www.fathersoffice.com; Umami Burger: 850 SOUTH LA BREA AVENUE IN LOS ANGELES. 323-931-3000. www.umami.com/umami-burger

446. *Bar Marmont vs. 25 Degrees.* Housed in rival hotels, these upscale burgers come with a side of fries and some vintage Hollywood ambiance. And since both stay open quite late (Bar Marmont's kitchen closes at 12:30 a.m. and 25 Degrees is open 24 hours), determining a winner might just depend on when and where your next burger craving strikes.
Bar Marmont at the Chateau Marmont: 8171 WEST SUNSET BOULEVARD IN HOLLYWOOD. 323-650-0575. www.chateaumarmont.com/barmarmont; 25 Degrees at the Hollywood Roosevelt Hotel: 7000 HOLLYWOOD BOULEVARD IN WEST HOLLYWOOD. 323-785-7244. www.25degreesrestaurant.com

447. *Original Tommy's vs. Fatburger.* To chili burger or not to chili burger, that is the question.
Original Tommy's: 2575 WEST BEVERLY BOULEVARD IN LOS ANGELES. 213-389-9060. www.originaltommys.com; Fatburger: 3026 SOUTH FIGUEROA STREET IN LOS ANGELES. 213-747-0101. www.fatburger.com

448. *Pie 'n Burger vs. The Apple Pan.* Burgers and pies are the perfect combo and these two have the best of both. Start with a cheeseburger and a slice of banana cream pie and go from there.
Pie 'n Burger: 913 EAST CALIFORNIA BOULEVARD IN PASADENA. 626-795-1123, www.pienburger.com; The Apple Pan: 10801 WEST PICO BOULEVARD IN WEST LOS ANGELES. 310-475-3585.

PASTRAMI. No matter how you slice it (thick or thin) or how you like it (traditional or with a twist), just one bite will convert you into a newly devout pastramitarian.

449. *Langer's vs. Brent's.* Old school eateries slug it out for your pastrami loving palates.
Langer's: 704 SOUTH ALVARADO STREET IN LOS ANGELES. 213-483-8050. www.langersdeli.com; Brent's: 19565 PARTHENIA STREET IN NORTHRIDGE. 818-886-5679. www.brentsdeli.com

RAMEN. The Japanese have a way of adopting something and making it entirely their own. In their hands, ramen—Chinese in origin (just like sushi)—has been transformed into a culinary art comprised of noodles and broth.

They've made the mastery of ramen making and ramen eating almost a religion and even have a museum dedicated to it in Yokohama, Japan. Whether you prefer your noodles thick or thin, or your broth flavored with *shio* (salt), *tonkotsu* (pork bone), *shoyu* (soy sauce), or miso, when eating ramen, take a cue from the Master Noodle scene in *Tampopo* and "observe the whole bowl, appreciate its gestalt, savor the aroma, admire the jewels of fat glittering on the surface, and caress the surface with your chopsticks to express affection." Ramen connoisseurs know this is really the only way, and there are plenty of them in Los Angeles.

---

450. *Santouka vs. Asa.*

Santouka Ramen. 21515 SOUTH WESTERN AVENUE IN MITSUWA MARKET PLACE IN TORRANCE. 310-212-1101. www.santouka.co.jp/en; Asa Ramen: 18202 SOUTH WESTERN AVENUE IN GARDENA. 310-769-1010.

---

451 *Daikokuya vs. Ramen Jinya.*

Daikokuya. 327 EAST 1ST STREET (IN LITTLE TOKYO) IN DOWNTOWN LOS ANGELES. 213-626-1680;. www.daikoku-ten.com; Ramen Jinya Ramen Bar: 11239 VENTURA BOULEVARD IN STUDIO CITY. 818-980-3977. www.jinya-ramenbar.com

---

PIZZA. This edible Frisbee has incited food battles all over the world. We'll just stick to those within driving distance.

---

452. *Casa Bianca vs. Mozza.* After more than half a century in delicious business, Casa Bianca is a pizza legend. But two celebrity chefs behind one pizzeria at Mozza—Nancy Silverton and Mario Batali, the go-to guy for fine Italian—this contest is a real nail-biter. (Or, rather, a crust-biter...)

Casa Bianca: 1650 COLORADO BOULEVARD IN LOS ANGELES. 323-256-9617. www.casabiancapizza.com; Mozza: 641 NORTH HIGHLAND AVENUE IN LOS ANGELES. 323-297-0101. www.pizzeriamozza.com

---

HOT DOGS. It's all about the snap and burst of flavor in this battle for top dog.

---

453. *Pink's vs. Skooby's.* Fans of long lines and Gray's Papaya will definitely have a hard time choosing between these two.

Pink's: 709 NORTH LA BREA AVENUE IN LOS ANGELES. 323-931-4223. www.pinkshollywood.com; Skooby's: 6654 HOLLYWOOD BOULEVARD IN HOLLYWOOD. 323-HOT-DOGS. www.skoobys.com

454. *Let's Be Frank Dogs vs. SlawDogs.* Hot dogs are usually made from all the animal parts you don't want to know about (remember the Weenie Tots episode from *Married with Children*?), but at Let's Be Frank Dogs, they make up for its bad rap by producing ones that are hormone and preservative free. At The Slaw Dogs, the fancy toppings—goat cheese, roasted garlic, kimchi, truffle oil, a fried egg, and Thai slaw—have fans foaming at the mouth.
Let's be Frank: Food stand in HELMS BAKERY COMPLEX, HELMS AVENUE BETWEEN WASHINGTON BOULEVARD AND VENICE BOULEVARD IN CULVER CITY. 888-233-7265. www.letsbefrankdogs.com; The Slaw Dogs: 720 NORTH LAKE AVENUE IN PASADENA. 626-808-9777. www.theslawdogs.com

SUSHI. When it comes to sushi there are many rules, like don't drown your fish in soy sauce, wasabi is for your rice, it's okay to use your hands, and a California roll is not sushi, but the most important one is to eat whatever the chef gives you. *Omakase*, also known as "chef's choice," is the best way to get into any sushi chef's good graces.

455. *sugarFISH vs. Sasabune.* Sushi master Kazunori Nozawa is pitted against former apprentice, Nobi Kushuhara, and with both offering the same excellent quality of fish on their sushi-and sashimi-only menus and Nozawa's signature warm rice, this is a tough one. Although Sushi Nozawa is now closed, sugarFISH still maintains the once dubbed "Sushi Nazi's" philosophy of only offering the best. When deciding between these two it all boils down to whom you trust the most.
sugarFISH: 11288 VENTURA BOULEVARD, #C, STUDIO CITY. 818-762-2322, www.sugarfishsushi.com; Sasabune: 12400 WILSHIRE BOULEVARD IN LOS ANGELES. 310-820-3596. www.trustmesushi.com

456. *Sushi Gen vs. Hama Sushi.* Just a block apart, but patrons at each of these sushi places swear that theirs is the best.
Sushi Gen: 422 EAST 2ND STREET (IN LITTLE TOKYO) IN DOWNTOWN LOS ANGELES. 213-617-0552. www.sushigenla.com; Hama Sushi: 347 EAST 2ND STREET (IN LITTLE TOKYO) IN DOWNTOWN LOS ANGELES.

FRIED CHICKEN. Soaked in buttermilk, flavored with Lawry's seasoned salt, single fried, doubled fried, whichever way you make it, the perfect fried chicken is much sought-after. And the key to finding the best is always in the crunchy crust.

457. *Roscoe's vs. Honey's Kettle.* As you're deciding between these two, it's best to have a side of waffles at Roscoe's or a hot buttermilk biscuit at Honey's Kettle to ensure that the decision-making process is made that much more difficult.
Roscoe's: 1518 NORTH GOWER STREET IN HOLLYWOOD. 323-466-7453. Honey's Kettle: 9537 CULVER BOULEVARD IN CULVER CITY. 310-202-5453. honeyskettle.com

CUPCAKES

458. *Sprinkles vs. Big Man Bakes.* Candace Nelson has been called the "progenitor of the haute cupcake craze"—she even opened the first cupcake ATM in Beverly Hills. But if we're talking just taste and not reputation, the cupcakes at Big Man Bakes are equally moist and delicious. I don't know who'd win in this food war, but if there was a cage match between Candace Nelson and William "Chip" Brown, my money would be on Chip. He's six feet five inches with a linebacker's frame. Where else would you put it?
Sprinkles: 9635 SOUTH SANTA MONICA BOULEVARD IN BEVERLY HILLS. 310-274-8765. www.sprinkles.com; Big Man Bakes: 413 SOUTH MAIN STREET IN DOWNTOWN LOS ANGELES. 213-617-9100. www.bigmanbakes.com

STEAKS

459. *Dan Tana's vs. Taylor's:* This is old school vs. old school all the way. Which red Naugahyde booth will you decide to scoot into?
Dan Tana's: 9071 SANTA MONICA BOULEVARD IN WEST HOLLYWOOD. 310-275-9444. www.dantanasrestaurant.com; Taylor's: 3361 WEST 8TH STREET (IN KOREATOWN) IN LOS ANGELES. 213-382-8449. www.taylorssteakhouse.com

ICE CREAM. When looking for something cool and delicious during the summer months, one must decide upon old-fashioned or newfangled. And with all the competition out there, let's hope it hasn't melted into soup by the time you choose.

460. *Mashti Malone's vs. Scoops.* A taste of the old world with exotic hints of rosewater and orange blossom, Mashti offers you a fragrant approach to ice cream. Don't under estimate their insanely delicious chocolate peanut butter either. But at Scoops they throw old world to the wind as they play off of fun and gimmicky flavors. Brown bread ice cream flavored with grape nuts? Sure, why not. They serve vegan options as well.

Mashti Malone's: 1525 NORTH LA BREA AVENUE IN LOS ANGELES. 323-874-0144. www.mashtimalone.com; Scoops: 712 NORTH HELIOTROPE DRIVE IN LOS ANGELES. 323-906-2649.

461. *Sweet Rose Creamery vs. Carmela Ice Cream.* The same and yet so different, these two ice cream shops have die-hard fans screaming through the streets that their place is best. Especially about their salted caramel. As they battle it out over who makes it best, just stand on the side lines and try not to get hurt.
Sweet Rose Creamery: 225 26TH STREET #51 IN SANTA MONICA. 310-260-CONE. www.sweetrosecreamery.com; Carmela Ice Cream: 2495 EAST WASHINGTON BOULEVARD IN PASADENA. 626-797-1405. www.carmelaicecream.com

Eat on the go at a food festival

462. The Taste. For several days this gourmet food festival "celebrates all that is epicurean." And what better way to do that than with a lot of celebrity chefs. From Beverly Hills to Downtown L.A., the *L.A. Times* and *Food & Wine* bring together a great mix of cooking demonstrations, wine seminars, and the ever-important local tasting events to showcase L.A.'s vibrant culinary scene. It's a way to get to know food and your city a whole lot better.
September. Paramount Pictures Studios, 5555 MELROSE AVENUE IN HOLLYWOOD. events.latimes.com/taste

463. Los Angeles Food and Wine Festival. After almost two decades as the premier food festival in Los Angeles, the American Wine and Food Festival started by Wolfgang Puck and Barbara Lazaroff and held at the back lot of Universal Studios, said good-bye in 2010. In its place is a newer more updated version known as the Los Angeles Food and Wine Festival. Still helmed by Wolfgang Puck, LAFW's inaugural event in 2011 blew the doors off this city's food scene. With over sixty citywide events, 140 celebrity chefs worldwide, 300 wineries, and more than fifteen thousand attendees in its first year, this four-day event was a smashing success. Although now more celebrities and chefs than just celebrity chefs, the event still follows some of the ideals of the old AWFF with spectacular food, entertainment, star-studded auctions and all proceeds going to support St. Vincent Meals on Wheels.
www.lafw.com.

464. Planned Parenthood Food Fare. When culinary legend Julia Child is present at the launch of your food fair, it's safe to say that your event has received the food world's gold stamp of approval. More than thirty years later, the annual Planned Parenthood Food Fare is still going strong with over 150 of L.A.'s finest restaurants and caterers, wineries, and vendors taking part in a worthwhile and fun event. Daytime tickets cost $150; evening tickets cost $225.

March. Santa Monica Civic Auditorium: 1855 MAIN STREET IN SANTA MONICA. 213-284-3200 ext. 3700. www.pplafoodfare.com

465. Redondo Beach Lobster Festival. There's nothing like eating fresh seafood by the sea, and the Redondo Beach Lobster Festival is as good as it gets. It's a great opportunity to gorge on your favorite crustacean and not worry if things get a little messy, while listening to live music and having fun with your friends. And after you've walked along the pier and your meal has settled a bit, why not go for a ride on the mechanical bull to work up your appetite for round two.

September. Seaside Lagoon, 200 PORTOFINO WAY IN REDONDO BEACH. 310-376-6911. (Redondo Beach Chamber of Commerce and Visitors Bureau), www.lobsterfestival.com

466. Swiss Fair. You don't have to be neutral here—at this Swiss Fair it's all about having fun. From the land that gave us cuckoo clocks, Le Corbusier, Swiss army knives, and Renée Zellweger (her dad's Swiss) comes another reason to celebrate—the food! This fair showcases the gastronomic treasures of Switzerland, and from the moment you enter (complimentary chocolates are given when you pay your $5 admission fee), it's all about the food. A mix of French- and German-influenced cuisine: raclette, fondue, züpfe bread, spätzli, and more await to tantalize your taste buds. And to wash it all down, some alphorn horns, a little yodeling, and a glass of Rivella, the popular Swiss soft drink.

July. Swiss Park: 1905 WORKMAN MILL ROAD IN WHITTIER. 800-242-2433. www.swisspark.com/swissfair

467. Mitsuwa Umaimono Gourmet Fair. You wouldn't expect a supermarket chain to take food so seriously, but then again, you don't know Mitsuwa. It hosts an annual festival that takes place at their various locations in Southern California to celebrate "good things" pertaining to food. From Takoya Kukuru's *takoyaki* (octopus balls) to Anchindo's *Deka Kintsuba* (azuki red bean dessert) and delectable baked goods, vendors are invited from all over to sell their delicious foods. But the biggest draw is the ramen. Big-name noodle masters from Japan prepare interesting and flavorful dishes like Chiba Kenji from Chibaki-Ya, the famous ramen specialist from Sendai, and Kawahara Shigemi from Hakata Ippudo Ramen in Kyushu, and people come from all over to experience noodle nirvana. They offer hot bowls of specialty ramen, shark fin soup and simple shoyu. In past years a big draw has been the *gyu tan shio* ramen, beef tongue in a salt-based soup. And for only $10 a bowl and

prepared by a true ramen master from Japan, how can you say no.
21515 SOUTH WESTERN AVENUE IN TORRANCE. 310-782-0335. www.mitsuwa.com

468. Annual Gilroy Garlic Festival. This festival technically isn't in Los Angeles, but for those who adore garlic, the Gilroy Garlic Festival is heaven on Earth. Over the course of three days you can stuff your face full of everything garlic, from garlic pizza to garlic ice cream, while browsing garlic-related vendors and enjoying live entertainment. The festival also raises money for charity, so grab a bulb and munch away.
July. CHRISTMAS HILL PARK, 7050 MILLER AVENUE, GILROY. 408-842-1625. www.gilroygarlicfestival.com

469. Cochon 555's Traveling Pork and Wine Bacchanalia. This is all about how pigs should be prepared and eaten. The organizers of Cochon 555 seem to have taken a page—several pages, in fact—out of Chef Fergus Henderson's cookbook, *The Whole Beast: Nose to Tail Eating* when they created this event. This porkapalooza, filled with pork lovers and lushes, brings together five chefs, five pigs, five winemakers and a whole lot of eating. Fasting a few days beforehand is encouraged. Event locations and dates vary.
www.cochon555.com

470. Nisei Week Japanese Festival. Little Tokyo not only houses the only Noguchi in the city (p. 139), but it also can boast having the oldest ethnic festival as well. For more than seventy years, the Japanese-American community has celebrated Nisei Week. Originally created to help lift spirits during the Great Depression and also bridge the gap between Issei (first generation) and Nisei (second generation), it's become the unifying hallmark of the community of Little Tokyo. Spend the week noshing on the different types of Japanese cuisine from sushi to katsu, as well as playing games and watching the Grand Parade. If you're still hungry, take part in a time-honored tradition and enter the gyoza-eating contest.
August. Event organizer: 244 SOUTH SAN PEDRO STREET, SUITE 303. 213-687-7193. www.niseiweek.org

471. Long Beach Crawfish Festival. New Orleans is rich in culture. It's the home to jazz, Mardi Gras, and last but not least, the crawfish boil. But when you can't go to New Orleans, Long Beach brings New Orleans to you. At the largest Crawfish Festival outside of Louisiana, expect to dine on tons of fresh crawfish and classic New Orleans fare prepared by authentic Cajun chefs while listening to amazing Cajun and Zydeco music.
August. Rainbow Lagoon, 400–403 SHORELINE VILLAGE DRIVE IN LONG BEACH. www.longbeachcrawfishfestival.com

472. Santa Barbara Wine Festival. If you're an oenophile (wine-lover) on a liquid diet, this festival has your name written all over it. The "Biggest Wine Festival under the Sun," offers over two hundred of California's finest wines from around the state for your tasting pleasure. So grab your glass, start swirling and sipping and let the inebriation begin.

June. Santa Barbara Museum of Natural History, 2559 PUESTA DEL SOL IN SANTA BARBARA. 805-682-4711. www.sbnature.org/winefestival

Santa Monica Farmers' Market

California is blessed with great weather almost all year-round, which equals a bountiful crop. At the Santa Monica Farmers' Market you'll find local farmers and vendors, some who drive hours to get there, selling fresh, seasonal, organic foods that are unbeatable. The variety of produce is unequaled as well. It is simply one of the best greenmarkets in the country, and there's no doubt you'll see some of the city's best chefs there every Wednesday. It's difficult to go wrong if you've got the time to explore and an open culinary mind—so take it slow and let your gastronomic senses guide you to some of the finest produce you'll ever have the pleasure of driving home.

ARIZONA AVENUE AT 2ND STREET IN SANTA MONICA. 310-458-8712 x 6. www.smgov.net/portals/farmersmarket

473. *Coleman Family Farms.* When you come across this stall at the Santa Monica Farmers' Market it's as if you've stumbled upon a cornucopia of biodynamic greenery. With unique produce like broccoli spigarello, arugula selvatica, New Zealand spinach, amaranth, chocolate mint, cherimoya, Portuguese kale, Syrian oregano, and red dandelion (that's just the tip of the iceberg), it's no surprise that Coleman Family Farms, now overseen by Romeo Coleman, is the go-to for top chefs and foodies alike. And if you're ever stuck on what to make for dinner, patriarch and not-so-retired Bill Coleman is great at providing simple and delicious recipe recommendations. In fact, all the Colemans are! Those in need of a different type of greenery can find Bill's wife Delia next to the lettuces, creating beautiful floral arrangements to take home.

474. *Coastal Organics.* When they're in season, Paul, Mark, and Maryann Carpenter have some of the best heirloom tomatoes at the market.

475. *Schaner Farms.* Although Peter Schaner offers a wonderful variety of citrus (fresh and freshly squeezed), lovely shallots and cippolini onions (seasonal), and other produce, it's the eggs that'll really peak your interest. Schaner has an eclectic mix, from pheasant to pharaoh quail, blue Swedish duck, emu, red bourbon turkey, and guinea hen. And yes, he even has chicken eggs. But if you expect them to look "normal," the yolks on you. His chicken eggs come from Rhode Island reds and Araucana, the latter's eggs being bluish green.

476. *Clearwater Farms.* Don't expect to find a button mushroom here. David West, "the mushroom man," and his assistant Karl, sell only the best fungi around. Hedgehogs, lobster, porcini, chanterelle, shitake, maitake, and, when they're in season, fragrantly divine truffles all await you under his makeshift canopy.

477. *Windrose Farm.* Bill and Barbara Spencer offer antique apples for eating, baking, sauce, and cider—varieties you normally can't find anywhere else, so why bother. Just come here. And their sun-dried tomatoes are utterly addictive.

478. *Weiser Family Farms.* Ozette, red thumbs, Russian banana, Chilean red, ruby crescent, and purple Peruvians—if you've ever heard of any of these potatoes then you've been fortunate enough to shop at Weiser. This is carb-lover heaven. Be sure not to overlook their colorful carrots, delicious melons, sunchokes (Jerusalem artichokes) and other seasonal offerings.

479. *Pudwill Farms.* From blackberries to red, yellow, and orange raspberries, figs, and mulberries, at Pudwill it's all about berries. But during certain times of the year, starting around June, they have something special, *Marais de Bois* (a type of wild strawberry), but only for a limited time.

480. *Harry's Berries.* There are strawberries and then there are Harry's Berries. One box of the seascape strawberries is never enough, and be forewarned: once you've tasted them, there's no turning back.

481. *Maggie's Farm.* The Farm was started by Nate Pietso's mother, who grew produce for Alice Waters at Chez Panisse. Now you can taste a piece of that heritage when you buy a bag of the family's signature "stellar mix" of spring lettuces. When available, they also sell edible flowers.

482. *McGrath Family Farms.* Phil McGrath offers up a great selection of produce at his corner stall. From delectable haricots verts to Chioggia beets, you can't go wrong at McGrath's.

483. *Bautista Family Organic Dates.* Jeffrey Steingarten, Food Editor at *Vogue* magazine, couldn't help but notice these chewy, sweet, and sticky dates. Pick up a box of Medjhool or Khadrawy before they sell out.

484. *Hollywood Farmer's Market.* Don't have time during the weekday to make it over to the Santa Monica Farmer's Market? You're in luck. Several farmers venture back into the city on Sundays to sell their goods. At the Hollywood Farmer's Market you'll find Pudwill Farms, McGrath Farms, Clearwater Farms and many other familiar Santa Monica Farmer's Market faces and an array of their delicious produce for sale. Come early, go for a stroll and if you get hungry, take advantage of the market's large number of prepared food vendors. Grab a bite, take a seat and enjoy a little people watching. After all, you're in Hollywood.
1600 IVAR AVENUE IN HOLLYWOOD. 323-463-3171. www.hollywoodfarmersmarket.net

485. Get a packed lunch at the **Larder at Tavern**...

Suzanne Goin's Tavern houses a small gourmet market and bakery, the perfect foodie destination. The Larder's selection of cured meats, olives, bread, and prepared foods is great to take out. But a nice touch is the tavern brown-bag lunch. Available only during the week, you can get the sandwich of the day, house-made potato chips, a Windrose Farm apple, and a cookie for $16—all of which comes in a tidy little paper bag.
11648 SAN VICENTE BOULEVARD IN BRENTWOOD. 310-806-6464. www.tavernla.com/larder

486. ...or a picnic box at **Clementine.**

This family-owned bakery-café uses only the freshest ingredients when preparing its meals. You can also find fresh or frozen dishes to take home and enjoy. During the summer months, you can get picnic boxes that make for a perfect visit to the Hollywood Bowl. Picnic-box options include crostini and dips, Spanish tapas with cheese and cured meats, Mexican-style shrimp cocktail, and deviled eggs, among others. Or if you want to build your own, choose from grilled steak, wild king salmon, or even cold meatloaf. And don't skimp on dessert, especially when you can order a banana caramel parfait with custard, sea salt, and chunks of chewy butterscotch brownie. Cap it all off with a thermos full of homemade hot chocolate or homemade chai.
1751 ENSLEY AVENUE IN CENTURY CITY. 310-552-1080. www.clementineonline.com

487. When British expats get nostalgic, they turn to **Ye Olde King's Head Gift Shoppe** for a taste of home.

Since 1974, expats and anglophiles have made their way to Santa Monica to stock up on imported British necessities. With three rooms full of essential items like PG Tips, Marmite, HP Sauce, delicious steak and kidney pies, canned haggis, and genuine Cadbury chocolates, who wouldn't shop here for a taste of the home country.

116 SANTA MONICA BOULEVARD IN SANTA MONICA. 310-451-1402. www.yeoldekingshead.com

488. Get a sandwich at **Larchmont Village Wine and Cheese**.

People line up day in and day out to get one of the gourmet sandwiches on offer. Whatever option you choose will include a heaping handful of mixed greens, a healthy swipe of sun-dried tomato spread and a drizzle of balsamic vinegar and olive oil. For extra salt and zing, sandwiches also come with a small side of kalamata olives and cornichons. The international chocolate bars placed near the cash register make for the perfect impulse buy.

223 NORTH LARCHMONT BOULEVARD IN LOS ANGELES. 323-856-8699. www.larchmontvillagewine.com

489. Go green at **M Café**.

Every once in a while it's good to eat a few veggies. Get your fill here with healthy and delicious vegetarian and vegan offerings. If you're looking for a natural pick-me-up, don't forget to try one of the fresh fruit and vegetable juices—tastier than a Red Bull and a whole lot better for you.

7119 MELROSE AVENUE IN HOLLYWOOD. 323-525-0588, www.mcafedechaya.com; 9433 BRIGHTON WAY IN BEVERLY HILLS. 310-858-8459. www.mcafedechaya.com

490. Grab a wheel at the **Cheese Store of Beverly Hills**.

If you're lactose intolerant but love cheese, jump to the next entry, this one's going to be a tough read... But if you can muster the strength to continue, you'll discover that this store is cheese heaven. At The Cheese Store of Beverly Hills you'll find wheels stacked high into towers, gooey richness oozing out of rinds, salt crystallization formed to perfection, and rare handmade farm fresh cheeses that'll melt in your mouth. If you find yourself lost in this cave of a store, just ask for owner Norbert Wabnig. He's been helping Angelenos navigate their way through the curds and whey since 1967. You might come for a quick nibble but will most likely leave a few hours later with a belly full of cheese and your arms laden with milky treasures. Told you it was going to be tough.

419 NORTH BEVERLY DRIVE IN BEVERLY HILLS. 310-278-2855. www.cheesestorebh.com

---

491. Make your own soup and sandwich combo at **Joan's on Third**.

Welcome to L.A.'s version of Dean & Deluca. Many venture here to buy fancy, expensive pantry items and to see a celebrity or two outside, but the real reason to come to Joan's is for a bowl of the roasted corn soup (seasonal) and the short-rib sandwich with melted jack cheese, pickled, caramelized onions, and arugula. Though not offered together, they should be. This is by far the best soup and sandwich combination in the city.

8350 WEST 3RD STREET IN LOS ANGELES. 323-655-2285. www.jonesonthird.com

---

492. Less is more at **Porto's Bakery & Café**.

Come and fill up on small savory treats like the flash-fried ham croquettes, soft mashed potato balls filled with ham and fried till they're golden brown, or the chicken croquette rolled in panko and fried. Are you beginning to pick up on the theme here? Be sure to take advantage of their delicious sandwiches and cakes as well.

3614 WEST MAGNOLIA BOULEVARD IN BURBANK. 818-846-9100. www.portosbakery.com; 315 NORTH BRAND BOULEVARD IN GLENDALE. 818-956-5996. www.portosbakery.com

---

493. Get the Godmother sub at **Bay Cities**...

At this combination Italian specialty store-deli, you come for a lot of things, but what you order is the Godmother sandwich. It's an Italian sub packed with genoa salami, mortadella, capicola, ham, prosciutto, provolone, vegetables, spicy pepper salad, spicy mustard, and pickles, all barely contained in a chewy Italian-style baguette. How can you order anything else?

1517 LINCOLN BOULEVARD IN SANTA MONICA. 310-395-8279. www.baycitiesitaliandeli.com

---

494. ...or make like the Godfather at **Guidi Marcello**.

Right around the corner from Bay Cities you'll find Guidi Marcello. Smaller in size, but still packed with a great selection of top quality Italian products, Guidi's offers buttery green olives, frozen pastas, and even Crucolo, a cheese made from miniature cows. And if you want to make that perfect bowl of bucatini all'amatriciana, you'll definitely need their guanciale (dried pork cheek).

Cash only unless your purchase is over $100. 1649 10TH STREET IN SANTA MONICA. 310-452-6277. www.guidimarcello.com

Dinner with In-House Entertainment

Dinner alone just doesn't seem to cut it anymore, especially since the idea of dinner and a movie isn't as special as it used to be. Instead, try a restaurant that offers more than just the experience of a meal. The following restaurants cleverly incorporate some signature flourishes into their dinner fare.

495. *El Mercado.* Head to the top floor, order dinner and be the judge as two mariachi bands on opposite sides of the venue battle each other for your applause. Just remember to bring your earplugs: it can get loud.
3425 EAST 1ST STREET IN EAST LOS ANGELES. 323-268-3451.
www.elmercadodelosangeles.com

496. *The Baked Potato.* Get a meal stuffed into a gigantic potato and a side of live jazz. The music will provide momentum that will help you eat your way through a potato the size of a small chicken.
3787 WEST CAHUENGA BOULEVARD IN STUDIO CITY. 818-980-1615.
www.thebakedpotato.com

497. *Guelaguetza.* At this authentic Oaxacan restaurant, located in a former Korean banquet hall, moles are a specialty and the clayudas are delish. At Guelaguetza not only will you see a diverse mix of people from all cultures, a perfect microcosm of L.A., but you'll enjoy a tasty meal with some entertainment as well. Most evenings there is live music, but on Thursdays classic Mexican films are shown on big screens.
3014 WEST OLYMPIC BOULEVARD IN LOS ANGELES. 213-427-0608.
www.guelaguetzarestaurante.com

498. *Lawry's the Prime Rib.* Order a prime rib dinner and wait as nearby guests turn their attention to your table to watch your waitress dress and toss the Famous Original Spinning Bowl Salad with flair. It's as delicious as it is entertaining.
100 NORTH LA CIENEGA BOULEVARD IN BEVERLY HILLS. 310-652-2827.
www.lawrysonline.com

499. *La Fonda.* For years La Fonda has provided its patrons not only with delicious Mexican cuisine but also with good music. For $25, either spent on food or drinks, you'll get to see one of the best Mariachi bands in Los Angeles, Mariachi Los Reyes, perform during your meal. And don't be surprised if your food gets cold: once these guys hit the stage you'll be too busy

clapping to eat. Call ahead to find out when Mariachi Los Reyes is performing before booking a reservation.
2501 WILSHIRE BOULEVARD IN LOS ANGELES. 213-380-5053. www.lafondasupperclub.com

---

500. *Palms Thai Restaurant.* At Palms Thai, you can enjoy classic Thai food with a little twist: dishes such as wild boar in curry and crisp-skinned sour sausages sizzling hot from the grill come with a side of entertainment. Although main act Kavee Thongpreecha, aka Thai Elvis, has left the building and retired, various musical acts still come on stage to belt out a song or two. But without Thongpreecha, the Palms Thai could use a little lift: any budding performers out there who love the King should definitely come on down and get that stage all shook up.
5900 HOLLYWOOD BOULEVARD, SUITE B, IN LOS ANGELES. 323-462-5073. www.palmsthai.com

---

501. *Fogo de Chao.* Order the meat course at this popular Brazilian churrascaria and sit back as your front-row meat-a-thon experience commences. A myriad of different types of meats and sausages arrives at your table on large skewers and are sliced and served with flair. Just make sure you turn over your card to signal that you want to stop, otherwise this meat show will go on all night.
133 NORTH LA CIENEGA IN BEVERLY HILLS. 310-289-7755. www.fogodechao.com

---

502. *Benihana.* When Rocky Aoki came up with Benihana he created a place that combined good food with charming entertainment and made it fun for all ages—the key to its success. Diners here enjoy the theatrics of slicing and dicing, and when the chef offers to toss a piece of food into your mouth, lean your head back and pray his aim is good.
Several locations. www.benihana.com

---

503. Find real green eggs and ham at **Huckleberry Bakery and Café**.

Patience is a virtue when it comes to this place, especially on the weekends. But once you place your order and grab a table, in that order, you can enjoy the delicious pastries created by chef/owner Zoe Nathan. Her buttery prosciutto-and-gruyère-stuffed croissants, her flaky bacon-maple biscuits (just one will not do), or even her reinterpretation of Dr. Seuss's green eggs and ham drizzled with pesto makes waiting among the hordes of stroller-wielding, khaki- and flip-flop-wearing weekenders worth it.
1014 WILSHIRE BOULEVARD IN SANTA MONICA. 310-451-2311. www.huckleberrycafe.com

504. Bitchin' butcherettes Amelia Posada and Erika Nakamura will help you find the right "cut" at **Lindy & Grundy**.

As you gaze into their refrigerated displays full of meat, you can't help salivate. This sustainable, "nose-to-tail" butcher shop, stocks a delectable selection of meats such as Rancho San Julian beef, Reride Ranch pork, Sonoma Direct lamb, and Rainbow Ranch Farms chicken, all of which are locally sourced. And just how fresh is it? Everything arrives whole and is butchered on site. And those hesitant to touch meat because they "don't know what's in it" can rest assured. All the meat here is antibiotic and hormone free. Be sure to call ahead to check their stock as they do sell out.

801 NORTH FAIRFAX AVENUE IN LOS ANGELES. 323-951-0804. Lindyandgrundy.com

505. These **coffee shops** will give you a jolt.

L.A.'s coffee culture has been kicking up a caffienated storm. An excellent cup requires the precision of a scientist and sometimes the patience of a saint—but it's worth it. And at the ***Coffee Commissary*** (*www.coffeecommissary.com*), ***Handsome Coffee Roasters*** (founded by three Intelligentsia alums, ***www.handsomecoffee.com***), ***Spring for Coffee*** (*www.springforcoffee.com*), ***Espresso Cielo*** (*www.espressocielo.com*), ***Cognoscenti Coffee*** (*www.milstudio.com*) and ***Paper or Plastik*** (*www.paperor-plastikcafe.com*), the best coffee you've never had might just be waiting for you.

VARIOUS LOCATIONS. Check websites for details.

506. Broaden your palate at **UMAMIcatessen**.

What happens when you combine the idea of international street bazaars with the classic American delicatessen? UMAMIcatessen, that's what. Located inside the Orpheum, this table-service dining hall has five different kitchens preparing an interesting mix of food concepts by chefs from around the country. From P!GG, a tribute to all things pork, to And a Donut, where donuts are fired to order, at UMAMIcatessen there's plenty to choose from.

852 SOUTH BROADWAY IN DOWNTOWN LOS ANGELES. 213-413-8626. www.umami.com

507. Start your day off right at the **Shabu Shabu House**.

If you're hungry, don't arrive here at 11:30 a.m. and expect to get a seat. Just because the place opens at that time doesn't mean people haven't been showing up almost an hour in advance to add their names to the waiting list. Once inside, sit at the counter and enjoy shabu-shabu, the Japanese hot pot, where you bathe (more than cook) thinly sliced fatty beef, tofu, noodles, and vegetables in hot water and dip them into a

sesame or ponzu sauce. Do you need any more reason than that to sneak out of work to add your name to the list?
127 JAPANESE VILLAGE PLAZA MALL IN LITTLE TOKYO IN DOWNTOWN LOS ANGELES. 213-680-3890. shabushabuhouse.menutoeat.com

---

508. Learn to share at **Lazy Ox Canteen**.

With a chef hailing from the hallowed kitchen of Ferran Adrià's El Bulli in charge, it's no wonder that the Lazy Ox's menu is so appealing. With so many tempting dishes, you'll need more than a few minutes to decide on what to order. Once you narrow it down and the dishes start arriving at your table, you'll wish your stomach was twice its size so you could order more. Next time bring some friends and order the lot!
241 SOUTH SAN PEDRO STREET IN LITTLE TOKYO IN DOWNTON LOS ANGELES. 213-626-5299. Lazyoxcanteen.com

---

509. Get your goat at **Tar & Roses**.

After putting in time at some noteworthy kitchens in Los Angeles (Joe's in Venice, Axe, and Wilshire), local chef Andrew Kirschner has finally opened his own. Deeply focused on fresh ingredients and influences from all over the world, each dish here passes through the belly of a wood-burning oven, giving it that special touch. Come and indulge in the three-course prix fixe special goat menu. Dine on spicy goat so tender that it's falling off the bone. It's rich, gamey, and amazingly worth getting your hands dirty as you pick at its succulent flesh. Tar & Roses also offers other special menus: goose, standing rib rack, and a shellfish pot. Be sure to get a side of vegetables. Their wood-roasted English peas are a must. Orders required in advance.
602 SANTA MONICA BOULEVARD IN SANTA MONICA. 310-587-0700. Tarandroses.com

---

510. Go on, drink it–at **Harvard & Stone**.

Once a dive in Hollywood, Harvard & Stone has been transformed into an industrial-inspired space (exposed pipes and faux weathered walls) that's become a popular hangout spot for many. Grab an artisanal cocktail from the whisky-focused cocktail list at the front bar and enjoy some unique concoctions while catching a burlesque act in the performance space. But if you're looking for something different to wet your whistle head to the back. At R&D, the back bar, you'll find drinkers with more refined palates lining up to become guinea pigs. Guest mixologists test their weekly experiments on those willing to pour unknown libations down their throats, and so far there have been only positive side effects.
5221 HOLLYWOOD BOULEVARD IN HOLLYWOOD. 323-466-6063. Harvardandstone.com

511. Go for simple at **Cooks County Restaurant**.

Chef Daniel Mattern (Campanile, A.O.C., Ammo) and pastry chef Roxana Jullapat have joined forces to open a restaurant where their approach to food is simple but with amazing results. A constantly rotating market menu that is easy and delightful makes coming to Cooks County a surprise in what you'll find, but not in what you'll taste.

8009 BEVERLY BOULEVARD IN LOS ANGELES. 323-653-8009. www.cookscountyrestaurant.com

Have Dinner in a Restaurant Garden

Eating outdoors in the middle of the city always feels like a decadent pleasure. And in Los Angeles, we're fortunate to have warm weather all year long, so you'll have plenty of opportunities. But not all outdoor eateries are created equal. Sidewalk cafes can be good for people watching, but they've got nothing on the transporting, deliciously smug feeling that comes from eating your meal tucked away in a back garden.

512. *Dominick's.* Come and hang out to get a feel of that old Rat Pack vibe. Frank might not be around, but the spirit of that era still lingers on sixty years later with mahogany booths and Italian-grandmother-inspired decor. It also has not one but two bars, one inside and one outside. So grab a seat, preferably near the giant fireplace, or cuddle up to some greenery, the inedible kind, and enjoy the cool atmosphere, which draws a great mix of hip locals and longtime customers. (Visit Dominick's small hipster spot, ***Little Dom's***, in Los Feliz.)

Dominick's: 8715 BEVERLY BOULEVARD IN WEST HOLLYWOOD. 310-652-2346. www.dominicksrestaurant.com; Little Dom's: 2128 HILLHURST AVENUE IN LOS ANGELES. 323-661-0055. www.littledoms.com

513. *Lucques.* Come here to enjoy the ridiculously delicious Sunday Supper, a three-course prix fixe for only $48, but don't forget to request the patio area. Though technically not the real outdoors, the patio, a simple yet elegant space with a large skylight and ivy-strewn walls, is very convincing.

8474 MELROSE AVENUE IN WEST HOLLYWOOD. 323-655-6277. www.lucques.com

514. *Red Lion Tavern.* You'll find everything you need to have a good time inside this traditional German beer garden. Lots of sustenance by way of sausages heaped onto a plate, waitresses dressed in traditional German garb, and reasonably priced German beers are here ready and waiting for your enjoyment. The atmosphere is casual, and if you head upstairs to the Red Lion's rooftop beer garden, you can fully experience the style of drinking from the old country.

2366 GLENDALE BOULEVARD IN LOS ANGELES. 323-662-5337. www.redliontavern.net

515. *The Little Door.* Not exactly outdoors, the Little Door has taken the "out" and brought it in. With candles overhead, ivy on the walls, and Chef Nicolas T. Peter's delectable California French fare on your plate, dining in this romantic patio setting could impress any date.

8164 WEST 3RD STREET IN LOS ANGELES. 323-951-1210. www.thelittledoor.com

516. *Alcove Cafe & Bakery.* This restaurant, housed in two historic cottages in Los Feliz, has a homey feel. But its outdoor setting with giant umbrellas, mix 'n' match lawn furniture and the perfect blend of locals and tourists reveals that it's more fun than cozy.

1929 HILLHURST AVENUE IN LOS ANGELES. 323-644-0100. www.alcovecafe.com

517. *Cliff's Edge.* This city hides many secrets, and none is as surprising as the Cliff's Edge in Silverlake. Hands down, this is the most romantic garden you can eat in anywhere in the city.

3626 WEST SUNSET BOULEVARD IN SILVERLAKE. 323-666-6116. www.cliffsedgecafe.com

518. *Geoffrey's Malibu.* On its fabulous terrace, California dreamin' is taken to another level. With spectacular vistas that are worth a million bucks, be glad you're only paying a fraction of the cost. Enjoy the perfect Sunday brunch dolphin watching and celebrity spotting, but be careful which way you lean: with the ocean so close, you might fall in.

27400 PACIFIC COAST HIGHWAY IN MALIBU. 310-457-1519. www.geoffreysmalibu.com

519. *Michael's.* There's no rustic here. It's all about lush and precise gardening that's so well done there's no doubt that Los Angeles's plastic surgery skills have crossed over into landscaping. You'll find that same precision in the kitchen, with its well-earned reputation for fresh and creative dishes. Innovation plus lovely scenery is always win-win.

1147 3RD STREET IN SANTA MONICA. 310-451-0843. www.michaelssantamonica.com

520. *The Polo Lounge.* Since 1941, the outdoor patio at The Polo Lounge has been a favorite haunt for the rich and famous and for those who wish to gaze upon them. The airy surroundings are full of character—and characters; it's a frequent celebrity hangout. And during the day, when the sun hits you like a spotlight, you'll feel like a star yourself.
9641 SUNSET BOULEVARD IN BEVERLY HILLS. 310-276-2251.
www.beverlyhillshotel.com/the-polo-lounge

521. *Saddle Peak Lodge.* This restaurant can seduce a carnivore at twenty paces with its offering of exotic game. No other restaurant serves buffalo, antelope, elk, and venison all on the same menu. During the summer the terrace is the perfect place to eat while you revel in the landscape and inhale the scent of pine and sage that tinges the air. And when the breeze is right, you'll get a hint of the salty sea. It's just what you need to build up an appetite.
419 COLD CANYON ROAD IN CALABASAS. 818-222-3888.
www.saddlepeaklodge.com

522. *Inn of the Seventh Ray.* On a balmy summer evening there's nothing better than kicking back with a glass of organic wine and enjoying the idyllic setting of this restaurant. You won't find hippie food in this Topanga hideaway, not after the revamp. Instead, Executive Chef Bradley Miller has replaced it with organic produce spruced up with a hint of molecular gastronomy. Linger and relax under the twinkling fairy lights dangling from old California sycamores, and since tables are set far enough apart, your magical night's conversation won't interfere with anyone else's. And if you're wondering why the napkins are purple—or, more specifically, violet—just think the seventh ray of the color spectrum.
128 OLD TOPANGA CANYON ROAD IN TOPANGA. 310-455-1311.
www.innoftheseventhray.com

523. Unwrap a sweet surprise at **Little Flower Candy Co.**

Delicious fresh candy with no artificial ingredients is what Christine Moore, a pastry chef turned stay-at-home mom, concocted while raising her kids. Moore might remind you of Diane Keaton à la *Baby Boom*, and her fresh homemade marshmallows, her chewy sea salt caramels, and an assortment of other goodies, including gluten-free cookies, could make you rethink your position on SAHMs.
1422 WEST COLORADO BOULEVARD IN PASADENA. 626-304-4800.
www.littleflowercandyco.com

524. Get a taste of Belgium via Los Angeles at **Syrups Desserts.**

The crepes, brownies, and madeleines could make any sweet tooth buckle under pressure, but what really draws customers all the way downtown is the Liège waffle. A hot Belgian waffle dotted with chunks of sugar and dressed up however you like screams "eat me." Thought Jean-Claude Van Damme owned all the muscles from Brussels? Think again. This waffle packs a sugary, chewy, delicious punch. Finding parking around here might be a downer, but eat enough waffles and you'll be up all day.

611 SOUTH SPRING STREET IN DOWNTOWN LOS ANGELES. 213-488-5136.

525. Get your kicks at **Fair Oaks Pharmacy and Soda Fountain** on Route 66.

If you're looking for serious nostalgia, then head over to Pasadena to the oldest soda fountain shop in the city. But be forewarned, the people that work here are jerks—soda jerks, that is—and can whip up some of the best hand-dipped shakes, malts, and egg creams around. And if you end up having one shake too many, there's a pharmacy on-site. How's that for service.

1526 MISSION STREET IN SOUTH PASADENA. 626-799-1414. www.fairoakspharmacy.net

526. Spend your summer eating frozen treats at **Fosselman's Ice Cream Co.**

For over ninety-one years, this ice cream parlor throwback has been making the same rich and chewy homemade ice cream. And with over forty-eight ice-cream flavors, like real vanilla, mint chip, and the more exotic macapuno, taro, and lychee, you can celebrate summer with a new flavor every day. If you're the type who enjoys ice cream year-round, be sure to try the special monthly flavors.

1824 WEST MAIN STREET IN ALHAMBRA. 626-282-6533. www.fosselmans.com

527. Indulge your sweet tooth at **Twohey's Restaurant.**

Known for its burgers and onion rings, the real cherry on top of Twohey's, pronounced 2EEs, is its award-winning decadent bittersweet hot-fudge sundae. Sinfully rich and silky smooth, no other sundae compares.

1224 NORTH ATLANTIC BOULEVARD IN ALHAMBRA. 626-284-7387. www.twoheys.com

528. Get in a festive mood at **Logan's Candies.**

Logan's has been hand-making candy since 1933, and here you can pick up old-fashioned ribbon candy in different flavors to get you in the holly jolly mood year-

round. If that doesn't cut it, it's also the home of the world's largest handmade candy cane. Try saying bah, humbug to that.
125 WEST B STREET IN ONTARIO. 909-984-5410. www.loganscandies.com

---

529. At Dylan's Candy Bar at the Grove, you're in for a sugar rush.
Dylan Lauren, daughter of legendary fashion designer Ralph Lauren, has finally expanded her candy empire to Los Angeles; dentists couldn't be happier and neither can we. Candies from all over the world and a few local ones can now be found under the lollipop branches at Dylan's. From Australian licorice to sour gummies to even the unusual bacon-flavored treats, the bins here are brimming over with sweet goodies that will be put a smile on anyone's face. Is there anything better than being a kid in a candy store?
6333 WEST 3RD STREET AT THE GROVE IN LOS ANGELES. 323-930-1600. www.dylanscandybar.com

---

KOREAN BBQ

530. *Get a pig lighter at* Honey Pig. If you're having trouble deciding what to order here, it's best to remember the name of the restaurant: pork is what you should get. Tasty cuts of pork (the black variety being the best) are cooked alongside heaps of *kimchi* (fermented spicy cabbage), marinated bean sprouts, and a selection of veggies, creating that perfect, all-in-one eating experience. Instead of devouring every last piece of sizzling deliciousness, opt to leave a few scraps on the grill, and let the server know that you're ready for some rice. They'll prepare savory fried rice on your grill that mixes in every bit of that remaining goodness. Be sure to ask for a pig lighter before you leave; it's a great souvenir of a great meal.
3400 WEST 8TH STREET IN KOREATOWN IN LOS ANGELES. 213-380-0256.

531. *You'll smell like the real deal when you leave* Soot Bull Jeep. Here you'll get a genuine Korean barbecue experience as you grill and char different cuts of flavorful, marinated meats over a hot flame. Cooking your own meat always ensures it's just the way you like it; it comes with rice and Korean side dishes known as *ban chan*. And with a name like Soot Bull Jeep (it means charcoal fire house), it won't be easy to forget: the smell will linger on your clothes for days. Note: If the flames on the grill get too hot to handle, douse them with a bit of ice to bring them down to a manageable temperature.
3136 WEST 8TH STREET IN KOREATOWN IN LOS ANGELES. 213-387-3865.

532. *Get your first taste of Korean Barbeque at* ChoSun Galbee. In this faux Marc Newson–designed restaurant, everything is "perfect." The staff is wired up

with headsets and walkie-talkies, the women wear traditional Korean *hanboks,* and the menu is full of options other than barbecue. With effortless service and good-quality but pricey food, ChoSun is ideal for first-timers.
3330 WEST OLYMPIC BOULEVARD IN LOS ANGELES. 323-734-3330. www.chosungalbee.com

---

533. ***You'll pay the price for eating at* Park's BBQ.** At Park's you'll find premium meats at a premium price. And with American wagyu (aka Kobe-style beef) on the menu, they're not messing around. But the meats aren't the only things that'll have you spending your hard-earned cash in this place. It has a great menu offering options for meat-eaters and veggie-lovers alike, making it no wonder that people pay a little extra to eat at Park's.
955 SOUTH VERMONT AVENUE SUITE G IN KOREATOWN IN LOS ANGELES. 213-380-1717. www.parksbbq.com

---

534. Grab sushi on a budget at **Sushi Karen.**

"Lunch special," usually isn't something you want to order at a sushi restaurant. The phrase connotes that the sushi isn't fresh or doesn't taste good. Sushi Karen begs to differ. For $13, Toshi-san serves you an assorted sushi lunch with six pieces of nigiri and six pieces of roll sushi.
10762 WASHINGTON BOULEVARD IN CULVER CITY. 310-202-0855. www.sushikaren.com

---

535. Get lost in the canyon at **PACE restaurant.**

For over a decade, Sandy Gendel has been transporting eaters to this bohemian hideaway, tucked in a nook off of Laurel Canyon Boulevard. Its cozy, candle-lit setting, solid wine list, and delicious market-fresh menu ensure that after one visit here you will find "peace in the canyon."
2100 LAUREL CANYON BOULEVARD IN LOS ANGELES. 323-654-8583. peaceinthecanyon.com

---

536. Go fishin' at **Thiên Ân Bò 7 Món.**

Fans of seven courses of beef make the trek out to Rosemead in the San Gabriel Valley to eat at Thiên Ân Bò 7 Món. Here they serve up authentic Vietnamese dishes that are well spiced and delicious. Although seven courses of beef sound like a carnivore's paradise (they serve everything from grilled juicy meatballs wrapped in caul fat to boar cooked at your table), pescartarians are in for a treat, too. The whole fried Vietnamese catfish is the stuff of dreams. Incredibly crispy skin, hot, and tender, the catfish cooked with scallions and garlic is eaten wrapped in a rice paper roll with different

Vietnamese herbs and dipped into a sauce of your choice: nuoc cham (fish sauce) or mam nem (fermented anchovy dip). If you're hungry, call ahead, as the fish can take up to 30 minutes to prepare.

8837 VALLEY BOULEVARD IN ROSEMEAD. 626-286-6665.

---

537. Track down **Cool Haus** for an ice-cream sandwich.

If you have a penchant for sweets, Cool Haus is the truck to find. Savvy businesswomen with licenses to drive, owners Natasha and Freya have transformed the simple ice-cream sandwich into a masterpiece. Sustainable, handmade, and organic whenever possible, their flavors are fun and the combinations delightful. Try candied bacon ice cream on chocolate chip cookies, or go for the classic Mies Vanilla Rohe (vanilla and chocolate chip cookies) or a Richard Meier (meyer lemon peel ice cream on ginger cookies); you can even eat the wrapper. With treats so big you'd consider missing dinner and going straight to dessert, Cool Haus is giving the Good Humor man a serious run for his money.

Eatcoolhaus.com (or follow them on Twitter @COOLHAUS)

---

538. Find **DwitGolMok** (DGM).

Just because you have the address doesn't guarantee you'll find DwitGolMok, but it'll get you close. To make it to the finish line, just follow your nose and head behind the main drag down South Berendo Street and through the parking lot toward the alleyway. All the aromas lead to spicy intestine soup; *budae jjigae*, a broth invented following the Korean War; and other delicious treats, including lots of soju (Korean rice liquor). Ask about any discounts and don't forget to bring a Sharpie so you can leave your mark, along with the other doodles on the walls, to prove that you made it.

3275 WILSHIRE BOULEVARD IN KOREATOWN IN LOS ANGELES. 213-382-8432.

---

539. No need to wait behind any velvet ropes to grab a drink at **Golden Gopher**.

Barman Cedd Moses has transformed the historic downtown scene, making it that much easier to find a stiff drink and have a good time.

417 WEST 8TH STREET IN DOWNTOWN LOS ANGELES. 213-614-8001.
www.213nightlife.com/goldengopher

---

540. Get a taste of French-Vietnamese history for less than $3 at **Báhn Mý Tho**.

Encased in a lighter-than-air baguette—leave the chewiness to the French—and Jam-packed with flavors that are savory, sweet, sour, and spicy, báhn mì sandwiches are the essence of colonial Vietnam. No matter what fillings you choose, you can't go wrong; they're always just right.

304 WEST VALLEY BOULEVARD IN ALHAMBRA. 626-289-4160. www.banhmimytho.com

---

541. Get your hands dirty at **Boiling Crab**, but wash up first.

That way you're prepared when they bring you your big plastic bags filled with seafood (crab, shrimp, crawfish, lobster) ordered by the pound and boiled to perfection in the seasoning of your liking. The "whole shebang" is a popular option. Then strap on your bib and start to dismember, suck, and strip every delicious morsel out of the hot shells. It's a messy job, but someone's got to do it. Avoid ordering spicy, it'll blot out the seafood taste altogether and leave you seeing red—lobster red.

3377 WILSHIRE BOULEVARD, #115 IN KOREATOWN IN LOS ANGELES. 213-389-2722. Several locations. www.theboilingcrab.com

---

542. Get your tea fix at **American Tea Room**.

You no longer need to travel the four corners of the planet in search of your favorite teas. Not when the folks at American Tea Room have done all the legwork for you. At their store, they've amassed a large selection of the finest teas, teaware, and accessories in the world. And with the help of their knowledgeable staff, you'll be able to brew the perfect pot of your favorite blend, and it'll taste as if the leaves were picked from the tea estates of Sri Lanka only yesterday.

401 NORTH CANON DRIVE IN BEVERLY HILLS. 310-271-7922. www.americantearoom.com

---

543. Get slow fast food at **Oinkster**.

There's always time to eat, but there's not always time to eat well. Oinkster offers high-quality food served fast—relatively fast, that is. Slow-smoked pastrami prepared like a French dip, juicy slow-cooked pulled pork with house-made barbecue sauce, and even the twice-fried Belgian fries are proof enough that there is such a thing as good fast food.

2005 COLORADO BOULEVARD IN EAGLE ROCK. 323-255-6465. theoinkster.com

---

544. Once you go **Planet Raw** you may never go back . . .

Chef Juliano Brotman is the embodiment of his restaurant's motto, "all organic raw vegan life energy." Everything here—from the food, sourced at the Santa Monica Farmers' Market, to the water-based paint job—has been curated not only to make you feel

better, but to be good for the planet as well. After you're done feasting (I recommend the "sushi" and the "cheeseburger"), pick up some biodynamic vegan wine to take home to keep those healthy vibes going.
609 BROADWAY IN SANTA MONICA. 310-587-1552. www.planetraw.com

---

545. At **BierBeisl** you'll find schnitzels, sausages, and Schnapps, oh my!

At Chef Bernhard Mairinger's authentic Austrian restaurant you'll get your fill of some of that country's finest dishes and drinks. Sit at the Stammtisch, a communal table, and indulge in sausage and beer tastings from käsekrainer, similar to a Polish sausage infused with swiss cheese, to the classic bratwurst and wash it all down with the finest in Austrian beers. Or try the delicious schnitzel, gulasch, and trio of pork. Be sure to finish your meal with a Schnapps from the special bar.
9669 LITTLE SANTA MONICA BOULEVARD IN BEVERLY HILLS. 310-271-7274. www.bierbeisl-la.com

---

546. Order the Newport Special Lobster at **Newport Seafood**.

This dish—large chunks of lobster stir-fried with heaps of garlic, scallions, and the lobster roe—is the best dish on Newport's menu. It's a rich feast you should definitely indulge in.
518 WEST LAS TUNAS DRIVE IN SAN GABRIEL. 626-289-5998. www.newportseafood.com

---

547. Run, don't walk, to **Go's Mart**.

In an unassuming strip mall in Canoga Park, you'll find an even more unassuming sushi restaurant. You're greeted with a display of VHS tapes and bland decor instead of a smiling hostess announcing your arrival with an "Irashai." Here, your focus is on the fish and the restaurant's creative dishes. Crowd pleasers include grilled shrimp stuffed with roe and topped with *uni* (sea urchin), creamy *shirako* (male genitalia from a snapper), a sandwich of crab and uni topped with caviar and gold leaf, and delicate tempura made with *sakura ebi* (small shrimp from Shizuoka), shishito peppers, and okra. And if you're looking for more traditional touches, you can order fugu (blowfish) in the winter. A meal can easily run you over $200, so mention a price limit when you make your reservation. The chef will prepare accordingly to adhere to your set amount.
22330 SHERMAN WAY IN CANOGA PARK. 818-704-1459.

Late Night

548. ***The party doesn't stop at Kitchen 24.*** Just because the clock strikes midnight doesn't mean the restaurant is going to turn into a pumpkin. Kitchen 24, open all day every day, serves tasty options like their famed "Smac and cheese" to the late-night crowd. Live music courtesy of a DJ keeps the good times going. And if you need a place to nurse that hangover the morning after, visit the build-your-own-Bloody Mary bar on the weekends from 9:00 a.m. to 3:00 p.m.

8575 SANTA MONICA BOULEVARD IN WEST HOLLYWOOD. 424-777-0959. www.kitchen24.info; 1608 NORTH CAHUENGA BOULEVARD IN HOLLYWOOD. 323-465-2424. www.kitchen24.info

549. ***Enjoy another late-night episode of "Kitsch and the Kitchen" at Fred 62.*** After driving around for almost an hour looking to fill a late-night craving, Jason and Ryan finally stumble upon Fred 62. Open twenty-four hours a day, this diner with bowling alley–style decor looks busy and promising. They order the Mac Daddy & Cheese and the Charles Bukowski, a hefty grilled ham and cheese sandwich, and sit back and wait. Will the duo eat soon? Will it be any good? The food arrives and the smiles that spread across their faces say it all. Next time a late-night craving strikes they know just where to go.

1850 NORTH VERMONT AVENUE IN LOS ANGELES. 323-667-0062. www.fred62.com

550. ***Rub elbows and chopsticks with members of the L.A. Philharmonic post-performance at Shibucho.*** You can thank Flea from the Red Hot Chili Peppers for introducing this author to his favorite sushi spot. This unassuming Japanese restaurant is a night owl's dream. Musicians finishing up their gigs and sushi lovers with jet lag all come here for a sushi fix. Shige Kudo, who honed his skills in Hokkaido and serves "Edo" style sushi/sashimi, seemingly has every fish available at his counter every night—all of it fresh, pristine, and ready to eat. Instead of ordering, leave it to Shige-san to create a delectable *omakase* ("chef's choice") feast. Just don't forget to tell him when you've eaten enough or your bill may be as eye-opening as your experience.

3114 BEVERLY BOULEVARD IN LOS ANGELES. 213-387-8498, www.shibucho.com

551. ***When it's late and you're in Koreatown, head toward the neon lights of Hodori.*** The Korean bat signal for late-night clubbers in need of post-partying sustenance, it's been the mainstay of the Koreatown scene for a long time.

1001 SOUTH VERMONT AVENUE IN KOREATOWN IN LOS ANGELES. 213-383-3554. www.hodorirestaurants.com

552. Chow down at **El Tepayac**.

Head to Manuel's Original El Tepayac Cafe in Boyle Heights, and attempt to tackle the "Manuel's Special," a five-pound burrito. If you don't have the guts or the stomach for that hefty challenge, settle on the famous Hollenbeck Burrito, pork meat in chile verde sauce. It is so famous it has spawned a legion of imitations, but as Manuel would say, "Ours is the original."

812 NORTH EVERGREEN AVENUE IN LOS ANGELES. 323-268-1960. www.manuelseltepeyac.com

553. Eat an Indian pizza at **Paru's**.

When you walk up to Paru's, you'll suspect you're in the wrong place—it seems more like a dive than a restaurant. But once you're inside, the cozy atmosphere will immediately put you at ease and prepare you for an Indian feast that may include samosas, dosa, and pizza from another mother, *uttapam*.

5140 SUNSET BOULEVARD, HOLLYWOOD. 323-661-7600, www.parusrestaurant.com

554. Savor a taste of Cuba at **El Cochinito**.

Sometimes you just need more pork, and at this small restaurant the chefs know how to make it right. The *lechon asado*, slow-roasted pork that is crispy on the outside and soft and juicy on the inside, is divine. When the pork is accompanied by a healthy smear of the *mojo de ajo* (garlic sauce) and a side of savory black beans and sweet fried plantains, you'll begin to wonder whether the strained relations between Cuba and the US are about Castro's government or, perhaps, Cuba's refusal to share the secrets of a true *lechon asado*.

3508 SUNSET BOULEVARD IN SILVERLAKE IN LOS ANGELES. 323-668-0737. www.elcochinitola.com

555. Trick your friends at **Bulan Thai Vegetarian Kitchen**.

Order the chicken, order the steak, just don't tell them what they're missing. Bulan prepares all its dishes with lots of traditional Thai flavors, which makes it hard to tell that the soy meat options aren't genuine. But one taste of the mock duck curry and you'll swear it's the real deal.

4114 SANTA MONICA BOULEVARD IN LOS ANGELES. 323-913-1488. www.bulanthai.com

556. Watch beautiful people make beautiful food at **Gjelina**.

It's one thing to open your restaurant to local fanfare; it's another when your chef is featured in a *Vogue* magazine spread with a supermodel. The kitchen staff at this Venice hot spot is possibly the best looking in Los Angeles, and the chef, Travis Lett, is a golden-haired demigod who labors over everything from organic salads to entrees. Although the service can be slow at times, the food is spot on. And since you're really here for the eye candy, no experience is ever bad.

1429 ABBOT KINNEY BOULEVARD IN VENICE. 310-450-1429. www.gjelina.com

557. Make everything seasonal at **The Tasting Kitchen**, where James Beard Award–nominated chef, Casey Lane, shows off his skills.

His seasonal menu is easy to navigate, and everything, consistently good, from the simple sides of delicately seasoned vegetables to the hearty, country-style entrees. Try the house-made pâté, with a side of toast, cheese, and figs. You'll see what I mean.

1633 ABBOT KINNEY BOULEVARD IN VENICE. 310-392-6644. www.thetastingkitchen.com

558. Treat your body to a healthy meal at **Real Food Daily**.

Since 1993 a popular destination for those seeking tasty, good-for-you vegan gourmet, RFD has made its inventive meals using tempeh and seitan a well-liked trend among the hipsters and Hollywood types. All of the "bad stuff" is taken out of food, and what's left is only the good. Enjoy the specials of the month or the yummy Salisbury seitan.

414 NORTH LA CIENEGA BOULEVARD IN LOS ANGELES. 310-289-9910. multiple locations. www.realfood.com

559. Make a mess at **Millie's Cafe**.

Sounds like something your mother wouldn't approve of, but at this cafe on Sunset, you can order a "mess" and eat one. Three eggs with lots of ingredients like smoked salmon and cream cheese (Neptune's Mess) or Cajun-spiced turkey sausage and cheddar cheese (Devil's Mess) are thrown together and served in a hot, hearty pile on your plate. But don't worry, mom, by the end of the meal the plates always end up clean.

3524 WEST SUNSET BOULEVARD IN SILVERLAKE IN LOS ANGELES. 323-664-0404. www.milliescafe.net

560. Fight off a food coma after you eat at **Huarache Azteca Restaurante**.

Huarache means "sandal" in Spanish, and that's exactly what you'll get. A large piece of masa is worked into the elongated shape of a sandal and topped with beans, meat, cheese, and vegetables. It's delicious, it's hearty, and if the weather's warm and relaxing, it's more than likely you'll want to take a nap. Have one of the agua frescas (fresh juices) to help wash it all down.

5225 YORK BOULEVARD IN HIGHLAND PARK IN LOS ANGELES. 323-478-9572. www.elhuracheazteca.com

561. Buy a T-shirt and a wrap at **Zankou Chicken**.

This Armenian chain has a cult following thanks to its garlic sauce and delicious chicken *tarna*, which is marinated in thirty different seasonings and served with pickled turnips. If you're a fan, make sure you buy a Zankou T-shirt. You'll be surprised how many conversations that yellow shirt can start.

7851 WEST SUNSET BOULEVARD IN LOS ANGELES. 323-882-6365. www.zankouchicken.com

562. Get a mulita at **La Taquiza**.

If you don't know what a *mulita* is, the staff at La Taquiza will be more than happy to tell you—but it'd be better if they could show you. They take two handmade corn tortillas with cheese and meat, and melt those together with guacamole, using it as a kind of cement, and voilà: a *mulita*. Just don't call it a quesadilla.

3009 SOUTH FIGUEROA STREET IN LOS ANGELES. 213-741-9795. lataquizaktown.com

563. It's okay to be a creature of habit at **Versailles**.

The staff appreciates diners who know what they like so don't worry if you only order the same thing here. They've been serving the same guests the same dishes since 1981. Be sure to go for the oxtails and the garlic and onion chicken.

1415 SOUTH LA CIENEGA BOULEVARD IN LOS ANGELES. 310-289-0392. www.versaillescuban.com

564. Indulge in the real K.F.C. at **OB Bear**.

At this Koreatown favorite, people come for the fried chicken. One bite and you'll know that Colonel Sanders had it all wrong; K.F.C. should really be "Korean Fried Chicken."

3002 WEST 7TH STREET IN LOS ANGELES. 213-480-4910.

565. Pretend you're in Paris and sit outside to people watch at **Figaro Bistrot**.

A French sidewalk cafe in the heart of Los Feliz Village, Figaro Bistrot has all the stereotypical elements of a Parisian bistro down cold, from the fixtures to the menu. Offering traditional French bistro fare like freshly baked croissants in the morning and escargot and steak frites for dinner, it's a must for Francophiles or even Frenchmen themselves looking for a taste of home. While you're here, strike a pose and vogue as you have your photo taken inside; pop icon Madonna shot her Louis Vuitton ad campaign here with famed photographer Steven Meisel.

1802 NORTH VERMONT AVENUE IN LOS ANGELES. 323-662-1587. www.figarobistrot.com

566. You might get lost looking for **R23**.

This hard-to-find treasure down an alleyway near Little Tokyo has been around for almost twenty years. It remains one of the coolest grown-up restaurants in town. In a loft building with soaring ceilings and weathered brick walls, it serves up vast slabs of pristine sushi. But it's the cooked dishes that shine. Go for something with crab, when they have it, and anything—*anything*—with rib-eye.

923 EAST 2ND STREET IN DOWNTOWN LOS ANGELES. 213-687-7178. www.r23.com

567. Don't go for half; go for whole at **Pollo ala Brasa**.

On the corner of 8th Street and Western Avenue you'll see a small restaurant that's been there forever. Nothing in particular about the place makes it look very special, but as you turn the corner just a hair, the mounds of split oak piled high against the wall will make you pull over. The smokiest, crispiest Peruvian-style chicken in town is cooked right here in their brick oven in the center of the restaurant. Order your bird, slide into a booth, and wait for one of the tastiest chicken feasts of your life.

764 SOUTH WESTERN AVENUE IN LOS ANGELES. 213-387-1531.

568. Chase down a dim sum cart at **888 Seafood**.

While it is a lucky number to the Chinese, when you come to 888 it'll be so crowded you'll be lucky to be seated in less than an hour. Once you're in, you can enjoy the dance of the dim sum carts. Moving backward, forward, left, right, and in between tables, the women with their carts offer you hot steaming pork buns, shrimp dumplings, chicken feet, sweet tofu, and more. The trouble: finding the cart with what you like. Since most of the dishes are covered, you often get repeats. It's best to keep your eye out for who's coming from the kitchen because that indicates the food is fresher. And if the situation gets desperate, you can either chase down your favorite cart or wave over a waiter to help you.

8450 VALLEY BOULEVARD, SUITE #121 IN ROSEMEAD. 626-573-1888.

---

569. **Sea Harbour Seafood Restaurant** isn't your normal dim sum.

There are no carts here. Instead, you place your order by marking off a checklist, then wait for the waves of food to come to your table, piping hot and always fresh. Your neck will thank you for not craning it around every two minutes looking for what to order next.

3939 ROSEMEAD BOULEVARD IN ROSEMEAD. 626-288-3939.

---

570. Cool down with a cold bowl of *naeng-myun* from **Yu Chun**.

Naeng-myun, a cold noodle dish from northern Korea, was originally a winter delicacy. Now it's the unofficial summer dish for Koreans and the perfect way to cool off. At Yu Chun, *chic mul naeng-myun* consists of black arrowroot noodles (typically *naeng-myun* is made with buckwheat) in a bowl of cold broth with flecks of ice, cucumber, Asian pear, half a hard-boiled egg and slices of beef brisket. It may not look like a lot when the server brings the dish to the table, but the chewiness of the noodles will make it seem like you're eating a never-ending bowl. Just ask the waitress to make a few extra snips with her scissors and the noodles will be easier to manage. You can also try the spicier option known as *chic bi bim naeng-myun*.

3185 WEST OLYMPIC BOULEVARD IN KOREATOWN IN LOS ANGELES. 213-382-3815.

---

571. Take down *Das Boot* at **Wurstküche**.

Since its opening, this modest sausage and beer hall in downtown's Arts District has been getting a lot of buzz. With its large selection of gourmet grilled sausages (anything from buffalo to rattlesnake), its double-dipped Belgian fries, and nearly two dozen German and Belgian beers on tap that can be served in a glass-shaped boot, everything about this place is *sehr gut*.

800 EAST 3RD STREET IN DOWNTOWN LOS ANGELES. 213-687-4444. www.wurstkuche.com

---

572. Go for greasy at **Yang Chow**.

Often referred to as the Chinese-food equivalent of Nate 'n Al, it's popular for its greasy and delicious dishes. Order up a plate of orange shrimp before you head out on the town for a night of drinking.

819 NORTH BROADWAY IN CHINATOWN IN DOWNTOWN LOS ANGELES. 213-625-0811. www.yangchow.com

573. Play bumper carts at **Elat Market**.

If you can navigate the streets of L.A., you'll be able to get down the aisles of this Middle Eastern specialty market relatively unscathed. With a fine selection of Persian, Indian, and Israeli products, especially the dried fruits like mulberries and figs, it's a popular destination and parking can be difficult. Once inside, be careful. Shopping is a full-contact sport here, and defensive elbow-throwing occurs frequently.

8730 WEST PICO BOULEVARD IN LOS ANGELES. 310-659-7070. www.elatkoshermarket.com

574. Pick your pork at **Assi**.

Not all Korean markets are the same, and at 2:00 p.m. on Thursdays and Saturdays the meat section of Assi reveals why: a whole fresh pig is butchered to order. If you're interested, come a bit early as shoppers wait in line at the meat counter for a chance to get the perfect cut.

3525 WEST 8TH STREET IN KOREATOWN IN LOS ANGELES. 213-388-0900. www.assisuperus.com

575. Get a crash course in Korean food.

Love the "Land of the Morning Calm" but can't comprehend its cuisine as easily as Chinese or Japanese? Head to the food court in **Koreatown Galleria**, where you can take your pick of a dozen Korean dishes. Easily navigate your way through soups, rice dishes, grilled meats, and noodles, all there for your tasting pleasure. And afterward, if you're suitably inspired, venture downstairs to the Galleria Market and pick up some ingredients for your own Korean feast.

3250 WEST OLYMPIC BOULEVARD (BASEMENT FLOOR) IN KOREATOWN IN LOS ANGELES. 323-733-6000. www.koreatowngalleria.com

576. Wander the aisles to create your custom twelve-pack at **Galco's Soda Pop Stop**.

John Nese slings around five hundred varieties of sodas at his red-brick store. Finds like Boylan's Sugar Cane Cola, Bauser Extra Dry Champayno, the perfect non-alcoholic celebratory drink, Kickapoo Joy Juice, and, of course, exclusive bottlings of flavors like Sweet Blossom Rose and Elderflower line its shelves. Throw in a good selection of old-fashioned treats like Abba-Zaba bars, Beemans Chewing Gum, Big Hunk, and Clark, and some rare ales from Europe (there are more than five hundred different beers from around the world) and anyone would be in paradise. Galco puts the "pop" back in soda.

5702 YORK BOULEVARD IN LOS ANGELES. 323-255-7115. www.sodapopstop.com

577. Get to the farmer's market early to pick up some **Bigmista's Barbecue**.

This mobile meat paradise owned and operated by Neil and Phyllis Strawder at the Atwater Village Farmers' Market on Sundays provides grub that is slow-smoked to perfection. In four short years it has become L.A.'s favorite barbecue sauce, dribbling down chins everywhere.

Atwater Village Farmers' Market: 3250 GLENDALE BOULEVARD (WELLS FARGO PARKING LOT) IN LOS ANGELES. Bigmista's Barbecue: 562-423-4BIG. www.bigmista.com

578. Get the ribs at **Baby Blues BBQ**.

At this popular barbecue spot in Venice, you're tempted to order everything on the menu, which includes pulled pork with that Carolina vinegar sauce and braised brisket and pork with all the fixings. But start with a rack of ribs and you'll soon discover that's about as far down the menu as you need to go.

444 LINCOLN BOULEVARD IN VENICE. 310-396-7675. www.babybluesvenice.com

SOME LIKE IT HOTTER THAN HOT

579. *Alondra Hot Wings:* There are hot wings, and then there are atomic hot wings. If you want to try the latter at Alondra in Montebello, get ready to sign a waiver. And whenever a waiver is involved, rest assured that you are in for some serious heat.

616 WEST WHITTIER BOULEVARD IN MONTEBELLO. 323-722-2731. www.alondrawings.com

580. *Jitlada Thai's Dynamite Challenge:* When a warning reads, "If you do not eat spicy food do not order this. This is REAL CHILI REAL SPICY," how can a chili-head say no? Order and get ready to blow your mind with the spicy "dynamite" Chef Tui concocts in his kitchen. The burn will be slow and painful, much like Jitlada's service, but if you're a fan of that painful ear buzzing only truly achieved by eating liquid fire, here you go.

5233 WEST SUNSET BOULEVARD IN LOS ANGELES. 323-663-3104. www.jitladala.com

581. *Orochon Ramen Special #2 Challenge:* Create your own version of "Man vs. Food" at Orochon by attempting to eat the hottest ramen on the planet. If you succeed, not only do you get a Polaroid on the wall of fame,

you also get definitive proof that you are a total masochist. Adam Richman would be proud.
123 ASTRONAUT E. S. ONIZUKU STREET, LITTLE TOKYO, IN LOS ANGELES. 213-617-1766.

582. ***Chichén Itzá's Habanero-Eating Contest:*** The prizes are $50 gift certificates. Is it worth it?
3655 SOUTH GRAND AVENUE, #C6 IN DOWNTOWN LOS ANGELES. 213-741-1075. www.chichenitzarestaurant.com

583. Become a wine collector overnight after a visit to **Wally's Wine**.

Steve Wallace will not only have you swirling and spitting better after one visit to this wine emporium, but he'll also help unlock the world of oenology (the sciences of wine and winemaking). Be sure to ask for his expert advice on picking out some good wines from his extensive inventory—and don't be afraid to be frank and honest, since the more he knows about what you're going to eat or what you like, the better his advice will be.
2107 WESTWOOD BOULEVARD IN WEST LOS ANGELES. 310-475-0606. www.wallywine.com

584. Line up for a smart cup of coffee at **Intelligentsia**.

Intelligentsia quickly earned a reputation for making the best coffee in the area when it opened in 2007. Every day they roast their own coffee beans in special roasters to achieve that unique flavor; the beans are then meticulously transformed into cutely decorated cappuccinos, lattes, macchiatos, Americanos, and perfect espressos. But since Intelligentsia sells coffee to almost every place in town, one has to wonder: How intelligent is it to wait in a line?
3922 WEST SUNSET BOULEVARD IN SILVERLAKE. 323-663-6173. www.intelligentsiacoffee.com

585. Hang out at **The Edison**.

One of the coolest, most unique bars in downtown L.A.—the space is a converted private power plant—The Edison is definitely trendy. With its 1920's speakeasy vibe, beautiful décor, and bar offerings—they serve absinthe—it's no wonder there's usually a line. But if you're not dressed to impress and willing to shell out $14 for a drink, you might want to rethink your Saturday night.
108 WEST 2ND STREET #101 IN DOWNTOWN LOS ANGELES. 213-613-0000. www.edisondowntown.com

586. Get a feast on a budget in **dineLA Restaurant Week**.

Twice a year Angelenos get a chance to taste the fancier side of the city, but on a more modest budget. During dineLA, in January and October, over two hundred restaurants all over the city, from the fanciest to more casual neighborhood joints, offer three-course prix fixe meals at lunch and dinner. And at a bargain price, it's perfect for the adventurous and curious pennypincher. How good a deal it is depends on the restaurant, but at least you'll be able to dine there without breaking the bank.
www.discoverlosangeles.com/dinela-los-angeles-restaurant-week

587. Homemade is better than store bought at **Nickel Diner**.

Abandon that Ding-Dong for one of Nickel's fabulous homemade desserts. The bakers take the Ding Dong and make it taste ding dang delicious. Sure it's more expensive than the packet you normally pick up at the store, but it's moist, creamy, and a heck of a lot better. And you know it hasn't been sitting around longer than a day or two. Also try the mouthwatering crunch fest that is the maple bacon doughnut.
524 SOUTH MAIN STREET IN DOWNTOWN LOS ANGELES. 213-623-8301. nickeldiner.com

588. Crack the code to get into the **R Bar**.

Behind the nondescript entrance of this Koreatown dive lies a dark and moody wood-paneled setting perfect for some laid-back debauchery. But to get in, one needs to get past the password-protected front door. With a decent bar menu, killer jukebox, and a good mix of people waiting on other side, you'll definitely want to succeed. Luckily, you won't have to tap into your psychic powers to enter; all you need to do is call ahead to ask the bartender for the secret word/phrase of the day.
3331 WEST 8TH STREET IN KOREATOWN LOS ANGELES. 213-387-7227. www.myspace.com/4rbar

589. Grab a drink at the **Stark Bar** and see art through beer goggles.

You gotta love it when recent improvements to LACMA included the addition of a bar. Set in architect Renzo Piano's open-air plaza, the Stark (named after art collector and Hollywood producer Ray Stark) is chic, minimalist, and fully stocked. Go from studying the inanimate to the animate when you grab a seat and watch people stroll by.
5905 WILSHIRE BOULEVARD IN LOS ANGELES. 323-857-6180. www.patinagroup.com

590. The Varnish at **Cole's French Dip**.

Cole's has been serving French Dip in the Pacific Electric building since 1908 (p. 181). And in its recesses lies a bar. Head past the bathrooms and look for the door with the picture of a champagne glass on it. It leads to The Varnish, a dimly lit, modest speakeasy that serves up specialty cocktails and a taste of old-time history. And if you're lucky, your waitress might let you order a French dip from Cole's and bring it to your booth. French dip to go with your cocktail concoction? Perfect.

118 EAST 6TH STREET IN DOWNTOWN LOS ANGELES. 213-622-4090. www.213nightlife.com/thevarnish

Taconnoisseur: or, a Connoisseur of Tacos

591. *Best Fish Taco in Ensenada.* The closest thing to being in Baja is eating here. Think simple battered fish and shrimp fried to perfection and served in a warm tortilla. And for the prices—$1.00 for the fish and $2.00 for the shrimp—it's a steal of a meal. Order a couple so you can try all of the different salsas offered.

1650 NORTH HILLHURST AVENUE IN LOS ANGELES. 323-466-5552. www.bestfishtacoinensenada.com

592. *Yuca's Hut.* Mother-and-daughter team Socorro and Dora Herrera have been serving mouthwatering Mexican food out of a tiny shack in Los Feliz since 1976. The biggest draw is the *cochinita pibil* tacos, pork slow cooked in a banana leaf and laced with achiote. It's so good that after one bite you'll know exactly why this place won a James Beard Award.

2056 NORTH HILLHURST AVENUE IN LOS ANGELES. 323-662-1214. www.yucasla.com

593. *El Taurino.* Choosing which sauce, red or green, you're going to have with your carne asada taco is like asking Neo which pill he's gonna take in the *Matrix*.

1104 SOUTH HOOVER STREET IN LOS ANGELES. 213-738-9197. www.eltaurino.com

594. *Antojitos Guerrero.* This family-run restaurant is the perfect place to enjoy breakfast, brunch, and lunch. Their beef and chicken tacos, served in homemade corn tortillas, are always hot and savory with a hint of sweetness from the maize. Be sure to also try their huevos rancheros, chilaquiles with salsa verde, and machaca con huevos (scrambled eggs

with savory shredded beef). Everything is tasty and always served with a smile.
5623 YORK BOULEVARD IN HIGHLAND PARK IN LOS ANGELES. 323-254-6118

---

595. *Taco Zone Truck.* When this taco truck burned down several years ago, the local community quickly rallied together, threw a fundraiser, and got enough money for a new truck. Everyone can be thankful they did. Where else would club-goers in Silverlake and Echo Park go to eat such yummy food? Parked on the street outside of a Vons supermarket on Alvarado, Taco Zone's *suadero* (brisket) tacos are so good, you'd drive across town after a night in Hollywood just for a taste.
NORTH ALVARADO STREET NEAR MONTANA STREET IN ECHO PARK. 818-763-4085.

---

596. *El Siete Mares.* Cheap and cheerful, if you can call eating in a parking lot cheerful, you can't go wrong with their fish or crispy shrimp tacos (dorados). Be sure to wash down all that goodness with a cold bottle of Mexican Coca-Cola.
3131 WEST SUNSET BOULEVARD IN SILVER LAKE. 323-665-0865.

---

597. *Ricky's Fish Tacos.* Fresh and delicious, hot and crispy, the fish tacos at Ricky's food stand would make a seafood lover out of anyone.
1400 NORTH VIRGIL AVENUE IN EAST LOS ANGELES.
Follow them on Twitter @rickysfishtacos

---

598. *Los Cinco (5) Puntos.* Yes the tacos here are delicious, but opt to make your own. Buy some of their delicious *chicharrones*, some handmade thick tortillas, a tub of guacamole, and salsa and let the feasting begin.
3300 EAST CESAR E. CHAVEZ AVENUE IN EAST LOS ANGELES. 323-261-4084.

---

599. *Mariscos Jalisco.* From delicious shrimp tacos to *aguachile*, raw shrimp marinated in lime and chile, one bite and you'll wonder why it took you this long to discover the magic that is Mariscos Jalisco.
Only open for lunch. 3040 EAST OLYMPIC BOULEVARD IN EAST LOS ANGELES. 323-528-6701.

Expert Contributor: Ludo Lefebvre

Ludo Lefebvre is a highly acclaimed chef, cookbook author, TV personality (*Top Chef Masters*, *Iron Chef America*, and *Ludo Bites America*), and founder of the wildly popular LudoBites and LudoTruck. *www.ludolefebvre.com*

MY FAVORITE SPOTS FOR FOOD IN L.A.

Sometimes I love vegetarian food, and the restaurant I go to when I want to clean out my body to balance out my week is ***Akasha***. Everything there is great and organic. I've spent a lot of time and cooked with the chef, Akasha Richmond. She was a yogi for twenty years. It's beautiful.
9543 CULVER BOULEVARD IN CULVER CITY. 310-845-1700. www.akasharestaurant.com

I'm obsessed with kimchi. I use kimichi for my foie gras dishes. I make some pretty good kimchi myself. But I buy my kimchi from ***Kimchi House*** in Gardena.
1434 WEST GARDENA BOULEVARD IN GARDENA. 310-532-8678.

My favorite place for chocolate is ***Madame Chocolat*** in Beverly Hills. She's the wife of chocolate wizard Jacques Torres. They met when she was taking a chocolate class with him. I go to see the chocolate displays. When I was a kid growing up in France, I went to go see Easter displays and holiday stuff, and her place really reminds me of that. My favorites there are the sea-salt caramels.
417 NORTH BEVERLY DRIVE IN BEVERLY HILLS. 310-205-0025. www.madame-chocolat.com

Best baguette is at ***Bread Bar***. Seriously, it's good.
10250 SANTA MONICA BOULEVARD IN SANTA MONICA. 310-277-3770. www.breadbar.net

I know there are a lot of sushi restaurants in Los Angeles but for me, I love sushi at ***Katsuya*** in Studio City. Their albacore tuna with fried onions and ponzu is the best.
11680 VENTURA BOULEVARD IN LOS ANGELES. 818-985-6976. www.katsu-yagroup.com

For sandwiches I go to ***Gram and Papas*** for their Jambon Beurre. It's French for ham and butter. It's the best, and I'm not just saying that because I gave them the recipe. It's really good. Just like it is in Paris. Only butter and ham with French radishes on the side. Simple and delicious.
227 EAST 9TH STREET IN LOS ANGELES. 213-624-7272. www.gramandpapas.com

I really like ***Park's BBQ*** for Korean BBQ. I love the different banchan (side dishes) they serve. My first taste of Korean food was there. They have so many types of kimchi—I especially like the spring kimchi and the galbi, Korean short ribs.
955 SOUTH VERMONT AVENUE IN LOS ANGELES. 213-380-1717. www.parksbbq.com

When I want to eat at a fancy restaurant, I opt for ***Hatfield*** or ***Melisse***, two restaurants and two chefs I really enjoy. The food is great.
HATFIELD: 6703 MELROSE AVENUE IN LOS ANGELES. 323-935-2977. www.hatfieldsrestaurant.com
MELISSE: 1104 WILSHIRE BOULEVARD IN SANTA MONICA. 310-395-0881. www.melisse.com

I love cheese, and when I want the best cheese I go to the ***Cheese Store of Beverly Hills*** and see Norbert. I've known Norbert for almost twenty years. Epoisse is my favorite, and any cheeses from Burgundy. I'm French, don't forget—we need cheese!
419 NORTH BEVERLY DRIVE IN BEVERLY HILLS. 310-278-2855. www.thecheesestorebh.com

As a French person, I love desserts. I get my macarons from ***Lette Macarons*** in Beverly Hills. Paulette Kourmetz, the owner, does a great job.
122 NORTH LARCHMONT BOULEVARD IN LOS ANGELES. 323-469-3620. www.lettemacarons.com

The best fried chicken spot in town is my ***Ludo Truck***! It's fresh, it's delicious, and it's cooked on the spot. *Oui*, it's the best!
Check twitter.com/LudoTruck for current location.

CHAPTER 6

The Great Outdoors

Despite what you may have heard, Los Angeles isn't just traffic jams and freeways. We've got the ocean and beaches, rivers, lakes, wildlife, and acres upon acres of parks and gardens across this city—not bad for a place widely regarded as a giant parking lot.

But in all seriousness, even with all of its cars, freeways, concrete, and skyscrapers, Los Angeles also has an awe-inspiring natural beauty. The city appeals to those with athletic passions and offers a multitude of outdoor options that can be found in the city's arts and culture, scenes, and cuisines. Along with activities like baseball, basketball, running, and cycling that can be found anywhere, L.A. also has cricket leagues, a trapeze school on a pier, canoeing, and surfing spots up and down the coast, to name but a few.

In this chapter I cover the best of the city's outdoor experiences, from parks to gardens, zoos and nature preserves, water activities, and sports. L.A.'s natural resources—including the ocean, rivers, beaches, and mountain ranges—provide plenty of opportunities to have fun outside. Hidden amid and around this great metropolis are some unique surprises as well: Nonprofit TreePeople with their moonlight hikes; a Japanese garden next to a water reclamation plant; and paddling excursions down a river in the middle of a city. You'll be amazed at how easy it is to access outdoor activities. With all kinds of country on the city's doorstep, there's no need to plan a long weekend to go horseback riding, hang gliding, or wind surfing, or to visit a national park—they're all right here.

Take advantage of the good weather and the many opportunities to bring the indoors outside: go to al fresco movies, concerts, festivals, fairs, and yoga and tai chi classes; the offerings explode like wildflowers during warmer months. Al fresco isn't just a dining experience in L.A., it's a way of life—and in many instances, it's completely free and ready for you to enjoy.

600. Traverse the globe in one visit to the **Gardens of the World**.

Since they couldn't take their community on their travels abroad, Ed and Lynn Hogan, founders of the travel group Pleasant Holidays, decided to bring their travels home with them instead. Enjoy the pristine Japanese Garden, complete with an authentic Japanese pagoda; the Mission Courtyard, with its hand-painted murals that are straight from the pages of California's history books; the Italian Garden, filled with cypress trees and grapes; and the French Garden, with a stunning waterfall centerpiece. All are tributes to different cultures from around the world. After a stroll around the grounds, and a relaxing moment spent listening to a jazz concert held at the bandstand, you just might consider booking a trip and visiting the real places. Call ahead to schedule a docent-led tour, or just explore on your own.

2001 THOUSAND OAKS BOULEVARD IN THOUSAND OAKS. 805-557-1135; www.gardensoftheworld.info

601. Find your Zen at **Suiho En**, the Japanese Garden.

When visiting Suiho En, don't expect to be immediately bowled over by its beauty, as this peaceful refuge's charm lies in its subtlety. At first, you only get a glimpse of what may be in store for you, but as you venture farther in, the garden gradually opens up and reveals a truly resplendent sight. Beautifully designed down to the placement of each stone, the 6.5 acres of this garden *are* harmony. Located next to the Donald C. Tillman Water Reclamation Plant and originally intended to show how reclaimed water can be used, Suiho En (meaning "the Garden of Water and Fragrance") is the perfect example of yin and yang. It is the epitome of harmony as it finds a balance between the beauty and tranquility in nature while being supported by the polluted waters that are purified (up to seventy-five million gallons a day) next door. Take a seat in the viewing arbor and observe the waterfall, where three million gallons of reclaimed water flow down into the lake daily, or go to the viewing platform to watch the water-filtering process up close and understand how these two places co-exist. Come for weekend tours, where guides dressed in red kimonos wait on you in the teahouse. From the end of May through the end of August, go for a docent-led evening tour and see the park at twilight.

6100 WOODLEY AVENUE IN VAN NUYS. 818-756-8166; www.thejapanesegarden.com

→ ***FACT:*** *The Japanese Garden was once used as a frequent film location for the television series Star Trek as Captain Kirk's alma mater, Starfleet Academy.*

602. Discover **Ernest E. Debs Regional Park.**

Hop on the 110 freeway (heading north from downtown L.A.) and you'll soon find yourself among towering trees and a menagerie of wildlife hidden within 282 acres of wilderness in Highland Park. Stop by the Audubon Center before you begin your exploration of the park's many trails, which are seldom crowded and always fairly serene. Visit the hilltop pond, inhale the soothing scent of eucalyptus, and unwittingly discover one of the most stunning views of downtown Los Angeles. With dogs allowed, lush trees to sit under on a hot day, and yet to be discovered by many locals, this park will feel at times like it's all your own.

Ernest E. Debs Regional Park: 4235 MONTEREY ROAD IN HIGHLAND PARK. 213-847-3989. Audubon Center: 4700 NORTH GRIFFITH AVENUE. 323-221-2255. debspark.audubon.org

603. Walk around the second-biggest park in the city, **Elysian Park.**

There's nothing wrong with coming in second behind Griffith Park. Just because Buzz Aldrin (the moon), Tenzing Norgay (Mount Everest), and George Lazenby (James Bond) were all runners-up doesn't mean they didn't make an impression, and Elysian Park does just that. This placid sanctuary in the middle of the city is full of lush greenery and different terrains and is perfect for picnics and outdoor activities. You have your pick of grassy meadows, canyons, hills with winding roads, and a fair portion of forested land—all of which puts Elysian Park on par with Griffith Park. NOTE: Feel safer knowing that the park is home to the Los Angeles Police Academy.

835 ACADEMY ROAD IN ECHO PARK. 213-485-5054. www.laparks.org

604. Stop and smell the roses at the **Exposition Park Rose Garden.**

The gardens in Los Angeles have a lot of history, and none more so than this. This seven-acre sunken space is filled with in excess of twenty thousand blooming bushes of more than two hundred different varieties of roses. It has a colorful past that includes camel, horse, dog, and car races; the longest bar in the city; and housed not just a brothel but one of the most stylish in the city. Garden enthusiasts come from all over to view the blooms, and though the roses are undoubtedly the star attraction, don't forget to go see the award-winning statues designed by Danish sculptor Thyra Boldsen or grab a seat around the central fountain. A green thumb is not required to visit; just remember to watch out for the thorns. Note: The Rose Garden is closed every year from January 1 to March 15 to prune back the roses. Located right behind the California Science Center (pp. 145 and 351) and near the Natural History Museum of Los Angeles (p. 141).

701 STATE DRIVE (IN EXPOSITION PARK) IN LOS ANGELES. 213-765-5397. www.laparks.org/exporosegarden

605. Have lunch between a rock and a hard place at **Santa Monica's Douglas Park**.

You can see from its three duck ponds, its spacious grounds perfect for learning how to ride a bike — it includes tennis courts and a lawn bowling area — and its fully loaded playground that Douglas Park is an ideal place to spend a day with the kids. But what makes this place special is the *Tables of Content* installation, by artists Ellen and Allan Wexler. Ten works of art that incorporate functional elements are placed throughout the park for everyone to enjoy. If you're hungry, sit at one of the Wexlers' wooden picnic tables. With one built around a mature tree and another around a boulder, not only do these tables invite you to eat in nature, but they also invite nature to join you. You couldn't ask for a better lunch date.

2439 WILSHIRE BOULEVARD IN SANTA MONICA.

606. See some eye-catching sculptures in **Beverly Gardens Park**.

Along Santa Monica Boulevard in Beverly Hills you'll find varying works of public art. A giant bronze bunny playing a drum, a zany oversize polka-dot garden of tulips, and a boulder made out of stainless steel are surprising reminders of this city's fondness for putting its eclectic art on display.

NORTH SANTA MONICA BOULEVARD AND NORTH BEVERLY DRIVE IN BEVERLY HILLS.
www.beverlyhills.org

607. **Shane's Inspiration** is *the* playground for all children.

There are many things to do in Griffith Park among its vast, sprawling acres, but none are as "open" to the public as Shane's Inspiration. Located near the merry-go-round, this two-acre space is "the first universally accessible playground in the western United States and the largest in the nation." It's more than just swings and slides—here children with physical disabilities can play alongside those without. Inspired by the loss of their son Shane, who suffered from spinal muscular atrophy, Catherine Curry-Williams and Scott Williams turned their tragedy, and the idea that their son would not have been able to enjoy his childhood properly had he lived, into an opportunity to improve the lives of disabled children. With a mock airline jetway, a space station, a "Ship of Dreams," and a mini-bicycle city, Shane's Inspiration allows all those who once couldn't, realize they now can.

4800 CRYSTAL SPRINGS ROAD (IN GRIFFITH PARK) IN LOS ANGELES. 323-913-4688.
www.shanesinspiration.org

608. Watch the balls fly at **Holmby Park.**

Located within one of the most expensive residential areas in Los Angeles, you'll find the idyllic Holmby Park. Meticulously maintained, this 8.5-acre park is one of the nicest in the city. It's home to the Holmby Park Lawn Bowling Club, which offers free lessons Tuesdays, Thursdays, and Saturdays, with free use of its equipment, and the par-three (eighteen-hole) Armand Hammer golf course. If you're in the mood to stretch your legs, follow the paths that circle around the park for some lovely views, but be sure to keep your eyes peeled and your reflexes sharp for wayward golf balls.

601 CLUB VIEW DRIVE IN HOLMBY HILLS.

→ ***DID YOU KNOW?:*** *You can see the Spelling Manor aka The Manor, which overlooks the park. Built for television producer Aaron Spelling (*The Mod Squad*,* Dynasty*,* Charlie's Angels*, and* Beverly Hills 90210*), it's the largest home in Los Angeles and was once the most expensive in the country with a $150-million price tag in 2009. It sold in 2011 for $85 million to Formula One heiress Petra Ecclestone.*

609. Investigate the old **Griffith Park Zoo.**

It's quiet in this secluded canyon area tucked away in Griffith Park, where the old zoo resides. Originally built in 1912, it was abandoned several decades later, when the animal collection outgrew the site, and relocated to the zoo's current location (p. 23). Now it's just a spooky but beautiful abandoned space with grubby, dark cages set amid boulder-lined grottoes that once housed their fair share of wild beasts. Tap into your inner detective like Fred and Velma of Mystery Inc. and discover the secrets of this reportedly haunted zoo (there are rumors of human and animal sacrifices). Look for clues as you walk around the large enclosures, and dare to go up the stairs, which have "zoinks" and "jinkies" written all over them.

4730 CRYSTAL SPRINGS DRIVE (IN GRIFFITH PARK) IN LOS ANGELES. Off Griffith Park Drive just north of the merry-go-round and west of the Wilson golf course.

610. Pay to play in **Lacy Park.**

It's not often you have to pay an admission fee to get into a park that doesn't have the word "amusement" preceding it, but when that park is in San Marino and mansions line the road that leads to its entrance, you begin to understand why. The City Council, to ensure the availability of Lacy Park to its residents and their guests, set up a list of regulations that, among other things, require a permit from City Hall for large functions, govern the length of dogs' leashes, and even dictate how much time you have to clean up after your dog. Don't think it's worth paying $4? Come on a weekday, when gaining access to thirty acres of beautifully maintained grassy fields, six tennis courts, and a charming rose garden is absolutely free. Being a resident does have its benefits, especially if you live in San Marino.

1485 VIRGINIA ROAD IN SAN MARINO. Admission on weekends for non-residents: $4. www.ci.san-marino.ca.us

---

611. Ride a dolphin at La Laguna de San Gabriel at **Vincent Lugo Park.**

Creatures of the sea come to life in this make-believe lagoon playground. Dozens of oversize ocean-themed concrete sculptures, designed by artist Benjamin Dominguez in the 1960s, are as fun as they are noteworthy. You can crawl over a sea serpent, climb and perch on top of a giant octopus, and even slide out of the mouth of a pink whale. If you're looking to actually get wet, there's a one-foot-deep gated pool for kids to splash around in.

CORNER OF WELLS AND RAMONA STREETS IN SAN GABRIEL. 626-308-2875. www.friendsoflalaguna.org. (NOTE: You can also find great examples of Benjamin Dominguez's work at the Atlantis Play Center in Garden Grove. 13630 ATLANTIS WAY IN GARDEN GROVE. 714-892-6015. www.ci.garden-grove.ca.us/?q=commserv/atlantis.)

---

612. Go watch a cricket match in **Woodley Park.**

England's version of baseball has its own home in Los Angeles at the Leo Magnus Cricket Complex. Considered the best cricket field in the country, where the top clubs in L.A. come to play, visitors can try their hand at deciphering the sport. Yes, it's a bat-and-ball game played between two teams, but that's pretty much where the similarities end. If you're interested in learning or watching a game, come during cricket season, when you'll find all five fields crowded with players—international and local—and the sidelines packed with cricket lovers. Just sit next to one, ask a few questions and the next thing you know you'll be getting your own personal over-by-over commentary in Cricket 101.

6350 WOODLEY AVENUE IN VAN NUYS. 818-756-8060. www.laparks.org/dos/parks/facility/woodleypk.htm

---

613. Play a basketball game with a view at **Briarwood Park.**

Head up the steep path near the park's entrance and you'll find the outdoor basketball court. The court, nestled in this scenic location, is surrounded by nature. Granted, it might not make for the best basketball game of your life, as the court is

sporadically maintained—but at least you won't feel as bad when you throw an air ball. You were distracted by the view; we understand...
461 ALMADEN COURT IN LOS ANGELES. 310-840-2186. www.laparks.org

---

614. Ditch the art inside the Getty Center and head outside to the **Central Garden.**

When you feel as if your brain can't handle any more art as you go from gallery to gallery, head out to the Central Garden for a breather. Out here, no two visits are ever the same, as everything is constantly changing and new vegetation is often added. It's all part of artist Robert Irwin's original concept—he created the garden as a reminder of the power of nature. Go see the floating azalea maze pond and the specialty gardens that surround it, watch the waterfall, or walk around the outdoor sculpture garden and admire works by René Magritte, Barbara Hepworth, Henry Moore, and William Turnbull. Or just rest under the bougainvillea arbors in the garden plaza and enjoy the view.
1200 GETTY CENTER DRIVE IN BRENTWOOD. 310- 440-7300. www.getty.edu

---

Cinema al Fresco

Los Angeles's answer to the classic small-town drive-in are the summer movie series shown in different parks around town. They're one of the most universally beloved of the city's activities—a fun and easy way to spend a few hours outdoors.

615. *Outdoor Cinema Food Fest.* This movable movie feast takes place during the summer. Outdoor movies, live music, and a slew of gourmet trucks rotate to various locations throughout Los Angeles, providing diverse and cool environments for everyone to kick back and relax while watching a movie on the largest outdoor screen on the West Coast (three stories tall and fifty-two feet wide). It makes for a fun viewing with lots of people. And of course, there's no need to bring food—the fest provides the ultimate picnic, with your choice of top-quality food truck vendors. Various locations. Every Saturday during the summer.
eatseehear.com.

616. *Movies on the Terrace at the Westfield Century City Mall.* Take a break from spending all your hard-earned money shopping by grabbing a seat on the outdoor terrace and watching a free film. Every Wednesday, shoppers at the Westfield Century City Mall can eat, drink, or just relax while indulging in possibly the only free thing there: a movie screening in the outdoor dining area. And though they don't show any of the new flicks being screened at the mall's theater, at least they're cheaper than the $15 you would have spent inside.

10250 SANTA MONICA BOULEVARD IN CENTURY CITY. Wednesdays. 310-277-3898. www.westfield.com/centurycity

617. *Sunday Summer Cinema at the W Hotel in Westwood* Indulge your inner movie star as you lounge in comfort in the "backyard," sipping drinks and nibbling on snacks while watching a flick at the W in Westwood. Head over early to score one of the coveted poolside cabanas.

930 HILGARD AVENUE IN LOS ANGELES. Doors open 7 p.m., movies start at sunset. 310- 208-8765. www.wlosangeles.com/movienight

618. *Pershing Square Friday Night Flicks* Every Friday night, when commuters head home and traffic dies down, head over to Pershing Square (pp. 37 and 235), in the middle of downtown LA, to watch a free movie surrounded by skyscrapers. On top of the usual fare, they've added a "Summer *Camp* Series" to their calendar, showcasing films that feature overacting and are sure to cause laughs as well as moans.

532 SOUTH OLIVE STREET IN LOS ANGELES. Fridays (July–October), after 8 p.m. 213-847-4970. www.laparks.org

619. Make like Tarzan in the Jungle Garden at the **Huntington Library's Botanical Gardens**.

The high forest canopy alone signals the drastic change in the environment. As you walk among the understory filled with shrubs, bromeliads, ferns, and leaves so big they could double as umbrellas, you feel as if you should be wearing khakis and a pith helmet while cutting back the dense foliage with a machete. If swinging from the vines seems tempting, just think of George of the Jungle to fight off the urge.

1151 OXFORD ROAD IN SAN MARINO. Check Web site for summer hours and additional admission information. 626-405-2100. www.huntington.org

620. While you're at the Huntington, expose your kids to the elements at the **Children's Garden**.

Earth, fire, air, and water—the science behind the four elements is on display for kids to explore and investigate. Kids can walk or run through the Rainbow Room to see what happens when light shines through a prism, observe the effects of sound waves as they cause ripples across the Sonic Pool, or play with magnetic sand and learn about force fields while creating neat designs. The coolest section is the Fog Grotto, where one hundred high-pressure nozzles create swirling clouds of fog. If your kids get a little hyper, take a walk with them and sniff out the soothing aromas of plants such as rosemary and lavender in the Fragrance Garden. A trip here should help answer a lot of those "How come?" questions they're always asking, or at least wear them out for the ride home.

Check Web site for summer hours and additional admissions information. 626-405-2100. www.huntington.org

---

621. Beware "the watchful eyes of Argus" at the **Los Angeles County Arboretum and Botanic Garden**.

This 127-acre arboretum might be smaller than the Huntington Library's Botanical Gardens, but that doesn't mean you'll find any less of an array of things to do and view. Opened in 1956 on land jointly purchased by California and Los Angeles around Lucky Baldwin's original development site of the modern-day Arcadia, the arboretum is home to exotic towering trees, a turtle-filled lake, the Queen Anne House (an ornately decorated and reportedly haunted Victorian gem), a waterfall, a "house" made of intertwined branches, and vegetation from all over the world. The gardens, grouped geographically, feature plants from the Americas, the Mediterranean, Australia, and Asia—each section is an environment unto itself. When walking under the native oaks or having a relaxing picnic on Bauer Lawn, keep an eye out for the ample number peafowls that roam free on the grounds. Original descendants of the birds imported from India by Baldwin in 1880, these beautiful creatures have a tendency to peck and chase. And during mating season, when the males have their beautifully iridescent plumage out on full display, they also like to surprise you with an ear-shattering shriek, for good measure.

301 NORTH BALDWIN AVENUE IN ARCADIA. 626-821-3222. www.arboretum.org

→ ***DID YOU KNOW?:*** *According to Greek mythology, the eyes on a peacock's tail come from Argus, Hera's watchful servant. With one hundred eyes that were always on alert, he was in charge of guarding Zeus's lover Io. In order to free Io, Zeus ordered Hermes to kill Argus. He put his eyes to sleep and then slew him with a rock. Hera took Argus's eyes and placed them upon the peacock's feather in his memory.*

622. Swim with the fishes at **La Jolla Underwater Park and Ecological Reserve.**

Not all parks are on dry land and down in San Diego, you'll find this 6,000-acre park/refuge underwater. This ocean playground, with two artificial reefs, two underwater canyons, and a kelp forest is a great place to snorkel and scuba dive.

www.sandiego.gov/lifeguards/beaches/shores.shtml or www.sandiegobikeandkayaktours.com

623. Go fly-fishing in **Deep Creek.**

Cast a fly out into this state-designated wild trout stream and patiently wait to reel in your catch. Located in the San Bernardino Mountains, this serene and picturesque creek flows year-round, and offers up two types of trout—rainbow and brown. Deep Creek is the perfect place for those who love to catch and release as it has a two-fish limit that is strictly enforced.

909-337-2444. www.deepcreekflyfishers.org/about-us/about-deep-creek

624. When you're done fishing, head down to **Deep Creek Hot Springs** for a good soak.

On the less-traveled northern face of the San Bernardino Mountains, down toward the privately owned Bowen Ranch, for just $5 per person and a two-mile trek (hiking shoes recommended), you can sit in the hot mineral springs that flow through a series of man-made terraced pools along Deep Creek. Be sure to bring enough drinking water for your hike, as consumption of spring water is not recommended and potentially dangerous. Camping is not permitted near the springs so you'll have to head back to Bowen Ranch where it's $10 to camp overnight. Check Web site for directions and additional information on curfew and nudity.

Deepcreekhotsprings.com and www.deepcreekvolunteers.com

625. Learn how to water-ski at the **McKenzie Water Ski School.**

When Memorial Day weekend hits Lake Arrowhead Village, you know it's time to get wet. Open to people of all ages, the McKenzie Water Ski School will teach you the basics—including the ever important standing up on your skis—during a beginner lesson on a two-mile course for $55. Whatever skills you're looking to master on water, McKenzie is here to teach. Soon you'll be hotdogging all over the lake with your newfound bag of tricks. Sure, Jesus could walk on water, but he never carved it up like this. Those not looking to get wet, but still looking to spend time on the water, can take a cruise around Lake Arrowhead in a ski boat. (Even better, make a special reservation for a sunset cruise.)

LAKE ARROWHEAD VILLAGE IN LAKE ARROWHEAD. Water Ski season runs from Memorial Day weekend in May to the end of September. 909-337-3814 (reservations and information); 909-214-4917 (reservations after hours). www.mckenziewaterskischool.com

---

626. Come worship the wind at **Cabrillo Beach**.

Head toward the San Pedro shoreline to Hurricane Gulch, a fitting nickname for an area that consistently gets strong winds. When the conditions are just right, you'll find the waters crowded with colorful windsurfer rigs. When wind and surf are perfect, speeds can reach 25 m.p.h. and higher.

3720 STEPHEN M. WHITE DRIVE IN SAN PEDRO. www.sanpedro.com/sp_point/cbrobch.htm

---

627. Sunbathe *au naturel* at **More Mesa** in Santa Barbara.

Buffered by more than two hundred acres of undeveloped land and plenty of boulders, you'll be able to enjoy the warmth of the sun all over your body on these soft, sandy shores. Not brave enough to strip all the way down? Try going topless to avoid some of those pesky tan lines. To get to the nude section of More Mesa, avoid the steep trail to the beach and walk farther along for twenty minutes to find the stairs. Make a right at the bottom, and stay north of the trail to avoid being fined or hassled. NOTE: Tar is found along the shore. To remove from skin, use any oil-based substance.

***PUENTE DRIVE NEAR MOCKINGBIRD LANE IN SANTA BARBARA.
wanr.earthbiz.net/MoreMesaDirections.html***

---

628. Kayak to a Starbucks in **Alamitos Bay**.

Rent a kayak and head out on the water for a trip that's more peaceful than driving and has better views. Alamitos Bay provides flat and calm conditions perfect for paddling around and enjoying the outdoors, with sightings of seasonal moon jelly and wild birds that inhabit the area. Afterward, head over to the Naples Island Canals, located just across the way. These recreational waterways make a complete circle through the center of the island and have several restaurants and shops you can kayak directly up to. All you have to do is tie up your kayak in the proper designated area and disembark. Kayak rentals require that you know how to swim.

5411 EAST OCEAN BOULEVARD IN LONG BEACH. 562-434-0999. www.kayakrentals.net

629. Kayak through the Painted Cave on **Santa Cruz Island**.

Take a ferry from Santa Barbara Harbor and head to California's biggest island, home to the largest and deepest sea cave in the world (nearly a quarter mile long and one hundred feet wide). At the Painted Cave, named for its colorful walls, explorers can paddle or float down into its deepest, darkest chambers. For those worried about getting "trapped," visit in the spring when a waterfall flows over the entrance/exit. The cave can be difficult to access due to the Nature Conservancy, which owns and manages the northwest portion of the island where it's located, so it's best to go through a travel company.

Stand-up paddle boarding, snorkeling, and fishing are optional. 805-899-4925. www.channelislandso.com/painted-cave-kayaking.php

Outdoor Music

Like the movies, outdoor concerts are an excellent way to enjoy nature in an urban environment. On evenings and weekends during warmer months, it's hard to find a park or public space that doesn't have some music going on, with informal performances by musicians of all kinds playing for your aural enjoyment. And of course, many parks and public outdoor spaces have extensive organized concert series.

630. *Jazz at LACMA:* Already well into its twentieth season, Jazz at LACMA, the museum's free outdoor concert series, is a Los Angeles music staple. Every Friday night from April till November, you can come check out jazz legends as well as emerging artists performing at the BP Grand Entrance as you sit back and enjoy a drink at the Stark Bar.

5905 WILSHIRE BOULEVARD IN LOS ANGELES. 323-857-6000. www.lacma.org

631. *Grand Performances at California Plaza:* This free downtown series showcases artistic happenings in and around L.A. with a fun and eclectic lineup of music, film, dance, and theater. Arrive early to get your choice of seats, as they tend to fill up. To avoid having your view obstructed by fellow attendees who love to dance, head higher up in the bleachers. And though it's summer, it can still get pretty chilly at night, so bringing a blanket or jacket is recommended.

350 SOUTH GRAND AVENUE AT WEST 3RD STREET IN DOWNTOWN LOS ANGELES. 213-687-2159. www.grandperformances.org

632. *Grand Performances' Lunch Box Series:* This Friday series offers a free hour of music at noon for everyone. See above for information.

633. *Hollywood Forever Cemetery:* Nowhere else in Los Angeles do musicians come to play for the living and the dead. Belle and Sebastian, Bon Iver, and the Flaming Lips have taken the stage at Fairbanks Lawn to perform at this unique concert venue. Troubadour booking agent Brian Smith and Hollywood Forever's Jay Boileau continue to line up stellar performances, finding acts that mesh perfectly with the intimate and special environment. Come with blankets and picnic baskets in hand and experience the magic. NOTE: Concerts are also held inside at the Masonic Lodge.
6000 SANTA MONIC BOULEVARD IN HOLLYWOOD. 323 469 1181. www.hollywoodforever.com

634. *UCLA JazzReggae Festival:* Every year, UCLA hosts a two-day outdoor concert on the Intramural Field. This event, entirely organized by students, showcases some of the best names in jazz and reggae. Come on both Jam Day and Reggae Day to experience a diverse mix of jazz, hip-hop, indie rock, and reggae—with the likes of Lupe Fiasco, the Miguel Atwood-Ferguson Ensemble, Tanya Stephens, the Wailing Souls, Bilal, and Little Dragon. Amazing performances, live art demonstrations, and a diverse crowd make this event a great way to kick off your summer. While you're here, head by the sustainability tent, where you can pick up a few tips on how to make your time at the JazzReggae Festival a little greener.
405 HILGARD AVENUE (AT UCLA) IN LOS ANGELES. Memorial Day weekend. www.jazzreggaefest.com

635. *Griffith Park Free Shakespeare Festival:* Hark! For outdoor theater head to Griffith Park to watch the internationally renowned Independent Shakespeare Co. perform the works of that brilliant master playwright William Shakespeare. Here, under the nighttime sky at the height of summer, you can enjoy some of Shakespeare's finest works for free. Pack a picnic full of cakes, ale, short-legged hens, a joint of mutton, and good wine, bring a blanket, and spend an evening with friends and family. Only a visit from Oberon and Titania themselves could make the night even better.
GRIFFITH PARK, 4730 CRYSTAL SPRINGS DRIVE IN LOS ANGELES. July–August. 213-479-0952. www.iscla.org

636. *Shakespeare by the Sea:* This annual series of Shakespeare performances is set in an outdoor theater overlooking the Pacific, among other venues. Here you'll observe that Shakespeare's genius is almost as boundless as the sea, and discover that your love for his works is just as deep. Seating is on a first-come, first-served basis.

June–August. 310-217-7596. www.shakespearebythesea.org

637. *Eagle Rock Music Festival:* Taking over several blocks of Colorado Boulevard in Eagle Rock isn't the hard part—it's trying to narrow down who to go see (one day just isn't enough). Members of L.A.'s underground music scene head here to perform for the crowds and support their community every October. With local musicians and musical collaboratives like Mochilla, Dublab, and Low End Theory taking turns rocking out for the crowds on three stages, you can bet everyone will have a great time.

ON COLORADO BOULEVARD BETWEEN ARGUS AND EAGLE ROCK BOULEVARD. cfaer.org/eagle-rock-music-festival or www.myspace.com/eaglerockmusicfestival

638. *Coachella:* This festival is the perfect place to kill numerous musical birds with one stone, so head to the Empire Polo Club in Indio and try to see as many of your favorite bands as humanly possible. Though it's technically not in Los Angeles, we've made an exception for Coachella, which takes place in the Colorado Desert, due to its legendary status as literally and figuratively the hottest music festival in Southern California. For six days (the line-up now repeats over two separate weekends) in April, headliners and emerging talents from all over the world play for your viewing and listening pleasure. Major groups have had reunions here and others have had meltdowns; one deceased artist was even resurrected as a 3D hologram. And with consistently strong line-ups, this festival always incites sheer pandemonium. Sure, three days packed with music and parties sounds tough and you might end up fighting your way through crowds, suffering from sunstroke, and not bathing, but for a Coachella experience, it's worth it. Note: While you're in the Indio area, be sure to try a sweet, delicious date milkshake. Dates are the star produce in the Coachella Valley, which produces 95 percent of the dates sold in the United States.

EMPIRE POLO CLUB, 81-800 AVENUE 51 IN INDIO. www.coachella.com

639. *Indie West Fest:* If you're tired of the mainstream and want to discover something new, head to Ventura and tap into the Indie West Fest.

Established artists perform alongside emerging acts, and here, their top priority is playing for their fans.
VENTURA THEATER, 26 SOUTH CHESTNUT STREET IN VENTURA. Every summer. indiewestfest.com

640. *Pershing Square Summer Series:* This series of free concerts and performances at Pershing Square in July and August is quickly becoming a major event in downtown LA. One of the highlights is the music performances curated by Spaceland Productions (Echoplex, the Echo, Malo), veterans of the city's alternative music scene, on Thursday nights.
532 SOUTH OLIVE STREET IN LOS ANGELES. July–August. 213-847-4970. www.laparks.org/pershingsquare

641. *Skirball Cultural Center's Sunset Concerts:* More than one thousand visitors head to the Skirball (p. 132) each week during the summer for their free Sunset Concerts series. On six Thursdays in July and August, you'll find a diverse lineup of artists from around the globe serenading the crowd in the outdoor courtyard. Make the moment even more memorable and join in on the merriment and music-making by bringing your own instruments.
2701 NORTH SEPULVEDA BOULEVARD IN LOS ANGELES. July–August. 310-440-4500. www.skirball.org

642. *Mariachi Festival:* Every year in Boyle Heights, mariachi musicians gather to perform at the Mariachi Festival, a free event. Originally from Jalisco, Mexico, mariachi music has found a home in the thriving Latino population of East L.A. Each November, international and local groups alike come to Mariachi Plaza, a neighborhood landmark, and perform for a full day. Men and women dressed in silver-studded and beautifully embroidered *charro* outfits, complete with wide-brimmed hats, play a mix of instruments—violin, trumpet, classical guitar, *guitarrón* (a large acoustic bass), and *vihuela* (a high-pitched guitar)—as they sing to the audience that gathers. A visit here will get you in that fiesta mood.
BANDSTAND AT MARIACHI PLAZA, EAST 1ST STREET AND NORTH BOYLE AVENUE IN BOYLE HEIGHTS. www.mariachifestival.info

643. Go on a full-moon hike with **TreePeople**.

Seasoned hikers, laidback walkers, and leisurely strollers head to Coldwater Canyon Park once a month to meet up with TreePeople. This nonprofit group, whose focus is on "helping nature heal our cities," takes nature lovers on a full-moon hike every month. The hour-long excursion is a great way to spend some time outdoors by yourself or with your family. You won't see any bad moons rising over here, but you will be inspired to care more about preservation.

Registration is required. www.treepeople.org

644. Find and sit under the **Giving Tree**.

Author Shel Silverstein's *The Giving Tree* is a classic childhood story about a relationship between a boy and a tree. The tree provides the boy with everything he desires and, in the end, gives itself up to be cut down. Don't worry—this isn't about finding a stump. Instead, you're on the lookout for a large tree with wide spreading branches that look like arms, just waiting to give you a hug. What a way to be embraced by nature! (Keep your eyes peeled as this tree often goes unnoticed.)

hiddenlosangeles.com/adventure-the-giving-tree

645. Celebrate summer for free with **free national park admittance**.

In June, park admission is waived to honor the first day of summer. You'll get free access to Joshua Tree, Death Valley, Yosemite, and more. Mark your calendar, pick a park, and have fun. Thank goodness it's summer.

For more information, including additional fee-free days, go to www.nps.gov/findapark/feefreeparks.htm

646. Find treasures and surprises at the **El Dorado Nature Center**.

The original "Lost City of Gold" was never found by Orellana and Pizarro, but you'll discover this El Dorado in Long Beach. At the entrance, cross over the wooden bridge that spans the lake, and you'll find the riches of nature. The nature center was created in 1965 by re-landscaping nearly one hundred acres of flat farmland and transforming it into an oasis for animal and plant life, with lakes, streams, and forested areas. Along with all the lovely vegetation, a tunnel made of intertwined tree branches, and little critters, you'll also discover that underneath its surface, the lake is teeming with aquatic life. Grab a hiking guide and trail map from the visitor center before embarking on your journey.

7550 EAST SPRING STREET IN LONG BEACH. 562-570-1745. longbeach.gov/naturecenter/default.asp.

647. Swing from the rings at **Venice Beach.**

Indulge your inner gymnast at this outdoor playground just south of Santa Monica Pier. Here you can swing back and forth to test your endurance, rope-climb to the top, and practice making your way across a balance beam without falling off.

VENICE BEACH NEAR SANTA MONICA PIER IN SANTA MONICA.

648. Have a rockin' good time at **Vasquez Rocks.**

The colossal cliff formations that protrude dramatically out of the earth at sloping forty-five degrees in Agua Dulce, just north of L.A., are an unforgettable sight. Named after Tiburcio Vasquez, a bandit known as "the Scourge of California," it's no surprise that he used this spot as his hideout. The rocks, formed by the infamous San Andreas Fault's movements, are not only a perfect hiding place, but also a popular filming location because of their ability to look like another world.

VASQUEZ ROCKS NATURAL AREA AND NATURE CENTER, 10700 WEST ESCONDIDO CANYON ROAD IN AGUA DULCE. 661-268-0840. parks.lacounty.gov

→ ***FACT:*** Star Trek, Bonanza, A Single Man, *and* Planet of the Apes *are among the TV shows and movies that have shot there.*

649. Beware the bees at the **Cave of Munits, a.k.a. the Bat Cave.**

According to legend, this cave was once the home of a Chumash shaman (hence the cave's other moniker: Shaman Cave) who met his end after murdering the son of a tribal chief. Located on the edge of El Escorpion Park in the Upper Las Virgenes Canyon Open Space Preserve (formerly Ahmanson Ranch), a narrow entrance leads into a huge cave. With its rugged and worn edges, large crevices, and the light that shines down through the openings above casting an eerie glow—it's easy to see why people still claim to feel the shaman's presence. The hive of bees guarding the entrance also adds to the lore.

UPPER LAS VIRGENES CANYON OPEN PRESERVE.
www.lamountains.com/parks.asp?parkid=28

→ ***FACT:*** *The Chumash are a Native American people who have lived in central and southern California for several millennia, with some settlements dating back at least ten thousand years.*

650. Get your toes wet at **Sturtevant Falls.**

Angeles National Forest is full of waterfalls, but Sturtevant in Arcadia's Santa Anita Canyon is one of its finest. Take Santa Anita Avenue north to Chantry Flats Road, and on to the parking lot and trailhead inside the forest. From there, begin your hike by heading toward Roberts Camp, a quaint collection of cabins. Then rock- and river-hop the rest of the way till you find yourself at the beautiful Sturtevant Falls. Relax and refresh while dipping your feet in the cool waters below the falls before heading back. Don't forget to pack a picnic, and get a National Forest Adventure Pass to park near the falls.

www.modernhiker.com and www.fs.usda.gov/angeles

Golf

Some head to the hills and some to the courts, but a lot of people head to the greens. Chip a birdie, putt, yell out "Fore!"—even if your handicap is higher than most, you'll still have a memorable time. Weekdays are best—fees are lower, crowds are lighter.

651. ***Trump National Golf Club.*** With a stunning view of the Pacific, an eighteen-hole round here can run $275. Did you expect anything less from the Donald?

1 TRUMP NATIONAL DRIVE IN RANCHO PALOS VERDES. 310-265-5000; www.trumpnationallosangeles.com

652. ***Angeles National Golf Course.*** The course features legendary golfer Jack Nicklaus's signature left-to-right play and is easy enough to maneuver on that you might reconsider your handicap. Carts have GPS systems, and bringing extra balls is recommended—you're not allowed to search for any lost balls in the protected wilderness. Considering playing here often? Sign up for the loyalty program to save money.

9401 FOOTHILL BOULEVARD IN SUNLAND. 818-951-8771. www.angelesnational.com

653. ***Roosevelt Golf Course.*** You'll get challenges and views galore on this nine-hole course in Griffith Park. See a panoramic view of downtown at the sixth hole, the Observatory at the eighth, and a glimpse of the Ennis House (p. 40) to round it all out.

2650 NORTH VERMONT AVENUE IN LOS ANGELES, 323-665-2011. www.ci.la.ca.us/rap/golf/index.htm

654. *Aroma Wilshire Center golf range.* Perfect your swing in the heart of Koreatown. This multilevel, 150-yard driving range is the largest outdoor venue of its kind in the city and is completely state-of-the-art. Its automated tee-up system means you'll never have to break your form to bend over and place a ball on the tee again.
3680 WILSHIRE BOULEVARD IN LOS ANGELES. 213-387-0111.
www.aromaresort.com

655. *Sherman Oaks Castle Park.* If you're more about decor and kitschy architecture than the landscaping of the greens, then head to Castle Park. Play on one of the three eighteen-hole courses in what feels like the golfing equivalent of Disneyland.
4989 SEPULVEDA BOULEVARD IN SHERMAN OAKS. 818-756-9459.
www.laparks.org

656. If you're looking for a leg-busting hike, head to **Mount Baldy**.

For serious hikers, a trek up Mount Baldy, the highest peak in Angeles National Forest, is a must. It's a ten-mile journey to the top, and along the way you'll pass the San Antonio Falls and venture through the treacherous Devil's Backbone Trail. For those less avid hikers who still appreciate a good view, take a ride up on the Sugar Pine Chair Lift. It'll reduce your hike by around three miles and drop you off on Baldy Notch, where the Top of the Notch restaurant is located. NOTE: It's best to refrain from hiking Mount Baldy when there's ice and snow to avoid any accidents. Also dress in layers, as temperature zones during your hike can vary as dramatically as the views.
701 NORTH SANTA ANITA AVENUE IN ARCADIA. 626-574-1613. www.fs.usda.gov/angeles; www.mtbaldyskilifts.com

657. Climb the *other* **Eagle Rock**.

Don't confuse this Eagle Rock with the neighborhood. You'll find this particular Eagle Rock, a mammoth cliff overhang, jutting out over the Topanga Canyon. Climbing up is not for the faint of heart, and the rock could give someone acrophobia just by looking at it, but if you can muster the courage and make your way to the top, you'll be rewarded with one killer view.
TOPANGA STATE PARK. 310-455-2465. www.parks.ca.gov/?page_id=629

658. Get high for free at the **Orange County Great Park.**

Thursday to Sunday, the park offers free rides in a hot-air balloon that can hold twenty-five to thirty people and flies up to four hundred feet in the air. The balloon doesn't go anywhere but up—it's tethered to the ground—but you'll still get an awesome view. First come, first served.

866-829-3829. www.ocgp.org/visit/balloon

659. Have the hot-air balloon come to you, with **Dreams Unlimited.**

You don't really see hot-air balloons in the city. In fact, as a rule, they steer clear, preferring less-congested areas, reducing the likelihood of hitting power lines and getting electrocuted. Not a good look. But Dreams Unlimited isn't like other companies—they're willing to come to you and take off from your lawn. For around an hour they'll fly you and four other passengers ten thousand feet above the ground to soar amid the clouds. Watch for the chase trucks that follow in hot pursuit and take you home after your high-flying adventure is done. In order for Dreams Unlimited to launch from your lawn, it has to be at least three hundred feet by three hundred feet, with no trees or power lines close by. Time to pull out the ruler and start measuring.

14210 CHOLAME ROAD IN VICTORVILLE. 800-246-8247.

660. Take a leap off of **Nowhere.**

Up East Fork Road in the San Gabriel Mountains, you'll find the Bridge to Nowhere. And since you have nowhere to go on the bridge except down, here's your chance to take a dive. Bungee America uses this abandoned bridge as its launching pad. For $70 you can take the plunge headfirst into the wild.

www.bungeeamerica.com

661. Defy gravity—or at least try to—at the **Venice Skate Park.**

Between the boardwalk and the sea you'll find a skating sanctuary, a throwback to the days when Tony Alva and Stacy Peralta skated in empty pools. Generations old and new come and continue that grand tradition here—skaters swoop in and out of the bowls and flip a few tricks, and once in a while you'll hear the slapping of boards against the ledge as they sound their approval of a good run. Some come to skate, others to watch, and when the light is right, you get a perfect picture of Venice as they float up and silhouette against the setting sun.

1800 OCEAN FRONT IN VENICE

→ **FACT:** *The palm trees synonymous with Southern California aren't native to these parts. They were originally imported to beautify our streets, and soon became one of our most famous calling cards. The city grows more than twenty-five different varieties, and most of the palm trees in Las Vegas are grown here and shipped.*

DAY TRIP

Los Angeles is a great city to visit, but sometimes even the most die-hard Angelenos need a bit of a break. If you're not looking to venture out too far and only have a day or two to spare, why not take a day trip? They're fun and full of adventure, so go explore!

662. *Take a day trip to San Simeon and Cambria.* See two amazing places in one trip by heading to San Simeon and Cambria. These two coastal towns, located minutes from each other, make the four-hour journey by car worth the drive. In San Simeon, visit the palatial ***Hearst Castle.*** Former *Harper's Bazaar* fashion editor Diana Vreeland joked in her autobiography that she was paid so little while working at the magazine (owned by Hearst Corporation) because "San Simeon must have been where the Hearst money went, I certainly never saw any of it." What began as a plan to build a bungalow so wealthy newspaper magnate William Randolph Hearst wouldn't have to camp in tents anymore up on the hill, turned into something more. Instead, he built a castle on his 250,000-acre estate. (That's almost half the size of Joshua Tree National Park.) "La Cuesta Encantada" or "The Ranch," as it was commonly referred to, features more than one hundred rooms, 127 acres of gardens, indoor and outdoor swimming pools, a movie theater, an airfield, the world's largest private zoo (now empty), and even real gold tiles in the pool room. One of the highlights is the outdoor Neptune Pool. Located near the edge of the hilltop, this painstakingly designed pool (it was rebuilt three times, until Hearst was satisfied) features four seventeenth-century Italian bas-reliefs on the sides of the colonnades, holds 345,000 gallons of water, and offers awe-inspiring views. Book an Experience Tour for $24 ($12 for children), which includes a short documentary IMAX film on William Randolph Hearst. In Cambria, visit the polar opposite of Hearst Castle, ***Nitt Witt Ridge***. Where Hearst Castle is over-the-top and filled with opulence and was constructed using only the best building materials and decorated with only the finest furnishings, Nitt Witt Ridge is a house made from salvaged junk. Artist and recluse Arthur "Art" Beal spent fifty years making his "castle on a hill" with the aid of a pick and a shovel. As Cambria's garbage collector, he found his materials in what the town threw out, and also used items found in surrounding forests and beaches—even, reportedly, remnants from the construction of Hearst Castle. Shells, toilet seats, car parts—you name it, he used it to build his home. Reservations required. The $10 tour includes a four-minute video.

HEARST CASTLE: 750 HEARST CASTLE ROAD IN SAN SIMEON. 800-444-4445. www.hearstcastle.org. NITT WITT RIDGE: 881 HILLCREST DRIVE IN CAMBRIA. 805-927-2690.

→ **FACT:** *Luminaries and stars from all over the world—including Charlie Chaplin, Franklin D. Roosevelt, Joan Crawford, Charles Lindberg, Winston Churchill, and Clark Gable—stayed at Hearst Castle. It was also the inspiration for the Xanadu mansion in Orson Welles's* Citizen Kane.

---

663. Also near San Simeon, you'll ***find the Piedras Blancas rookery***, home to around fifteen thousand northern elephant seals—named for the large elongated snout of the adult male that resembles an elephant's trunk. At any given time, hundreds of these blubbery creatures can be found along the shores, sleeping and working on their tans. They're there year-round, but the biggest groups are from mid-April to mid-May.

HIGHWAY 1, FOUR MILES NORTH OF HEARST CASTLE. www.elephantseal.org

---

664. *Take a fairytale trip to Solvang.* Fans of Hans Christian Andersen and all things Danish will love visiting this village—whose name means "sunny fields"—just fifty minutes north of Santa Barbara. Solvang was founded in 1911 by a group of Danes traveling to set up a colony far away from the bitter winters of the Midwest. They settled in the Santa Ynez Valley and brought a taste of Denmark to California. You'll find Danish-style architecture as well as replicas of Copenhagen's Round Tower and the famous Little Mermaid statue in the town center. And don't worry; they didn't forget the windmill. Spend a day enjoying Danish music and folk dancing, eating Danish specialties available at the many bakeries and restaurants, and getting a feel for what inspired famed fairy-tale author Hans Christian Andersen to pen all those marvelous stories. Visit in September to attend Solvang's annual Danish Days Festival, already in its 77th year. Just outside the town center, which is less Denmark-centric, you can also visit the Quicksilver Ranch; there they raise miniature horses, and it's free to visit. You'll also find Ostrich Land close by, where for $5 ($4 for admission, $1 for food) you can feed the ostriches and emus. Be careful: they bite.

www.solvangusa.com.

665. *Go see the swallows at Mission San Juan Capistrano.* You first encountered stories about the missions of California back in elementary school. But since then, actually going to visit one hasn't been high on your to-do list—until now. Originally erected to spread the Christian faith among Native Americans, missions are now popular travel destinations. And since this is your first mission experience, you might as well start off with the most popular, Mission San Juan Capistrano. The mission has remained an active site since it was established back in 1776. Visitors can spend hours walking around the grounds, visiting the gardens, and viewing the extensive and long-standing buildings that have survived the barrage of time, including the oldest building in California, the adobe Serra Chapel. Inside the chapel is a gold-covered altar originally from Barcelona and thought to be more than three hundred years old. But Mission San Juan Capistrano is best known for the swallows that return every year and remake their nests in the chapel. These small birds are celebrated on St. Joseph's Day, March 19, but any day is a good day to come and visit the mission.
26801 ORTEGA HIGHWAY IN SAN JUAN CAPISTRANO. 949-234-1300.
www.missionsjc.com

666. *Travel to the mystical land known as Joshua Tree National Park.* You begin to realize you're not in Kansas anymore when you pull up to this never-ending stretch of wilderness dotted with huge rock temples. The park's mountains and ranges are a result of tectonic plate movement along the San Andreas Fault, and it is home to more than 750 miles of hiking trails and incredibly diverse landscapes, making it the perfect example of the great outdoors. Wander around in the Wonderland Wash and let your imagination run wild—it's filled with "animal"-shaped rock formations that sometimes require some creativity to be seen. Pitch a tent, cool off by a mountain stream, find yourself alone in the serene sandstone canyons, get lost in the palm oases, and try climbing a rock or two. A rock-climbing novice? Head to the Joshua Tree Climbing School for your first "ground course." Soon you'll be bouldering and rappelling off of anything. Temperatures vary during the year and during the day, so dress in layers. Note: Pick up a guidebook from the visitors center so you don't get lost.
74485 NATIONAL PARK DRIVE, TWENTYNINE PALMS. 760-367-5500;
www.nps.gov/jotr/index.htm

667. *Enjoy an evening of stargazing.* If you're more interested in what's going on up above than down below, then you'll love the nighttime sky in Joshua Tree. From late July through August, the sky transforms from an existential void into a Disney light show. During this time, the Perseid meteor shower appears and shoots as many as one hundred meteors every hour. Head toward Ryan Campground, or anywhere in the middle of the park, to avoid the city lights that might divert your attention from the real luminaries at night. And don't forget to check out the sunset, when the sky is transformed into a rainbow of colors.

668. *Go back in time at the Indian Canyons just outside Palm Springs.* With their towering palms, rock formations, and streams, the Indian Canyons looks more like the *Land of the Lost* than the real thing. But one touch will confirm that it is in fact all there. Sadly, it's no longer a well-kept secret—weekenders flock there to hike around the different canyons and explore the ancient surroundings. If you're not a fan of the crowds, and if the swimming hole and waterfall at the end of the popular Murray Canyon prove a little claustrophobic, head up Palm Canyon Trail to Lost Paradise. You'll find pools to swim in, palm trees aplenty, and—since it's an eight-mile hike—a lot fewer people.
760-323-6018. www.theindiancanyons.com; www.hiking-in-ps.com/index.php

669. *Stop by the Elrod House.* While you're in Palm Springs, make it a point to visit this dazzling and distinctive midcentury home designed by John Lautner, Frank Lloyd Wright's former apprentice and the creator of Googie-style architecture. This five-bedroom, six-bath home was built in 1968 for interior designer Arthur Elrod. You might remember its interior and the beautiful women who graced it—the house was used in the James Bond movie *Diamonds Are Forever* (remember Bambi and Thumper?) as well as in numerous *Playboy* shoots. But its exterior is equally memorable. With its enormous domed concrete roof, with wedge-shaped sections cut out to accommodate skylights providing indirect light and shielding the home from the intense desert sun, the structure as a whole emphasizes the relationship between space and nature. A lasting example of Lautner's great architectural style. Private residence; please be courteous.
2175 SOUTHRIDGE DRIVE IN PALM SPRINGS.

670. *Walk the Yellow Brick Road at Salvation Mountain.* South of Joshua Tree near the Salton Sea, in Niland, you'll find the desert's answer to Simon Rodia's Watts Towers (p. 36) in Leonard Knight's Salvation Mountain. This man-made three-story mountain and monument to universal love, emblazoned with the words "God Is Love," has been a labor of . . . love. Knight started on his project in the mid-1980s after failed attempts at his lifelong

goal of launching a hot-air balloon with the same phrase written on it. Instead he focused his attention on building a monument, which led to Salvation Mountain. Using adobe clay, bales of straw, and more than one hundred thousand gallons of paint, he fashioned himself a colorful mountain that sticks out from its bleak surroundings. Walk up the mountain's "yellow brick road," see the different colorfully painted rooms hidden within, go see the hogan (a dome-shaped home), and stop by the museum.
www.salvationmountain.us

671. *Remember to hydrate when visiting Death Valley National Park.* It's the hottest, the driest, the lowest—Death Valley National Park is a land of extremes. Spanning three million acres of wilderness, Death Valley is the very definition of a desert, with snowcapped mountains, water-fluted canyons, and picturesque layers of colored rock. Here you'll also find resilient plants and animals that have adapted to survive the harsh desert weather. During the main visitor season (November through April), park rangers give a variety of talks and guided tours. Catch a glimpse of the transient wildflower population, explore historic mining sites, and if you're game, re-create the famous scene from Michelangelo Antonioni's *Zabriskie Point* that was shot at . . . Zabriskie Point. Schedules for programs change weekly, so call the visitors center for information. Note: While you're here, be sure to visit Dante's View, Eureka Dunes (the tallest sand piles in the state), and the bleakness of the Badwater Basin salt flats (at 282 feet below sea level, it's the lowest point in Death Valley).
760-786-3200. www.nps.gov/deva/index.htm

672. *Hang out at the San Diego Zoo.* Lions, tigers, and bears are great, but if you're looking for a bit more oomph with your zoo experience, then head down to Balboa Park and spend the day at the San Diego Zoo. One hundred acres of land house one of the most progressive zoos in the world. The idea grew out of the exotic animal exhibitions closed after the 1915 Panama-California Exposition. A permanent space was set aside in 1921, and so it began. The zoo has its fair share of special features. It's one of the few zoos in the country that exhibit giant pandas, on long-term loan from China, and it also houses the largest population of albino koalas outside Australia (including the only one born in captivity). It also grows some rare animal food: more than forty types of bamboo for the pandas and eighteen varieties of eucalyptus tree for the koalas. Talk about a smorgasbord! For an up-close and personal encounter with the animals—you can help clean and feed them—book a tour, and take the kids to learn from one of the many educational programs. Since there are more than four thousand animals from eight hundred species, there's plenty to see, so it's best to take the guided tour bus that makes its way through 75 percent of the park and save your energy to explore the remaining 25 percent on foot. You can even get an aerial view by taking the Skyfari gondola lift. Too tired, but still want more? Haven't even made it over to Safari Park? Inquire about a zoo sleepover, which varies in theme. Fans of the Beach Boys and *Citizen Kane* may experience a sense of déjà vu. Parts of Orson Welles's acclaimed movie were filmed here, and it was the setting for various Beach Boys photos, including the cover of *Pet Sounds*.

2920 ZOO DRIVE (in Balboa Park) IN SAN DIEGO. 619-231-1515.
www.sandiegozoo.org

→ **FACT:** *The idea of cageless exhibits with grotto areas left exposed without protective wiring to ensure an open-air feel was pioneered at this zoo.*

673. *See the horses at the Del Mar Thoroughbred Club.* The racetrack built right next to the Pacific is "Where The Turf Meets The Surf." Built in partnership with actor Bing Crosby, Jimmy Durante, and Paramount Pictures, Del Mar has been a destination for horseracing lovers since 1937. Stop by to catch a race, eat trackside, and if you don't have any plans afterwards, stay for a concert.
www.dmtc.com

→ **FACT:** *Del Mar was closed during WWII and used as training grounds for the U.S. Marine Corp. Later it was a manufacturing site for B-17 bomber parts. It was also a frequent hangout for former head of F.B.I., J. Edgar Hoover and his colleague Clyde Tolson. Hoover dined in the Turf Club, located on the fourth floor.*

674. Start off your year one step at a time at the **Santa Monica stairs.**

Many New Year's resolutions involve some ambitious form of exercise—biking, running, hiking, and whatnot. But if all you're looking for is a basic workout that provides you with an ocean breeze, a woodsy scent, and sunshine, then head to the stairs. Yes, climbing these stairs just south of the Pacific Palisades is simple, but it won't be easy. After a few trips up and down, you'll definitely start to feel the burn. And when your legs start to wobble like a newborn calf trying to stand, it's time to take a break.

4TH STREET AND ADELAIDE DRIVE IN SANTA MONICA.

675. If Santa Monica is too much of a trek, head to the **Beachwood stairs.**

Go up and down these historic steps for a grueling workout. Italian stonemasons built these 148 steps (and five other staircases in the area) in 1923 as part of the original design of Hollywoodland, using local granite from the Union Rock Quarry in Bronson Canyon (now the Bronson Caves). Built to appeal to potential homeowners, these stairs now appeal to fitness freaks, who enjoy the challenge of the steep incline. Frequent stair climbers include athletes, locals, nannies, and—as if you need another reason to come here—members of nearby Fire Station 19.

NORTH BEACHWOOD DRIVE AND WOODSHIRE DRIVE IN HOLLYWOOD.
www.beachwoodcanyon.org

676. Go "play" at **Sand Dune Park.**

When you see a big pile of sand, your inner child's first reaction is "Fun!" But at the sand dune in Manhattan Beach, the first thing your body is going to say is "Ow!" People of all ages come to walk, climb, or crawl their way up the one-hundred-foot-high dune to get their blood pumping. You'll work your quads, your calves, and, surprisingly, everything else. Need a moment to catch your breath? Linger at the top and look out at views of the city. And since LAX is close by, you'll spot planes coming and going throughout the day. To climb up the sand dune, it's best to go barefoot or invest in a pair of scuba-diving booties. They work better than tennis shoes filled with sand. Because of neighborhood complaints of overuse and parking issues due to visitors, the city closed the dune for many months. It's now open again, but you must register to visit online and pay an entry fee of $1.

33RD STREET AND BELL AVENUE IN MANHATTAN BEACH. ci.manhattan-beach.ca.us

677. Go running in **Franklin Canyon Park.**

Nestled in a valley below the Hollywood Hills between Sherman Oaks and Beverly Hills, this park boasts historic reservoirs built in 1914 by William Mulholland (p. 63), the duck-filled Heavenly Pond, and lush woods. Ascending the trails to literal heights, past lakes and ponds, gives you a great sense of seclusion and takes you into the Santa Monica Mountains overlooking Century City. At a combined 5.5 miles, these are great long-distance running trails, with gradual inclines so you won't burn out too early.

2600 FRANKLIN CANYON DRIVE IN BEVERLY HILLS. 310-858-7272.
www.lamountains.com/parks.asp?parkid=14

→ ***FACT:*** *A frequent filming location for television and film since the 1930s, Franklin Canyon Park can be seen in* True Blood, Twin Peaks, The Silence of the Lambs, Platoon, *and the opening credits to* The Andy Griffith Show.

678. Take your best-kept friend and set him or her free at **Bailey Canyon Park**.

Being a pooch sure does have its benefits, but none are as great as being let off the leash to go explore. In Bailey Canyon Park, dogs are let loose upon the wilderness of the Sierra Madre mountain ranges. With so many things to see and sniff here, your dog won't know where to begin. Let your four-legged friend have fun and get dirty, and then lead him around the canyon-view nature trail to run along the creek and a few streams to cool off, while you reward yourself with a view of the forty-foot waterfall.

451 WEST CARTER AVENUE IN SIERRA MADRE. 626-355-5278. www.cityofsierramadre.com

679. Dogs can make a splash at **Arroyo Burro Beach**.

It's hard to find a leash-free beach, but Arroyo Burro Beach in Santa Barbara is a rare exception. Here, man's best friend can frolic in the waves and go for a swim. Four-legged freedom never tasted so salty or so sweet.

Take Las Positas off-ramp from the 101 North and turn left. Turn right at road's end. www.countyofsb.org

Go to Disneyland.

During a visit with his wife overseas, Walt Disney went to Copenhagen and visited Tivoli Gardens, the second-oldest amusement park in the world (it was built in 1843), which is said to have inspired Disneyland. Disney even took something that Tivoli founder Georg Carstensen once said—"Tivoli will never, so to speak, be finished"—and adapted it to describe his theme park: "Disneyland will never be finished as long as there is imagination left in the world."

And who doesn't want to visit a world filled with imagination? For any kid, or even just kids at heart, a trip to the "Happiest Place on Earth" is a dream come true, but navigating it in one day can wear down even the biggest fan. Here are the twelve must-dos for visitors to the magic kingdom."

680. *Celebrate by starting off on the right foot!* Is it your birthday? Did you just get married? Are you celebrating another anniversary? Head to City Hall and get a free button to mark the occasion—and, for birthdays, a special call from Goofy. Even if you aren't visiting for a special event, you can still get an "I'm Celebrating" button to let everyone know you're here to have a good time.

681. *Take advantage of the FastPass.* This system allows you to pick up a ticket and come back at a set time to bypass the long lines. Wait times are reduced significantly for the more popular rides.

682. *Head to the Enchanted Tiki Room in Adventureland.* The Enchanted Tiki Room is classic Disneyland. Created by Walt Disney to translate film animation to the real world, the once groundbreaking audio animatronic technology, which has captivated audiences since this attraction opened in 1963, has remained relatively untouched, adding to the overall charm. Inside this South Seas–inspired paradise, you'll be serenaded for fifteen minutes by macaws, toucans, cockatoos, tiki statues, and more—over 225 animatronic performers. Feel free to lend your voice and sing along while you're in the "Tiki Tiki Tiki Tiki Tiki Room." Note: While waiting for the next show, purchase a delicious Pineapple Dole Whip from the Tiki Juice Bar and use the restrooms located in the waiting area. They're never really busy.

683. *Find the entrance to Club 33.* In New Orleans Square, near the exit from Pirates of the Caribbean, you'll find the doorway to Disneyland's exclusive members-only club. Opened in 1967, Club 33 has hosted presidents, dignitaries, and other special guests in its beautifully decorated five-star restaurant, bar, and lounge filled with rare Disney memorabilia. How do you become a member? The waiting list for club membership is currently closed, and names already on the list can take up to fourteen years to process. But if you're willing to wait, email: club33interest@disneyland.com for more info.

CLUB 33, ROYAL STREET, NEW ORLEANS SQUARE. www.disneylandclub33.com

684. *Ride the Big Thunder Mountain Railroad in Frontierland* during the day—and at night. There's nothing like riding an outdoor high-speed roller coaster to put you in a good mood. Surround yourself with the American West, inspired by Utah's Bryce Canyon, and brace yourself for the fast and tight turns. Come back at night to experience a different side of the Big Thunder. Nothing feels better than the cool evening wind whipping through your hair.

→ ***FACT:*** *This rollercoaster cost $16 million to build, almost the total cost of all the original Disneyland attractions combined.*

685. *Grab a hefty snack.* Look around the Central Plaza, in the middle of Disneyland, for carts with large green umbrellas. Here you'll find giant turkey legs to snack on. Considering all the money you'll spend on food here, this is actually worth the price. Don't forget to try it with salsa.

686. *Enjoy a taste of the future—ride Space Mountain in Tomorrowland.* This popular roller coaster might have opened back in 1977, but it still packs a punch today. Ride along in the dark through galaxies and blaze past stars, all to a spacey soundtrack.

687. *Help Buzz Lightyear and Star Command fight the evil Emperor Zurg at Buzz Lightyear Astro Blasters.* Your whole family will have fun on this interactive ride as you help Buzz dispatch Zurg while racking up as many points as possible.

688. *Strategize.* Make note of what time the Disneyland fireworks begin and stake out a spot near the Central Plaza to watch the projections on Sleeping Beauty Castle at the entrance to Fantasyland.

689. *Make your own memories.* Instead of spending money on the same old souvenirs, create your own with a pocketful of change. Inside various stores along Main Street, you'll find penny machines that can make souvenirs that are fun and cheap. For as little as 51¢ you can walk away with the perfect Disneyland memento.

690. *Buy a year pass.* If you're a local and go to Disneyland more than twice a year, consider paying the extra money to get a yearly pass. The Southern California Select, the cheapest option, allows you to go to Disneyland 170 out of 365 days of the year. A one-day pass to Disneyland alone is $81 for children ages 3–9 and $87 for adults. To get a one-day hopper ticket that allows you into both Disneyland and Disney California Adventure Park is $119 for children and $125 for adults.

691. *Get a room at the Grand Californian.* If you didn't do enough your first time around at Disneyland, why not hang out and go again tomorrow? The Grand Californian is the most expensive of the Disney hotels, but it's also the best. Designed and decorated like an oversize log cabin, the aptly named Grand is big enough for everyone to enjoy. Its back entrance opens onto California Adventure and also puts you steps away from Downtown Disney. You can also get a jump on the crowds the next day, as guests of the Grand can enter Disneyland and California Adventure an hour before the general public. If you're going to go the next day but didn't buy a two-day pass, just head to Guest Services at the end of Main Street near Central Plaza and pay the difference.

DISNEYLAND: 1313 SOUTH DISNEYLAND DRIVE IN ANAHEIM. 714-781-INFO (4636). disneyland.disney.go.com

692. Experience a winter wonderland at **Snow Summit.**

During the winter, when the conditions are just right, snow lovers head to this resort in the San Bernardino Mountains and ski or snowboard down its perfectly powdered hills (it gets the heaviest snowfall in the area).

SNOW SUMMIT MOUNTAIN RESORT. 880 SUMMIT BOULEVARD IN BIG BEAR LAKE. 909-866-5841 (reservations). www.snowsummit.com

693. Take a full-moon horseback ride into the **Santa Monica Mountains.**

Saddle up and head out on a breathtaking ninety-minute horseback ride through the mountains. Experience a different side of the wildlife you normally see during the day as you ride under the glow of a full moon, and glimpse an abundance of nighttime critters coming out to play.

LOS ANGELES HORSEBACK RIDING, 2623 OLD TOPANGA CANYON ROAD IN TOPANGA. 818-591-2032. www.losangeleshorsebackriding.com

694. Go camping in style at **Malibu Creek State Park.**

Some people weren't born to rough it, and luckily you won't have to here. Head out toward the coast for the weekend, set up camp, and enjoy the less-than-rugged facilities, including flushing toilets and coin-operated showers. Enjoy the beautiful landscape filled with oaks and sycamores, and take advantage of the thirty miles of park trail that are just outside your tent door. Early reservations are advised. Ask for site 27; it's got the best shade.

1925 LAS VIRGENES ROAD IN CALABASAS. 818-880-0350. www.malibucreekstatepark.org

695. Have a *Pretty Woman* moment at the **California Polo Club.**

Garry Marshall's 1990 film *Pretty Woman* did a lot of things: it propelled Julia Roberts into the A-list stratosphere and landed her a Golden Globe Award and an Oscar nomination, it introduced us to the pitfalls of mouth kissing, and it gave

moviegoers a taste of the Beverly Hills good life. More than twenty years later, people still come here to walk along Rodeo Drive, look at expensive cars, and eat at fancy restaurants. But what about polo? Although a match was at the heart of a big scene in the movie, polo never seemed to catch on as a spectator sport in Los Angeles. But that'll change once you head over to the California Polo Club and watch your first match. Here you'll see members, various professionals, and guests engage in a proper polo competition much like in the film, but better. Founded in 1995 in the Sylmar district in Los Angeles, the CPC has opened up this complex sport, once reserved for the elite, to the public. Come and enjoy a game, partake in a potluck barbeque, and if you're up for it, take a lesson with one of the club's pros. And yes, to voice your approval, Arsenio Hall fist-pumping is allowed.
11035 OSBORNE STREET (IN SYLMAR) IN LOS ANGELES. 818-558-7656. www.californiapoloclub.com

696. Go exploring with **Friends of the Los Angeles River**.

Want to check out the Glendale Narrows, an interesting section of the L.A. River, but don't want to do it alone? Don't worry. Friends of the Los Angeles River have a Car Caravan Tour guided by author, veteran L.A. River guide, and great storyteller Jenny Price. Head over with a group of fellow explorers to learn about the concrete canyon, see the foliage and wildlife, and enjoy discovering something new about the city. If you'd like to get to know the river up close and personal, take a guided kayak tour. While paddling down reinvigorated portions of the L.A. River in the Valley, including the scenic Sepulveda Basin, you'll learn first hand that there's more to this river than meets the eye. Tickets sell out fast, so book early.
Meet at the Los Angeles River Center and Gardens and form carpools. 570 WEST AVENUE 26, LOS ANGELES. 323-223-0585. mail@folar.org; folar.org; for kayaking information: www.paddlethelariver.org

Outdoor Yoga

In nicer weather, yoga instructors bring their classes outside. For devoted practitioners, these classes offer a change of pace without changing the activity; for newcomers they are a way to try yoga in a setting that may be less intimidating than a studio.

697. *Runyon Canyon Yoga:* Classes take place in a small grove just inside Runyon Canyon Park (p. 79). A rotating roster of instructors, fresh air, and friendly faces make this a great way to spend time outdoors. Note: The Sunday session is the most popular; also, check the MySpace page

for additional classes (including sunset sessions).
2001 NORTH FULLER AVENUE. 323-666-5046. runyoncanyon-losangeles.com

698. *Liberation Yoga:* They've brought the outside into their "garden studio," complete with wood flooring and vegetation. Your first class is free.
124 SOUTH LA BREA AVENUE IN LOS ANGELES. 323-964-5222. www.liberationyoga.com

699. *Hiking Yoga:* Head to Griffith Park (p. 20) to take a class that's more a hike than yoga but still works up a sweat. You'll explore nature while you hike, and get in tune with your body at the same time. Classes meet at the Astronomers Monument in front of the Observatory in Griffith Park.
888-589-2250. www.hikingyoga.com

700. Try your hand at **outdoor tai chi.**

From Santa Monica to Studio City, Westwood to Mar Vista, and with locations opening in Malibu and Thousand Oaks, TC Society's classes seem to have a monopoly on outdoor tai chi. Maybe it's because they practice and teach authentic Yang-style tai chi, which consists of three sections and more than one hundred stances, or because Master T. C. Hou guides you through the basic techniques to help you have a better understanding. But most likely it's because Master Hou passes along generations of knowledge and training in each lesson. The forms he teaches were passed down from Yang Lu Chan, the founder of Yang-style tai chi, to Yang Chien-Hou (his son), to Yang Shao-Hou (his grandson), to Hsiung Yang-Ho (T. C. Hou's master). Private lessons with Master Hou himself are also available.
626-475-3404. tcsociety@gmail.com; tcsociety.com

701. Run with **Nike.**

Every week, runners of varying skill levels hit the pavement and head to the Nike store in the Grove for their Run Club. Here you get your pick of different degrees of running depending on your personal fitness, and then head out with your "new friends." You'll make your way around Park La Brea in sweaty herds, and afterward, when all you can think about is a shower, you'll find yourself lingering a bit longer. Post-run, Nike offers a refreshments-and-socializing session with water, protein bars, and a chance to meet the other runners. Just because you couldn't keep up with that person who caught your eye earlier doesn't mean you can't chat with them now. They'll be standing still. Nike also offers running clinics by experts, frequent-runner rewards, and product trials and demonstrations.

189 THE GROVE DRIVE IN THE GROVE IN LOS ANGELES. Wednesdays. 323-954-0450. Twitter: @NikeTheGrove

---

702. Go on a Fun Run with the **Los Angeles Frontrunners**.

The Frontrunners, a running and walking club for lesbian, gay, bisexual, and transgendered people and their friends and supporters, welcome *everybody* to come join their outings. A club formed to build friendship in the LGBT community, the Frontrunners is not only a great way to participate in running events and stay fit, but also supportive and fun.

Monday–Thursday. www.lafrontrunners.com

---

703. Train for the L.A. Marathon with the **L.A. Leggers**.

With the help of the L.A. Leggers, a nonprofit organization, you might just run your first marathon this year. For just $65 you get thirty-one weeks of training, experienced mentors to guide you, lectures with nutritionists, medical, and athletic experts, and more. Not to mention a snazzy T-shirt, and discounts on sports massages and physical therapy to keep you on track to reach your goal. The Leggers' training program definitely has a leg up on the competition.

www.laleggers.org

---

704. If you think the L.A. Marathon (p. 33) is a walk in the park, try the **Badwater Ultramarathon**.

Running twenty-six miles seems like an eternity to the athletically challenged, but the thought of running 135 miles seems like something only Forrest Gump could comprehend. Superathletes, who have honed a level of unbelievable endurance and embrace the extremity of their sport, relish the opportunity of embarking on this ultramarathon of epic proportions. For them, running 135 miles nonstop from Death Valley to Mount Whitney in the middle of summer, in 130-degree temperatures, must feel like Christmas in July.

www.badwater.com

---

705. Find your urban oasis downtown at the **Kyoto Gardens**.

You don't find much green among the concrete and metal of downtown L.A., and the views are cluttered with buildings. If you're looking to escape the hustle and bustle, head to the third-floor terrace of the DoubleTree Hotel, where the Kyoto Gardens, a half-acre garden filled with greenery and reminiscent of Japan, is a nice and calming

surprise. Smell the flowers, enjoy the waterfalls, and soon everything else will fade away, with only the skyline there to remind you where you really are.
120 SOUTH LOS ANGELES STREET (IN LITTLE TOKYO) IN DOWNTOWN LOS ANGELES. 213-629-1200. doubletree3.hilton.com/en/index.html

---

706. Join in on a ride with the **Los Angeles Wheelmen**.

Since their beginning in 1945, the Wheelmen have been about the sheer enjoyment of riding with friends. They're not a racing club, but more of a group exploration on wheels, and they offer different rides based on skill level, from basic to downright difficult (four hundred miles!). With weekly rides in Griffith Park, a South Beach ride, and one through the San Fernando Valley, the Wheelmen go everywhere. Newcomers are welcome to take part in a few rides before deciding whether to join, but with an individual membership at $20, and considering that you'll get discounts with your new Wheelmen ID at several area bike shops, choosing to sign up should be as easy as riding a bike.
www.lawheelmen.org

---

707. Ride through the streets at night with the **Midnight Ridazz**.

Cruising with the Ridazz is another way to see Los Angeles, as well as a cool way to hang out with fellow riders including bicyclists, unicyclists, and skateboarders. This popular "party on wheels" is filled with hipsters, art students, lawyers, and others, and offers you sights and sounds around the city at night that you'd normally miss if you were stuck in a car. It's a chance to break free and have fun. Rides have been on the second Friday of every month since the Ridazz first started in 2004. Not only do the eight original members still ride, but so do more than thirteen hundred others. On nights when the rides are especially big, the LAPD follows along to assist with traffic in order to help prevent accidents. Check their Web site for more information, and a free online guide to safe cycling.
www.midnightridazz.com

---

708. It's all uphill on the **Fargo Street Bike Ride**.

Although it's only one city block long and undoubtedly the shortest organized bicycle ride, it sure is a toughie. Fargo Street in Echo Park goes up the steepest hill in the city. Since 1974 the Los Angeles Wheelmen (above) have sponsored this annual springtime ride, known as "the Climb," along Fargo's 33-percent-grade hill. The results can range from relief to comedy to downright scary—many cyclists have been battered and bruised rolling backward down the intimidatingly angled ascent.

Note: If you're brave enough to attempt to tackle Fargo Street, making a zig-zag pattern uphill is apparently the easiest way.

FARGO STREET BETWEEN ALLESANDRO STREET AND ALVARADO STREET IN LOS ANGELES. Every March. www.lawheelmen.org

709. Skate on the **Venice Boardwalk**.

With a setting like the boardwalk, where weird is normal, and locals and tourists mingle effortlessly, it's all about enjoying being outside. Instead of walking or riding a bike along this famously eclectic boardwalk, strap on some skates and glide down the concrete walkways. Skates are easier to maneuver through crowds than a beach cruiser, and will get you around faster than just walking—and besides, skating along the coast is fun and is just one of those things you have to do. You can rent skates on the boardwalk from Boardwalk Skate & Surf.

201-1/2 OCEAN FRONT WALK IN VENICE. 310-450-6634. www.boardwalkskate.com

Surfing

Sean Penn's portrayal of surfer dude Jeff Spicoli in *Fast Times at Ridgemont High* personified America's stereotypical view of Los Angeles's laidback beach lifestyle. Surfers were viewed as slackers who didn't do anything but surf. But what was once a subculture that grew out of the 1960s and '70s and a lot of Beach Boys songs has moved into the mainstream.

The surf culture here was popularized and immortalized by the surf photographer LeRoy Grannis, who captured the sense of nostalgia inherent in the sport's evolution. To catch that perfect wave was often the goal, but sometimes it was being a part of something larger than themselves that drew people to surfing and its culture. As Spicoli said, "All I need are some tasty waves, a cool buzz, and I'm fine."

Come hang ten, get stoked, and go rhino hunting (looking for big waves) at these top surfing beaches.

710. *Surfrider Beach:* This is one of the most-surfed spots in L.A. County. Located next to Malibu Pier, it's one of the most iconic beaches in the history of surf culture. You'll find the water dotted with new surfers and old pros like surf god Laird Hamilton. Just remember that in Malibu, wave etiquette is key—your fellow surfers do not tolerate bad behavior, and they're not shy about letting you know. Not the best for beginners.

711. *Mondos:* With its east-to-west-traveling waves, you'll get a little taste of Hawaii in Los Angeles. And if you head a bit farther north, you can catch a wave you'll be able to ride for miles. Surf's up!
www.wannasurf.com/spot/North_America/USA/California/Ventura/Mondos

712. *Venice Beach:* The break wall here makes this the perfect place for beginners to try their hand at surfing on mellow waves. Don't worry, there's a lifeguard close by just in case.
AVENUE 26 AND OCEAN FRONT WALK IN VENICE.

713. *Trestles:* For a totally radical experience, head to Trestles. This world-class beach hosts several professional surf contests each year. It's a collection of three spots: Upper, Middle and Lower Trestles. Head to the Lower for the best waves.
www.parks.ca.gov

714. *The Wedge:* It's one thing to sing along to "Wipe Out" by the Surfaris—it's another to actually wipe out. This beach has some of the most powerful breaks around, so unless you know what you're doing, you'll want to stay away.
www.visitnewportbeach.com

715. Learn from the pros how to handle your board.

Local surf shops such as **ZJ Boarding House** in Santa Monica, **Zuma Jay** (the oldest surf shop in Malibu), and **Mollusk** in Venice provide lessons and have wet suits and foam long boards available for rent for beginners looking to catch their first wave.
ZJ: 2619 MAIN STREET IN SANTA MONICA. 310-392-5646; www.zjboardinghouse.com; Zuma Jay: 22775 PACIFIC COAST HIGHWAY IN MALIBU. 310-456-8044. www.zumajays.com; Mollusk: 1600 PACIFIC AVENUE IN VENICE. 310-396-1969. mollusksurfshop.com

716. If you're not into surfing but still want to get out on the water, try **Stand Up Paddle Lessons**.

Popular among celebrities like Cameron Diaz, Jennifer Aniston, and Marisa Miller, stand up paddling is more than just standing—it's an actual sport. And at Poseidon Stand Up Paddle (SUP), they'll teach you everything you need to know about SUP during an hour and a half lesson. From launching to basic paddling to proper

equipment usage, you'll learn it all. Soon you'll be paddling with the best of them.
310-694-8428. info@poseidonstandup.com; www.poseidonstandup.com

717. Learn to fly through the air with the greatest of ease at **Trapeze School New York** in Los Angeles.

Head to this trapeze school on Santa Monica Pier and you'll soon find yourself soaring with the seagulls. If you like to be challenged or just entertained, take one of the aerial arts classes that are available for every skill level. From trampoline jumping to silk dangling, they all provide a fun and challenging experience, with a boost of self-confidence and a great view. Soon you'll be unleashing your inner acrobat and possibly considering a career change. Cirque du Soleil, anyone?
200 SANTA MONICA PIER IN SANTA MONICA. 310-394-5800. losangeles.trapezeschool.com

718. Place a bet at **Santa Anita Park**.

Spend a day at the track watching the horses and hoping to win big. Santa Anita, a thoroughbred racetrack, is the oldest in Southern California. It hosts several celebrated national racing events including the Santa Anita Derby and the Santa Anita Handicap. General seating is super cheap, which means you'll have some money leftover to try your hand at picking a winner. Afterwards, you can celebrate winning by grabbing a drink at The Derby (p. 352). Fact: From 1942 to 1944, Santa Anita was used as a Japanese American internment center, with up to seventeen thousand people living in horse stables, including Star Trek actor George Takei.
285 WEST HUNTINGTON DRIVE IN ARCADIA. General admission: $5. 626-574-7223. www.santaanita.com

719. Go watch a Class A baseball game at the **Sam Lynn Ballpark**.

Ever since the Dodgers filed for bankruptcy, baseball fans have looked for a new outlet to reignite their love for America's favorite pastime—and I'm not talking about the Angels. At Sam Lynn Ballpark, home to the Bakersfield Blaze, a league with a mixed roster of rookies and experienced first-year players, fans can finally find new teams to get behind. They might not have big-name draws like the major league teams, but the Blaze have more heart, and in the end it's all about the love of the game. Since the field faces west, games have a later start time than at most parks, to avoid getting sun in the players' eyes as they bat.
4009 CHESTER AVENUE IN BAKERSFIELD. 661-716-4487. www.milb.com

720. Swing for the stands at **Rex's Baseball Batting Cage**.

Whether you choose baseball or softball, fast or slow, just remember to keep your eye on the ball and swing as if the bases were loaded.

11723 SOUTH WESTERN AVENUE IN LOS ANGELES. 323-756-8101. rexsbaseball.com

721. Practice your backhand at the **Cheviot Hills Park** tennis courts.

Put on your tennis whites, grab your racket and a bucket of balls, and head to one of the fourteen courts at Cheviot Hills. Here you can pretend to be a tennis great as you return each ball with a deft touch and perfect your net play. No one, not even Roger Federer or Maria Sharapova, can hold a candle to you. Eat your hearts out, tennis pros! But if it turns out your forearm is more Barry Bonds and less Rafael Nadal, be grateful for the high fencing that'll help keep more balls in than out. Just don't throw a John McEnroe and everything will be fine.

2551 MOTOR AVENUE IN LOS ANGELES. 310-836-8879.
www.laparks.org/dos/sports/tennis/facility/cheviotHillsTC.htm

722. Hit a bull's-eye at the **Rancho Park Archery Range**.

If tennis isn't your thing, head over to the archery range in Cheviot Hills Park. Before using the range here, a safety orientation class is required, and since the range, the equipment, and instruction are free, classes tend to fill up quickly. Come early so you don't get turned away, and remember: "be the arrow."

CHEVIOT HILLS PARK, 2551 MOTOR AVENUE IN LOS ANGELES. 310-837-5186.

723. Channel your inner Robin Hood at the **Pasadena Roving Archers**.

Arroyo Seco becomes Sherwood Forest every Saturday morning from 9 to 11. Archers here teach you the basics of how to stand, shoot, and retrieve. Instruction is free, but equipment is limited, so it's best to arrive around 8 a.m.

BROOKSIDE PARK, 415 SOUTH ARROYO BOULEVARD IN PASADENA. Range is across the footbridge from the parking lot. 626-571-7252. www.rovingarchers.com

724. Drag race legally at the **Toyota Speedway** at Irwindale.

Get fast and furious, or just watch the DVD, to prepare for the one-eighth-mile-drag-strip action that goes down at this speedway. Thursday nights, hundreds of cars compete in an event that started as an alternative to illegal street racing. Anyone can join in as long as they have a valid license, $20, and a street-legal car or motorcycle. It's an adrenaline rush, but it's also safe— a fire and medical crew is on hand.

500 SPEEDWAY DRIVE IN IRWINDALE. 626-358-1100. www.irwindalespeedway.com

---

725. Get trigger-happy at the **Oak Tree Gun Club**.

There's plenty of room at this outdoor firing range for you to try your hand at shooting. Trap, skeet, sporting clays, rifle, and pistol—they've got it all. Guests can enjoy a game of Trap and Skeet or participate in friendly competitions with Oak Tree's shooting leagues. They even have a pistol range with moving metal targets and three bays that are big enough to make you feel as if this were your own private club. Range masters are on hand to help beginners with advice and rentals. Open to the public; all experience levels are welcomed. Remember to abide by all the rules of safety here so everyone can have a great time.

23121 COLTRANE AVENUE IN NEWHALL. 661-259-7441. www.oaktreegunclub.com

---

Beach volleyball

In the early 1900s, private beach clubs brought volleyball out of the gym and onto the sand. Since then popularity for this sport has risen; it's even part of the Summer Olympics Games. Why is it so popular? Because it's cheap and affordable; all you need is a leather ball. In Los Angeles, nets abound at many public beaches, but few sites maintain the rope lines that mark court boundaries, so you may have to bring your own. You won't see a lot of jungle ball here. The beaches below are some of the best for playing or just observing the fine art of beach volleyball.

726. *Manhattan Beach:* The birthplace of beach volleyball, and home to the first beach volleyball tournament in the world. This is the quintessential L.A. beach.

MANHATTAN BEACH BOULEVARD AND NORTH OCEAN DRIVE IN MANHATTAN BEACH. www.ci.manhattan-beach.ca.us

727. *Sorrento Beach:* The sand is shallow here, making for better jumps. Don't believe me? Just ask Sinjin Smith, Jim Menges, or some of the other greats who've played here. (Sorrento versus Manhattan: Both claim to have started beach volleyball, but Manhattan has the upper hand as it hosted the first tournament.)

OFF PACIFIC COAST HIGHWAY IN SANTA MONICA.

728. *Hermosa Beach:* The sand is deeper, making it more difficult to jump, but if you can jump and move here, you can do it pretty much anywhere. Park in the structures on 13th Street near the pier-side courts to avoid pregame headaches.
HERMOSA AVENUE AT 13TH STREET.

729. *Will Rogers State Beach:* Great for the ladies as several of the nets are set at women's height.
17000 PACIFIC COAST HIGHWAY, PACIFIC PALISADES.

730. *Playa del Rey:* Isolated enough that before the Beijing Olympics in 2008, the Chinese teams came here to practice. If that doesn't give this beach's street credit a boost, I don't know what will. The erratic wind makes for a lot of wild balls, but that might be the kind of training you're looking for to keep you on your toes and your reflexes sharp.
PACIFIC AVENUE AT CONVOY STREET.

Expert Contributor: Michael Leon

Michael Leon's work utilizes skateboarding's DIY ethos as a means of mixing multi-generational counterculture, pop art, and life experiences. He projects all of the results onto multiple mediums: from graphic design and film, to sculpture and skateboard decks.

THE FIVE BEST PLACES TO SKATEBOARD IN L.A.

Downtown Car Wash banks. This spot consists of two twelve-foot banks and waxed ledges—it's very noticeable from the street and harder to skate than it looks. These can't be hit straight on unless you first ollie onto the sidewalk from the street. So you'll mostly be doing a little push and swerve to hit the waxed ledge two feet up the bank, or just surfing the length of the building on your cruiser board.
811 WEST OLYMPIC BOULEVARD IN LOS ANGELES. 213-629-1273. www.downtowncarwash.com

Wilshire Gap to Ledge. There are two gap-to-ledge things. Unfortunately, the spot is super exposed to Wilshire Boulevard and a bust during business hours. But it's been a popular L.A. spot for many years and has been seen in countless videos. If you're like me, you're going to stick to the small ledge next to the three-stair behind the black sign. The great things about this spot are the many possibilities and levels of difficulty packed into a small area. Try it, get kicked out, come back in a few days, and try it again.
3700 WILSHIRE BOULEVARD IN LOS ANGELES.

Hollywood Walk of Fame. Ah, Hollywood. This is just a great surface to roll on, which means any bump or curb cut is that much better because it's super easy to keep speed. The walk heads slightly downhill heading east, so start at the Chinese Theatre and head down from there. Not a place you would go often just to skate, but when you find yourself rolling here it can be fun—especially with a big crew so you can channel those old Bones Brigade videos.
HOLLYWOOD BOULEVARD BETWEEN GOWER STREET AND LA BREA AVENUE IN HOLLYWOOD. www.walkoffame.com

Stoner Skate Plaza. For me, an almost perfect skatepark design. This is a great place to meet up with friends and cruise around. If you're visiting L.A. and you want to watch pro skateboarders do their thing, this is the place—there's always someone there you will recognize. Skaters are actually starting to move into the neighborhood just to be

close. Most of the obstacles are mellow and manageable, and the locals are younger and cool so you will not get vibed.
1835 STONER AVENUE IN LOS ANGELES. 909-949-1601. www.californiaskateparks.com

Lincoln Skatepark. A new skatepark designed by Lance Mountain and Paul Rodriguez, this cool and mellow snake run for us old folks slams you into a huge wall topped by a Jersey barrier. The rest of the park features a few low hips with three to four gap/stair/rail options at the lower end of the park. Doesn't have the flow of Stoner, but if you like more transition, this is fun. Plus, if you find yourself on the East Side, this is your local.
3501 VALLEY BOULEVARD IN LOS ANGELES. 213-847-1726. www.laparks.org

CHAPTER 7

Bargains and Splurges

If shopping were to debut as an Olympic sport, L.A. would be the host city. For Angelenos, shopping isn't a pastime, it's a sport at which they excel. From custom-made shoes to exotic spices and everything in between, this commercial mecca draws in people from around the world who come looking for the best and are eager to part with their money; the array of unique shopping opportunities is dizzying. But it's not just the variety of things you can buy that makes Los Angeles special, it's also about the experiences you'll have. Whether you indulge in a truly *Clueless* moment and go down Rodeo Drive *à la* Cher Horowitz searching for that perfect Alaïa dress; find the gourmet market of your dreams; get lost in a maze of first-edition books; or score huge discounts at sample sales, L.A. is your oyster and shopping is its pearl.

In this chapter I've chosen my favorite Los Angeles shopping experiences. Specialty stores in the best neighborhoods, perfect places to enjoy window-shopping, book and record stores where you can lose yourself for hours; it's the ideal mix of highs and lows in shops and on the street and includes the chance to be caught off-guard by some genuinely unpredictable price tags. So whether you scoop up a designer dress for $1 or splurge on a $1,000 bottle of wine, both will exceed your wildest expectations.

With everything that can and will tempt you, remember to stay in control. Stripes might be flattering on some people, but orange prison jumpsuits are a bad look for everyone.

731. Enjoy the star-studded view at **Barneys New York.**

Is it the *New York* in Barneys New York that makes it seem cooler than its competition along Wilshire Boulevard? It might have to do with the light, airy decor and the architectural use of natural light, but, let's face it, it's most likely the cool vibe and selection of in-demand designers that has celebrity shoppers coming back time and time again. Stop by the shoe salon and you might find yourself next to that famous size 0 celebrity stylist; peruse a rack of the newest season at Co-Op where you're sure to see a familiar tabloid face or two. Just waiting in line for a dressing room yields many close encounters of the famous kind. Head spinning from all the shopping and celebrity gawking? Go upstairs to Barney Greengrass to refuel and relax. Grab a seat outside on the patio and enjoy a view of the city—though chances are you'll find a star distracting you from that, as well.

9570 WILSHIRE BOULEVARD IN BEVERLY HILLS. 310-276-4400. www.barneys.com

732. Get pampered head-to-toe at **Saks Fifth Avenue.**

The moment you enter, Saks exudes sophistication. With its chic, minimalist decor it's more classic than trendy. The staff here may seem icy to match the decor but don't fret, they're very warm. Feeling blah? Head to the makeup counter to pick up a tip or two to take you from dull to glowing. The shoe department is one of the best in the city for that waiting-on-hand-and-foot experience and selection. And the best part, with mini Chanel and Louis Vuitton storefronts on the ground floor, you don't need to pound the pavement any farther to get what you need.

9634 WILSHIRE BOULEVARD IN BEVERLY HILLS. 310-275-4211. www.saksfifthavenue.com

733. Shop and refuel at **Neiman Marcus.**

For over 100 years, Neiman Marcus has been selling the best in high-end fashion to its customers. Come here to find anything, and if you can't find it, they'll find it for you. It's a shoppers' paradise with floor upon floor of lust-worthy purchases. If you get hungry during your shopping adventure, head downstairs to the ground floor and buy the most affordable—and most infamous—item at Neiman Marcus: the chocolate chip cookie. A piece of Neiman Marcus urban legend: a shopper who loved the cookie so much bought the recipe for $250. Though there's no evidence that this story is true, it's something you can sink your teeth into and tell your friends about. Note: If you love the cookies as well, the recipe can be found on the company website, free of charge.

9700 WILSHIRE BOULEVARD IN BEVERLY HILLS. 310-550-5900. www.neimanmarcus.com

734. Shop off the beaten "rack" at **Nordstrom**.

Though you won't find a storefront in Beverly Hills alongside the other retail palaces, Nordstrom is well worth a detour. With a more approachable feel than Saks or Barneys, there are still plenty of items well within splurge territory. Nordstrom has a wide range of products from clothing to bedding, housewares to jewelry, and a huge shoe area that is often packed on the weekends.

MULTIPLE LOCATIONS. shop.nordstrom.com

→ ***FACT:*** *The store is named after John W. Nordstrom, who got the money to start his business by prospecting for gold in Canada's Klondike Gold Rush.*

735. Navigate your way through **Opening Ceremony**.

During his heyday, Charlie Chaplin got around the Los Angeles real estate market. The Hollywood legend owned prime property ranging from a movie studio (today Jim Henson Productions p. 61), an office building (once Campanile and La Brea Bakery p. 170), and a dance studio. Fashion forward duo and Opening Ceremony owners Humberto Leon and Carol Lim have revamped the latter into an avant-garde, unisex boutique that houses some prime fashion real estate of its own. Navigate its 10,000 square foot layout—meant to emulate driving on the L.A. freeways— and discover their collection of trend-setting designers, art books, zines, and footwear without having to worry about sudden stops—which may occur if something catches your eye.

451 NORTH LA CIENEGA BOULEVARD IN WEST HOLLYWOOD. 310-652-1120. www.openingceremony.us

736. Pull over for jeans and more at **Fred Segal**.

When driving down trendy Melrose Avenue, a pit stop at Fred Segal is a must. Opened in 1960 as the world's first jeans only store, it's grown exponentially over the years, becoming a favorite shopping destination for fashionistas and celebrities alike, and expanding with different "stores" within Fred Segal featuring different areas of expertise. You'll still find the jeans section it's famous for, but now it also has shoes, bags, an apothecary, pricey high-end designer duds, and Mauro's Café where you can grab an iced tea and relax, or indulge in a big plate of pasta—only best enjoyed after you've visited the fitting rooms and not before. It also has a location in Santa Monica complete with a salon/spa, and its semiannual sales are a must. Note: A popular reference point in pop culture, Fred Segal has been featured in movies *Less Than Zero*, *Clueless*, and *Legally Blonde*.

8118 MELROSE AVENUE IN LOS ANGELES (Mauro's Café). 323-651-1800; 500 BROADWAY STREET IN SANTA MONICA. 310-907-4022. www.fredsegal.com

SHOPPING ON THE CHEAP
Sample Sales:

First rule of sample sales is: you do not talk about sample sales. Second rule of sample sales is: you do not talk about sample sales. But since secrets like this rarely stay secret for long, there are key things to keep in mind when attending a sample sale. Comfortable clothes that are easily removable are a plus. If you're shy about changing in public, you'll have to conquer your fear. Most sample sales don't have dressing rooms for theft reasons. Tights are an easy solution. And if you "drop trou," just make sure you're wearing clean underwear sans holes. Bring a friend to help hunt and gather and keep a sharp eye on the piles of clothes you're hoarding in a corner. People can be ruthless and will take any opportunity they can to snag those hard-to-find items. As they say: when it comes to sample sales, everything is fair game. And, last but not least, hold on to every piece of clothing you like so you don't give up any potential finds. Even if you're not sure, never put it down. Leaving a sample sale regretful of what you could have bought is worse than not finding anything at all.

Samples sales are fashion-conscious Angelenos' best-kept secret. These hidden caches of discounted designer clothing stock plenty of fashionable Los Angeles closets and keep many a young fashion or magazine assistant in office-appropriate apparel. Technically, most of the clothes sold at the sample sales listed here aren't actually designer samples, as they once were when the term "sample sale" was coined. The clothes you find at the sample sale are usually overstock from inventory; after designers ship that season's merchandise to stores, they sell what's left over to what are essentially cleaning houses, at a big discount, which offer it to the public through sample sales. This means that, one, the stuff tends to be from the current season; and two, there's usually a range of sizes.

Sample sales take place all the time. Many are held in the Downtown Garment District at designer showrooms, but others are held in stores or other spaces round the city. DailyCandy (www.dailycandy.com), and Apparel News (www.apparelnews.net/calendar/sample-sale) list current sample sales and are good places to check to see who's offering what, where, and when. In addition to sample sales, outlets and warehouse sales are great places to find deals. The following are some favorite places to go.

Outlets & Warehouse Sales

737. *Desert Hills Premium Outlet:* Head out to a real shopping oasis. With over 130 outlet stores featuring top designer brands and shops like Bottega Veneta, Barneys New York, Brooks Brothers, Levi's Converse, Ugg Australia, and Lancôme, the Desert Hills Premium Outlet is a real shoppers'-on-a-budget dream come true. With its selection of heavily discounted designer goods, you can spend the day shopping without breaking the bank. Be careful, even with big markdowns, the desert heat has been blamed for causing some questionable purchases, so remember to stay hydrated.
48400 SEMINOLE DRIVE IN CABAZON. 951-849-6641. www.premiumoutlets.com

738. *Barneys Warehouse Sale:* Join the well-heeled fashion editor, the stockbroker, your next-door neighbor, even the dog walker . . . in February and August, you'll find crowds waiting at the crack of dawn for first grab at the sales racks and bins to stock their closets with fashionable finds at incredibly discounted prices. With markdowns between 50 and 80 percent on all of Barneys remaining stock from that season (women's, men's, and shoes), it's open season. It's kill or be killed when it comes to sales like this so don't be surprised if you get knocked down, stepped on, and have a few items snatched out of your hands as people dart from rack to rack in hopes of finding that perfect score. Your arms will ache with the mountain of items you've managed to collect, and once you're ready, shed any modesty—and your clothes—as you'll find yourself undressing in front of strangers to make sure everything fits. Don't worry, you'll find men and women alike changing all over the floor wherever they can. After a trip or two to the Barneys Warehouse Sale, worrying about standing around in your underwear will be a distant memory. Your goal here is to score big on great finds; everything else is secondary.
LOS ANGELES CONVENTION CENTER, 1201 SOUTH FIGUEROA STREET IN LOS ANGELES. 213-741-1151. www.lacclink.com

739. *American Apparel Retail Outlet:* If you love basics, but find them a tad on the pricey side, then head downtown to American Apparel's giant warehouse, home to the brand's factory store. You'll find all your favorite AA basics here, but cheaper. With tops, bottoms, undergarments, and more, the brand has made a name for itself among the masses—both young and the old—as the go-to when looking for that perfect (very) deep v-neck t-shirt or fleece with a better cut than your normal gym sweats.

Overruns of fleece hoodies, cotton v-necks, jeans, swimwear, bags, and a lot of sparkly spandex are all here for your purchasing pleasure. Be sure to inspect your clothes before you buy as some items are damaged and all sales are final.

747 WAREHOUSE STREET IN LOS ANGELES. 213-488-0226.
www.americanapparel.net

---

740. *FIDM Scholarship Store:* Take notes from the students at the Fashion Institute of Design & Merchandising who, no matter how hectic their schedules, always leave time for a little shopping. And with prices at 50–98 percent off, could the incentive be any better? FIDM's Scholarship store, located on campus, is loaded with clothes, jewelry, and fabric from major department stores, boutiques, and wholesalers, all donated to teach students how to run and properly operate their own retail space. And if you're looking for a steal of a deal and know how to sew, check out the "repairable corner" where you'll find designer goods for as cheap as $2! The needle and thread will probably cost you more.

919 SOUTH GRAND AVENUE IN LOS ANGELES. 800-624-1200.
fidm.edu/resources/scholarship-store/index.html

---

741. *ZGallerie Outlet:* Look beyond the scuffs and embrace the blemishes and all you'll get are great deals at the ZGallerie outlet. Located at one of their distribution warehouses, this outlet sells overstock, cancelled orders, floor models, and pieces that have scratches or dents. "Flawed goods"—something as simple as backward knobs—can yield huge discounts upwards of 90 percent. With items that are usually in good condition and new furniture arriving daily, it's best to arrive early for first pick. There are no returns, holds, or exchanges so make sure you take your time to examine everything before buying. If you're prepared to buy, be prepared to take your purchases with you: They deliver for a $135 fee.

1855 WEST 139TH STREET AT WESTERN AVENUE IN GARDENA. 310-808-1850.
www.zgallerie.com

---

742. *J. Brand Factory Outlet:* Head here if you want to get the skinny on designer jeans. Overruns, discounted, or samples—whatever it is—J. Brand takes 50 percent–80 percent-off on items that usually retail around $170 to $300, making a visit a no-brainer. Beloved by fashionistas, celebrities, and even *Vogue*'s Editor in Chief, Anna Wintour, J. Brands are the staple jeans for your wardrobe. Pricing is easy as boxes are marked, racks are organized, and the staff is attentive and there to help you with all your denim needs. You'll find a variety of sizes, cuts, and washes for men and women, as well as a maternity section with plenty of stretch.

1225 EAST WASHINGTON BOULEVARD AT ESSEX STREET IN LOS ANGELES. 213-740-1408. jbrandfactoryoutlet.com

743. *Outdoor Outlet:* If you've never had a reason to venture out into the wilderness—or have come up with too many excuses not to—Outdoor Outlet will change that. Here you'll find yourself shedding your urban skin and embracing your new role as Outdoor Weekend Warrior. Amidst the tents, sleeping bags, food stuffs, clothing, camp stoves, and accessories (at reduced prices), you'll find several reasons to start daydreaming about a mountain trek, a weekend camping getaway, or heading downriver to your favorite fishing spot. Not everything in the store is on sale, but there are more than enough items to make it a good shopping trip.

304 SOUTH DATE AVENUE IN ALHAMBRA. 626-537-2180. www.outdooroutlet.com

744. Go treasure hunting for antiques at a **Hughes Estate Sale**.

Attending an estate sale can be an exciting event. Not only do you get to see interesting items that people have been hoarding in their homes, you get to bid on them. They offer the promise of something new and interesting, and if you're willing to wake up at the crack of dawn, the Hughes Estate Sale will give you first stab at bidding on the item of your dreams. Known for putting on estate sales all around Los Angeles County, during their monthly warehouse sales, Hughes sells off furniture and other items they weren't able to set up formal sales for. You'll find multiple lots from different estates all in one place, which saves time because all the legwork has been done for you. Come early, get a good look around, see what you're in the mood for, and start bidding on these ridiculously low-priced items. They even offer coffee and donuts to take the ease off of waking so early. Every sale is different, so sign up for their mailing list and if you see something you like, be sure to set your alarm.

711 WEST WOODBURY ROAD IN ALTADENA. 626-791-9600. hughesestatesales.com

745. Decorate your home on a budget at **St. Vincent de Paul**.

One of the upsides of not having much cash, when you think about it, is your ability to see how far it can stretch and at second-hand superstore Society of St. Vincent de Paul Thrift Store, it can go farther than you imagined. Furnish your apartment for less than a couple hundred with unique furniture finds, dishware for the kitchen, a piano for your living room; get great deals on electronics, and different outfits to lounge around in your fabulous apartment once the decorating is done—and get good karma for supporting St. Vincent de Paul. The store is always packed with people on the lookout for a great find: come and discover your own. You'll need ample time to explore all the nooks and crannies, and if you're lucky, the staff may make a deal on the big-ticket items—just make sure to come prepared with a truck to get them home.

210 NORTH AVENUE 21 IN LINCOLN HEIGHTS. 323-224-6280. www.svdpla.org

---

746. Pretend you're a Top Chef at **Surfas**.

If you've ever wanted to engage in culinary warfare with your neighbor by having an *Iron Chef* cook-off but lack proper tools, then head to the Surfas warehouse space in Culver City. For years, foodies and restaurateurs have flocked here to browse through the generous selection of pots, pans, knives, utensils, and more to create a gourmet kitchen. Not sure how to use some of the items you just bought? If you can find one of the staff wandering around, they'll be more than happy to help you out. And just in case you need to kick your kitchen skills up a notch, they also host food events and classes. So next time a food challenge is issued, you'll be ready.

8777 WEST WASHINGTON BOULEVARD IN CULVER CITY. 310-559-4770. www.surfaslosangeles.com

---

747. Capture your baby's first memories with **Monkeys and Peas**.

Even with no actual storefront, Monkeys and Peas has become very well known for a simple yet beautiful style of baby photography. Photographer Trina Yin and her small team, known for keeping things easy and stress-free, are the ideal solution for expectant and full-time mothers. And with their amazing portfolio, hush-hush celebrity clientele list, and top-notch customer service, you'll soon be calling them, as well. Indoor or outdoor, black-and-white or color, wherever or however you decide to capture your child's first moments, Monkeys and Peas will work to make sure that they're memories you'll cherish for a lifetime. And if you refer a friend, you'll have even more memories, as you'll receive an additional $50 print credit for your next session.

www.monkeysandpeas.com

---

748. Find yourself in tchotchke heaven at **Shine Gallery**.

Almost hidden within the Farmer's Market (p. 27) you'll find a store that's full of Americana pop culture. More kitschy than trendy, Shine Gallery houses pop culture artifacts going back as far as the 1930s. All of the offerings are authentic and in great condition, so if you're looking for something unique to buy as a gift, this is the place. Toys, matchbook covers, Stork Club cigarette holders, gag gifts, and magic tricks rescued from old stores and warehouses now have a home where they can shine.

FARMER'S MARKET, 6333 WEST 3RD STREET #134 AT FAIRFAX AVENUE IN LOS ANGELES. 323-954-4700. www.shinegallery.com

---

749. Brew your own potions at **Panpipes Magickal Marketplace**.

The nation's oldest occult shop likes to take things seriously, and once you step foot into Panpipes you'll find out how serious. The owners here take the time and care to talk to every customer about all their pagan needs. Pentagrams, stones, crystals, ankhs, tarot cards, candles, and dragon's blood—this full service occult shop has it all. They even have an in-store alchemist on site to hand blend incenses, potions, and lotions customized to fill any of your spell needs.

1641 NORTH CAHUENGA BOULEVARD IN LOS ANGELES. 323-462-7078. www.panpipes.com

---

750. Buy a diamond on a budget at **St. Vincent Jewelry Center**.

Who doesn't love going shopping for jewelry? It's something anyone would love to do, but it's rarely something most of us can really afford. If you're in the market for something sparkly and are on a budget, the best place to head is downtown to the Jewelry District to visit to St. Vincent Jewelry Center. Here you'll find a labyrinth of stalls and dealers hoping to strike a bargain. You'll be pleasantly surprised how many carats your dollars can buy.

650 SOUTH HILL STREET IN LOS ANGELES. 213-629-2124. svjc.com

---

751. Encounter six degrees of celebrity separation via jewelry at **Neil Lane**.

Neil Lane loves beautiful things and as a celebrated designer and vintage jewelry collector, he prides himself on outfitting the very best of Hollywood's elite during awards season. His vintage jewelry stunners give that extra star-wattage to celebrities like Reese Witherspoon, Angelina Jolie, and Julia Roberts on the red carpet. And when love is in the air, they head here for his custom wedding rings that have graced the hands of many a celebrity bride. Come and look, and if you can afford it, pick up one of Neil's beautiful vintage pieces. Be sure to ask who's worn it where and when, so you have a great story to go along with it. Neil Lane is also the official engagement ring designer for the *Bachelor* TV series, but don't worry, a ring from here will boast better odds for you than the people on that show.

708 N LA CIENEGA BLVD IN LOS ANGELES. 310-275-5015. www.neillanejewelry.com

---

752. Buy a crazy gift at the **Wacko Soap Plant**.

Spend an entire day at this fun-filled, warehouse-sized store, which is decked out like

Pee Wee's Playhouse. Tired of getting the same, standard gifts for friends and family? Then browse through Wacko's selection of the artsy, random, and kooky, such as art books, trinkets, bug jewelry, comics, toys, the Mexican Cinema, soaps, and more. A gift from here will certainly draw *oohs* and *ahhs*—or some serious laughter, depending on what you find—all in the name of good fun. Be sure to check out the La Luz Art Gallery (p. 149) in back to see up-and-coming artists who often have their work on display.
4633 HOLLYWOOD BLVD IN HOLLYWOOD. 323-663-0122. www.soapplant.com

---

753. Buy a basket of books at **Storyopolis**.

Many of us don't spend enough time nurturing the minds of our youth. Instead we plop them in front of a TV or computer screen and leave them to their own devices. Instead, try taking them to Storyopolis for a chance to use their imaginations and expand their minds. This bookstore—complete with art gallery, huge, couch-lined room for story time, and shelves filled with classics—is a great place for kids to spend their day. Pick up one of the great gift baskets with themes like pirates or Caldecott award winners; they are a refreshing and welcoming change from the digital world.
16740 VENTURA BOULEVARD IN ENCINO. 818-990-7600. www.storyopolis.com

---

754. For something other than Harry Potter books for the kids, head to **Children's Book World**.

With an inventory of more than 80,000 titles, Sharon Hearn's Children's Book World is hard to beat for kid-lit. Here you'll find popular titles mixed with often-neglected categories like nonfiction and in-between readers. A full-service store filled with music, educational aids, and audio books, it's the perfect place to feed kids' minds. Be sure to stop by on Saturday mornings for storytellers and book signings by some of the best children's authors out there.
10580 WEST PICO BOULEVARD IN LOS ANGELES. 310-559-2665. www.childrensbookworld.com

---

755. Personalize a gift at **Color Me Mine**.

You may not be the best artist, but nothing says "I love you," or "Hey, You're special!" better than something handmade. At Color Me Mine, you can choose from different types of ceramic items like skulls, vases, bowls—and even unicorns—to personalize your present. Sit at one of the paper-covered tables, sketch out a design, and get ready to get a little messy as you paint your masterpiece. Once you're done painting, the staff will take your piece to fire it in the kiln. Come back in a few days and voila, you'll have a work of art.
Check website for various locations: www.colormemine.com

L. A. Designers

Los Angeles is home to some great established and up-and-coming designers. They are artistic, creative, and innovative, and able to design stellar pieces that will turn into closet staples. Forget Juicy Couture velour tracksuits, L.A. style is so much more like Raquel Allegra's bo-ho pieces, A.L.C.'s dresses, or a Cerre leather jacket. While you're here, take home a real piece of Los Angeles back with you. Or, as a local, support emerging artists! Here are a few you should keep your eyes open for while checking out the racks.

756. *Vena Cava:* Los Angeles natives Lisa Maycock and Sophie Buhai are back in Los Angeles and designing up a storm. After several years in New York City where their designs shone on catwalks and were featured in the pages of fashion magazines like *Vogue* and *Harper's Bazaar*, Vena Cava has come home. The duo has brought with them beautifully designed dresses and separates, and must-have prints. Viva Vena Cava.
www.venacava.com

757. *Jasmin Shokrian:* With her clean lines, neutral palette, and meticulous draping, its no wonder that Shokrian, an art school graduate (in film, sculpture, and painting) has such a devoted fan following. And with a line of accessories that include intricate leather belts and now bags, there's just more of Jasmin Shokrian to love.
310-300-0377. www.jasminkrian.com

758. *Kova&T:* Christina Tang and Dasha Zhukova, the best friends and designers/partners behind this L.A.-based line made a name for themselves with their leggings, which have been knocked off by hundreds. Not only did their leggings in cashmere, latex, and lace become a wardrobe staple for fashionistas, but also their take on the LBD is a hit season after season. Their creative clothes are classic with a chic twist, perfect for the style savvy shopper.
213-627-6664. www.kovaandt.com

759. *Creative Growth for Everybody:* What do you get when physically and mentally disabled artists working at the oldest, largest non-profit visual arts center in the world collaborate with The NEWS and the Knoernschild family (Hurley and KZO)? A line of fun, thought-provoking, and inspirational clothing called Creative Growth. This collaboration not only

gives the artwork a larger audience through fashion, it raises money for the artists and Creative Growth. Good fashion for a good cause.
www.creativegrowthforeverybody.com

760. *Rodarte:* Sisters Kate and Laura Mulleavy have been on the fashion fast-track to superstardom since 2005 with no signs of slowing. Beloved by almost every heavy-hitter in the fashion industry, they've won accolades and prizes galore and were the first women to win the prestigious Swiss Textiles Awards (trust me, it's big). They've redesigned movie posters, guest-edited publications, costume-designed for movies and ballets, and their works are included in the permanent collections of the Costume Institute of the Metropolitan Museum of Art, the Fashion Institute of Technology Museum in New York, and the Los Angeles County Museum of Art.
www.rodarte.net

761. *THVM:* The amazing Olga Navaroza and Brian Kim, co-founders of the Echo Park–based brand, THVM Atelier, have created the perfect balance between men's and women's wear. More that just a denim brand, they work to design unique, and even custom-made jeans that are affordable and unisex. They also publish a biannual fashion and art magazine, *THVM Rag*, and have a multi-brand boutique called THVM which houses various L.A. brands such as Endovanera and Cast of Vices, as well as their eponymous label.
1317 PALMETTO STREET IN LOS ANGELES. 213-617-0667. shop.thvm.com

762. Go sit in a chair at the **Eames Workshop**.

For those who appreciate modern American furniture and design, a trip to the Eames offices is a must on your list of things to do. The Eames Office is a nondescript office, gallery, museum, and gift shop rolled into one. It is *the* place—other than the Eames House (p. 41)—where fanatics of the influential designing duo come to pay tribute and ogle their goods. Here, in their original workshop, you'll get a history lesson on the Eames family, see an entire collection of Eames chairs, and have a chance to sit in an original chair. After a renovation of the space by architect Frank Israel, the Workshop remains an important space in design history. You might not walk out with a lounge chair for $4,000, but you can pick up the Eames House of Cards, a deck of cards that come in various sizes, the prefect present for the design lover in your family.
901 ABBOT KINNEY BOULEVARD IN VENICE.

763. Break the bank at **Maxfield's**.

This high-end boutique tucked away in a cement building with minimal signage is where you'll find fashion at its finest. For years, Maxfield's has been carrying unknown, cutting edge designers, as well as the most coveted labels in fashion. You won't find $100 jeans here. Instead you'll find pieces with price tags that read more like mortgage payments than anything else. And for those looking for pieces with a bit more history than straight off the runway, Maxfield's carries a great collection of vintage Hermès, Chanel, and amazing art and photography books, all expensive and all for sale.

8825 MELROSE AVENUE IN LOS ANGELES. 310-274-8800. www.maxfieldla.com

764. Pamper your pets with only the best at the **Barkley**.

The Barkley Pet Hotel & Day Spa in Westlake Village is the world's most luxurious pet hotel in the world, with custom towels, fur-lined dressing gowns, and toy pillows in the shape of Balenciaga handbags. But what really makes this pet palace stand out is the lavish treatment given to each of its furry guests. Personal swim instructors provide swimming lessons; there are daily exercise routines and natural hair dye treatments and massages; and there's a spa menu that can provide your pet with a steak from the Four Seasons Hotel across the street and tuna sushi for your finicky feline friend. The Barkley also provides trans"paw"tation via a customized limo service, and if you're a pet owner who wants to see how your four-legged friend is doing, you can check the "paw"parazzi gallery, which includes a live streaming webcam.

31166 VIA COLINAS IN WESTLAKE VILLAGE. 818-889-BARK. www.thebarkleypethotel.com

765. Shop like the stylish girls do at **Satine**.

Though Satine may look like your typical trendy L.A. boutique, it's far more. It's a style leader that houses well-known brands as well as the up and coming. Come here and treat yourself to everything from Alexander McQueen to Jen Kao, Jenni Kanye to Andrea Liberman, and make a note to come by during their sales events when those drool-worthy pieces are actually within your price range with markdowns—sometimes 80 percent off. Everything is spaciously laid-out and easily accessible—the only problem you'll have is deciding if being able to afford food is really a priority on your list, as you might want to spend that money on something you just spotted and decidedly cannot live without.

8134 WEST 3RD STREET IN LOS ANGELES. 323-655-2142. www.satineboutique.com

766. Find something for the hard-to-buy-for person in your life at **New Stone Age**.

This magical curio shop is part science lab, part knick-knack wonderland, part global gift store, and all parts interesting and fun. The shelves are chock-full of pleasant surprises from the beautiful to eclectic, and at every turn you'll find something special and unique. When it comes to birthdays or the gift-giving season, your finicky friends won't know what hit them.

8407 WEST 3RD STREET AT ORLANDO AVENUE IN LOS ANGELES. 323-658-5969. www.newstoneagela.com

767. The clumsy need worry only a little when at **Plastica**.

Though people tend to think of plastic as a cheap material and not very chic, you'll be surprised how many fun and well-designed plastic bits and bobs you'll find at Plastica. A place that blends art form, function, and sustainability, the store has a great selection of items like vases, bento boxes, toys, utensils, and chairs—items that can put any accident-prone person at ease.

8405 WEST 3RD STREET IN LOS ANGELES. 323-655-1051. www.plasticashop.com

768. Grab a surfboard at **Mollusk Surf Shop**.

This Venice surf shop is the epitome of the laidback surfing lifestyle. Housed in a store handcrafted from salvaged wood, Mollusk has a retro, fun feel in a tree-house-type space. The boards here mimic the atmosphere and also have that retro vibe, imbued with a craftsman's touch. They have a good selection to choose from, but the next time you're here, ask their totally radical staff to see the special board designed by shapers Josh Farberow and Scott Anderson called the "Slide and Glide"—it's far out. Note: When the waves are good, call ahead to check what time the store will open.

1600 PACIFIC AVENUE IN VENICE. 310-396-1969. www.mollusksurfshop.com

769. Buy hand-rolled cigars at **Leon Cigar**.

Cuba is famous for its cigars, so leave it to Cuban cigar-rolling veteran Gilberto Leon to show us what's what when it comes to cigars. Born in Pinar del Rio, a town known for the best tobacco in Cuba, great cigars are in Leon's blood. For 73 years in Cuba and the U.S. Leon has been crafting these tightly rolled bundles of premium tobacco, and since 1979, he's been selling them here in Los Angeles. Housed in a narrow storefront, this old-school and unpretentious space features a handful of select smokes on its menu, each hand-rolled on site and made from specially selected leaves grown in the Dominican Republic from Cuban seed. The freshness, taste, and easy draw is what sets

Leon's apart from the rest and has cigar aficionados coming from all over the city to get their stogies.

3956½ WEST 6TH STREET IN KOREATOWN. 213-385-3375. www.leoncigars.com

---

770. Buy your beauty products at the beautiful **Le Pink & Co. Beauty Apothecary**.

Avoid the harsh fluorescent lights of your local CVS, the mish mash of generic products at Rite-Aid, and head to Silver Lake and the warm pink glow of Le Pink & Co. Here you'll find a touch of old world European decadence lining its white cabinets and shelves with colorful and fragrant soaps; rare perfumes; vintage glass jars filled with bath salts, oils, and lotions that require serious accents in order to pronounce properly; and hard to come by imports from around the world. And once you're done indulging in products that'll make you look good, how about something that'll make you feel good? Le Pink & Co. also offers a great choice in sweet treats from classic candy bars to candy sticks and even a Violet Crumble all the way from the land down under.

3820 W. SUNSET BOULEVARD IN SILVER LAKE. 323-661-7465. lepinkandcompany.tumblr.com

---

771. Find yourself in book-lover heaven at **Mystery Pier Books**.

It's ironic when one can't find the words to describe how fantastic a bookstore is, but you'll be at a loss as well when you arrive at Mystery Pier Books. For over 12 years, father and son Harvey and Louis Jason have been compiling a treasure trove of first edition classics that will make you fall to your knees in rapture, as well as signed scripts and other incredible ephemera. You'll find yourself slowly browsing through editions signed by Ernest Hemingway, Raymond Chandler, Ayn Rand, Jack Kerouac, Kurt Vonnegut, and more. Mystery Pier is a go-to gift store for winners and nominees for award shows. Actor Michael Caine described this place as "the most wonderful museum, except you get to buy the exhibits"—and if you've got the money, whether it's tens of thousands for Charlie Chaplin's personal script, or a few hundred for a signed John Steinbeck, you'll definitely find something you'll love and treasure.

8826 SUNSET BOULEVARD IN WEST HOLLYWOOD. 310-657-5557. mysterypierbooks.com

---

772. Think outside the box when buying clothes at **Noodle Stories**.

If you're looking to spruce up your wardrobe with workable, unique, and stylish clothes, go to Noodle Stories. Here they shun trends and the mass-produced and opt for classic, well crafted, and somewhat avant garde pieces by the quietly adored heroes of the fashion world, Comme des Garçons, Margiela, and Junya Watanabe. Items can be expensive, but that's the price you pay for quality and a chance to be a little different. Ask the friendly and professional staff about any upcoming sales, and receive free alterations with your purchase.

8323 WEST 3RD STREET IN LOS ANGELES. 323-651-1782. www.noodlestories.com

---

773. Buy something for your artsy designer friends—or make your own house look cooler with something from **OK Store**,

where the most perfect, kooky meld of art and design can be found. From handmade jewelry to a selection of cool bookends, fun kids' stuff that even adults would enjoy, and other interesting items with a great design aesthetic, picking up something from here will yield more than one surprise. You might finally get that that looking-over-their-glasses, approving nod of satisfaction from one of your highbrow friends. A bonus.

8303 WEST 3RD STREET IN LOS ANGELES. 323-653-3501. okthestore.com

---

774. Get ready for your next big trip at **Distant Lands Travel Bookstore and Outfitters**.

This bookstore not only has a huge selection of great travel books and maps, but also great travel gear, from durable luggage to travel accessories like the ever-important document organizer, electrical adaptors, and packing kits, that actually makes packing easy. Even if you're not going away, you might want to pick up a few interesting guides, a book to brush up on your high school French, or maybe some eye-opening inspiration—that's always free. Be sure to check out the calendar of events for lectures on travel and more.

20 SOUTH RAYMOND AVENUE IN PASADENA. 800-310-3220. www.distantlands.com

---

775. Get your lingerie custom made at **Trashy Lingerie**.

It's far from trashy at this famous lingerie store that custom designs its intimates. In 1973, Mitchell Shrier and his wife opened a shoe store where they sold a popular shoe known as the "Trashy." Mitchell soon found himself dying stockings to go with the shoe and even lingerie to match and two years later, opened Trashy Lingerie. They not only make lingerie, but their five onsite seamstresses create costumes—making this a popular costume destination for women on Halloween—as well as bathing suits. For only a $2 yearly membership fee, you to can shop where Madonna, Drew Barrymore, Cameron Diaz, Janet Jackson, and other sexy celebs buy underthings that are original, handmade—and for that extra special touch, customizable.

402 NORTH LA CIENEGA BOULEVARD IN LOS ANGELES. 310-652-4543. www.trashy.com

776. Go to celebrity hot-spot **Kitson**.

Everyone knows the name Kitson. The store has been featured in the pages of *US Weekly*, *People*, *InTouch*, and a slew of other magazines for over a decade. Why? The Kardashians, the Hiltons, the Lohans, to name a few famous clients. Everyone loves coming to this store on Robertson to shop and be photographed, in that order. It is the go-to boutique for trendy, pop-culture-related men's, women's, and children's fashions, from t-shirts to denim, dresses, and shoes, so be sure to drop by and see what this store is all about. If you didn't have time to make it to Kitson during your visit, stop by their LAX store in Terminal 7 (United) for a quick stop and shop.

115 SOUTH ROBERTSON BOULEVARD IN LOS ANGELES. 310-859.2652; 700 WORLD WAY AT LAX. 310-642-0971. www.shopkitson.com

777. Buy a piece of art at the **CAFAM Museum Shop**.

To visit this tiny, global bazaar filled with artsy treats, you won't have to travel far. However, you will need to employ some self-restraint, as all the wonderful gift items you find here will tempt you. Everything is handcrafted, one of a kind, and free trade. Works by local artists are featured, as well as toys and trinkets from as far away as India and Zimbabwe. The stock list changes often to reflect the museum's exhibitions, so each trip here is a cultural and shopping adventure.

5814 WILSHIRE BOULEVARD IN LOS ANGELES. 323-937-4230. www.cafam.org

778. Tap into your inner Basquiat at **Blue Rooster**.

This independent, neighborhood art supply store in Los Feliz is just what you need to get your creative juices flowing. Custom canvases and panels, screen printing classes, free lectures on how to use natural pigments—becoming a starving artist never looked so good, or sounded so fun.

1718 NORTH VERMONT AVENUE, LOS ANGELES. 323-661-9471. www.bluerooster artsupplies.com

779. Start—or reignite—your comic book collection at **Meltdown Comics and Collectibles**.

One of L.A.'s best comic book sellers for two decades, Meltdown Comics is a sanctuary for lovers of comics and memorabilia. A place where the nerdy congregate for exhibits, signings, and even stand-up comedy. Whether you're a newbie or a seasoned expert, their amazing staff of knowledgeable know-it-alls is always helpful and friendly.

7522 SUNSET BOULEVARD IN HOLLYWOOD. 323-851-7223. www.meltcomics.com

780. To fill the void left by the closing of Cook's Library, head over to **Janet Jarvits's Cook Books.**

Anybody with the slightest hint of an epicurean sensibility could spend hours in here, surrounded by the stacks of cookbooks, brushing up on such things as the fine art of whisking. Jarvits has more than 30,000 titles accumulated from thrift stores, estate sales, and private clients. The store has books that date back to the 1800s as well as signed first editions of Julia Child's cookbooks and everything in between.

1388 EAST WASHINGTON BOULEVARD IN PASADENA. 626-296-1638. www.cookbookjj.com

781. Ditch the dull at **Gary's Knife Sharpening Service.**

Who knew that Gary Silverstein would switch professions from medical biller to professional knife sharpener after he realized he enjoyed knife sharpening a whole lot more? Now this self-taught sharpener sets up his stall in seven farmers markets around the city, where he takes care of the neglected contents of your kitchen knife drawer, as well as sharpening the knives of chefs from restaurants around the city.

At various farmers' markets. 310-560-3258. www.garysknifesharpening.com

782. Buy tableware at **Heath Ceramics.**

Artist Edith Heath was the first non-architect to win the prestigious AIA gold medal award, for the exterior tiles at the Norton Simon Museum (p. 133). High praise indeed, though considering Heath handmade all of those richly-toned brown tiles, you can see why the award is apt. Heath's legacy, which focuses on design and handcrafted techniques, lives on in the company she founded, Heath Ceramics, one of the few remaining mid-century American potteries in existence today. Here, tableware and tiles are still made by skilled craftsmen, who make everything on site. Visit Heath Ceramics and pick up some great mix-and-match tableware.

7525 BEVERLEY BOULEVARD AT SIERRA BONITA AVENUE IN LOS ANGELES. 323-965-0800. www.heathceramics.com

Bookstores

Not long ago neighborhoods like Hollywood, Westwood, and Long Beach were rife with used bookstores. Wafts of musty leather seduced wayward pedestrians, hinting at the undiscovered texts piled haphazardly inside. But as browsing the aisles has given way to scouring websites and using eReaders, many of L.A.'s best-known purveyors of secondhand books have vanished. Those that remain have a large niche to fill. Where rare and antiquarian bookshops sate the desires of the serious collector, used bookstores serve as part lecture hall and living room, part book club and hiding place.

Ray Bradbury once wrote, "I go to Acres of Books, as I go to Paris, or Rome, or London, or New York, to be—lost." But Acres of Books is no more. For those of us who are saddened by the loss of the largest secondhand bookstore in California, we have no choice but to move forward.

783. *Arcana Books:* Have Arcana track down your dream book. Though known for its incredible collection of rare and out-of-print editions of almost every artsy book out there, one of the great things about Arcana is if they don't have it, they'll find it for you—they don't mind at all.
THE HISTORIC HELMS BAKERY, 8675 WASHINGTON BOULEVARD, CULVER CITY. 310-458-1499. www.arcanabooks.com

784. *Skylight Books:* Shop where the writers work—the best indie bookstore in town. With its selection of contemporary fiction, liberal politics, and periodicals, as well as a staff full of writers—and writers are always on the ball—Skylight has no match. Watch out for store events, which offer you a chance to see and hear some of L.A.'s most stimulating authors.
1818 NORTH VERMONT AVENUE IN LOS FELIZ. 323-660-1175. www.skylightbooks.com

785. *Book Soup:* You can always get what you want at Book Soup. They know what you're looking for and continue to give it to you—it's no wonder this bookstore opened in 1975 is still around. The shop provides its customers with books on arts, photography, film, music, and noir, as well as champions hard-to-find books by university, international, and small presses. While its selection of 60,000 titles is a huge draw, it's the author signings every week and the possibility of seeing someone famous that has people coming back. It is Hollywood, after all.
8818 SUNSET BOULEVARD IN HOLLYWOOD. 310-659-3110. www.booksoup.com

786. *Charlene Matthews Bindery:* Turn your treasured pages into a work of art at Charlene Matthews Bindery. She has over 20 years of experience under her belt, and can do much more than bind books. Her personal touch certainly beats any of the more straightforward online self-publishing fads out there.
5720 MELROSE AVENUE IN LOS ANGELES. 323-962-2109. www.charlenematthews.com

787. *Vroman's in Pasadena:* Support the largest independent and family-owned bookstore in Southern California. The store was started by voracious bibliophile and passionate photographer, Adam Clark Vroman, who sold his extensive collection of books to open it, and whose passion for books remains the ethos for Vroman's to this day. The store has expanded to include fine writing instruments and stationery, as well as notebooks—anything to keep the written word alive and kicking.
695 EAST COLORADO BOULEVARD IN PASADENA. 626-449-5320. www.vromansbookstore.com

→ **FACT:** *Pasadena native and food world icon Julia Child had her first book signing at Vroman's.*

788. *Don't expect to find clowns at Circus of Books*—still, this porn shop in Silver Lake is fascinating. With its laid-back staff and impressive collection of imported design and fashion magazines sitting nonchalantly alongside fetish material, you can't help wonder where the cerebral ends and the carnal begins.
4001 SUNSET BOULEVARD IN SILVER LAKE. 323-666-1304. www.circusofbooks.com

789. *Family Bookstore:* Get a breath of fresh air at Family—chain stores can't compare. Although it's relatively small, this much-beloved store—filled with rare, independent publications—hosts book signings, installations, and fun performances with local artists, whose work Family sells and supports.
436 NORTH FAIRFAX AVENUE IN LOS ANGELES. 323-782-9221. www.familylosangeles.com

790. *Lead Apron:* Spend your fortune at the Lead Apron. First editions of modern and contemporary art books, Andy Warhol screen prints, and other random and expensive things you didn't know about and now want are all here just waiting for you.
8445 MELROSE PLACE IN WEST HOLLYWOOD. 310-360-0554. www.leadapron.net

791. *Hennessey + Ingalls:* Pick up that perfect gratuitously over-sized coffee table book here. "The largest bookstore dealing in visual arts in America," Hennessey + Ingalls has an impressive collection of rare and out-of-print art titles, as well as a great selection of design magazines from all over the world.
214 WILSHIRE BOULEVARD IN SANTA MONICA. 310-458-9074. www.hennesseyingalls.com

792. *Ivanhoe Books:* Come for Ivanhoe's large selection of mid-century modern architecture, interior design, and decorating books. They also have special vintage photography monographs from photo luminaries Edward Weston, Deborah Turbeville, and Annie Leibovitz.
1618 SILVERLAKE BOULEVARD IN SILVERLAKE. 323-660-1500

793. Dress like your parents—or your grandparents—at **Hidden Treasures**.

Whether you like vintage or antique clothing, you'll find both at Hidden Treasures. Located in the heart of Topanga, this unique store, decorated with old props, waterfalls, and pirates, has a clothing collection dating back to the Victorian era through the 1970s that draws in a great mix of regulars, stylists, and tourists. Be sure to check out their Treasure Trunk out front where items are $1.75. If you're lucky, you'll find some pieces formerly owned by the ex-Mrs. Lenny Kravitz, the beautiful Lisa Bonet, who lives in the neighborhood and often sells her clothes here.
154 SOUTH TOPANGA CANYON BOULEVARD IN TOPANGA. 310-455-2998

794. Gain a higher tolerance for scrutiny, while perusing premium vintage fashion at **Lily et Cie**.

Owner Rita Watnick has amassed over half a million pieces of vintage clothing over 30 years, and everyone in town knows it. If you have seen an actress wearing pristine vintage during awards season, it's highly likely she got her dress here. Though Watnick tends to look down her nose and often wrinkles it with distain if you're not a wealthy celeb, that doesn't mean you can't go by and have a look. If you can ignore the somewhat icy treatment, and want the opportunity to see some truly amazing vintage fashion, adopt a stiff upper lip, follow all the rules, and let the images of all the vintage finery wash over you.
9044 BURTON WAY IN BEVERLY HILLS. 310-724-5757. www.lilyetcie.com

795. Look over your shoulder while you're shopping at **Mister Freedom**.

This nondescript brick building on Beverly Boulevard houses owner Christophe Lorion's huge and methodically merchandised collection of vintage clothing, footwear, and accessories ranging from French gentleman farmer to Madras haberdashery for men and women dating from the 1850s to the present. When going through the racks here it feels more like a treasure hunt than vintage shopping, and with an additional selection of rare textiles, vintage books and props, as well as just random vintage items from around the world, it looks like it. Be warned that its no photo policy is strongly enforced to avoid any industrial spying, so you will feel like you're being watched. Mister Freedom also has its own line of clothes, which it stresses is a registered trademark and all infringements will be prosecuted. I wonder how William Klein feels about that one.

7161 BEVERLY BOULEVARD IN LOS ANGELES. 323-653-2014. www.misterfreedom.com

---

796. Make a fashion journey and visit **Cameron Silver at Decades**.

If you want vintage, Silver is the person you go to in this town. Silver, a native Angeleno and one-time cabaret singer, found his calling while hunting for men's clothing for his cabaret act. While trying to get his hands on some of the best in historical men's clothes, he discovered that there were far too many women's garments out there to pass up. He ended up buying them all, and in 1997 opened Decades, his vintage salon. Singlehandedly responsible for bringing vintage to the forefront of fashion, he was named one of *Time* magazine's "25 Most Influential Names and Faces in Fashion." He dresses A-list actresses for the red carpet, consults with multiple fashion brands, and even launched his own line of denim. The premier fashion house Hermès has created the "Cameron" bag in his honor. Though the allure of Decades and all its vintage finery is great, once you meet Silver himself, a handsome man swathed in a suit cut from fashion's glowing light, you'll realize the pull of the two are indiscernibly the same. Silver's second store Decadestwo is just next door, and if you're looking for more vintage, head down the street and visit Katy Rodriguez and Mark Haddawy's Resurrection.

8214 MELROSE AVENUE IN LOS ANGELES. 323-655-1960. www.decadesinc.com

---

797. Furnish your closet while you furnish your home at **Mohawk General Store/Amsterdam Modern**.

If you like to get the most out of shopping trips then head to this great two-in-one shop where you may find everything you need. At Mohawk General Store/Amsterdam Modern, owned by Kevin Carney and Ellen LeComte, not only will you find amazing mid-century home furnishings and twentieth-century Dutch designs that would spruce up any home, you'll also find a great selection of clothes and accessories that will smarten you up as well. So whether you're in the market for a Cire Trudon candle, a Jielde floor lamp, or a new pair of pants, all you have to do is walk through one door. Returns and exchanges are not appreciated, so be sure you're happy with what you want to buy before making a purchase.

4011 WEST SUNSET BOULEVARD IN SILVER LAKE. 323-669-1601.
mail.mohawkgeneralstore.net

798. Relish the past at **Counterpoint Records and Books,**

and browse its floor-to-ceiling selection of used books—from art books to poetry—as well as its mountains of out-of-print VHS and great vinyl. Painstakingly kept in alphabetical order, the selection of '60s and '70s records, which range from jazz to classical and Disney, is always worth flipping through. And with merchandise constantly moving in and out, Counterpoint always has something for somebody with some affection for the analog era.

5911 FRANKLIN AVENUE IN HOLLYWOOD. 323-957-7965.
www.counterpointrecordsandbooks.com

799. Thank the shopping gods for **Church Boutique.**

To enter paradise, shopping isn't mandatory, which makes coming to Church that much more appealing. Instead people come to Rodney Burns and David Malvaney's chic and discreet boutique, to hang out, look at their collection of interesting knick-knacks, and more often than not, avoid the paparazzi. If you feel like shopping, choose from their praiseworthy collection of unknown and need-to-know brands, like BiJules and John Malkovich's Technobohemian label, that will definitely leave you feeling enlightened.

7277 SANTA MONICA BOULEVARD IN WEST HOLLYWOOD. 323-876-8887.
www.churchboutique.com

800. Fall down into a rabbit hole of vintage finds at **Shareen Vintage.**

Rich in history as it is in fashion, Shareen Vintage in downtown Los Angeles is a sprawling fashion warehouse perfect for the serious vintage shopper. Stacks of racks filled with clothes from every era imaginable are strewn about the space where women dress and undress randomly while Shareen walks around the floor, helping with advice and styling tips. Being a regular has its benefits. Every Saturday, regulars get first dibs on several racks of 300 new vintage pieces each. Open to the public on Wednesdays, Saturdays, and Sundays only.

1721 NORTH SPRING STREET IN LOS ANGELES. 323-276-6226. www.shareen.com

801. Ride tall in your custom saddle from **Superior Saddlery.**

Olympians, Grand Prix competitors, and discerning riders get their saddles custom made by Master Saddle Maker Paul Selvey. Originally from Walsall, England, the saddle making capital of the world, he painstakingly builds his saddles with perfected technique and expertise ensuring the quality of each saddle. Made from the smooth leather of the water buffalo for maximum grip, and featuring beechwood spring

tree, wool panels, and an extra soft, deep seat to accommodate the most sensitive of backsides, all saddles are fully adjustable and ready to ride.
11700 LITTLE TUJUNGA CANYON ROAD, LAKE VIEW TERRACE. 818-899-8600. www.superiorsaddlery.com

---

802. When the ink well has run dry, stop for a refill at **The Fountain Pen Shop**.

In an age where *letters* are really code for emails and texts, it's refreshing to know that stores like The Fountain Pen Shop still exist. Located in Monrovia and filled with over 1,000 antique, collectible fountain pens, this is a writing paradise. For as low as $25 to as high as $500 you can outfit yourself with a great writing instrument that is either old or modern depending on your taste. They also repair pens and sell ink stain removers, which is always a good thing. So make like Max Fischer from Wes Anderson's *Rushmore* and flex your writing prowess. Calligraphy is actually a lot of fun.
2640 SOUTH MYRTLE AVENUE IN LOS ANGELES. 626-294-9974.

---

803. Dress up your noggin at **Baron Hats**, where the world's finest custom-made hats are made.

Create your dream hat or buy one of their classic reproductions from their huge inventory, featuring hats seen in tons of Hollywood films. Choose among the Indiana Jones, John Wayne Tribute Hats, the perfect straw or fedora, or my favorite, the Jack Thompson from *The Man from Snowy River*, all of which will become treasured possessions. The staff teaches you how to extend the life of these handmade treats with simple cleaning lessons—and even show you the proper way to pick them up.
1619 WEST BURBANK BOULEVARD IN BURBANK. 818-563-3025. www.baronhats.com

---

804. Say "yes" to decadence and indulge at **Sweet Lady Jane**.

For someone who didn't start out her career as a baker, Jane Lockhart has done a bang-up job. By creating mouth-watering baked goods using only the freshest and finest ingredients, she has made dessert an irresistible indulgence. Everything from her red velvet cake to triple berry shortcake and praline cheesecake is sinfully delicious and worth buying the whole cake. If you're a big fan of pie, the 10-inch deep-dish apple pie is perfection encased in a double thick crust. Although the $55 price tag might make some appetites abate, keep in mind that returning the pie pan automatically yields a $10 refund. Cakes start at around $37 and can go up to $400 depending on the size.
8360 MELROSE AVENUE IN WEST HOLLYWOOD. 323-653-7145. www.sweetladyjane.com

805. Be one with the beach by decorating your home with pieces from **Surfing Cowboys**.

Whether you're a surfer or just love the lifestyle, Surfing Cowboys has a great selection of vintage furniture and home décor to help bring a taste of the beach indoors. Whether you're shopping for something special or just browsing, each piece here has a unique history featured on a placard, just in case you want to know more. Enjoy the vibe and appreciate the nostalgia.

12553 VENICE BOULEVARD, LOS ANGELES. 310-915-6611. www.surfingcowboys.com

806. Sift through vintage while partying at **A&D Vintage Clothing**.

Last Saturday of every month, A&D throws a vintage party, usually open until 2 a.m. with an open bar and DJ. Here you'll find piles of clothes to dig through for just $7 a pound. Late night dancing, piles of cheap clothes, and free booze... Who would have guessed that shopping could be this fun?

35201 UNION PACIFIC AVENUE IN LOS ANGELES. 310-701-5126. www.advintageclothing.com

807. Snag cheap seats at the **Hollywood Bowl**.

The venerable Hollywood Bowl, one of the best music venues in Los Angeles, has been a staple for more than 80 years. Every summer thousands of locals and out-of-towners, come to picnic at this outdoor amphitheater, but few realize that seats can be bought for as little as $1 during the week, and $3 on weekends for big-name artists. Next time your friends ask if you want to take care of the picnic basket or the tickets, choose tickets.

2301 NORTH HIGHLAND AVENUE IN HOLLYWOOD. 323-850-2000. www.hollywoodbowl.com

808. Pick a card, any card at **The Magic Apple**.

With a great selection of props and magic effects, it's easy to pick up a few kid-friendly tricks for the budding Harry Houdini or Blackstone in your family. If you want to see a trick performed before you buy, you won't have to draw upon your powers of persuasion, the staff is more than happy to share a secret or two. Looking for something special? Wave your wand or simply ask and they'll special order it for you. This is not a trick; magic here really is this friendly.

11390 VENTURA BOULEVARD, 2ND FLOOR, IN STUDIO CITY. 818-508-9921. www.themagicapple.com

809. Buy a vintage timepiece at **Wanna Buy a Watch? (WBAW?)**.

For over twenty years, WBAW? has been one of the most popular vintage shopping destinations in Los Angeles for watch lovers. They have hundreds upon hundreds of beautifully restored watches on display that range from the moderately priced to the eye-poppingly expensive. Whether you like Art Deco pocket watches, vintage Omega Aqua Terras, or custom dial Rolex watches, you'll be more than pleased with what you find here. Soon you'll be shouting out the time, instead of waiting for someone to ask.

8465 MELROSE AVENUE IN LOS ANGELES. 323-653-0467. www.wannabuyawatch.com

810. Buy some jewelry, real or fake, at **Wertz Brothers**.

There's no shortage of vendors here at the Wertz Brothers Antique Mall: 190 dealers occupy this 20,000-square-foot treasure trove housed under one roof that sells a great mix of furniture, collectibles, cameras, art, and more. Here you'll find some beautiful estate and costume jewelry to choose from that ranges from the delicate and beautiful Trifari Tremblant pins to outlandish rhinestone creations. All that glitters here doesn't have to break the bank, so take a good look around and bring cash if you're planning on bargaining.

11879 SANTA MONICA BOULEVARD IN LOS ANGELES. 310-477-4251. www.wertzbrothers.com

811. See what develops from a trip to **Samy's Camera**.

Don't be surprised if you're suddenly overcome with the urge to yell, "Lights, Camera, Action!" when you first walk in. Since 1976, this has been the ultimate resource for professional and budding photographers, as well as a few directors. This full-service store, bursting at the seams with photo equipment, has a great and knowledgeable staff, offers digital processing, film development, and even camera repair. Hesitant to spend a huge amount of money on a camera without knowing if you'll be happy? Head to the rental department on the ground floor and see if it's available to rent. Try it out for a few days at a nominal cost before you decide. And don't be afraid to ask for advice, the customer service here is fantastic and they're more than happy to spend as much time as you need to ensure that you pick the right stuff.

431 SOUTH FAIRFAX AVENUE IN LOS ANGELES. 323-938-2420. www.samys.com

La Brea Avenue

La Brea Avenue is to Los Angeles what Lafayette Street is to New York: a shopping mecca that mixes high and low, chic and hip. On this stretch you'll find streetwear brands like Stüssy mingling with vintage veterans like Golyester and The Way We Wore, and in-between you'll spot classic, hard-to-find spectacles at Jacks Eyewear—and much more.

812. *American Rag CIE:* Home to the best denim bar in L.A., the World Denim Bar at American Rag is unparalleled. They've even installed cameras in the dressing rooms at booty-level, which send a streaming view of your derriere on a closed-circuit loop to a screen embedded in your dressing room mirror, ensuring that you see all necessary angles before making your choice.
150 SOUTH LA BREA AVENUE IN LOS ANGELES. 323-935-3154. www.amrag.com

813. *Jet Rag:* If *Bloodsport* and vintage shopping had a baby, that baby would be the Jet Rag $1 sale that happens every Sunday morning. People wake up at the crack of dawn and then wait for hours as bales of clothing are slowly cut loose throughout the morning, pouncing upon them as if these clothes were brains and they were starved zombies. Hold on tight and protect your face because people push, crawl, grab, and snatch whatever they can when you're not looking (and even when you're looking). Tempers do flare over fashion, especially when every item is a dollar. Be sure to grab a laundry bin if you get a chance so you have someplace to store all your finds. And if you can't find anything outside, head inside where every piece of vintage is meticulously organized by eras and categories. The prices are significantly higher, but then everything looks expensive when you compare it to a dollar.
825 NORTH LA BREA AVENUE IN LOS ANGELES. 323-939-0528

814. *UNDFTD:* Owners Eddie Cruz and James Bond know shoes and have made it their business for years. For the past decade they have stocked the shelves to reflect their fanatical passion for footwear with hard-to-find colorways and up-and-coming brands intermixed with all the classics. Go and pick up one of their special collaborations with Nike, New Balance, Converse, and Puma; try to score the ultimate limited edition, as they're often released at this outlet; or if you're just looking for a cool pair of sneakers, this place has it all. Be sure to check out their in-house label, sold in-store and online.
112½ SOUTH LA BREA AVENUE IN LOS ANGELES. 323-937-6077. undefeated.com

815. *Union L.A.:* You'll find a great selection of menswear brands from all over the world, all housed under Union's roof. Owner Chris Gibbs works hard so you can dress well, as he scours the globe for the best in well-designed menswear to fit any aesthetic. With brands like Visvim, White Mountaineering, Parabellum, Sacai, Wtaps . . . the legwork is done; all you need to do is shop. *110 SOUTH LA BREA AVENUE IN LOS ANGELES. 323-549-6950. www.unionlosangeles.com*

816. *Nick Metropolis:* The prop and furniture store on the corner of La Brea and 1st is iconic and as un-Ikea as you can get. You can see a life-size version of the Simpsons, buy retro plastic furniture, or just sit next to a weird statue of Barack Obama and have your picture taken. Whatever you do, it's fine at Nick Metropolis—"where furniture is famous 7 days a week." *100 SOUTH LA BREA AVENUE IN LOS ANGELES. 323-934-3700*

817. Give your movie memories a longer shelf life with a piece of Hollywood from **Larry Edmunds Bookshop**.

This trove of movie posters, books, photos, and other memorabilia reeks of the Golden Age of Hollywood—and, God, it smells good. Movie goddesses Kim Novak, Bette Davis, and Lauren Bacall are all signed and waiting for you to take them home and worship them on your mantle. Your love of classic films can only be fueled after a visit to this place—with all the Hollywood that surrounds you, you won't be able to get enough. Buy a classic movie poster, signed autobiographies, or even a postcard. For a moderate fee you'll have a piece of Hollywood to call your very own.
6644 HOLLYWOOD BOULEVARD IN LOS ANGELES. 323-463-3273. www.larryedmunds.com

818. Get happily lost in huge piles of stuff at **Junk for Joy**.

This space is filled to the brim with everything you could want to find for costumes, funky vintage outfits, and fun, out-there clothing. Stop by, but clear out a good chunk of time, 'cause there are nooks and corners that are worth exploring. There is literally no way of knowing what you might walk out with...
3314 WEST MAGNOLIA BOULEVARD IN BURBANK. 818-569-4903. www.junkforjoy.com

819. Spend hours going over toe shape, shoe design, colorways, and leathers to create the shoes of your dreams at **George Esquivel Shoes**.

Let's make no bones about it: these shoes are expensive. A bespoke pair of George

Esquivel brogues or boots will set you back a few hundred dollars or even a cool grand, but having shoes handmade by this former CFDA *Vogue* Fashion Fund Nominee is a necessary splurge. You'll definitely have some happy feet once you slip into your very own pair.

8309 WEST 3RD STREET IN LOS ANGELES. 714-670-2200. www.esquivelshoes.com

---

820. Protect your eyes from the sun—and the star wattage of celebs and fake-tanning victims—with a pair of specs from the original **Oliver Peoples**.

Oliver Peoples is a brand that's known world-wide and renowned for its high-quality materials and design, and it all started with Larry and Dennis Leight's first optical boutique on Sunset Boulevard. You can buy Oliver Peoples almost anywhere, but to buy at their original store is something different entirely.

8642 WEST SUNSET BOULEVARD IN LOS ANGELES. 310-657-2553. www.oliverpeoples.com

---

821. See a movie for cheap at **Highland 3 Theater**.

You won't find $16 tickets at this historic 1924 movie theater designed by L.A. Smith. Instead you'll find a relic of the old Highland Park area that was once an entertainment hot spot. Come on Tuesdays and Wednesdays when ticket prices are $4; the neighborhood vibe and a concession stand that won't gouge you will surely have you coming back for more.

5604 NORTH FIGUEROA STREET IN LOS ANGELES. 323-256-6383. www.highlandtheatres.com

---

822. Find some fun Swedish trinkets at **Yolk**.

Scandinavians must spell success Y-O-L-K because this Silver Lake boutique isn't anything but successful. Classic Scandinavian styles (Marimekko) and amazing Stokke kids furniture are mixed in with international finds sought out from all over the world, as well as a large selection of local goods from artists in the area.

1626 SILVER LAKE BOULEVARD IN SILVER LAKE. 323-660-4315. www.shopyolk.com

---

823. Give the gift of Japan from **Rafu Bussan**.

Of all the little stores in Little Tokyo Rafu Bussan stands out for its ceramics. Meticulously organized and beautifully packaged, Rafu Bussan has a ceramic something, whether it's a bowl or a sake set, for everyone.

326 EAST 2ND STREET IN LOS ANGELES. 213-614-1181. www.rafubussaninc.com

824. Indulge your naughty side at the **Pleasure Chest.**

Can't tell a Pocket Rocket from your Rabbit? The people at the Pleasure Chest can help you. Like a personal trainer finding the workout routine to best suit you, this one-stop sex shop launched a personal shopper program, which pairs customers with in-store experts to navigate the boutique's selection of goods—from crops and candles to lubes and lingerie.

7733 SANTA MONICA BOULEVARD IN WEST HOLLYWOOD. 323-650-1022. www.thepleasurechest.com

825. Slow down to notice the thoughtfully chosen treasures at **Tortoise General Store.**

Every item in this impeccable store on Abbot Kinney in Venice has been hand picked by Keiko and Taku Shinomoto, the Japanese couple behind the scenes. Only the best-crafted and designed items are right for their discerning clientele. Baby kimonos, Noguchi-designed paper lamps, sculptures, Japanese folk crafts, and ceramics. For more, head down the street and visit their other space, Tortoise.

1208 ABBOT KINNEY BOULEVARD IN VENICE. 310-314-8448. www.tortoiselife.com

826. Go global at **A+R.**

Owners Andy Griffith and Rose Apodaca give shoppers a concentrated dose of well-edited global design at their store. Browse through their amazing selection of products from international and local designers, for items to help up the design ante in your humble abode—or wardrobe. A favorite among style-conscious and design-savvy Angelenos, so you're always bound to rub well-dressed shoulders with a hip crowd.

1121 ABBOT KINNEY BOULEVARD IN VENICE. 800-913-0071. www.aplusrstore.com

827. Shop at the L.A. County Coroner's Office gift shop, **Skeletons in the Closet,**

which offers one-of-a-kind and slightly morbid gifts that are perfect souvenirs. Choose from t-shirts, towels, totes, and key chains, all displaying one of the County Coroner's unique designs, such as a skeleton in a Sherlock Holmes outfit, the instantly recognizable chalked body outline, or the Coroner's seal. And yes, the gift shop is located at the actual coroner's office.

1104 N MISSION ROAD IN LOS ANGELES. 323-343-0760. www.lacoroner.com

828. Get your money's worth at **99 Cents Only Stores.**

You can't go wrong with a trip to the 99 Cents Only Store, where every visit yields savings and surprises. Finding anything for less a dollar used to be easy, and is now becoming an anomaly. A fading blinking light on our shopping horizon. Thank goodness the 99 Cents store is still around and still offering a myriad of different products for less than a dollar. The best part of visiting one of the stores is to see just how much you can get for your money's worth. Make a game of it and start with $5. If you go any higher than $100, you might walk out with half the store.

www.99only.com; check website for locations.

→ ***FACT:*** *Photographer Andrea Gursky's image of the interior of the Hollywood 99 Cents Only Store became the most expensive photograph ever sold in February 2007, auctioned for $3.3 million.*

829. Find inner peace at **Sahaja Meditation.**

Yogis from all over the world come to find self-realization through meditation—and at Sahaja, they not only offer you this experience first-hand, but for free. As they say at Sahaja, "Your self-realization is your birthright. You should never have to pay for the experience of Divine Love." If only every journey to self-discovery were this peaceful and cost-efficient.

19530 VENTURA BOULEVARD IN TARZANA. 866-972-4252. www.sahajameditation.com

830. Engage your senses at **Spice Station.**

Step inside and inhale the heavily fragranced air of this culinary perfume store. Here you'll breathe in the heady aromas of spices from around the world, learn about their histories, and get a little taste. There are so many to choose from you may have to step outside for some fresh air, as the spices have a tendency to overpower your senses in a good way. Another sensory overload, Vacation Vinyl (p. 296), is just down the street.

3819 WEST SUNSET BOULEVARD IN LOS ANGELES. 323-660-2565.
www.spicestationsilverlake.com

Vinyl Sources

Record collectors and people who amass music as others collect books or antiques will travel all over the world to fill the holes in their libraries, but lucky Angelenos have no shortage of places carrying classic LPs, EPs, and 45s, if they know where to look. There are scores of independent, new, and used record stores across the city to keep vinyl enthusiasts of all kinds happy, but to find the best ones you'll have to roam east to west and scour the streets of some unlikely neighborhoods. The ones highlighted are special not only for keeping astonishing collections of vinyl, from classic oldies to life-changing rarities, but also for being unique places that are worth the journey itself.

831. *Amoeba Music:* Stepping into Amoeba is a lot like visiting L.A.: it's crowded and vast. You look out onto a sea of people and find the scene so daunting at first, you're not sure what you've gotten yourself into. But once you get past the initial shock, you'll discover that the real joy of coming to Amoeba is in its hidden pleasures. Saddle up next to the Goths and the Hippie rockers, the Jazz and Hip Hop heads, and start digging through acres of bins. With the largest collection of vinyl in town, you can easily spend a day just exploring. As you stumble across interesting finds you may want more information: the large and well informed staff is more than happy to help. Come looking for nothing and expect to find everything. Don't forget to check the in-store calendar to see what big names will be gracing the Amoeba stage for a free show. From Paul McCartney to DJ UNKLE sets; from Cut Chemist and Elijah Wood (yes Sauron, even Frodo has performed here), to poets and comedians; signings by Guillermo del Toro, movie casts, and more—at one point or another, they'll all pass through Amoeba's doors. All free, all ages. Sign up for the Amoeba Music Newsletter for upcoming live shows.
6400 SUNSET BOULEVARD IN LOS ANGELES. 323-245-6400. www.amoeba.com

832. *Origami Vinyl:* Come for their intimate in-store live music that is slowly rivaling Amoeba (on a smaller scale), with performers such as Jonsi from Sigur Ros and Superchunk. Even with its small selection of vinyl, this record shop/label has become a fun hang out spot for locals.
1816 WEST SUNSET BOULEVARD IN LOS ANGELES. 213-413-3030. www.origamiorigami.com

833. *Vacation Vinyl:* Say yes to a heaping serving of psychedelia—in vinyl form. Niche music and weird formats in all their glory reside here. Vacation

produces free live in-store shows every week, works directly with bands and labels to stock the store—and in a crazy recent coup, stole away the legendary used record buyer and store operator Pete Majors from Amoeba.
3815 WEST SUNSET BOULEVARD IN SUNSET JUNCTION. 323-666-2111. www.vacationvinyl.com

834. *Record Surplus Shop:* Get lucky, and hit the motherload—local radio station KCRW is known for dropping off some of its fabled vinyl collection here to be sold to the masses. This store's tagline is "The Last Record Store"—and if it was, indeed, the last record store, that would be just fine. It's the perfect place for the casual collector and the forward thinking DJ. At this Westside vinyl staple, you'll find no pretense and a selection heavier on the classics than pop music.
12436 SANTA MONICA BOULEVARD, LOS ANGELES. 310-979-4577. www.recordsurplusla.com

835. *Records L.A.:* Get your fill of soul and funk on the weekends while throwing back a cold one and flipping through bins filled only with vinyl. Could there be anything better? They update their MySpace page occasionally, letting you hear some of the latest music they've received.
5654 WEST ADAMS BOULEVARD IN LOS ANGELES. 213-399-9806. www.myspace.com/recordsla

836. *Wombleton:* Forget funk and soul, this counterpart to Records L.A. is the place for rock, psych rock, folk, rare, and imported records. The New Arrivals Party is a their way to celebrate the arrival of tons of original pressings with a DJ that spins the real vinyl (!) in a fun-filled environment. Bring your portable player with you so you can listen to the interesting and unique records you'll discover: Cosmic Disco or Goth/Darkwave anyone? Come check out their sidewalk sales during the weekend.
5123 YORK BOULEVARD IN LOS ANGELES. 213-422-0069. www.wombletonrecords.com

837. *Poo-Bah Records:* If you never associated the music scene in Pasadena with anything other than the famous Jan and Dean song about a certain little old lady, it's time to give Poobah's a visit. Poo-Bah Record Shop has been Pasadena's source for underground hip-hop, experimental, and other music since 1971.
2636 EAST COLORADO BOULEVARD IN PASADENA. 626-449-3359. www.poobah.com

Expert Contributor: Kristin M. Burke

Kristin M. Burke is a costume designer for motion pictures in Los Angeles. She is the author of *Costuming for Film: The Art and the Craft, Going Hollywood: How to Get Started, Keep Going, and Not Turn Into a Sleaze,* and *I Wanna Be Your Vegan: The John Johnson Cookbook*.

MY TEN FAVORITE PLACES TO SPEND OTHER PEOPLE'S MONEY

Santee Alley. This is L.A.'s version of a souk—vendors yelling, haggling, babies crying, salsa music blasting, dirty, overcrowded streets, the enticing aroma of street meat wafting above the crowd . . . For all its surface-level disgustingness, there are bargains to be had if you are an adept negotiator. It's a cash-only situation, and receipts are sometimes hard to come by. Worth a trip: see a minimum of fifty varieties of knock-off Louis Vuitton handbags.
SANTEE STREET AT 12TH STREET IN LOS ANGELES. www.thesanteealley.com

Slauson Swap Meet. Also called "The Slauson Super Mall," here is a place where you can get a custom airbrushed T-shirt, brand-new sneakers, custom embroidery, lingerie that would make your granny blush, custom gold jewelry, and your nails done—all under one roof. Yes, you can haggle (but be nice, as the booth owners are notoriously cantankerous), and yes, you should bring cash. Worth a trip for the wide array of fake luxury brand names alone—"Couch," "Roolex," "Cucci," "Lewis Witten." Awesome.
1600 WEST SLAUSON AVENUE IN LOS ANGELES. 323-778-6055.

Burlington Coat Factory. It's a bit like picking blackberries in extreme heat—you're sweating, there are scratchy brambles, and there are a lot of things that look good but aren't berries. So if you like scrounging, BCF is fantastic. They have a very good selection of men's suiting sizes (not high quality, but they do have many 52L and 46S options). They also have a great selection of cheap bathrobes. If you look hard enough, you can find designer jeans at a fraction of the cost of retail. And where else can you find a down coat in the middle of summer?
22835 VICTORY BOULEVARD IN WEST HILLS. 818-340-2494. www.burlingtoncoatfactory.com

International Silks and Woolens. Without question, this is the best fabric store in L.A. Why? They carry an enormous selection of vintage fabric, and they are the nicest fabric vendors you will ever meet. Attentive, personal service, beautiful fabrics, and a family feeling will keep you coming back. Look upstairs for the vintage silks and be

blown away. Worth a trip: special-occasion fabrics and notions, and service with not just a smile, but also a hug.
8347 BEVERLY BOULEVARD IN LOS ANGELES. 323-653-6453. www.internationalsilks.com

Madison Shoes. These shoes aren't cheap, but they are *soooo* beautiful. Boasting designers like Chloe, Lanvin, Caleen Cordero, Miu Miu, and Yves St. Laurent, this is the place to shop when you have earned the right to purchase something fabulous.
9630 BRIGHTON WAY IN BEVERLY HILLS. 310-273-4787. www.madisonstyle.com

Amy Ming Jewelry. The great thing about Amy Ming Jewelry is that you can find pieces for $12, and you can find pieces for $1200. There is something for every taste and style, and the selection is wonderful. Many items are handmade and one of a kind. Bracelets, earrings, necklaces, rings, and pendants—it's all here, and in exquisite stones and metals. You will not leave empty-handed; it's a great place to buy a gift.
5652 WEST 3RD STREET IN LOS ANGELES. 323-938-8889. www.amyming.com

The Cooper Building Sample Sales. On the last Friday of every month, the streets of the garment district hum with the unmistakable buzz of bargain seekers flying in and out of the Cooper Building. It's a cash-only situation, and all sales are final, but I have had extraordinary luck purchasing very expensive garments for like $10. This is a scrounger's paradise, and it helps if you set a limit or bring a list of garments you are looking for. The atmosphere is intoxicating, and it is easy to get caught up in the rapture of amazing bargains.
860 SOUTH LOS ANGELES STREET IN LOS ANGELES. www.cooperdesignspace.com

Golyester. Beautiful antique and vintage treasures abound at Golyester. It's an exquisite collection, and the prices are accordingly more than you'd find at a thrift store. Knowledgeable, helpful staff are a real plus. It's easy to get lost in the dreams and nostalgia of the atmosphere—the accessories alone will blow your mind: hats, gloves, shoes, belts, and jewelry, oh my.
450 SOUTH LA BREA AVENUE IN LOS ANGELES. 323-931-1339. www.golyester.com

Shelly's Dance and Costume Wear. This is a one-stop shop at Halloween time. Shelley's has been here for absolutely ever, and they really have a niche carved out for themselves. There are dance costumes—leotards, tutus, sequined tap-dance numbers, pointe shoes—and there are also costume-costumes, from devils to the *Wizard of Oz*, aliens, clowns, princesses, slashers, and pirates. Sales clerks are sometimes quite crabby, but that's half the fun of the experience, *non?*
2089 WESTWOOD BOULEVARD IN LOS ANGELES. 310-475-1400.
www.shelleysdanceandcostume.com

Samuel French. Everything you ever need to know about filmmaking or theater or writing or directing or costuming can be found at Samuel French bookstore. With locations in Hollywood and in Studio City, hold on to your wallet when you walk in the door. It's a great place in which to get lost for a few hours. I've purchased many great research books here, and the clerks are very knowledgeable and helpful if you are searching for something hard to find.
7623 WEST SUNSET BOULEVARD IN LOS ANGELES. 866-598-8449. www.samuelfrench.com

CHAPTER 8

Enrichment and Renewal

Improving one's well-being is key when living in any city, especially one like Los Angeles. Let's face it, the traffic alone could make your blood pressure spike! But fear not, the city is well-equipped to help you with all your revitalization needs. From education to recreation and the all-important relaxation, L.A. has a wide range to choose from.

This city encourages open minds and active bodies and helps those looking to do more. Dynamic classes, sports, or pastimes have a home here, and the city attracts people from all over the world who are willing to share their creativity and expertise. And finding what you're looking for in terms of enrichment is easier than you think. From yoga classes to book readings, public lectures, performances, university courses on art, dance lessons, and language classes, this city is full of wonderful resources. Who knows, a few expert chess lessons could have you feeling like Bobby Fischer, and a class or two at the Silver Lake Conservatory might give you the courage to ask Flea if you could go on tour with the Red Hot Chili Peppers.

And once you've fed your mind, don't neglect to feed your body and soul. Be sure to refresh, relax, and rejuvenate at one of the city's many spas or meditation centers, or by doing a bit of exercise. No matter what you want or need, there's a wealth of resources at the ready to fulfill your every desire—be it to sharpen the mind, warm the soul, or just help you burn off all that Korean barbecue.

838. Listen to stories at Mark Taper Auditorium at the **Central Library**.

There's nothing better than going to a library and having someone else do all the reading for you. At [ALOUD] at the Central Library, all you have to do is sit back and listen. Since 1993, this award-winning series has brought lectures by professors from numerous universities, readings from celebrated authors, performances by musicians and actors, film screenings, and forums for discussion to the people of Los Angeles, giving them the opportunity to listen to key figures in the arts, humanities, business, and science. Generally provided free of charge, they stimulate conversations and provide an arena for civic dialogue. Exchange a few ideas through active audience participation and a question-and-answer session with local authors, academics, and experts from within their fields.

RICHARD J. RIORDAN CENTRAL LIBRARY. 630 WEST 5TH STREET. 213-228-7500. Check the website for a calendar of events and exhibitions. www.lfla.org

839. Meet with foreign intellectuals at the **Villa Aurora**.

In this castle by the sea, you'll discover an international meeting of the minds. Villa Aurora is a place of encouragement where artists and scholars alike come to discuss anything, including literature, art, science, and politics. Purchased by German-Jewish writer Lion Feuchtwanger and his wife, Marta, in 1943, it became a meeting place for German and European exiles in Los Angeles. Willed to the University of Southern California (USC), it remains an artist residence and historic landmark. To promote and foster German-American cultural exchange and to remember the European exiles that settled in Southern California, Villa Aurora offers a variety of public lectures, screenings, and performances.

520 PASEO MIRAMER, PACIFIC PALISADES. 310-454-4231. www.villa-aurora.org

840. Speak your mind at **Zócalo Public Square**.

Since Aztec times, the word *zócalo* has meant gathering place. Here in Los Angeles, Zócalo Public Square is the town square and a forum to speak and connect. The Zócalo provides a venue where the public can connect through lectures, screenings, and conferences with Nobel Prize laureates, Pulitzer Prize winners, academics, innovators, and other highly regarded members of their fields in an open and accessible space. These discussions not only inform the public, they also educate. Check out where the community comes together to listen, speak, and discuss what is happening in the world today, and see if you have something to say.

213-381-2541. www.zocalopublicsquare.org

841. Ask a few questions at **Writers Bloc**.

For sixteen years, this independent literary and cultural series has engaged some of Los Angeles's favorite writers and thinkers in public exchanges, allowing us to hear what they have to say. It's one of the best places to see famous authors interviewed by other notable celebrities, and with free screenings and Q and As, not only do you get to spend an evening looking at someone great, you also get to listen to them.

www.writersblocpresents.com

842. Learn about the unknown from real experts at the **Jet Propulsion Laboratory**.

Space, the final frontier, might be light years away, but if you're interested in learning more, the NASA Jet Propulsion Laboratory is infinitely closer. Their Theodore von Kármán monthly lecture series, named after the founder of the JPL, offers the public a chance to come and learn about space- and technology-related topics from the pros. Lectures take place twice per month on consecutive Thursdays and Fridays, and admission and parking are free. No reservation is required but seating is limited so come early.

4800 OAK GROVE DRIVE, PASADENA. 818-354-4321. www.jpl.nasa.gov

843. You don't have to be enrolled to **sit in on a lecture at a university**.

Los Angeles is an intellectual and collegiate hub of knowledge and institutions. Those interested in attending university lectures and events will find many of them open to the public. With diverse subjects ranging from politics to Egyptology and health care to hip-hop, you can learn a variety of things without having to worry about tuition.

Check websites for more information. UCLA: www.ucla.edu, USC: www.usc.edu, California Institute of Technology: www.caltech.edu, Cal State LA: www.calstatela.edu, Los Angeles City College: www.lacitycollege.edu, Art Center College of Design: www.artcenter.edu, Otis College of Art and Design: www.otis.edu

844. See a strange show at the **Steve Allen Theater** at the Center for Inquiry Los Angeles.

This is the theater of the absurd, a place that oozes eccentricity in a city—Hollywood—that already has pretty high standards. Be adventurous and come see a show that's new and imaginative at this alternative, forward-thinking establishment that's not only a theater in a basement but also part of the Center for Inquiry Los Angeles. Founded by astronomer Carl Sagan and prolific science fiction author Isaac Asimov, this non-profit works to promote science and secular humanism and embraces controversy. So whether you catch one of former artistic director Amit Itelman's unique Trepany House productions or see Satan-worshipping and a virgin sacrifice when you visit, keep an open mind and remember that it's just theater.

4773 HOLLYWOOD BOULEVARD AT NORTH BERENDO STREET, LOS ANGELES. 323-666-4268. For tickets, call 800-595-4849. www.trepanyhouse.org

---

845. Learn the importance of the rook and pawn versus rook endgame at the **Los Angeles Chess Club.**

Do you dream of one day being a Chess Grandmaster but don't know a knight from a bishop? Come to the Los Angeles Chess Club and learn from some of the best chess players in the city; soon, you'll be pulling a Garry Kasparov! Well, you might not become a world chess champion like Kasparov overnight, but at least you'll know how to identify a rook properly. Private lessons can be pricey at $350 for six hours and $650 for twelve hours, but no one said it would be cheap to learn how to say "checkmate."

11514 SANTA MONICA BOULEVARD. 310-795-5710. www.lachessclub.com

---

846. Listen to stories from an ex-Scientologist at the **Tongue and Groove at the Hotel Café.**

The monthly Tongue and Groove series in Hollywood at the Hotel Café showcases short stories, poetry, personal essays, spoken-word pieces, and music from various notable authors and musicians who grace its stage. If you're lucky, you'll get a chance to hear something from host and Tongue and Groove founder Conrad Romo, who occasionally reads from a continuing series on his experience as an ex-Scientologist—everything L. Ron Hubbard and Tom Cruise wouldn't want you to hear. But I'm sure Katie Holmes won't mind.

1623½ NORTH CAHUENGA BOULEVARD. 323-461-2040. www.tongueandgroovela.com

---

847. Create art in a historic setting at **Barnsdall Art Park.**

Where else can you take part in a community art class in a historic architectural gem like Frank Lloyd Wright's Hollyhock House? Donated by art maven Aline Barnsdall in 1927 to the city of Los Angeles for use as an art center, Barnsdall Park has been a focal point for artistic expression on various levels. In addition to the youth art and music classes, it also offers classes for adults that range from jewelry making to ceramics, and hosts musical and performance artists at the Barnsdall Gallery Theatre.

4800 HOLLYWOOD BOULEVARD, LOS ANGELES. 323-660-4254. www.barnsdall.org

848. Take a class with some Japanese flair at **Tortoise General Store**.

In addition to selling an amazing selection of hand-crafted goods, Tortoise General Store offers expert wood carving, flower arranging (ikebana), and saori hand weaving classes. A few hours with master woodcarver Yo Takimoto held outdoors in a very intimate ten-person class will have you speaking the language of wood in no time.

1208 ABBOT KINNEY BOULEVARD. 310-314-8448. www.tortoisegeneralstore.com

849. Learn the art of painterly printing at **Josephine Press**.

Every other Saturday, under the watchful eye of an experienced print maker, you'll spend 7 fun hours perfecting the process of making art by monoprint. Open to beginners and advanced-level printers, you'll spend the day transferring images applied to Plexiglas plate to paper, creating your own work of art. Classes are limited to 5 participants and fill up quickly, so act fast. Sessions run from 10 a.m. till 5 p.m. with an $80 fee, plus $10 for materials. Tools are provided and paper is available for purchase. See website for more information.

2928 SANTA MONICA BOULEVARD, SANTA MONICA. 310-453-1691.
Email josephinepress@earthlink.net to resgister or visit www.josephinepress.com

850. Don't say a word at the **Mime Theatre Studio**.

If Marcel Marceau, the godfather and master of mime, once said that Lorin Eric Salm, the owner of Mime Theatre Studio, was "a very talented mime, very disciplined, very dedicated and constant," you should pay attention. Trained by Marceau at his Paris International School of Mimodrama and with thirty years in theatrical mime and theater under his belt, Salm creates the magic of illusion through the power of silence. Mime Theatre Studio offers three levels of classes and gives a discount to those willing to pay in advance. Call at least two weeks beforehand to ask about the discount. Just remember to speak up over the phone, as they can't hear mime.

6131 COLDWATER CANYON AVENUE, NORTH HOLLYWOOD. 310-494-MIME.
www.mimetheatrestudio.com

851. Reconsider a career under the big top after taking circus classes at the **Kinetic Theory Theatre**.

At Kinetic Theory Circus Arts, the only progressive skill-based circus classes and theater-training program in the Los Angeles area, they offer students of all ages and skill levels the opportunity to train with top-notch professionals in a variety of different fields. Classes include introduction to circus arts, circus conditioning, aerial arts, con-

tortion, and more. Whether you're interested in learning the basics, developing moves for a show, or just having fun, Kinetic Theory Circus Arts will help you attain your goals.
3604 HOLDREGE AVENUE, LOS ANGELES. 310-606-2617. www.kinetictheorytheatre.com

---

852. Bring the kids to the **Armory Center for the Arts** for the year-round youth-arts education program.

Here, instructors, most with Masters of Fine Arts degrees, provide the materials and tools to help students realize their creative visions at any age. And while the kids busy themselves with tapping into their imaginations, parents can observe everything from high above on the Armory's balcony.
145 NORTH RAYMOND AVENUE, PASADENA. 626-792-5101. www.armoryarts.org

---

853. Put your best made-up faces forward at **Cinema Makeup School**.

Hollywood is all about illusions, and what better place to learn the art of make-believe than at a real movie industry makeup school? Sign up for the Master Makeup course, where you'll learn a ton over eighteen weeks, including makeup techniques for high-fashion, character, prosthetic, and the ever-important special effects. Soon you'll be creating looks that will have everyone doing a double take.
3780 WILSHIRE BOULEVARD, SUITE 202, LOS ANGELES. 213-368-1234. www.cinemamakeup.com

---

854. Lavish your hair with love by visiting **Salon Benjamin**.

This light and airy space filled with artworks (curated by Sonja Teri), vintage artifacts, and an overstuffed Chesterfield sofa is not your typical salon. Then again, Benjamin Mohapi isn't your regular hair stylist. At his salon, you'll get the same star treatment he's been giving musicians, photographers, and celebrities for the past 23 years, and with a spot of afternoon tea to boot. It may cost you a small fortune ($300) for an appointment with Ben, but after your first, you'll wonder how you or your hair ever got on without him.
8910 MELROSE AVENUE IN WEST HOLLYWOOD. 424-249-3296. www.salonbenjamin.com

---

855. Get a haircut at **Vidal Sassoon Academy**.

Although it's the hair academy and not an actual salon, that doesn't mean you're not getting the real deal when you come here for a cut. Students here are trained to cut and style hair following the ethos of the man who "changed the world with a pair of scissors" and coined the phrase "If you don't look good, we don't look good."

Vidal Sassoon revolutionized hair with the Mia Farrow pixie cut, Nancy Kwon's sexy bob, and the geometric five-point bob once demonstrated on Grace Coddington, and at the academy they continue his work. Whether you're interested in a modern, low-maintenance, wash-and-go look, or something more drastic, make an appointment and come with an open mind. If you're worried about trainees cutting hair, don't be: supervisors are on hand overseeing each cut and sometimes stepping in to tweak the job to make sure that everything is perfect. Besides, it's hair; it'll grow back. Bring your student ID for an even bigger discount.

321 SANTA MONICA BOULEVARD IN SANTA MONICA. 310-255-0011. www.vidalsassoon.com

---

856. Perk up your color or try a new shade at the **Aveda Institute Los Angeles.**

When it comes to beauty, there's always a price, but at the Aveda Institute, it's a lot cheaper than you think. The Institute, located near UCLA, is a hands-on classroom filled with students enrolled in a 56-week program trained by a team of full-time and part-time instructors. Local college students and bargain hunters come here to benefit from the Institute's intense curriculum—from waxing to styling, cutting to coloring. Hair looking dull? Come for some color and a gloss. For only $25, not only will your hair be happy, you'll have enough left over just in case you'd like to pamper yourself some more.

10935 WEYBURN AVENUE IN WESTWOOD. 310-209-2000. www.avedainstitutelosangeles.com

---

857. Learn a real history lesson at the **Los Angeles National Cemetery.**

Los Angeles may be famous for the sheer number of stars laid to rest around the city, but heroes have been interred here as well. Head to Westwood and take a walk around the cemetery, where you'll find a somber history lesson among the graves of soldiers who fought in the Spanish-American War, World War I, World War II, and the Korean War. You'll also find more than one hundred Buffalo Soldiers as well as two war dogs and their handlers. The vast amount of people who lost their lives serving their country will leave you speechless.

950 SOUTH SEPULVEDA BOULEVARD, LOS ANGELES. 310-268-4675.
www.cem.va.gov/cems/nchp/losangeles.asp

---

858. Stitch your way to a new wardrobe at the **Sewing Arts Center.**

There's nothing like the allure of saving money on new clothes to help motivate you to learn how to make your own, and taking a class here is a great investment. You'll learn the basics, advanced fashion sewing, how to make accessories, and more. The center offers a popular children's camp during the summer, and if you thought sewing was a woman's job, you'll be surprised to find that a large number of the students are men. Sign up for the five-week jeans-making course, which is one of the most entertaining courses available.

3330 PICO BOULEVARD, SANTA MONICA. 310-450-4300. www.sewingartscenter.com

---

859. Add "bilingual" to your resume at the **Beverly Hills Lingual Institute**.

When living in such a multicultural city Los Angeles, you can't expect everyone to speak English. So why not broaden your own horizons and learn something new. The institute offers more than twenty-five language classes ranging from Korean to Spanish, and considering Los Angeles means "The Angels" in the latter, it might be a good place to start. Whatever you choose, be ready because whether you're a beginner or an advanced speaker, you'll be diving right in with an eight-week course. But don't worry, with class size limited to ten people, you'll get all the attention you need to get that accent just right.

439 NORTH CANON DRIVE, BEVERLY HILLS. 310-858-0717. www.bhlingual.com

---

860. Learn to throw clay on a wheel like a pro during the six-week pottery-making course at **Xiem Clay Center**.

Ghost and its memorable pottery scene made the medium famous, but there's more to clay than just Patrick Swayze and Demi Moore. Once you've stopped singing along with the Righteous Brothers and are ready to learn, head to Xiem. Each class includes twenty-five pounds of clay and twelve hours of instruction to get you started on throwing, trimming, and glazing. There are also private lessons available if you're shy about throwing clay around strangers.

1563 NORTH LAKE AVENUE IN PASADENA. 626-794-5833. www.xiemclaycenter.com

---

861. **Derby Por Vida**, the L.A. Derby Dolls' Roller Derby fitness program,

will whip you into shape. For $55 (the cost of the class plus membership and USARS insurance), you'll get to strap on some skates and learn how to stop and go, transition and jump, and employ basic blocking techniques with the best of them. You'll also participate in endurance drills and learn the all-important whip techniques as you work your way through Roller Derby 101. Some equipment and skates are on hand to borrow but be sure to bring your own wrist and mouth guards. All classes are held at the L.A. Derby Dolls' Doll Factory.

1910 WEST TEMPLE STREET, LOS ANGELES. www.derbydolls.com/fitness/

Bowling

The feeling of wax under your feet as you try not to slip and fall down the lane, the sound of the ball crashing against the pins, the smell of beer and nachos and socks...what's not to love? Bowling, you're like heaven on Earth. Tots and octogenarians alike can send pins flying and you don't have to bring your own shoes or ball to feel like you're a pro. Even as Wii and Xbox Kinect vie to take our attention away from the alleys, nothing beats the real deal. Here are a few lanes that are still scoring strikes.

862. *AMF Mar Vista Lanes.* Thoughts of *The Big Lebowski* come to mind as you set foot inside this old-timey bowling alley, with its faded interiors, greasy-spoon food, and cocktail bar that serves—you guessed it—White Russians. Don't let its age (it opened in 1958) fool you, though. The lanes are oiled, the scoring equipment is top-notch, and it gets so crowded with leagues that you'd consider joining just to throw a ball down a lane. Avoid league nights unless your ideal evening consists of watching other people bowl.
12125 VENICE BOULEVARD IN LOS ANGELES. 310-391-5288. amf.com/marvistalanes.

863. *The Spare Room.* Inside the Roosevelt Hotel is the hippest bowling lounge in town. It's classy and clean, but unfortunately there are only two lanes. Call ahead to make a reservation; while you wait for your lane to free up, grab a drink in the rec room bar, play a game of chess, or take part in an epic battle of Connect Four. Once you're up, slide your feet into a pair of custom-made George Esquivel bespoke bowling shoes and get ready to throw some serious strikes. Afterward, commemorate your evening with a photo in the secret photo booth, if you can find it. (Hint: it's hidden behind one of the walls.)
Hollywood Roosevelt Hotel: 7000 HOLLYWOOD BOULEVARD. 323-769-7296. www.spareroomhollywood.com

864. *Lucky Strike.* The Lucky Strike knows how to take care of its bowlers. At its Pasadena 300 location, everything about the game is upscale and upper class. A sizing guide helps ensure you get the right ball, shoes are delivered to your booth, and signature drinks and delicious appetizers are available for your snacking pleasure while you watch music videos on projection screens in between games. For a second, you might even forget why you came in the first place. For parties, the private 300 Club, with seven lanes and a separate bar, is definitely a perfect score.
3545 EAST FOOTHILL BOULEVARD, PASADENA. 626-351-8858. www.threehundred.com/pasadena.html

865. *Palos Verdes Bowl.* Although it's located in a strip mall, don't be fooled. Palos Verdes Bowl is filled with forty lanes of bowling heaven. More than fifty years of wear and tear haven't diminished the sturdiness and smoothness of these lanes, and you can't beat their Monday Mania special. For just $9, you can have unlimited bowling access from 6:00 p.m. to 9:30 p.m., and that's including shoes. If a deal like that doesn't enrich your soul (and wallet) and renew your being, you're not bowling enough. Check online to see their weekly happenings and other special events, and sign up for their Bowling eClub to receive two free games of bowling.
24600 CRENSHAW BOULEVARD, TORRANCE. 310-326-5120. www.pvbowl.com

866. *All Star Lanes.* These lanes have seen better days. The carpet is threadbare, its holiday decor reminds you that Santa isn't real, and although it once hosted the Beastie Boys' annual Grand Royal Christmas party, it hasn't seen Ad-Rock or Mike D. in years. But there's still something awesome about this place, especially at night when the lanes light up for some serious glow-in-the-dark bowling.
4459 EAGLE ROCK BOULEVARD IN LOS ANGELES. 323-254-2579. www.allstarlanesbowling.com

867. *Pinz.* People come to Pinz to bowl as much as they do to people watch. A celebrity favorite, their lanes are often occupied by the likes of Cameron Diaz and Justin Timberlake, among others. If there's no star power in sight, don't despair as they're there in spirit; you'll find their personalized bowing balls on display. Come to Pinz's Shake, Rattle & Bowl nights for some incredibly loud music and tons of bowling fun. The flashing lights can trick anyone into thinking they've spotted someone who might be famous.
12655 VENTURA BOULEVARD, STUDIO CITY. 818-769-7600. www.pinzbowlingcenter.com

868. *Montrose Bowl.* A small wonder of a bowling alley that's survived the test of time and the Roosevelt era, Montrose Bowl is a little gem. Established in 1936, this 1950s-style bowling alley is the oldest operating bowling alley in Los Angeles County. Most nights you'll find its eight lanes booked for parties and filming, with limited hours for open bowling. So make a reservation or get there early—if there's a wait, grab a seat at the diner and have a bratwurst. Note: If the orange-and-turquoise interior looks familiar, you probably recognize it from the film *Pleasantville*. The 1998 movie set in the 1950s was filmed here.
2334 HONOLULU AVENUE, MONTROSE. 818-249-3895. www.montrosepartybowl.com

869. *Shatto 39 Lanes.* The greatest thing about Shatto Lanes is not its location or reasonable pricing but rather the memories of what this place once was. It's a bowling throwback, with its aboveground ball returns, dozens of early arcade games, and simple architectural design that houses a whole lot of lanes. Come here to bowl for fun and health, or just come here for the sake of bowling.

3255 WEST 4TH STREET, LOS ANGELES. 213-385-9475. www.shatto39lanes.com

870. Enroll in the **cabaret vocal workshop** and channel your inner Liza Minnelli.

Sign up for the longest-running cabaret vocal workshop at Los Angeles City College, where you'll work on your pipes and get taught by the mother of a real *American Idol*, Peisha McPhee (mother of *American Idol* Season Five runner-up Katharine McPhee). Cost is $125 for six classes.

855 NORTH VERMONT AVENUE, LOS ANGELES. 323-953-4000. www.lacitycollege.edu

871. Discover your inner nerd at the **Machine Project**.

To call this place anything but extraordinary would be a massive oversimplification. This gallery space, an injection of intellect on the east side, has classes, workshops, lectures, and a performance series and is best known for its courses, which range from electronics and sound design to sewing and natural medicine. Sign up to learn how to make pizza dough, crochet a scarf, or program your iPhone. To become a member of this amazing movement, all one needs to do is just show up.

1200-D NORTH ALVARADO STREET, LOS ANGELES. 213-483-8761. www.machineproject.com

872. Learn hair and makeup techniques from the 1940s and 1950s at **reVamp**.

It's where you go to buy your favorite reproductions of vintage-inspired fashion, and now with their bimonthly hair and makeup classes, you'll be able to get the complete look. Held once every two months, this four-hour hands-on workshop will teach you the basic fundamentals to capture the look from bygone eras. Bring your own supplies (an extensive list is available on their website for both hair and makeup), a photo of the hairstyle you'd to learn, and let the transformation begin. ReVamp's website also offers tutorials in antiquated coiffure, complete with diagrams and instructions for creating hairstyles to try at home. Classes are limited to ten people and cost $50 each.

834 SOUTH BROADWAY, SUITE 1200, LOS ANGELES. 213-488-3387. www.revampvintage.com

873. Follow the fretwork of legends at the **Fender Center for Music Education**.

Known as the brand of choice for Jimi Hendrix, Kurt Cobain, and John Frusciante, to name just a few, Fender guitars are as legendary as the axe heroes who have wielded them. The Fender Center offers youth and adult courses at varying levels, with evening adult classes taught by university-grade instructors who are real Fender fanatics. After a few weeks, who knows? You might just be brave enough to challenge your friend to a duel—his Telecaster versus your Jaguar. Just remember: no "Stairway to Heaven."

365 NORTH MAIN STREET, CORONA. 951-735-2440. www.fendermuseum.com

874. Jam at your leisure in the School of Rock Band 101 adult class at the **Hollywood Academy of Music**.

Once a week, the School of Rock Band 101 class offers a pressure-free environment for those just looking for a chance to jam and have fun. After eight sessions, you'll perform onstage alongside other groups enrolled in the program and experience your first Battle of the Bands...but here everyone's a winner. Get ready to rock and roll. Lessons are $40 a lesson or $160 per month. Check the website for more information.

7469 MELROSE AVENUE, SUITE 34, HOLLYWOOD. 323-651-2395. www.hollywoodacademyofmusic.com

875. Enjoy a day of free music at **Make Music Pasadena**.

For twelve hours in June, downtown Pasadena is transformed into a musical playground. This annual one-day celebration of local and internationally renowned musicians is a free event that takes place in alleyways, courtyards, building lobbies, and other unique locations around town. Featuring the best of up-and-coming, indie, and even Grammy Award–winning singers, such as La Sera, Tita Lima, Best Coast, Kinky, Natalia Lafourcade, Warpaint, and Dengue Fever, and with an admission fee of $0, it's pretty hard to beat. The diversity and energy of this music event is what Los Angeles is all about.

www.makemusicpasadena.org

876. Drive backwards and sideways in no time at the **Rick Seaman Stunt Driving School**.

Nothing says "Hollywood" like some mind-blowingly reckless stunt driving. Sign up for the three-day Super Level I Class at Willow Springs Raceway and pick up a few tricks of the trade from a real stunt driver. A world champion from the famous Joie Chitwood

Thrill Show will teach you the kinds of techniques you've witnessed in frantic car chases on silver screens all your life—just what you need to get into that tight parking spot first. And don't forget the often needed but never fully appreciated defensive-driving classes for young drivers—a must when navigating your way through Los Angeles.
WILLOW SPRINGS RACEWAY, ROSAMUND. 818-341-9526. www.rickseamanstuntdrivingschool.com

---

877. Learn soba making from Akila Inouye, founder and master chef of Tsukiji Soba Academy, at **Mazumizu Autumn Soba Workshop**.

Soba noodles, made from buckwheat flour and water, require a knowledgeable touch to transform such simple ingredients into culinary delights, and no one does this better than Inouye-san. For more than fifteen years he has taught his logical and well-practiced approach to soba making (he focuses on mixing the water and flour, which is the first and most important step) to more than 20,000 people, many of whom have gone on to become soba masters. If you're ready to make soba, you're definitely in good hands.
310-600-4263. mazumizu.com

---

878. **Le Cordon Bleu** gives your inner Top Chef the chance to pursue a career in the kitchen.

During their rigorous twelve-month course, you'll learn techniques like sautéing, slicing, and braising which will give you the tools and freedom to express yourself through the medium of food. Soon, your talents might need a bigger stage than your home kitchen—is that the Food Network I hear calling?
530 EAST COLORADO BOULEVARD, PASADENA. 866-230-9450. www.chefs.edu/los-angeles

---

879. Become a sushi master in just twelve weeks at **California Sushi Academy**.

The first vocational school specializing in training and certifying sushi chefs, the academy trains you to be a master in just three months—saving you ten years' worth of painstaking work in Japan. Whether it's a career in sushi or just knowing the best way to fillet a fish, at the Academy, veteran sushi chefs teach you the art of Japanese cuisine by focusing on developing knife skills, traditional cooking techniques, fish preparation, and presentation.
11310 NEBRASKA AVENUE, #1, LOS ANGELES. 310-231-4499. www.sushi-academy.com

---

880. Learn the same techniques as acting pros at the **Stella Adler Los Angeles Academy of Acting and Theatre**.

This world-renowned acting school offers extensive training to those serious about a career in theater, film, and television. Adler, one of the world's foremost acting teach-

ers, crafted techniques for dramatic training interpretation while working with Constantin Stanislavski, the father of modern acting. Her methods have been practiced by some of Hollywood's biggest stars, such as Robert De Niro, Marlon Brando, and Benicio Del Toro. She must be good, or why would Brando be yelling for Stella?
6773 HOLLYWOOD BOULEVARD, 2ND FLOOR, LOS ANGELES. 323-465-4446. www.stellaadler-la.com.

---

881. Sharpen your comedic skills onstage at the **Upright Citizens Brigade**.

The UCB is the alma mater of such comedic heroes and heroines as Matt Besser, Amy Poehler, and Matt Walsh. Now a regular haunt for young, up-and-coming comedians—both on stage and in the audience—it's also the deep end into which any budding comic must jump into to learn how to keep up with the pros. Once you complete Improv 101 and Sketch Writing 201, you'll have them rolling in the aisles with laughter.
losangeles.ucbtrainingcenter.com

---

882. Make Italian for dinner with cooking classes at **Mozza**.

In the private kitchen and dining room next to Osteria Mozza (p. 170), you'll learn how to make pizza by kneading dough and shaping the crust. But if you're a newbie, don't worry—you only have to do the easy stuff in this class, as the chef does most of the work for you. While you wait to "make" your pizza, snack on antipasti, drink some wine, and indulge in the ultimate Italian experience of *dolce far niente*, the sweetness of doing nothing.
6610 MELROSE AVENUE, LOS ANGELES. 323-297-1130. www.mozzarestaurantgroup.com

---

883. You'll feel like Charlie Bucket after a bottle of **Wonka's Fizzy Lifting Drink**

when you do an iFly session. At Universal Studios Citywalk, step into a towering clear tunnel with blasting winds strong enough to float on. Once you watch a brief video on proper iFly techniques and learn hand signals to communicate with your instructor, it's time to suit up and fly away—no burping required to get back down.
UNIVERSAL STUDIOS CITY WALK, UNIVERSAL CITY. 818-985-4359. www.iflyhollywood.com

---

884. Find sanctuary within the invisible walls of the **Wayfarers Chapel**.

Lloyd Wright, son of famed architect Frank Lloyd Wright, built a see-through church with glass walls and ceiling in Palos Verdes that has become a favorite for those who want to sit inside and meditate on nature's beauty. A tree chapel built in the midst of a forest exudes a Zen-like serenity in its clear surroundings where nature and architecture meet. It is popular among the wedding set, which keeps the chapel busy, so be sure to call

ahead to see when it's open to the public. Parking and admission are free.
5755 PALOS VERDES DRIVE SOUTH, RANCHO PALOS VERDES. 310-377-1650. www.wayfarerschapel.org

---

885. Unwind with a few rounds at the **L.A. Gun Club.**

Shooting a gun sounds like it would have the opposite effect of releasing tension, but that's exactly what it does. At the Los Angeles Gun Club Indoor Pistol Range, you'll find yourself feeling loose and limber after letting off a few rounds with a weapon of your choice. Not sure which firearm to choose? Get a little dirty with a Smith & Wesson Model 29 or if you're feeling a bit more mysterious, the Beretta 418 or Walther PPK should do the trick. Once you're armed, pick from one of the many paper targets, take aim, and fire. If you're never fired a gun before, don't worry as the Club offers free firearms safety and handling instructions. Because it is a popular shooting destination with celebs, you might find yourself taking aim alongside Ryan Gosling or even members of Cypress Hill, but at the very least you'll see plenty of autographs gracing the club's walls.
1375 EAST 6TH STREET, DOWNTOWN LOS ANGELES. 213-612-0931. www.thelosangelesgunclub.com

---

886. Go skating at **Paramount Iceland.**

Skating around in a circle over and over again might sound uneventful, but it's pretty awesome when you're skating in the rink founded by the Zamboni family (inventors of the ubiquitous ice-cleaning machine). Bliss out in this Olympic-size winter wonderland; on Tuesdays, you'll find inner peace and outer harmony aided by the sounds of an ancient Wurlitzer pipe organ during family night.
8041 JACKSON STREET, PARAMOUNT. 562-633-1171. www.paramounticeland.com

---

Karaoke

Not everyone can sing like Whitney Houston or Michael Jackson but you sure can try. With karaoke, the joys of singing come with more than just a tune. You get disco balls, refreshments, freedom, fun with friends, possible public embarrassment, and maybe even the roar of thunderous applause. Whether you like to sing in public or private, here are some places where you can do so at the top of your lungs.

887. *Try and catch a celebrity belting out a tune at Caffe Brass Monkey.*

This popular Koreatown karaoke bar has been a favorite among locals, hipsters, and celebrities for a long time. Located behind an office building, it not

only has a huge selection of tunes to choose from, but it's also just a great place to meet up with friends and unwind. Grab a table, sign up with the DJ, and throw back a drink or two to get the courage you'll need for singing in public.
3440 WILSHIRE BOULEVARD, LOS ANGELES. 213-381-7047. www.cafebrassmonkey.com

888. *See if you can get an encore call at the Gaslite.* Rarely will you find a friendlier or more nerve-racking crowd than at the Gaslite—the karaoke-goers here are serious about their craft. So if you're heading up to the mic, you'd better have something to back it up. Try to make karaoke history by getting an encore…but that usually doesn't happen unless you're a famous singer in disguise à la Jewel.
2030 WILSHIRE BOULEVARD, SANTA MONICA. 310-829-2382. www.thegaslite.com

889. *Avoid the crowds and sing in the safe confines of a private room at Max Karaoke in Little Tokyo.* For those not so eager to share their musical talents (or lack thereof) with the world, rent a space at Max Karaoke. Here, you get one of the best selections of songs in English, Spanish, Korean, Japanese, and more. You'd be hard-pressed to find a wider selection of songs anywhere else.
333 SOUTH ALAMEDA STREET, #216, LOS ANGELES. 213-620-1030.
www.maxkaraokestudio.com

890. *Flog your guts out at Rosen in Koreatown.* Since public karaoke might be too much pressure and the crowds a bit too unforgiving, lock yourself away in your own private room. Formerly geared toward the Korean crowd, Rosen has expanded its musical horizons and is now more internationally friendly. You'll find songs in Korean and English. Take advantage of the call button in the room; if you need anything to eat or drink or have any technical difficulties, all you need to do is push and your attendant will be there in a flash.
3488 WEST 8TH STREET, LOS ANGELES. 213-387-0467. www.rosenla.com

891. Kids can let loose at the Kids Rhythm Club Drum Circle at **REMO Recreational Music Center**.

You won't have to worry about telling your kids to sit down and be quiet here. At this 10,000-square-foot warehouse-like space, filled with more than a hundred djembes, congas, mallets, drums, and sticks, dozens of kids get to energetically express themselves through music during their free weekly events on Saturday mornings at 9:30 a.m. and 11:00 a.m. Parents are welcome to join in the fun and blankets are available

in the center of the circle to accommodate the younger set. Parents will also be thrilled to hear that earplugs are available.
7308 COLDWATER CANYON AVENUE, NORTH HOLLYWOOD. remormc.com

---

892. For a mental workout on the beach, head to **Chess Park.**

About a city block or two south of the Santa Monica Pier along the beach, there is an area designated for chess players where it's more mental worship than body worship under the sunshine and palm trees. From sunup to sundown, chess lovers come to play the ultimate game of strategy at one of the 140 tables. You'll find more than just weekend players here; they range from novices to the occasional chess master. If you're not up to snuff, just watch—spectators are always welcome. And if you're good enough to put your money where your rook is, then place a friendly wager. If you're looking for a little more action, head over to the human chessboard and play a life-size version. When you have had enough and need a different kind of stimulation, just wander a few minutes and you'll find yourself at the pier or walking along the coast. Note: former World Chess Champion Bobby Fischer used to play chess here.
www.santamonica.com/visitors/what-to-do/attractions/chess-park/

---

893. Play at game of chess at any time at **Tang's Donut Shop.**

At the intersection of Sunset Boulevard and Fountain Avenue, you'll find a nondescript doughnut shop that doubles as a late-night hangout for chess players who love to gamble. Come on Friday or Saturday night to grab a doughnut, but stick around to see some real chess action.
4341 WEST SUNSET BOULEVARD AT FOUNTAIN AVENUE, LOS ANGELES. Open 24 hours. 323-662-4085.

---

894. Go see a show at **Largo.**

For years, Largo packed in audiences with some of the best musical and comedy shows in town, starring everyone from Elliott Smith (in his last show) to Patton Oswalt. It's moved from its original location on Fairfax to the former Coronet Theatre, a multistage, 280-seat complex on La Cienega, giving more people the opportunity to come and see their stellar lineup of continuously great performances.
366 NORTH LA CIENEGA BOULEVARD, WEST HOLLYWOOD. 310-855-0350. www.largo-la.com

---

895. Watch a rare screen gem at **Los Angeles Filmforum.**

You won't see any blockbusters at Filmforum's weekly Sunday-night presentations at the intimate Steven Spielberg Theatre in the Egyptian. Instead they screen rare,

independent films like documentaries, animation and other forms of progressive cinema that challenge the boundaries of film and art. Filmforum has been dedicated to preserving cinema since 1975, and this nonprofit arts organization continues to keep you engaged and curious.
Egyptian Theater: 6712 HOLLYWOOD BOULEVARD, HOLLYWOOD. www.lafilmforum.org

---

896. Enter **Sweeney Todd's Barber Shop,** and exit looking like a new man.

This cash-only barbershop, dating back to 1927, is an authentic blast from the past. Under new ownership since 2007, Todd "Sween" Lahman keeps the spirit of the classic haircut and famously close "cut-throat" shave alive in gentlemanly surrounds. Visitors are expected to write their name on a chalkboard before patiently waiting their turn, affording adequate time to peruse the selection of vintage men's magazines and kick back.

→ ***NOTE:*** *Getting a haircut here can sometimes take longer than expected, so be sure to keep an eye on your parking meter to avoid getting a ticket.*

4639 HOLLYWOOD BOULEVARD, LOS ANGELES. 323-667-9690. sweeneytoddsbarbershopla.com

---

897. Walk and meditate at the **Peace Awareness Labyrinth & Gardens**.

Relax in nature without ever leaving the city at this day retreat. Once the Beaux-Arts estate owned by famed musical choreographer Busby Berkeley, it's now home to one of the most peaceful spots in Los Angeles. Come and walk around the hand-carved stone labyrinth or their meditation garden filled with flowers and foliage. Listen to the Asian-inspired fountains to help soothe your frayed city nerves as you discover inner tranquility.
3500 WEST ADAMS BOULEVARD, LOS ANGELES. 323-737-4055. www.peacelabyrinth.org

---

898. Find harmony at the **Self-Realization Fellowship**.

Look out onto the huge, tranquil spring-fed lake inside the Self-Realization Fellowship, founded by Paramahansa Yogananda, and reflect upon life. Sit on one of their benches and you'll discover that when a view is this good, meditation isn't as hard as you think.
4860 WEST SUNSET BOULEVARD, HOLLYWOOD. Next to the Scientology Center. 323-661-8006. www.yogananda-sfr.org

---

899. Find **yoga** you like.

It may seem like there are as many places to take yoga as there are tanning salons in this city, and if you lump the gyms, centers, and private teachers in with the studios, there probably are. Some devoted practitioners may lament the mass production of this sanctified ancient practice, and to be sure, there are plenty of nontraditional teachers and classes out there. But if you look at it strictly in terms of accessibility and convenience, this is a great thing. If you live in the city and practice yoga, you may have a place that you are loyal to. But if you are visiting or are interested in beginning, then explore! Many centers offer free introductory classes or packages (p. 252). Classes and teachers vary greatly from one studio to another, from basics like the style of yoga practiced and the size and condition of the facilities to less tangible factors, including the atmosphere, clientele, and attitude. Some studios are very social and hold non-yoga gatherings as well as classes; some are very serious about one form of yoga and teach classes only in a single style; and some have even created their own signature practices that are particularly accommodating to people with special interests, such as beginners, mothers, pregnant women, or people very pressed for time. With so many different outlets available, you have the luxury to sample and compare, so don't feel limited to one style, teacher, or studio. Citysearch (losangeles.citysearch.com) has a comprehensive listing for studios all over the city. And YogaFinder (yogafinder.com) has an international database where you can search for yoga classes. A nice alternative to regular class in a studio is outdoor yoga. This change of pace lets you escape the confines of the studio and practice in a more ambient environment—particularly nice if you're suffering from urban claustrophobia. (Outdoor yoga classes are offered in parks and gardens, and some of the best are included in chapter 6, "The Great Outdoors.")

---

900. Transform yourself into a pop star at **Millennium Dance Complex**.

Your instructors are the very same choreographers who have worked with Britney Spears, Justin Timberlake, Cher, Prince, Janet Jackson, and so many other stars. Although you may not meet them or sing like them, at least you can steal some of their moves. You might even end up in a class taught by a former boy-band member or two.
5113 LANKERSHIM BOULEVARD, NORTH HOLLYWOOD. 818-753-5081.
www.millenniumdancecomplex.com

---

901. Perform a striptease after a few lessons at **Sheila Kelley's S Factor**.

What do you get when you combine the ideals of ballet, yoga, striptease, and pole dancing all into one? It's called the S Factor—something a little risqué but worth the possible embarrassment of slipping off the pole your first time in class. While preparing for a role as a stripper in the film *Dancing at the Blue Iguana*, actress Sheila Kelley discovered the power of movement and created this incredibly popular (Oprah's a fan) stripperesque workout. Enter a class awkward and unsure, and leave full of body confidence.
5225 WILSHIRE BOULEVARD, SUITE B, LOS ANGELES. 323-965-9685. www.sfactor.com

902. Train among super athletes and ninjas at **Tempest Freerunning Academy**.

When you enter the academy, it's like being transported into a video game—the moves you see here are almost unreal. Developed by the founders of Team Tempest and X-Games course designer Nate Wessel, the enormous space is a playground for those interested in the unconventional and usually urban pursuits of freerunning and parkour. Sign up for the Ninja Warrior Workshop to work on your athletic prowess and try to attempt all the gravity-defying stunts that freerunning is about. Just the word *ninja* alone will give you a slightly mysterious edge, even if your skills don't. Tempest has a great staff as well as classes for all ages and experience levels.

19821 NORDHOFF PLACE, #115, LOS ANGELES. 818-717-0525. www.tempestacademy.com

903. Take a serious dancing course at **Edge Performing Arts Center**.

From casual to immersion to conservatory to professional, Edge is world-renowned as one of the finest professional training facilities for commercial dance. It has a Who's Who roster of choreographers, teachers, and performers who have worked on countless music videos, films, and concerts and have instructed entertainers such as Beyoncé, Janet Jackson, Michael Jackson, Lady Gaga, Jennifer Lopez, Madonna, Prince, Rihanna, Shakira, Justin Timberlake, and even Ryan Gosling. So pick a class and learn belly dance with Layla, jazz funk with Nolan Padilla, jazz with Mandy Moore, or contemporary jazz with my favorite, Sonya Tayeh.

1020 COLE AVENUE, 4TH FLOOR, LOS ANGELES. 323-962-7733. www.edgepac.com

904. **The Dance Doctor** is exactly what you need if you're suffering from two left feet.

The first dance at a wedding is always nerve-wracking, but just a few visits with John Cassese (aka the Dance Doctor) will cure all your jitters. Whether you're looking for a few simple moves or are ready to cut a rug, he knows what to prescribe to get you on your feet and moving to the rhythm.

1440 4TH STREET, SANTA MONICA. 310-459-2264. www.dancedoctor.com

Study a martial art

The organized system of movement and postures that characterizes martial arts was developed originally as a means of self-defense, but each practice's individual principles, philosophy, and techniques provide benefits beyond fighting skills. Like yoga, martial arts can enhance both physical and mental fitness, and although the styles vary in approach and specifics, they are all quite beautiful to watch and perform. Karate, tai chi, and tae kwon do are only some of the many kinds of martial arts practiced in Los Angeles, and each of these can be found at gyms and studios all around the city. Following are several places that offer less well-known varieties.

905. *Learn from real kung fu masters at the Wushu Center.* The mastery of the East is brought west at the Shaolin Wushu Center, where a variety of classes are offered in kung fu and tai chi for all ages and levels. You can also try your hand or fist at other traditional and contemporary Chinese martial arts, such as northern and southern fist, staff, broadsword, grappling, and wrestling for self-defense. Classes are taught by living legend Hu Jianqiang, a two-time all-around Wushu champion and the highest-ranking Wushu master in the West, and his wife, Master Zong Jianmei. It might feel a little like *Crouching Tiger, Hidden Dragon* when you come to observe your first time, but with dedication and expert tutoring you can transform from a caterpillar into a butterfly in no time.

1647 SOUTH LA CIENEGA BOULEVARD, LOS ANGELES. 310-278-1688. www.wushucenter.com

906. *Go the way of the samurai at Shinkendo Japanese Society.* At the Honbu Dojo, the world headquarters for Shinkendo Japanese swordsmanship, the traditional fighting arts of the samurai are taught under the guidance of master Obata Toshishiro-kaiso. Shinkendo is a form of *budo*, or Japanese martial arts, created in 1990 by Obata. He continues his family's tradition of training others in hopes of maintaining the legacy of Japanese swordsmanship.

320 EAST 2ND STREET, 2ND FLOOR, BETWEEN SAN PEDRO AND CENTRAL AVENUES, LOS ANGELES. 626-688-7540. www.shinkendo.com

907. *Learn the official combat system of the Israeli Defense Forces, Krav Maga.* Used everywhere from Bratislavan ghettos to the battlefields of the Middle East, it evolved from an eclectic mix of street-fighting styles. Krav Maga, which in Hebrew means "hand-to-hand combat," focuses on neutralizing any threats while simultaneously using defensive and offensive tactical maneuvers to overcome any hostile approach.

11400 OLYMPIC BOULEVARD, SUITE 100, WEST LOS ANGELES. 310-966-1300. www.kravmaga.com

908. Get a $15 massage in the **San Gabriel Valley**.

On Valley Boulevard from Alhambra to Temple City, you'll find the streets chock-full of places advertising $15 massages. Although they might not be certified massage therapists, they definitely have what it takes to help you release some of that stress and tension.
VALLEY BOULEVARD BETWEEN ATLANTIC BOULEVARD AND WALNUT GROVE AVENUE.

909. Get your face touched by the same woman who touches Brad Pitt's face at the **Kate Somerville Clinic**.

Not a fan of plastic surgery but going for that years-younger look, Kate Somerville is the anti-aging guru you'll want to see—particularly for her Ultimate Kate Facial. They use everything from LED light therapy to Laser Genesis to erase years off your visage, and all of her products, including world-famous serums, work magic to rejuvenate your once dull skin.
8428 MELROSE PLACE, SUITE C, AT LA CIENEGA BOULEVARD, LOS ANGELES. 323-655-7546. www.skinhealthexperts.com

910. Work out your kinks at the **Shiatsu Massage School of California**.

Nothing can sort out a crick in your neck or lower back pain faster than a trip to the Intern Clinic at SMSC—the internationally recognized leader in massage therapy education. Here the healing hands of the SMSC students, in a safe and supervised environments, provide therapeutic 60-minute Shiatsu massages. Make an appointment, and indulge in the restorative benefits of this Eastern-style body massage. And at a discounted rate of $30, less than half the cost of a massage with a pro, not only will the pain in your neck disappear, so will all potential pain in your wallet.
2309 MAIN STREET IN SANTA MONICA. 310-581-0097. www.smsconline.com

911. Visit the only natural mineral spa in the city at **Beverly Hot Springs**.

This natural hot spring hidden under L.A. is the closest thing to a Turkish bath you can get. Come and recharge your muscles, let off some steam in the sauna, or sign up for one of their various massages and treatments used to help rejuvenate the body and mind. Although the prices might seem a bit high, each paid treatment includes the cost of the $40 entrance fee, adding up to a great value. After you're done with your pampering session, make sure you spend some time in the soothing hot waters, the real reason why you came.
308 NORTH OXFORD AVENUE, LOS ANGELES. 323-734-7000. www.beverlyhotsprings.com

912. Get your brain stimulated from the outside with **Linda Kammins.**

For more than twenty-five years, Kammins has kept herself relevant—she first opened her aromatherapy hair salon in West Hollywood in 1987. It's a testament to the follicular mastery of Kammins's nurturing and nourishing work. Get one of her famous homemade oil treatments that stimulate the scalp and leave hair thick, shiny, and gorgeous. And if you follow Kammins's advice of daily hair brushing and ten-minute scalp massages, your hair might start looking better sans treatment.

848 NORTH LA CIENEGA BOULEVARD, #204, WEST HOLLYWOOD. 310-659-6257. www.lindakammins.com

913. Be alone with your thoughts at **Float Lab.**

The idea of sealing yourself up in a pitch-black chamber and floating in salt water for an hour and a half might not appeal to everyone, but the adventurous at heart will love their experience at Float Lab. Located in Venice, it offers a unique and relaxing sensory-deprivation experience for just $40. Take a shower, put in your earplugs, and then float in a thick solution of water and Epsom salts while you mediate on nothingness. Once you're done, not only will you find yourself pleasantly relaxed, you'll also have noticeably softer skin. Call a week in advance to schedule an appointment, and be sure to hydrate and have a snack beforehand. If you come for the last session of the night, you're allotted an extended journey into otherworldly dimensions.

801 OCEAN FRONT WALK #5, VENICE BEACH. 310-396-3336. www.floatlab.com

914. Have your troubles pricked away at **Han Sung Acupuncture.**

Although the legendary Dr. Chung Kyu Lee is now retired, Han Sung Acupuncture remains open under the care of Dr. Hong Ki Yoon. They've been treating what ails the holistic set in Los Angeles here for decades. Celebrities, musicians, the elderly, and the young all come here for an alternative approach to healing and a multitude of Chinese herbal concoctions, custom-made for their conditions.

1010 ARLINGTON AVENUE, LOS ANGELES. 323-734-0088.

915. Relax and unwind at four in the morning at **Wi Spa.**

Open twenty-four hours, seven days a week, Wi Spa gives you access to its sauna and *jjimjilbangs* (Korean public bathhouses). Take advantage of the different rooms in the *jjimjilbang* area, which are customized, unique, and fun. Visit the clay room to detox or brave freezing temperatures in the cold room to help tighten pores. The jade room is perfect for rejuvenation, while the salt room does the trick in softening your skin. Go

on a Tuesday to take advantage of its low rate of $15, and if you're too relaxed to make it home, it's only an extra $5 to spend the night.
2700 WILSHIRE BOULEVARD, LOS ANGELES. 213-487-2700. www.wispausa.com

---

916. Have an organic experience at **Petite Spa**.

Using natural and organic products makes a difference, and at Petite Spa, they use only the best to yield the results you want. Get the hair and scalp treatment with organic nourishing oils; a warm coconut-milk scalp massage stimulates circulation and rejuvenates limp and lifeless hair. And enjoy an added massage on your neck and shoulders when you get the full package.
723 BROADWAY, SANTA MONICA. 310-393-3105. www.petitespa.net

---

917. Immerse yourself in Ethiopian coffee culture at **Messob**.

Ethiopians know a lot about coffee—after all, the rise of coffee culture around the world has been attributed to their country, where it was discovered. To really get a true Ethiopian experience, take part in a traditional coffee ritual at Messob, considered one of the most intricate in the world. Over the course of two hours, green coffee beans are washed, roasted, ground, and boiled right at your table, giving off a rich and heady fragrance that any coffee lover will appreciate. The coffee is served in small ceramic cups to sip and savor while socializing.
1041 SOUTH FAIRFAX AVENUE, LOS ANGELES. 323-938-8827. www.messob.com

---

918. Travel the world one sip at a time with the **Art of Tea's tea sommelier lessons**.

One cup after another, you're transported to the best tea destinations in the world—Asia, Africa, India, and the Middle East. At the Art of Tea's warehouse, company's CEO Steve Schwartz leads you on a multisensory journey at the only tea sommelier program in the nation. Attended by tea lovers from all over, these classes teach the history behind some of the most famous teas and how to appreciate the second most popular drink in the world. Slurp instead of sip for maximum flavor, learn how to distinguish Chinese from Japanese green tea, make tea blends, learn how to sniff tea, and learn how to describe a tea like an oenophile describes wine. To find out more about attending classes, call or check the website. If you don't have a budget, splurge for the extended tea course, which can set you back a few thousand dollars.
748 MONTEREY PASS ROAD IN MONTEREY PARK. 877-268-8327. www.artoftea.com

Expert Contributor: Mike Sonksen

Mike Sonksen, also known as Mike the Poet, is acclaimed for his spoken-word performances and legendary city tours, which combine poetry and history and have been covered in newspapers, such as *The New York Times*, *The Washington Post*, and *The Los Angeles Times*.

THE TEN BEST WAYS TO ENRICH YOURSELF IN LOS ANGELES

Since 2000, ***A Mic and Dim Lights*** has been held every Thursday night in Pomona. Cory Cofer, aka Besskepp, is the host of the show. An HBO Def Poet, award-winning high school teacher, and National Poetry Slam team member, his resume is deep. Beyond his own accomplishments he has mentored hundreds of poets in the Inland Empire. There are hundreds of writers who started their poetry career on Thursdays with Besskepp. The venue is a mix of hip-hop poets, emcees, slam poets, local poets, college poets from Cal Poly and Claremont, and others who have heard the good word about what a great night of poetry it always is.
300 WEST SECOND STREET IN POMONA. 909-469-0080.

Since 2002, ***Mozaic*** has been hosting a monthly night of spoken word in Venice. Held at the Talking Stick coffeehouse, there are usually some singer-songwriters and Venice performance artists, but the event is mostly performance poetry with some surprises. Hippies, hip-hop heads, and West Side college kids form an eclectic, positive crowd.
1411 LINCOLN BOULEVARD IN VENICE. 310-450-6052. www.venicemozaic.com

Capoeira Batuque is the oldest Capoeira academy in Los Angeles. Capoeira is a Brazilian art form blending dance, percussion, and song into a performance. Capoeira Batuque's space is in Culver City. Their founders are originally from Brazil and have been spreading the art of Capoeira in the city for two decades now.
11928 WASHINGTON BOULEVARD IN CULVER CITY. 310-397-3667. www.capoeirabatuque.org

Corazon del Pueblo is a community cultural center in Boyle Heights. The East Side underground magazine *Brooklyn & Boyle* was started here by Abe L. Salas. In addition to a thriving open-mic night on Wednesday nights, they have also been hosting theater productions and painting classes for local youth.
2003 EAST FIRST STREET IN LOS ANGELES. www.corazondelpueblo.org

Libros Schmibros is a lending library and used bookstore across the street from Corazon del Pueblo. Under the direction of the writer David Kipen, they have a great

collection of rare books. Kipen is the former book editor of *The San Francisco Chronicle* and knows more about books than just about anybody. There's always a rotating cast of personalities browsing books and talking shop with Kipen.
1711 MARIACHI PLAZA DE LOS ANGELES IN LOS ANGELES. 323-302-9408. librosschmibros.wordpress.com

Jack Grapes is one of the greatest poetry teachers this city has ever seen. Pioneering a technique called "Method Writing," Grapes utilizes a series of intense writing exercises for his students to hone their voices. Grapes has published two thousand poets in Southern California over four decades while teaching through UCLA Extension, privately held sessions, and at over one hundred schools around Los Angeles.
www.jackgrapes.com

Project Butterfly holds space in a large loft in the Arts District. Educators, guides, healers, shamans, artists, and activists present a wide range of programs and workshops several times a month. Their mission is to cross-pollinate with others actively engaged in positive transformation.
821 TRACTION AVENUE IN LOS ANGELES. 213-709-6696. www.projectbutterfly.org

Sushi Chef Institute is the only professional sushi school that properly trains sushi chefs in Southern California. It is the first sushi school to be granted institutional approval by a US Government bureau—and more importantly, they uphold traditional Japanese standards by teaching the essence of sushi technique. Any sushi chef not trained in Japan or schooled by the Sushi Chef Institute is faking the funk.
1123 VAN NESS AVENUE IN TORRANCE. 310-782-8483. www.sushischool.net

Tía Chucha's is a bookstore and gallery founded by best-selling author Luis Rodriguez. They hold poetry workshops, readings, and tribal ceremonies. Their popular workshops on native plants and gardening focus on improving communities and building local and ecological awareness. Also check out their music lessons, dancing classes, and puppeteering sessions.
13197 GLADSTONE AVENUE IN SYLMAR. 818-939-3433. www.tiachucha.com

The World Stage is an important jazz venue. Their motto is "Seeking light through sound." Wednesday nights are poetry workshops and Thursdays are jazz open-jam sessions. Founded by the great drummer Billy Higgins and the poet Kamau Daaood, the World Stage serves as a refuge for South Side Los Angeles youth. Leimert Park has become the West Coast Harlem, hosting a renaissance of jazz, hip hop, and spoken word.
4344 DEGNAN BOULEVARD IN LOS ANGELES. 323-293-2451. www.theworldstage.org

CHAPTER 9

City of Cars

Mars Bonfire summed up Los Angeles best when he wrote the opening lyrics for "Born to Be Wild." It's the best place to "Get your motor runnin'. . ." After all, you're in a city that has been built to accommodate our adoration for automobiles. The all-American ideology of cruising with the top down and the radio up that has been portrayed in art and cinema worldwide is exemplified by L.A.'s car culture.

In May 1897, Los Angeles began its long-term love affair with automobiles when the city's first car hit the downtown streets. In over a hundred years, nothing much has changed. From drive-thru to drive-in—even the former Bullocks Wilshire was designed to appeal to newly wheeled shoppers—L.A. has been crafted for our driving convenience. The sheer number of unique car rentals, car washes and car-friendly experiences—not to mention every Angeleno's lifesaver, the ubiquitous valet parking—speaks volumes.

But just because most Angelenos use their legs for pushing on and off the gas pedal, and the rubber that hits our streets is more radial than a running shoe, doesn't mean that there aren't other ways to get around this city. Our hearts don't just beat for horsepower; they also race for bicycles, the metro, and walking. This city provides many ways to get around for those who don't have a car, can't drive, or just want to see L.A. in their own way.

In this chapter we'll explore the best things to do in the City of Cars—whether that means getting behind the wheel of a legendary classic car yourself, embracing the city's public transit, or entrusting yourself to an alternative form of transportation—and you'll find that navigating this city and its motorized history can be fun with or without horsepower.

919. Unlike New York City, and indeed many great cities in America, in Los Angeles you can **make a right on red**.

This kind of freedom is not to be scoffed at, so if there are no pedestrians in the cross walk or any signs present preventing you from doing so, you're free to go.

920. Make like a real Angeleno and **carpool**.

Immortalized by Larry David, who recruited a prostitute to get him into the diamond lane on the way to a Dodgers game in *Curb Your Enthusiasm*, carpooling not only saves drivers time but also helps protect the environment by encouraging economy. If you're in a hurry to get somewhere and need to jump on the freeway, during certain hours you might consider grabbing a few friends to take advantage as well. The carpool lane, also known as the diamond lane for the diamond symbol intermittently painted on it, allows cars containing multiple passengers to zip through traffic more quickly than the vehicles of solo drivers. Some require only two passengers, while others require three—so make sure to check with the Department of Transportation if you're unsure of the rules of your intended route.

→ ***NOTE:*** *You cannot drive over the double white lines to get in or out of the carpool lane and must wait for designated breaks in the road that allow for entrance and exit.*

http://www.dot.ca.gov

At the carwash, yeah...

Like people and showers, some cars need a nice hot wash to get their week started on the right... pedal. And in Los Angeles, people love washing their cars. Whether you're looking to clean your ride or an excuse to show it off, here are the best we found:

921. *See how a good wash and perfect pancakes mix at Olympic Car Wash.* For over 25 years in the Koreatown area, Olympic Car Wash has been buffing, waxing, and detailing the cars of this fair city. But the majority of its clientele come for the wash. For $11 not only do you and your car get a real car wash experience, (you get to watch the whole spray and foam process from inside a walkway), but a team of dedicated car washers also scrub and wipe it dry by hand. Not clean enough? Just ask for Mike, the owner. He likes to make sure his customers are happy and the cars are clean. And while you wait, play a video game, grab a massage in one of the

coin-operated chairs, peruse the different knickknacks on sale in the gift store, or take a short walk to the House of Breakfast (Olympic Café) for a stack of buttermilk pancakes.
3554 WEST OLYMPIC BOULVARD IN KOREATOWN. 323-737-2100.

922. *Get a waterless wash at Eco Detail and put your green mind at ease.* Love to wash your car but can't handle the guilt of wasting all that water? At Eco Detail they provide an environmentally friendly option: a waterless wash. In the process of avoiding the use of toxic chemicals, their waterless technique also saves approximately 50 gallons of water that might otherwise be required to do the job. The staff are thoughtful, the job thorough, and with prices that range from $80 to $280—depending on what you want done and how big your car is—it's a good price for what you get. Detailing takes around 2–3 hours, so it might be the perfect time to delve into some serious reading.
Various locations. www.waterlessecodetail.com

923. *Get your car washed the old-fashioned way at the Hand Car Wash in Studio City.* A fixture on Ventura Boulevard for years, the Hand Car Wash, famous for its giant hand sculpture sign with a Corvette on top, is popular not only for its quality washes, but also for its friendly neighborhood vibe. Whether you're here for a spotless shine or to check out its mural (nicknamed "The Great Wall of Studio City"), a trip to the Hand Car Wash is always memorable.
11514 VENTURA BOULEVARD IN STUDIO CITY. 818-980-8999.
www.studiocityhandcarwash.com

924. If you're more concerned about what's going in and out of your car and can't afford a Prius, bring your diesel car over to Lovecraft.
Here they can convert any diesel car to run on biofuel—used vegetable oil—for around $900. Those with enough mechanical know-how can buy a converter kit for around $600. Sure, you'll smell a little like French fries, but smelling delicious in the name of helping the environment can only be a good thing. If you want to know where to buy the biofuel for your converted eco-vehicle, check out www.lacitybiodiesel.com for more information on biofuel retailers.
1400 NORTH VIRGIL AVENUE IN LOS ANGELES. 323-644-9072. www.lovecraft.com

925. Head east to see a drive-in movie at the **Mission Tiki**.

Built in 1956 and recently renovated with four Technalight screens and a high-tech sound system that transmits through your FM radio, the kitsch atmosphere of Mission Tiki is a perfect backdrop to a lazy double feature. From the tiki-themed bar to grass huts and Easter Island-esque statues, the Mission is a cinema-goer's paradise and feels like a movie set in itself—and is definitely worth the drive.

10798 RAMONA AVENUE IN MONTCLAIR. 909-628-0511. www.missiontiki.com

Where to Buy or Rent Classic Cars

You'll see more '40s, '50s, and '60s cars in Los Angeles than anywhere else in America. In this city, they are typically second to homes in cost, and considering the amount of time you spend navigating your way around and sitting in traffic, they are almost like a second home. And if you're going to be spending that much time in your car, more likely than not, you're looking for something that makes an impression.

926. *Classic car buffs need look no further than Heritage Classics.*

Heritage is the largest classic car showroom in Los Angeles, and for the past 25 years it has bought and sold some of the best classic and sports cars in the country. Just looking at its past inventory list online, you know this place is the real deal. Looking for a 1961 Porsche Roadster, or something a little more extravagant like a 1965 Rolls-Royce Mulliner Park Ward Drophead Coupe? What about a 1964 Aston Martin DB 5 Coupe for the weekends? If you've got the bank account for it, the sky's the limit. And if anyone has an extra $40,000 just lying around, there's a 1958 BMW Isetta Bubble Top Cabriolet waiting with your name on it. Even if you're not looking to buy, a visit here is a must if you've got a penchant for classic cars. Go over during showroom hours; it doesn't hurt to look, but it does hurt when you can't buy.

8980 SANTA MONICA BOULEVARD IN WEST HOLLYWOOD. 310-657-9699. www.heritageclassics.com

927. *If you can't afford to buy, try a rental from Regency Car Rentals.* Why buy when you can rent a classic for a fraction of the cost? Nothing says "Los Angeles" like driving through the streets in your classic Mustang Convertible or indeed any of the other timeless machines that can be found on Regency's well-curated lot. If you're looking to impress for one night only, or just feeling the need to make like an Angeleno and roll

down the PCH in the right kind of wheels for an afternoon, this might be the place for you.
4363 LINCOLN BOULEVARD IN MARINA DEL REY. 800 847-6493. www.regencycarrentals.com

928. Looking for something with a bit more "oomph"? ***Head over to Rent In Style for the exotic sports car of your dreams.*** You'll look good, you'll feel good—but for something this slick, you'll have to fork over anywhere from $900 to $3,000 a day, depending on the car. If the price doesn't faze you then get ready to hop into the car you've only dreamed about, let alone thought you'd ever drive—and get ready to reenact all the movie scenes that will be running through your mind as you zoom around the city behind the wheel of a Ferrari or a Lamborghini. Just try not to scratch the paint when you're parking.
13469 BEACH AVENUE, MARINA DEL RAY. 888-333-4117. www.rentinstyle.com

929. *If you're looking to rent for a while, Rent A Wreck is the perfect place.* Founded in 1968, Rent A Wreck is a great place for long-term renters as well as drivers under 21 years of age. Not only can you pick up a quality vehicle to rent, but you can also find your choice of quirky cars with humorous names like La Bomba that are full of character. For long-term visitors, Rent A Wreck is a blessing, because it's not only more affordable than your typical rental places (over longer periods), it's also a lot more fun and personal. The staff is great at offering advice on insurance, as well as finding local mechanics.
2270 SOUTH CENTINELA AVENUE IN WEST LOS ANGELES. 310-826-7555. www.carrentalwestlosangeles.com

930. Seek that extra protection insurance can't provide at the **Annual Blessing of the Cars**.

Held at Hansen Dam on the northern edge of the San Fernando Valley, the all day–all night affair, held in midsummer, attracts tens of thousands of car lovers. A Catholic priest first blesses all the cars together and then individually, and, if you ask nicely, you can request some holy water for your radiators. Sometimes it doesn't hurt to have a little help from the man upstairs while you're on the road.
HANSEN DAM PARK, 11770 FOOTHILL BOULEVARD IN SYLMAR. 818-899-6016. www.laparks.org

931. For more than fifteen years, the AAA has offered a 4th of July weekend free *"tipsy tow"* all across Los Angeles.

That means you can call them up and they'll take you and your vehicle home—absolutely free. The caveat is that it applies to trips only up to seven miles—but that kind of deal is worth waiting a year, and drinking your own weight in liquor on Independence Day.

800-400-4AAA. www.aaa.com

Gas stations

Ever since *Twentysix Gasoline Stations* by American pop artist Ed Ruscha was published in 1963, the symbolism of the gas station has held special fascination for Americans, and for Angelenos in particular. Although "Bob's Service" in Los Angeles, the first service station in Ruscha's famous book, is no longer around, there are still a few stations dotted across the city that are worth a drive by. Back in the 1960s, Ruscha may have chosen these places for their bland aesthetic or their suburban mediocrity; fifty years later, like the classic cars on the streets of Los Angeles, they are treasured icons of a bygone golden age.

932. *See contemporary architecture meet LA tradition at United Oil Gas Station.* This 24-hour station, designed by Kanner Architects, not only offers twelve pumps of low-price gas but also a car wash and a fully stocked mini-market onsite. Reminiscent in design of a typical freeway interchange, United Oil's station has two ramps—the concrete one takes patrons up and over the rear of the mini-market and back down to the car wash, while the metal one serves as the structural swooping roof of the mini-market—and its design cleverly reaffirms in contemporary terms L.A.'s longstanding love of cars.

4931 WEST PICO BOULEVARD IN LOS ANGELES. 323-939-6964.

933. *Go see Jack Colker's 76 gas station—but don't fill up.* Designed by William Pereira, the man behind LACMA, this landmark building on Crescent Drive in Beverly Hills was in fact originally designed to be a part of LAX airport. Only when it emerged that the structure was no longer necessary for the airport was this remarkable, Googie-inspired, futuristic piece of architecture repurposed as a gas station awning. Filling up here isn't recommended, since it's some of the most expensive gas in the city—not because of the architecture, but just because this is, after all, Beverly Hills.

427 NORTH CRESCENT DRIVE IN BEVERLY HILLS. 310-273-3891.

934. *See the future of gas station design at the Helios House.* On the corner of Olympic Boulevard and Robertson Boulevard you'll find a space-age structure made of stainless steel. At first glance you're not sure what it could be, but on closer inspection you'll realize that it's a gas station. But similarities between this and other stations that sell gas end there: from the renewable materials used to create it, to its futuristic Frank Gehry-like design, this structure, Leed Certified by the U.S Green Building Council, stands alone in Los Angeles. From wet wipes-dispensers built into the pumps to recycling bins, solar panels, and even clean bathrooms, the Helios House paints a bright, clean future for gas stations—if not for the petroleum industry itself. ***8770 WEST OLYMPIC BOULEVARD IN LOS ANGELES. 310-855-9346.***

Getting Around LA with BMW.

It's not all about the automobile. "BMW" is the acronym my Grandpa Han taught me to describe how he gets around the city without the aid of a car. As a non-car owner, I rely heavily on BMW—B for Bicycle, M for Metro, and W for Walking—as my means of getting around town, and despite what you may hear about Los Angeles, the ultimate driving alternative does in fact work wonderfully.

B

Biking is one of the most enjoyable means of transportation in the city. The stability of commute time (around the same time to get anywhere regardless of how many people are on the road), the ability to explore new neighborhoods you'd miss if you were in a car or on the freeway, the chance to save time as well as money, and the pure, unadulterated joy of knowing you'll never have to step foot in a gym ever again are all reason enough to strap on a helmet and get back in the saddle again. On a bike you see this city in a different light: from palm trees to mansions, beaches to mountains, and the people you meet riding next to you, there are things you'd never experience stuck behind the wheel of a car. Coasting on two wheels definitely beats sitting in traffic on four any day of the week.

To help improve the quality of life and provide another clean transportation option for Angelenos in their daily commute, Mayor Antonio Villaraigosa ordered the city to "build a 1,680-mile bikeway system and make the city more bike-friendly." The mayor has pushed for bicycle safety in the city ever since he fell and broke his elbow when a taxi pulled in front of his bicycle some years ago. The Bicycle Plan will result in every Angeleno having access to a bike path within one mile of their home.

With more craters than the moon, the unevenly maintained roads in Los Angeles weren't really built for biking, and it's far from what one would consider cyclist heaven—but that doesn't mean you won't have a great time. And luckily, the bicycle shops in this city have their fair share of sturdy bikes (to rent or buy) for your riding pleasure, and to help you with any of the obstacles, whether potholes or braking cars, you come across on your journey.

935. *Neglected bikes are resuscitated at Bicycle Ambulance.* Find a bike to fit your exploration needs at this Santa Monica bicycle haven. The bikes here are bought from police auctions and refurbished, allowing you to rent a very reliable bike for as little as $22 a day.
2212 LINCOLN BOULEVARD IN SANTA MONICA. 310-395-5026.

936. *Head to the epicenter of bicycle culture in Los Angeles at The Bicycle Kitchen.* A focal point of DIY bike culture in the city, this non-profit is dedicated to getting people out of cars and onto bikes. Here you can learn how to fix and build your own ride, from picking the right frame to the details of gears and brakes. The Kitchen provides tools, a large stockpile of parts, and a staff of friendly volunteers with the know-how and the patience to help you get you started.
4429 FOUNTAIN AVENUE IN LOS ANGELES. 323-662-2776. www.bicyclekitchen.com

937. *For those who fancy themselves more sophisticated cyclists, there's Orange 20 Bikes.* Started by two former volunteers from the Bicycle Kitchen, Orange 20 is a bit on the pricier side when it comes to some of its bikes, but it does offer nice touches like custom wheels and specialty gear for urban hipster bikers.
4351 MELROSE AVENUE IN LOS ANGELES. 323-662-4537. www.orange20bikes.com

938. *If you tire easily from pedaling you might consider investing in a Derringer Bike.* Designer Adrian Van Anz has taken the idea of the 1920s board-track racing motorcycle and given it a hybrid-drive system. With a Derringer, you can pedal it old-school or you can flip on the eco-minded Honda engine and zoom around at speeds up to 35 mph. The wide tires make it safer to ride, and its 180-mpg makes it unbelievably economical. The footprint it will leave on the environment will be light, even if the same can't be said of its impression on your wallet; a Derringer costs around $3,500. Riding one doesn't require a special license, but you do have to be 16 years or older.
7954½ WEST 3RD STREET IN LOS ANGELES. 323-944-0091. www.derringercycles.com

939. *Buying a bike from the Beverly Hills Bike Shop pays for itself.* If you buy a bicycle from the Beverly Hills Bike Shop, you get free-tune ups on your bike for life. How can you say no?
10546 WEST PICO BOULEVARD, LOS ANGELES. 310-275-2453.
www.bhbikeshop.com

940. *Join up and go ride with the Los Angeles Wheelmen.* Started over a century ago, the Wheelmen bicycle riding club began in 1893, and they're still going. A club dedicated to enjoying biking rather than racing, they offer easy, moderate, and difficult rides, as well as special events like the 24-hour ride or the exceedingly intimidating 400-mile ride. The Wheelmen offer multiple bike riding sessions during the week and recommend newcomers try out a few rides before deciding to join.
www.lawheelmen.org.

941. *Celebrate all things bicycle at the Bicycle Film Festival.* The last thing you'd assume someone who just got hit by a bus would consider doing would be create a film festival celebrating bicycles, but that's exactly what the Bicycle Film Festival's Founding Director Brendt Barbur did. After he was struck while riding his bike in New York City, he took a negative and made it into a positive, and created the BFF. The festival provides a platform on which to honor the two-wheeled apparatus through music, art, and film—and every event draws an amusing crowd that brings together cinephiles, casual cyclists, and the die-hard brakeless fixie crews of the city.
www.bicyclefilmfestival.com/los-angeles.

942. *Learn how to make bicycling a part of your everyday life with C.I.C.L.E.* C.IC.L.E. (Cyclists Inciting Change thru LIVE Exchange) is a not-for-profit group that helps riders of all ages and skill sets learn how to use bicycles as their main mode of transportation. They provide those interested in becoming dedicated bikers information and tips on what to look for when buying a bike, offer riding lessons, and recommend cycling routes that are just right for you. If you're looking to better acquaint yourself with the city, they also offer exploratory cycling sessions around Los Angeles.
4610 EAGLE ROCK BOULEVARD, #1001, LOS ANGELES. 323-509-4905. www.cicle.org

943. *For a mix of biking and hiking, sign up for a tour with Bikes and Hikes L.A.* This full service bike/hike tour company offers a healthy and fun way to explore the city. With two locations in Los Angeles (West Hollywood and Walk of Fame in Hollywood), this tour helps you see the city while reducing your carbon footprint. Designed for everyone, groups are paired with local expert guides who offer a unique insider's tour full of hidden gems to be discovered all over the city. Avoid traffic and have fun visiting celebrity homes; ride from Hollywood all the way to the beach; indulge in a special land and sea adventure with their special bike and sail tour; and, if you're looking for something specific, put together your own custom adventure. Each bike rental comes with a bicycle, a helmet, a safety vest, and a lock. Baby seats and trailers are also available for an extra charge.
8743 SANTA MONICA BOULEVARD IN WEST HOLLYWOOD. 323-796-8555.
www.bikesandhikesla.com

944. *If spectating is more your thing, head over to the south side of the Home Depot Center complex* to see the Los Angeles Velodrome Racing Association. The 250-meter indoor wood bicycle-racing track is part of the Velo Sports Center, where LAVRA —a nonprofit, volunteer organization established in 2006—hosts occasional weekend racing events that are free for spectators. Watching riders zip around the track, seemingly defying Newton's laws of physics at breakneck speeds, is a dizzying spectacle, and enough to give you the itch you get back on your bike again.
18400 AVALON BOULEVARD IN CARSON. 310-630-2000. www.lavelodrome.org

M

The Metro in Los Angeles comprises buses, subways, and light rail trains that eliminate the need to watch the road or find parking. You'd be surprised how efficient the subways are here—silver trains are zooming through tunnels right under our feet every day. The most common perception about Los Angeles is that it's a totally car-centric culture, but LA is also a city that is accommodating to those who are carless. With the Metro, locals and visitors alike can enjoy the city's world famous attractions, multicultural neighborhoods, and hidden gems without resorting to a battle with the traffic.

To find out how to get anywhere, visit www.metrola.org, and it'll route you to where you need to go via the Metro. Here are 10 great places it's best to go to via subway:

945. Jump on the Red Line and head to ***Hollywood and Highland.*** While you're there, visit ***Grauman's Chinese*** (p. 17), see the ***Walk of Fame***, go see the ***Capitol Records Building*** (p. 17), take a look at the ***Egyptian Theater*** (p. 317), visit the gift store at the ***El Capitan*** (p. 346), have your picture taken in front of the ***Dolby Theatre***, the home of the Oscars, also the permanent home of ***IRIS, A Journey through the World of Cinema™ from Cirque du Soleil®*** and walk up Highland Avenue to visit the ***Hollywood Bowl*** (pp. 153 and 289). You're also right near the Hollywood and Vine subway stop which drops you off in front of the Pantages Theater and is within walking distance of ***Amoeba Music*** (p. 296) and the ***Cinerama Dome*** (p. 158).

946. Take the Red Line one stop farther to get off at ***Universal City.*** Spend the day at ***Universal Studios Hollywood*** (p. 314) and when you're done, get your fill of shopping and eating at Universal City Walk.

947. At ***Wilshire/Western***, you'll find yourself in the heart of Koreatown. The subway drops you off in front of the ***Wiltern Theater*** (p. 81). Here you'll find restaurants, bakeries and markets, like the ***Galleria Market*** (p. 213), full of different Korean cuisine to sample. And if you're in the mood for a movie, the ***CGV Theater***, which shows Korean films and English-language films with Korean subtitles, is just a block away.

948. At the ***Wilshire/Western*** stop, grab the Metro Local 20 bus, which will take you to the ***La Brea Tar Pits*** (p. 130) and the ***Los Angeles County Museum of Art (LACMA)*** (p. 130)

949. ***7th Street/Metro Center*** drops you off in the heart of Downtown. Visit the ***Central Downtown Library*** (p. 18), go see some art at the ***Museum of Contemporary Art*** (p. 134), and walk around ***Pershing Square*** (p. 37), a popular spot for free concerts and outdoor screenings during the summer, which is one stop away, but easy to walk to from the 7th Street stop. You can grab a quick bite close by at ***Grand Central Market*** and take the ***Angel's Flight*** (p. 31) up the hill. Once you're at the top you can make your way over to the ***Walt Disney Concert Hall*** (p. 38), the ***Ahmanson Theatre*** (p. 154), the ***Mark Taper Forum*** (p. 154), and the ***Dorothy Chandler Pavilion*** (p. 154).

950. The last stop on the Red Line heading east is ***Union Station***. Get off here and visit the ***Terminal Annex*** (p. 112) where Bukowski worked, grab a French dip at ***Philippe the Original*** (p. 43), wander the pueblo style buildings of ***Olvera Street*** (p. 34), visit the birthplace of the city at ***El Pueblo de Los Angeles Historical Monument*** (p. 101), and explore ***Chinatown*** (p. 30).

951. The ***Hollywood/Western*** station off the Red Line delivers you within footsteps of Thai Town and many dining adventures. On the weekends, a shuttle from the Vermont/Sunset stop takes you directly to the ***Griffith Observatory*** (p. 21).

952. Start at Union Station and take the ***Gold Line*** for a cultural tour of Pasadena. Head north and get off at the Memorial Park Station area and visit the ***Norton Simon Museum*** (p. 133), the ***Pacific Asia Museum*** (p. 133), and the ***Pasadena Museum of California Art***.

953. Go south on the Gold Line and visit Little Tokyo/Arts District. There you'll find the ***Geffen Contemporary*** (an annex of MOCA) (p. 135). You can also go grab a bite at ***Hama Sushi*** (p. 184) or ***Wurstküche*** (p. 212). If you continue east, you'll find yourself at ***Mariachi Plaza*** (p. 235) in Boyle Heights, where mariachi musicians have gathered since the 1930s.

954. Take the ***Metro Rail Blue Line*** and visit the historic ***Watts Towers*** (p. 36), which can be accessed from the 103rd Street station. You can also visit the ***Queen Mary*** (p. 32) and the ***Aquarium of the Pacific*** when you go to the Transit Mall stop near the end of the Blue Line. ***Note:*** Off the Blue Line at the Imperial/Wilmington station you can transfer to the Metro Rail Green Line and can grab a free airport connection shuttle at the Aviation/LAX stop that will take you to ***LAX***.

W

Walking in LA sounds like an oxymoron. Who walks when they can drive? In Los Angeles people get in their cars just to go down the street to get a carton of milk. Still the saying goes, "nobody walks in L.A.," and that may be due to the inevitable distance between where you are and where you want to be. However, there are lots of walkable areas around the city, and plenty of guided tours and walking maps to help you find your way.

And don't be surprised while walking around Los Angeles if the concrete jungle you imagined isn't all concrete. You'll be pleasantly surprised how green this city actually is, when you know where to look...

955. ***Figure out where to stretch your legs with Walk Score.*** Walk Score is a great website that gives you a list of L.A.'s most walkable neighborhoods, from Downtown to Koreatown, the parks and beaches and beyond. And wherever you go, the best way to explore is always on foot.
www.walkscore.com

956. In November 2006, Mike Schneider led fifteen friends on a 15.8-mile trek from downtown to the ocean on a daylong journey along Wilshire Boulevard. Since then, ***the annual Great Los Angeles Walk***, which navigates its way down a different boulevard each year, has grown exponentially to include 300 people, food trucks, guest speakers, and even an after-party in Santa Monica. Held on the Saturday before Thanksgiving, Schneider's yearly walking excursions give locals a chance to see Los Angeles in a different light. It's the perfect way to start off the holidays—and gives you a chance to squeeze in a workout before the feasting begins.
323-356-2536. www.greatlawalk.com

957. ***Avoid Hollywood Boulevard with a Felix in Hollywood tour.*** Started by Philip "Felix" Mershon in 2011 as a Hollywood tour company that specifically avoids Hollywood Boulevard, the Felix in Hollywood tour covers nearly all forms of twentieth-century entertainment on a half-mile stretch along Sunset. From films and TV to record labels and radio, this 90-minute walking tour covers both sides of the Boulevard from Vine Street to Bronson Avenue. Taking your time to stroll along with the tour is as much fun as what you'll see and learn about along the way—and it sure beats the crowds on Hollywood.
1500 NORTH VINE STREET IN HOLLYWOOD. 323-929-0302. felixinhollywoodtours.com

Expert Contributor: Albert Yeh

Albert Yeh is a native Angeleno who bicycles almost daily, and is a brand manager for great fashion and product designers.

MY FAVORITE BIKE RIDES IN L.A.

Griffith Park and the Hollywood Sign. Living in Los Angeles City, this is a great quick ride to do in the morning during the week. I ride from the base of Nichols Canyon up to Mulholland Highway, then descend into the valley. From the valley side, one can head over to Griffith Park to begin the ascent of Mount Hollywood to the observatory. The Griffith Observatory is a great place to catch a classic view of Los Angeles. Also, it's a great melting-pot place, where you find residents from all over the city. From the observatory, you descend either Western or Vermont Boulevard with a quick stop at Trails Café for the fantastic coffee and heavenly scones.

San Vicente Boulevard, from Brentwood to Santa Monica to the Beach Bike Path. The 405 freeway is one of the key identifiers of Los Angeles residents: does one live east or west of the 405? Although I live east of it, a lot of the great cycling routes are west of the 405 along the Pacific Coast Highway. So I find myself crossing the 405 several days a week to ride on the West Side. San Vicente Boulevard is a great road for cyclists and runners. It's one of the rare roads in L.A. where one can ride continuously for three miles without running into a stoplight. And the roads are very bicycle friendly, with a wide bike lane. And the best news—it's gently downhill to the beach. From there, head north toward Malibu, then back south toward Venice, Marina del Rey, and Palos Verdes.

Pacific Coast Highway to Topanga Canyon, Latigo Canyon, Decker Canyon, and Mulholland Highway. Probably my favorite place to ride in Los Angeles is along the coast and through the canyons within the Santa Monica mountains. There are miles of great cycling roads networked between Mulholland Highway and the PCH. If you love to climb and descend, there's no better place. A favorite loop is from PCH to Topanga Canyon, Fernwood, Stunt Road, and Piuma, which takes one from sea level to 2,300 feet.

Mountain Biking in Santa Monica Mountains. I always like to mountain bike in the Santa Monica Mountains. From Brentwood, head up Mandeville Canyon to Westridge and then on to "Dirt Mulholland" and Backbone Trail. It's a well-maintained network of trails that allow one to escape the city . . . while being within city limits.

Cycling within ***West Hollywood and Mid City*** to run local errands—because the best way to discover the new shops in the community is by bike, and riding in the tree-lined neighborhoods is always a great reset and inspiration. And a visit to Venice Beach, riding the ***Venice Beach Bike Path/Abbot Kinney***, leads to a great day. Awesome shops, a great mix of L.A. residents gathering on the boardwalk, and the Venice community make for a welcome visit.

CHAPTER 10

Only in L.A.

Shakespeare once wrote, "All the world's a stage, and all the men and women merely players." For Los Angeles, that stage is Hollywood, and it has played the character and the backdrop for countless films and TV shows, including *Beverly Hills 90210, Curb Your Enthusiasm, Baywatch, Arrested Development, Swingers, Beverly Hills Cop, L.A. Confidential,* and *The Artist*. In fact, most people think Hollywood is Los Angeles—and in some ways it is.

In this final chapter, we celebrate all the things that make this city unique—the quirky and signature things that you just won't find anywhere else. Only here could you hear an order for "a half double decaffeinated half-caf with a twist of lemon," as Steve Martin did in *L.A. Story*. Even Larry David's hilarious antics in *Curb Your Enthusiasm*—like hiring a prostitute so he could use the carpool lane to make it to the Dodgers game on time—seem completely plausible because, after all, this is L.A.

Throughout this book I've tried to pick out the city's very best features—the entertainment, sites, and activities that stand out. From memorable and unknown movie locations to classic destinations that are in a league of their own. But there are things that define Los Angeles and are completely unique to this city. So whether you're looking to get a real taste of Academy Awards history at Musso & Frank, to soak up the sun and see street performer Harry Perry on the Venice Beach boardwalk, or to find out how things really blast off at NASA's Jet Propulsion Lab, you'll find that there are plenty of things that make this city one-of-a-kind. And if the things to do aren't convincing enough, just consider the number of stars that have made this city their final resting place. There's a reason Michael Jackson, the King of Pop, was laid to rest here.

I hope after reading this book and visiting all these wonderful places, you'll realize that when it comes to the great city of Los Angeles, just spending time here and appreciating the city for its endless variety and truly inspiring landscape is the best thing to do, in and of itself. There's no place like it on Earth.

958. Visit the **World's Biggest Dinosaurs museum**.

When you hear the word *Cabazon*, only one activity comes to mind: shopping. After all, it's home to the ever-impressive and very discounted Desert Hills Premium Outlets (p. 269). But next time you visit Cabazon, why not go hunting for dinosaurs? At the World's Biggest Dinosaurs museum, kids and adults can explore the known and unknown and learn all about creation theories by reading featured works from some of the world's most notable scientists. The dinosaurs were built more than thirty years ago, and the T. Rex (known as Mr. Rex) took seven years to build. Most of the work was done by hand, and Mr. Rex towers four stories above the ground. The Apatosaurus (formerly known as a Brontosaurus) is one of the largest land animals that ever existed and even contains a store in its belly. Dig up your own dinosaur at the Dino Dig, pan for gold, and learn about the mythical dinosaur of the Congo. Then, if you need a break with a view, head to Mr. Rex's mouth where you can sit, relax, and gather a new perspective through his teeth. Note: If you're not sure where to go, just look for the two giant dinosaurs staring at you from the Interstate Highway—you can't miss them.

50770 SEMINOLE DRIVE, CABAZON. 951-922-0076. cabazondinosaurs.com

959. Indulge in some delicious chocolates made right here in Los Angeles at **See's Candies**.

Founded by Charles See in San Francisco in 1921, this West Coast chocolate company has a kitchen right here in Los Angeles on La Cienega Boulevard, which churns out fresh chocolates and candies every day. Known by its motto, "Quality Without Compromise," for more than ninety years, the company, now owned by Warren Buffett's Berkshire Hathaway Inc., is still guided by the values introduced by Charles See. Whether you go and create a custom box of chocolates for a friend or indulge your own sweet tooth with their huge selection of sweets (my favorites are the nuts and chews), you'll taste the quality that is See's in every bite.

3431 SOUTH LA CIENEGA BOULEVARD, LOS ANGELES. 310-559-4919. www.sees.com

→ ***FACT:*** *The black-and-white shops were designed to resemble the home kitchen of Mary See, Charles's mother and the woman synonymous with See's.*

960. Get a taste of the original L.A. espresso at **Pasquini Espresso Company**.

Even if you don't drink espresso, you know the name Pasquini. Found in cafés and restaurants all over the city, Pasquini's machines have been serving up potent shots of this Italian invention for more than fifty years. This Milan-made machine was created

by founder Ambrose Pasquini, an Italian immigrant who missed the taste of home and decided to bring espresso stateside. He imported a machine and opened the first espresso café in Southern California (and the company is still based in Los Angeles). As interest grew, he began importing and rewiring machines for restaurants; soon, he began tinkering with them to improve what was already out there to make it easier to use. In the 1970s, Pasquini created the Livietta to use at home and it can still be found gracing kitchen counters today. For about a cool $1,000, you too can have a caffeine buzz all day, every day.
1501 WEST OLYMPIC BOULEVARD, LOS ANGELES. 213-739-0480. www.pasquini.com

---

961. Get in focus at the **Binoculars Building**.

There's not a lot of architecture along Main Street in Venice that is as eye catching as a massive sculpture of a pair of binoculars. Built in 1991, this commercial office building was designed by famed Los Angeles architect Frank Gehry for ad agency Chiat\Day (famous for their "1984" ad campaign that introduced Apple's Macintosh computer) as their West Coast headquarters. But it's the sculptural masterpiece in front of the building created by acclaimed Swedish artists and husband-and-wife team Claes Oldenburg and Coosje van Bruggen that is most iconic. The binoculars are so big they're used as both a car and pedestrian entryway, just walk or drive in between the lenses. Note: The Binoculars Building is currently leased out to Google.
340 MAIN STREET, VENICE.

→ ***FACT:*** *Just across the street on the corner of Rose Avenue and Main Street, you'll find the Ballerina Clown, by artist Jonathan Borofsky, which was made famous by the movie* Speed. *It's perched above the entrance to a CVS Pharmacy.*

---

962. Get a bona fide superstar haircut at **Sally Hershberger**.

Where else but Los Angeles could you get an appointment to have your hair cut by the woman who invented Meg Ryan's trademark shag? Über-hairstylist Sally Hershberger created the iconic 'do more than twenty years ago, and even with the $600 price tag, demand still hasn't stopped. Make an appointment and get the Meg done by the master or ask for the Jane Fonda, the Barbra Streisand, or the Hillary Clinton—Hershberger cuts their hair as well.
760 NORTH LA CIENEGA BOULEVARD, LOS ANGELES. 310-854-4922. www.sallyhershberger.com

→ ***NOTE:*** *If you're looking for another famous haircut, you can go see Chris McMillan on Burton Way and ask for the Rachel.*

963. Live the life of a Disnoid and go to **Disneyland** every single day.

Trekkies have the Star Trek Enterprise, witches and wizards have Hogwarts, and hobbits have Middle Earth, but unlike these three, Disnoids actually have a place to go to live out their fantasies. For die-hard Disney fans (known as Disnoids, a term coined by DreamWorks studio chief Jeffrey Katzenberg), living in Los Angeles does have its perks—namely, being able to visit the happiest place on Earth 365 days a year. Buy a Premium Annual Passport for admission every day. People get engaged, celebrate their weddings, and honeymoon here, and some Disnoids go as far as secretly burying their dead pets in various parts of the park. (Let's hope the last one doesn't become too popular.)

1313 DISNEYLAND DRIVE. www.disneyland.disney.go.com

→ ***FACT:*** *Disneyland is like the West Coast's Graceland. Elvis fans have an annual August pilgrimage to Disneyland, where tens of thousands take part in a candle-light vigil on the anniversary of Elvis's death.*

964. Enjoy an edible part of Academy Awards history with squab from **Carpenter Squab Ranch** in Ventura.

The squab ranch owned by Gary Carpenter, a third- generation pigeon farmer (his grandfather started it), has fed most of Hollywood's Golden Era elite. Served at the first Academy Awards dinner in 1929, Carpenter's squab was also offered at legendary establishments Romanoff's and Ciro's. If you're interested in tasting a piece of Hollywood history, they can still be found on the menu at Musso & Frank Grill (p. 25).

5207 CASITAS PASS ROAD, VENTURA. 805-649-1474.

965. In Los Angeles, you're not anyone unless you add a slash (/) to your credits, so it's no wonder that many celebrities have added *restaurateur* to their resumes. Eat at one of these celebrity-owned spots and tell everyone you've tasted the real L.A. Robert De Niro is famous for being a partner at Nobu, but in L.A. he also owns famed celebrity hangout **Ago**. This Italian restaurant serves quality fare with a side of celebrity sightings. Once a restaurant owned by director Vincente Minnelli (Liza's dad), the **Rainbow Bar and Grill** (p. 48) in 1972, became a hangout for rock musicians, metalheads, and their groupies under owners Lou Adler, a record producer; Elmer Valentine, who cofounded **Whisky a Go-Go** and the **Roxy Theatre**; and Mario Maglieri. For rock fans, this is the perfect place to grab a strong drink and run into some famed regulars like Lemmy from Motörhead. Grab a slice at **Mulberry Street Pizzeria**, and if you're lucky, owner and Oscar-nominated actress Cathy Moriarty (remember her from *Raging Bull*?) will be on hand to take your order—she waitresses here on occasion. **The Milky Way** in Beverly Hills isn't owned by a famous celebrity, but the owner did give birth to one: Leah Adler, Steven Spielberg's mother, runs this little kosher Jewish fusion restaurant. There's no meat on the menu, but they offer great fish and vegetarian dishes. Ask for the fried smelt, it's Steven's favorite. Actor Ryan Gosling built **Tagine** with his own hands, and that means he's left his mark all over this tasty Moroccan restaurant. Even though the Oscar-nominated actor is hardly present, with all the work he's put into it, it's almost like he is. **Dominick's** (p. 198) has a trio of famous investors: actress Rose McGowan, singer Ben Harper, and actress Laura Dern, making this restaurant the perfect celebrity ménage à trois. Johnny Depp's name is no longer on the deed to the **Viper Room**, but you can't help thinking of Johnny and River Phoenix when it comes to this famous music club. With all the memories this place is home to, stopping by for a drink is a must.

Ago: agorestaurant.com; Rainbow Bar and Grill: www.rainbowbarandgrill.com; Whisky a Go-Go, www.whiskeyagogo.com; Roxy Theatre, theroxyonsunset.com; Mulberry Street Pizzeria: www.mulberrypizzeria.com; The Milky Way: 9108 West Pico Boulevard, Los Angeles. 310-859-0004. Tagine: www.taginebeverlyhills.com; Dominick's: www.dominicksrestaurant.com; Viper Room, www.viperroom.com

---

966. "The tighter the better" is the motto when you see **Steel Panther** at the House of Blues.

If you miss big hair created with reckless amounts of hair spray, bigger egos, guyliner, never-ending guitar solos, and body-hugging spandex so tight it that limits blood circulation, then have no fear—'80s metal is still here. Steel Panther, formerly Metal Shop, has been keeping the art of hair metal alive and literally kicking. Every Monday night, this foursome takes the stage at the House of Blues, and serves up renditions of ear-piercing and tongue-wagging classics from Bon Jovi, Poison, Mötley Crüe, and Van Halen. Their covers are spot-on and incite zealous sing-alongs from the crowd, but where they really shine is the in-between. Never breaking character, Steel Panther embodies the true form of the ironic rock star with their hilarious onstage banter, and they even have rock-star fans such as Gene Simmons and Slash to boot. Expect them to see your Marshall Amp at 10 and raise it to 11.

6255 SUNSET BOULEVARD. 323-769-4600. www.steelpantherrocks.com

---

967. Get inked at the **Shamrock Social Club**.

There's a reason why stars such as Johnny Depp, Rihanna, David Beckham, Angelina Jolie, and Brad Pitt choose to get inked at the Shamrock: owner and legend Mark Mahoney. Mahoney is the Boston-born, L.A.-bred master of black-and-gray self-expression. He's been perfecting his craft for more than thirty years now, and it shows in his work. To get an appointment with Mahoney may take several months due to the long waiting list, but it's well worth it. You can also walk in and get a tattoo from his talented and professional staff, like Dr. Woo.

9026 SUNSET BOULEVARD, WEST HOLLYWOOD. 310-271-9664. www.shamrocktattoo.com

---

968. See a double feature in Quentin Tarantino's movie theater, the **New Beverly Cinema**.

Originally a 1920s vaudeville theater, New Beverly went through phases as a nightclub, foreign-film theater, porno theater, and grind house that incorporated live nude dancing, before finally settling on the double-feature format in 1978. One of the oldest revival houses in the city, it continues to run its double-features series from a wide variety of genres. In 2007, when owner Sherman Torgan died, the theater was in jeopardy of closing. Filmmaker and longtime fan Quentin Tarantino bought it, allowing the Torgan family to continue operations. Tarantino even makes programming suggestions from time to time—he was quoted as saying, "As long as I'm alive, and as long as I'm rich, the New Beverly will be there, showing double features in 35mm."

7165 WEST BEVERLY BOULEVARD, LOS ANGELES. 323-938-4038. www.newbevcinema.com

---

969. Go "kustom" with **George Barris Automotive**.

From the original Batmobile to the Munster Family's Koach, design and paint whiz George Barris made a name for himself as the King of Kustomizers by building unique and imaginative custom cars from scratch. With his brother, Sam, who was a metal craftsman, Barris created some of the most memorable cars in television history. If you're looking for something eye-catching to ride on the streets of Los Angeles, nothing says custom like a George Barris.

10811 RIVERSIDE DRIVE, NORTH HOLLYWOOD. 818-984-1314. www.barris.com

---

970. If you're going to watch a Disney film, there's no better place to do it than at the **El Capitan Theater**.

This old movie palace located across the street from Grauman's—Sid Grauman helped open the El Capitan with Charles Toberman—has been around since the 1920s. It opened a year before the Chinese Theatre did. Once home to dramatic plays performed by the likes of Clark Gable and Joan Fontaine, it even held the world premiere of Orson Welles's *Citizen Kane*. The Spanish Colonial Revival–style exterior and East Indian interior were swapped out for the moderne style, and it became the Hollywood Paramount. Disney bought it in the '80s, restoring most of the building's original decor as well as the original name. Now fully restored, El Capitan gives you more than just a movie when you come to watch a Disney flick here—it has live shows and a soda fountain and studio store next door that serves up shakes and sundaes, as well as some hard-to-find Disney merchandise for you to enjoy.

6838 HOLLYWOOD BOULEVARD, LOS ANGELES. 818-845-3110. elcapitan.go.com

---

971. A night at the **Echoplex** could be more memorable than you thought.

In Echo Park, the venue of choice for up-and-coming and established bands is the Echoplex. Why? The venue is intimate, the crowds are good, and it feels like home. Music performances here range from the soulful Jimmy Scott to indie darling Best Coast to the raging Nine Inch Nails. If you're lucky, you'll be pleasantly surprised by some of the secret acts that make it onstage for impromptu performances. Find yourself face-to-face with Thom Yorke from Radiohead accompanied by Flea from the Red Hot Chili Peppers—and if you think those two are awesome, the other guests will just blow you away. Enter through the alley.

1154 GLENDALE BOULEVARD, LOS ANGELES. 213-413-8200. www.theecho.com

---

972. Get a taste of Chinatown in Koreatown at the **Windsor Restaurant**.

In 1949, when the Windsor Restaurant was on the ground floor of the Windsor Apartments, building owner Ben Dimsdale created a classic dining establishment that had the perfect old-school vibe to fill the void left by the closed Brown Derby. In Roman Polanski's *Chinatown*, it took the place of the Derby when Jack Nicholson's JJ Gittes meets up with Faye Dunaway's Evelyn Mulwray. The original Windsor, like so many classic eateries, has swapped owners and is now The Prince. But the pleated red-leather booths and English beefeater iconography has remained virtually untouched, and it now offers a tasty mix of American and Korean food. Their Korean-style fried chicken is the stuff of dreams. And, as *Mad Men* can attest, it still provides the perfect setting for a throwback scene.

3198½ WEST 7TH STREET AT CATALINA STREET, LOS ANGELES. 213-389-2007. www.theprincela.com

---

973. When it's just too hard to say good-bye to man's best friend, head to **Bischoff's Taxidermy**.

Instead of getting your dog's name tattooed on your person à la Jennifer Aniston, when your best friend says his last bow-wow and heads to the great, big dog park in the sky, opt to take him to Bischoff's Taxidermy for a lasting tribute. Founded in 1922, this Burbank institution can handle just about any pet. They work on anything from mice and hamsters to larger animals like crocodiles and horses (they did Roy Rogers's

Trigger). Come for an estimate or just to stare at their showroom filled with stuffed animals, and if you're seriously interested in immortalizing your pets, they recommend you freeze the deceased immediately for best results.

54 EAST MAGNOLIA BOULEVARD IN BURBANK. 818-843-7561. www.bischoffs.net

---

974. Visit the address where magic lives at the **Brookledge Theater**.

Meet the Brookledge Follies, who perform vintage magic tricks and variety acts each month in an antique theater located behind a Spanish-style mansion in Hancock Park named Brookledge. Hosted by magician Rob Zabrecky and created by Erika Larsen, daughter and niece of Magic Castle founders Milt and Bill Larsen, the Brookledge is where the spirit of magic and the skill of the art form are kept alive and kicking. Conjuring up an invite to one of the hottest magic tickets in town is a feat in itself as guests are admitted by invitation only. Non-magic folk may find it nearly impossible to gain entry, but for those who are determined to go, start by inquiring at the **Magic Castle** (p. 19). Who knows, the spirits may be listening and willing to answer your prayers with an "Open Sesame."

BROOKLEDGE THEATER AT HANCOCK PARK.

---

975. Cruise the Venice Boardwalk and find **Harry Perry**.

If there ever were a street performer in Los Angeles noteworthy enough to make this book, it's Harry Perry. With his turban, electric guitar, and roller skates, Perry is a huge part of the L.A. landscape. A professional musician who has performed with the Grateful Dead and Jane's Addiction, as well as in small clubs, Perry enjoys playing on Venice Boardwalk, where he is undoubtedly the strip's star attraction. Buy a CD and a shirt to support the hardest-working street performer under the L.A. sun.

Venice Beach boardwalk. 310-890-6810. www.harryperryband.com

---

976. Get rid of your houseguest for a day with the help of **Tour du Jour**.

Out-of-town guests, although a pleasure to have, can sometimes slowly drive a person insane. Tour du Jour helps you regain some peace of mind and personal space by allowing you to book your houseguests on half-day (prices start at $129 per person, with a two-person minimum) or full-day ($359 per person, two-person minimum) private outings. Guests are swept away in anything from a Jaguar to a 1992 Cadillac limo and taken on shopping sprees or tours of movie stars' homes. Tour du Jour makes sure they get a different look at L.A. by visiting places that are off the beaten path, ensuring your guests have a great time—while you relax.

9663 SANTA MONICA BOULEVARD, #680, BEVERLY HILLS. 310-659-2929. www.tourdujour.net

977. Visit the infamous strip bar **Sam's Hofbrau**.

This strip bar, known as the Brau, is not for the faint of heart. It's as diverse as you can get in terms of clientele and the women who work here. The women stripping are as real as they get—all shapes and races—and that attracts some serious drinkers. Popular around lunchtime and late afternoon, it's worth a peek while the sun is out, as the neighborhood turns questionable once it gets dark. The Brau was featured in Quentin Tarantino's *Jackie Brown* in the scene where Robert De Niro picks up Samuel L. Jackson after the money drop.

1751 EAST OLYMPIC BOULEVARD, LOS ANGELES. 213-623-3989. www.samshofbrau.com

978. See where Courtney Love got her start dancing at **Jumbo's Clown Room**.

A strip club in a strip mall might seem odd, but Jumbo's is in a class of its own. For more than four decades, this intimate venue has allowed its girls to call themselves dancers without the ridicule. More burlesque than strip—there's no nudity—this small club, a favorite with locals, is also a great late-night bar to grab a drink. A perfect place to hang out with friends, Jumbo's still gives you a show… but with a bit more pizzazz.

5153 HOLLYWOOD BOULEVARD, HOLLYWOOD. 323-666-1187. www.jumbos.com

979. Enjoy billionaire David Geffen's view without spending a dime at **Carbon Beach East**.

With its beautiful, soft, clean sand surrounded by white lattice gates and million-dollar homes, this stretch of coast is really the high life. A 42-foot section of premium coastline was once closed off due to a legal battle between billionaire David Geffen and California beach officials, but the entire beach is now open. (Geffen was granted a 10-foot privacy buffer to protect him from metal-detecting beachcombers.)

DRIVE NORTH ON THE PACIFIC COAST HIGHWAY; look for parking as soon as you pass Carbon Canyon Road.

980. Catch a glimpse of the elusive **Grunion run**.

Along Southern California's sandy beaches, from March through September, one of the most remarkable life cycles in the sea is completed: the California grunion comes ashore to spawn. These small, silvery fish are found only along the coast of Southern California and northern Baja and have a unique spawning behavior. They make excursions out of the water only on particular nights to lay their eggs in wet sand on the beach. The grunions spawn with such regularity that their arrival can be predicted a year in advance. Shortly after high tide, sections of these beaches some-

times are covered with thousands of grunion depositing their eggs in the sand. Runs occur on most Southern California beaches, with ends of the beaches being the best spots. If you want to watch, plan on staying late and avoid using flashlights, as light may scare the fish and deter them from coming out of the water. If you'd like to take any home, you'll need to get a valid state fishing license—just because they're already out of the water doesn't mean it's not considered fishing.
www.dfg.ca.gov/marine/grunion.asp

---

981. Celebrate the holidays by going to see **Christmas lights**.

Los Angeles might not have the weather to call itself a winter wonderland, but it has the spirit and the electric bills to show for it. Every year, several neighborhoods go all out for the Christmas season by decorating their homes and streets with thousands upon thousands of glowing little lights. The **Balian House**, in Altadena, is the 1922 mansion owned by ice-cream magnate George Balian. During the holidays, the mansion and the three and a half acres of land surrounding it are decorated and set aglow with tens of thousands of lights and decorative scenes, a tradition that started back in 1955. Sometimes you can find Christmas carolers, and previous years have had photo ops with Santa as well as hot chocolate and coffee for free. For more than eighty years, the majestic deodars (cedar trees) on the Mile of Christmas Trees have been strung with 10,000 lights. Known as **Christmas Tree Lane** in Altadena (near the Balian House), it is not only the oldest large-scale Christmas lighting spectacle in the U.S., but it's also the oldest large-scale outdoor Christmas display in the world. Visit their annual tree lighting ceremony, which starts early and is held at the Altadena Library. In **Upper Hastings Ranch**, north of the 210 Freeway on Michillinda Avenue, you'll find a variety of beautiful homes decorated in holiday splendor. People drive from all over Los Angeles to take in the sights at **Candy Cane Lane** in Woodland Hills. With so many glowing lights and amazing nativity and Christmas scenes, you can't help but wonder how they haven't blown a fuse. Must be Santa working some of his Christmas magic.
Balian House: 1960 MENDOCINO LANE, ALTADENA. Altadena Christmas Tree Lane: www.christmastreelane.net
Candy Cane Lane: www.woodlandhillscc.net/candy_cane_lane.html

---

982. Grab a beer and hang out with some turtles at **Brennan's Pub**.

This is the only place in Los Angeles where you can get cheap eats, good drinks...and watch turtle racing. At this local Marina del Rey institution, they have been racing turtles every Thursday night since 1976 and are still going strong. Bring your own turtle or rent one there, but just make sure you don't point at the turtles, or you will be fined.
4089 LINCOLN BOULEVARD, MARINA DEL REY. 310-821-6622. www.brennanspub-la.com

983. See a space shuttle up close at the **California Science Center**.

The end of the historic Space Shuttle program of NASA marked the retirement of all its orbiters. And after its final flight in May 2011, the Endeavour, the fifth and final spaceworthy shuttle, which was originally constructed to replace the Challenger, soon needed a new home. It found one at the CSC's Samuel Oschin Space Shuttle Endeavour Display Pavilion. Transported to Los Angeles in September 2012 on the back of NASA's Boeing 747 Shuttle Carrier Aircraft (an airplane big enough to carry a space shuttle!) and driven through Los Angeles's wide streets before arriving at the CSC, one look at this amazing piece of machinery and you can't help but countdown and patiently wait for it to blast off. Once the Samuel Oschin Air and Space Center is complete, it will become Endeavour's permanent home.

700 STATE DRIVE, LOS ANGELES. 213-744-7400. www.californiasciencecenter.org

984. Get your fill of some real Mexican wrestling at **Lucha VaVoom**.

Wrestling has always been a sport known more for its entertainment value than its athleticism, and at Lucha VaVoom, they pump up the entertainment to the max. Burlesque dancers, drag queens, midgets, and ring girls are thrown together with luchadors (Mexican wrestlers) for a crazy night of theatrics you won't forget. Buy your ringside seats now.

1038 SOUTH HILL STREET, LOS ANGELES. 213-746-4674. luchavavoom.com

985. Go behind the scenes at **NASA's Jet Propulsion Lab**.

If you're a space buff, there's no way you'd miss out on a chance to visit the Jet Propulsion Lab. During their annual open house, NASA opens its doors to the public and gives you a peek at what really goes on behind closed doors. You'll visit the microtechnology lab, where they make everything that is teeny-tiny and microscopic, as well as the headquarters of deep-space operations, also known as Mission Control, where the Mars Rover Program is managed and all the satellites in space are monitored. You might even get a chance to touch a real satellite and go home with a few free goodies too. Space exploration will never seem the same after this visit.

4800 OAK GROVE DRIVE, PASADENA. 818-354-4321. www.jpl.nasa.gov

986. Go head-to-head against former *Jeopardy!* champions at **O'Brien's Irish Pub & Restaurant**.

Every Wednesday night at 8 p.m., in the back room, former *Jeopardy!* and *College Jeopardy!* champions come to flex their mental muscles and pummel the brain cells of those who dare challenge them at pub-quiz night. The *Jeopardy!* addition to quiz night at O'Brien's, the longest running pub quiz in Los Angeles, began in 2006 when Alan Bailey, playwright and director and previous *Jeopardy!* winner came by one day with two former champions, and, not surprisingly, won. Soon word spread and former champions in desperate need of cerebral challenges and adrenaline fixes began showing up to compete. Although you won't walk away with $3.5 million like Brad Rutter did as the show's all-time money winner, they do get $75 toward their bar tab, and the coveted title of Pub Quiz Champion.

2941 MAIN STREET IN SANTA MONICA. 310-396-4725. www.obriendsonmain.com

---

987. Hang out with jockeys at **The Derby**.

A day at the races just wouldn't be the same without a meal at The Derby. Located near the Santa Anita Race Track, the restaurant opened in 1922 and still remains the epitome of that classic bygone era with its decor and succulent cuts of steak—and a glass of bourbon to wash it all down. Once owned by George Woolf (aka The Iceman), the jockey who rode Seabiscuit in some of the most famous races in track history, this place is practically a shrine with memorabilia and photos all over.

233 EAST HUNTINGTON DRIVE, ARCADIA. 626-447-2430. www.thederbyarcadia.com

---

988. You'll find peace and happiness at the **Hotel Shangri-La**.

With its $30 million redesign, this historic Santa Monica hotel, built in 1939, is the embodiment of glamour. Thanks to a beautiful art deco design and fantastic beachfront location, it has only gotten better with age. Nearly all the rooms have an ocean view, the posh rooftop bar offers great sunrise and sunset views, and a walk along the shore is just steps away.

1301 OCEAN AVENUE, SANTA MONICA. 310-394-2791. www.shangrila-hotel.com

---

989. Spend a day eating olives at **Graber Olive House**.

Food lovers on the lookout for a day trip that doesn't involve the standard wine fest should head to Ontario to visit Graber. At this Spanish hacienda estate turned olive-processing plant, hungry visitors can come and stuff themselves with samples of Graber olives and take a free tour. Open since 1894, it offers a great selection of olives for sale, some only available on-site. Come during late fall or early winter, when the processing plant is in full swing. Just remember to avoid the pits.

315 EAST 4TH STREET, ONTARIO. 800-996-5483. www.graberolives.com

990. Unleash your inner M.J. at the **Thriller Zombies Festival** at Venice Beach.

July is a great month to spend some time at the beach, especially Venice. Here, you can learn how to do Michael Jackson's "Thriller" moves with members of Thrill the World Los Angeles (TTWLA), a dance group comprising everyday people performs to help various charities. The Thriller March, Performance, and Workshop is part of the Venice Beach Walk for Homeless Summer Festival and a lot of fun. Don't wait for darkness to fall across the land, dance your way into the sunshine; it's for a good cause.
www.thrilltheworld.com

991. Climb Los Angeles's version of Rome's Spanish Steps at the **Bunker Hill Steps**.

At the base of Bunker Hill (Hope Street) and Library Tower (5th Street), you'll find 103 steps designed by Lawrence Halprin, complete with a raised faux-rock-bottom water channel that starts at the top of the stairs in a fountain, which features a female form by sculptor Robert Graham, and ends at the bottom as a waterfall. Shaded partially by trees, the steps are a great place to stop, sit, and relax. If 103 steps are too many, don't worry; there are escalators and an elevator right next to the stairs for accessibility and ease.
5TH STREET, DOWNTOWN LOS ANGELES.

992. Get a little extra protection for your pets at the **Annual Blessing of the Animals**.

In April, people come from all over L.A. to Olvera Street on Holy Saturday to get their animals blessed. This tradition, which was started in the 4th century by Antonio de Abad, the patron saint of the animal kingdom, has continued in L.A. for more than eighty years. Here, Archbishop José H. Gómez does what he can to bless your animals with a little peace and protection.
El Pueblo de la Historic Monument: 125 PASEO DE LA PLAZA. 213-485-3730. Occurs annually on the Saturday before Easter Sunday.

993. Do **the Simpsons' list** of things to do in L.A.

On an episode of the Simpsons, Bart hands Homer a list of "must-see places" around Los Angeles to keep Homer away from the Academy Awards. Although the list contains places that are referenced mostly during radio breaks and traffic reports, here's Bart's list of must-see attractions. **Watts Towers** (p. 36) is a National Historic Landmark and a definite must-see. **Cerritos Auto Square** is a long street of auto dealerships in the city of Cerritos. **Keyes on Van Nuys** is an auto dealership in Van Nuys with a very catchy radio jingle that is reminiscent of the Beach Boys. The **El Toro Y** is the freeway interchange in Orange County where the 5 and 405 freeways meet, creating a Y shape. The **California Incline** is a natural incline where Santa Monica meets the ocean. **The Valley** is well, the San Fernando Valley. **LAX Long-Term Parking Lot C** is what locals try their best to avoid by getting dropped off at the airport. The **Beverly Connection** is a mini mall located across the street from the far more impressive Beverly Center. **405/10 Freeway Exchange** is where you change from the 405 to the 10 or vice versa in West Los Angeles. **Chatsworth** is a city in the Valley. **Long Beach City College** is the city college in Long Beach. A pretty creative list considering it's from Bart.

Cerritos Auto Square: www.cerritosautosquare.com; Keyes on Van Nuys: www.keyescars.com; The Beverly Connection: www.thebeverlyconnection.com; Long Beach City College: www.lbcc.edu

---

994. Dead stars are just as popular as living ones at **Westwood Memorial Park.**

Where else can you visit Dorothy Stratten (murdered), Natalie Wood (drowned), Minnie Riperton (breast cancer), and the ultimate blonde bombshell, Marilyn Monroe (drug overdose), all in the same place? At Westwood Memorial Park, you can drop in and show your respects to its share of actresses who met their untimely deaths—no diamonds necessary to visit, but flowers wouldn't hurt.

1218 GLENDON AVENUE, LOS ANGELES. 310-474-1579. www.dignitymemorial.com

---

995. Follow the **Rainbow Brick Road.**

In West Hollywood, also known as Boystown, on the corner of San Vicente and Santa Monica Boulevards, you'll find yourself walking over a rainbow. The colorful crosswalk, which was originally set up to celebrate Pride Month in June 2012, became so popular that it's now permanent. So next time you're in Boystown, follow this kaleidoscopic path and discover where the LGBT community calls home. There's no place like it.

CORNER OF SAN VICENTE AND SANTA MONICA BOULEVARDS IN WEST HOLLYWOOD.

996. Enjoy some fine art while looking for Michael Jackson's final resting place at **Forest Lawn Museum**.

A cemetery isn't usually the first place one thinks of to view fine art, which makes the extensive offerings at Forest Lawn Memorial Park in Glendale all the more alluring. More than a million visitors a year come to view its permanent gallery, which displays paintings, sculptures, and artifacts from all over the world, including two of the world's largest paintings, the *Resurrection* and the *Crucifixion*, the latter reportedly the world's largest framed canvas-mounted painting at 195 feet wide and 45 feet high. You'll also find a life-size stained-glass window re-creation of Leonardo da Vinci's *The Last Supper* and a reproduction of Michelangelo's *Moses*, which was originally created for the tomb of Pope Julius II in Rome. The King of Pop was laid to rest in the Grand Mausoleum, where he joined Hollywood legends Clark Gable, Jean Harlow, and W. C. Fields. Don't ask staff to point you towards the gloved one's hidden monument, as they are tight-lipped about celebrities' grave sites. Instead, pick up a self-guided map and search the extensive grounds.

1712 SOUTH GLENDALE AVENUE, GLENDALE. 800-204-3131. www.forestlawn.com

→ ***NOTE:*** Although it may seem a macabre place for a picnic, if you really want to dine with the stars, take a seat on the flat granite surface overlooking downtown L.A. I guarantee they'll be waiting.

997. Go see a gunfight in **Pioneertown**.

Located 56 miles east of San Bernardino—it's a bit of a drive—you'll find the village of Pioneertown, which started as a live-in Old West movie set built in the 1940s. Visit April through October to catch a mock gunfight that is staged along the village's Mane Street in honor of the history of this little made-up Old West village.

998. Take a day trip to **Calico Ghost Town**.

Donated to the county of San Bernardino in 1966 by Walter Knott of Knott's Berry Farm, Calico is one of the few remaining original mining towns of the West. Once full of silver miners, the streets are now filled with tourists, who come to explore some of the untouched buildings that remain from the silver-mining days. Come and ride the Calico and Odessa Railroad, take a tour through the Maggie Mine, or go panning for silver. On a clear day, you can look out onto the Mojave Desert and see for miles.

36600 GHOST TOWN ROAD, YERMO. 800-86-CALICO.
cms.sbcounty.gov/parks/Parks/CalicoGhostTown.aspx

999. See the famed **L.A. Derby Dolls** in action.

When going to see the Derby Dolls compete, you'll be met by a rambunctious crowd of fans cheering loudly as they witness some serious throw-down action taking place around the track. These ladies mean business, and they take no prisoners. Expect some spills and lots of thrills when you go see the Dolls—you'll be glad you did. Get there early to grab a good view of the action as the girls push, grab, and shove their way past the competition. Buy your tickets in advance, as they sell out, and if you'd like the VIP treatment, pay a little extra for a reserved bleacher seat.
www.derbydolls.com/la/

1000. Take a tour of a **studio back lot**.

The cities we've seen in films and shows, like Gotham (*Batman*), Sunnydale (*Buffy the Vampire Slayer*), and Hill Valley (*Back to the Future*) may be real in our minds, but on paper, they're just sprawling faux towns staged to reflect any occasion and adjusted to fit any scene. The back lots of Warner Bros., Universal, and Paramount have their own police stations, banks, and fire departments, and although they lack real-life occupants, they possess a sense of the real world we always imagined they would. Partake in one of their tours to get a look behind the scenes, and glimpse real Hollywood history. VIP packages are available to provide the ultimate experience.
Paramount Studios: $45 per person. 323-956-5000. www.paramountstudios.com. Warner Bros.: vipstudiotour.warnerbros.com. Universal Studios: Tour is included with park admission. universalstudioshollywood.com.

→ ***FACT:*** *When visiting Warner Bros., keep an eye out for the cats. They are descendants of James Cagney's cats and have the run of the back lot, where Clint Eastwood finances their care.*

1001. "Los Angeles According to Larry David" seems like an appropriate finale. You can't help but remember certain locations simply because of all the awkwardness that the man with two first names injects into them. He leaves his mark all over the city like an uncomfortable seal of approval. And even though I used to take Tae Kwon Do classes with onetime *Curb Your Enthusiasm* guest star Krazee-Eyez Killa at Sky Martial Arts, I realized not even I can do L.A. like Larry does. Here's a list of places that true *Curb Your Enthusiasm* enthusiasts can relate to, and which, after enough time in the City of Angels, you might relate to as well.

First, head to the **Brighton Coffee Shop** to have your very own whisper lunch. It's a must if you don't want everyone to hear your conversation. Then, if you need a place to meet a blind date, go to **Canter's**; if the date is bad, at least the food will be good. Grab some sushi at **En Sushi**, but try to avoid insulting your Japanese waiter. Head to **Starbucks** and order "one of the vanilla bullshit things," and see what you get back. Grab a delicious dinner at **Wilshire Restaurant**, where they serve great organic dishes—just don't ruin the meal by offering your date an ultimatum. Find a reason to celebrate at the **W Hotel in Westwood**. Grab a sandwich at **Sainsbury Market** deli, but don't lend anyone there any money. Enjoy a meal with family and friends at **Saddle Peak Lodge**. Take a big leap and discover the joys of Italian food just like Larry did at **Matteo's**. Or go find yourself a potential date at the **18th Street Coffee House**...but leave your cell phone in the car—it's not allowed on the premises.

Brighton Coffee Shop: 9600 Brighton Way, Beverly Hills. 310-276 7732. www.brightoncoffeeshop.com; Canter's: 419 North Fairfax Avenue, Los Angeles. 323-651-2030. www.cantersdeli.com; En Sushi: 11651 Santa Monica Boulevard, Los Angeles. 310-477-1551; 1972 Hillhurst Avenue, Los Angeles. 323-664-1891. www.ensushi.com; Starbucks: locations across the city. www.starbucks.com; Wilshire Restaurant: 2454 Wilshire Boulevard, Santa Monica. 310-586-1707. www.wilshirerestaurant.com; W Hotel in Westwood: 930 Hilgard Avenue, Los Angeles. 310-208-8765. www.wlosangeles.com; Sainsbury Market: 12200 Wilshire Boulevard, Los Angeles. 310-826-4388. Saddle Peak Lodge: 419 Cold Canyon Road, Calabasas. 818-222-3888. www.saddlepeaklodge.com; Matteo's: 2321 Westwood Boulevard, Los Angeles. 310-475-4521.www.matteosla.com; 18th Street Coffee House: 1725 Broadway, Santa Monica. 310-264-0662.

Expert Contributor: Flea

Flea is a musician, a bassist with the Red Hot Chili Peppers, and the co-founder of the Silverlake Conservatory of Music.

FLEA'S FAVORITE THINGS ABOUT L.A., IN NO PARTICULAR ORDER

Eating at ***Inaka*** macrobiotic restaurant on La Brea. I have been eating there for thirty years. The same guy has cooked my meal every time. I feel safe there and the vegetable *yosenabe* is the greatest thing I have ever had in the winter months, not mention the deep fried *mochi*.
131 SOUTH LA BREA AVENUE IN LOS ANGELES. 323-936-9353.

I consider myself a burrito connoisseur, and for the best fish tacos and burritos one must go to ***Lily's in Malibu*** just off the Pacific Coast Highway and Heathercliff. In Malibu, all the restaurants are expensive and fancy and of varying degrees of pretentiousness, but Lily's just costs a few bucks, Lily is the nicest lady in the world, and the food destroys. I've had all the best in East L.A., and Lily's rules.
29211 HEATHERCLIFF ROAD IN MALIBU. 310-457-3745.

Going to see high school basketball games. L.A. always has some of the best high school players in the country and going to games is inexpensive and fun as hell. I have seen kids take off from the free-throw line and dunk in front of a hundred people, in a great competitive game. The kid ends up in the NBA in a few years and you get to see it. *Amazing*.

Playing basketball at the Hollywood Y. There's the intense game in one gym, and the old farts/mellow guys game in the other gym. So fun. I love the Y, because it is for everybody, all flavors of humans: the sweet old folks getting their exercise on, the little kids on the Junior Lakers, all cultures, all ages, economic brackets—it is a great place for the community and what L.A. at its best is all about.
1553 SCHRADER BOULEVARD IN LOS ANGELES. 323-467-4161. www.ymcala.org

Running in all the ***fire trails*** in the hills around Griffith Park and the observatory on up to Mount Hollywood. Whoohooo! After a rain, L.A. is the greatest place on earth.

The Roosevelt Municipal Golf Course. It is an inexpensive course, it's beautiful, and you can get in and out in a couple of hours. You can meet some beautiful Korean peo-

ple there, too, and my friend Pete was once paired there with the great Teddy Edwards. The view of the Griffith Observatory from the 9th hole is an L.A. classic.
2650 NORTH VERMONT AVENUE IN LOS ANGELES. 323-665-2011. www.golf.lacity.org

Going to the ocean, mountains, and the desert. A few years ago I surfed Malibu in the morning, drove to Joshua Tree for a night in the desert, and woke the following morning and went snowboarding in the mountains—all a hop, a skip, and a jump from L.A. Hooray!

The best sushi in Los Angeles is to be had at **Shibucho** in the Rampart District. It is a small place, run by a man named Shige, who is the best sushi chef I have ever encountered. It is expensive though.
3114 BEVERLY BOULEVARD IN WESTLAKE. 213-387-8498. www.shibucho.com

Shane's Inspiration children's playground in Griffith Park. It is an awesome spot full of fun, and wheelchair accessible for handicapped kids. It makes me happy.
4800 CRYSTAL SPRINGS ROAD IN LOS FELIZ. 323-913-4688. www.shanesinspiration.org

Expert Contributor: Paul Mittleman

Paul Mittleman is a tastemaker and the former creative director of Stussy.

THE BEST THINGS TO DO IN L.A.

Bristol Farms. Just the best place to waste time and money and prepare for cooking and entertaining.
VARIOUS LOCATIONS ACROSS THE CITY. www.bristolfarms.com

Barney Greengrass. Lox, bagels, and strawberry lemonade, all with a great view.
9570 WILSHIRE BOULEVARD IN BEVERLY HILLS. 310-777-5877. www.barneygreengrass.com

Baja Fresh. It only makes sense how good it is after you move away.
VARIOUS LOCATIONS ACROSS THE CITY. www.bajafresh.com

Clear blue skies. Clouds are about as common as rain in LA.

Chateau Marmont. It's just darn comfortable.
8221 SUNSET BOULEVARD IN WEST HOLLYWOOD. 323-656-1010. www.chateaumarmont.com

Laurel Canyon Dog Park. A big 'ol dog park where all the dogs just have fun, and the people are pretty nice, too.
8260 MULHOLLAND DRIVE IN HOLLYWOOD. 818-769-4415. www.laparks.org

And the obvious: ***Nobu Matsuhisa*** is still very, very good.
129 NORTH LA CIENEGA BOULEVARD IN BEVERLY HILLS. 310-659-9639. www.nobumatsuhisa.com

In the end, before I lived in L.A., I did not visit it much, and when I did I made the rounds based on what other people thought I would like. As a resident, I really enjoyed getting to know the city. So the best thing you can do in Los Angeles is get a grill, invite some friends over, and fire it up for some BBQ. It's a great place to visit, but a sublime place just to ***stay home***.

INDEX

A

B

C

D

E

F

G

H

I

J

K

L

M

N

O

P

R

S

T

U

V

W

X

Y

Z

CALENDAR OF EVENTS

January

Kingdom Day Parade, page 94
People's Choice Awards, page 84
Rose Bowl/Tournament of Roses, pages 33, 93

February

Queen Mary Scottish Festival, page 102
Writers Guild Awards, page 84

March

Antelope Valley California Poppy Preserve, page 94
Festival of the Kites and Yo-yo Competition, page 92
L.A. County Irish Fair, page 102
Los Angeles Marathon, page 33
Planned Parenthood Food Fare, page 186

April/May

Anatolian Cultures & Food Festival, page 102
Blessing of the Animals, page 353
Cinco de Mayo, Fiesta Broadway, page 101
City of Lights, City of Angels French Film Festival, page 162
Coachella, page 234
Doo Dah Parade, page 92
Grilled Cheese Invitational, page 122
L.A. Comedy Shorts Film Festival, page 162
L.A. Times Festival of Books, page 95
Los Angeles Asian Pacific Film Festival, page 162
Original Renaissance Pleasure Faire, page 103
Topanga Banjo-Fiddle Contest and Folk Festival, page 152
UCLA JazzReggae Festival, page 233

June

Annual Brand X Santa Monica Drive-In, page 86
Artwalk Culver City, page 99
Dance Camera West Film Festival Los Angeles, page 162
Los Angeles Film Festival, page 161
Make Music Pasadena, page 312
National park free admission, first day of summer, page 236
Playboy Jazz Festival, page 153
Santa Barbara Wine Festival, page 189
Smiths/Morrissey Convention, page 95

July

AAA "tipsy tow" July 4th weekend, page 332
Bastille Day, Elysian Park, page 101
Colorado Street Bridge celebration, page 99
Gilroy Garlic Festival, page 188
International Laureates Music Festival, page 151
OUTFEST, page 162
Rubber Ducky Race, Venice, page 104
Swiss Fair, page 187
Thriller Zombies Festival, Venice Beach, page 353

August

Docuweek, page 161
Feel Good Film Festival, page 163
L.A. County Fair, page 92
Venice Canals Hot Summer Row-Ins Movie Nights, page 86

September

Cinecon Classic Film Festival, page 163
Feast of San Gennaro, page 103
Long Beach Crawfish Festival, page 188
Los Angeles International Short Film Festival, page 163
Nisei Week Japanese Festival, page 188
Redondo Beach Lobster Festival, page 187
The Taste, page 186

October

Canalloween, Venice, page 104
Eagle Rock Music Festival, page 234
Fright Fest, Six Flags, page 97
Ghostly Equestrian Ball, page 98
Halloween at Monster Massive, page 98
Halloween Horror Nights at Universal Studios, page 96
Haunted Hollywood Tour, page 98
Hollywood Film Festival, page 163
Knott's Scary Farm Halloween Haunt and Camp Spooky, page 97
Los Angeles Haunted Hayride, page 98
Los Angeles International Children's Film Festival, page 163
Mitsuwa Umaimono Gourmet Fair, page 187
Old Town Haunt, Pasadena, page 97
The Other Venice Film Festival (OVFF), page 163
Queen Mary Dark Harbor Halloween Terror Fest, page 97
Shelly's Dance and Costume Wear, page 299
West Hollywood Halloween Carnaval, page 96

November

AFI Fest, American Film Institute, page 161
Annual Artivist Film Festival, page 163
Annual Tree Lighting Ceremony, page 115
Great Los Angeles Walk, page 338
L.A. Scavenger Hunts, page 114
Mariachi Festival, page 235

December

Christmas lights, page 350
Holiday Boat Parade, Venice, pages 63, 104
IDA Documentary Awards Gala, page 84
Pershing Square ice skating, page 37

Sundays

drum circle, Leimert Park, page 28

Tuesdays

Downtown Art Walk, page 99

Wednesdays

Westfield Century City Mall, movies on the terrace, page 227

Fridays

Cooper Building Sample Sales, page 299
First Fridays, National History Museum, page 141
Grand Performances, Lunchbox Series, page 233
Jazz at LACMA, page 232
Pershing Square Friday Night Flicks, page 228

Spring

cherry blossoms, Descano Gardens, page 105
Payne Foundation wildflower hotline (March to May), page 95

Summer

Blessing of the Cars, page 331
Cinespia, page 38
Griffith Park Free Shakespeare Festival, page 233
Indie West Fest, page 234
Long Beach International Sea Festival, page 95
Outdoor Cinema Food Fest, page 227
Pershing Square Summer Series, page 235
Shakespeare by the Sea, page 234
Skirball Cultural Center's Sunset Concerts, page 235
Sunday Summer Cinema at W Hotel, Westwood, page 228

Monthly

Sierra Club moonlight hikes, page 22 various times, check website
Cochon 555's Traveling Pork and Wine Bacchanalia, page 188
Grand Performances at California Plaza, page 232
Grunion Run, March–September, page 349
L.A. Street Food Fest, page 100
Los Angeles Food and Wine Festival, page 186
Star Dedication Ceremony, page 84
Thai New Year Songkran Festival (Lunar New Year), page 100

ABOUT THE AUTHOR

JOY YOON is a writer, editor, and creative consultant. Fueled by her passion for the culinary arts, she began her career as a food researcher for *Vogue*. Since then her musings have appeared in *The New Order*, where she served as editor in chief, as well as in *Paper*, *DazedDigital*, *i-D online*, *Art Wednesday*, *Huffington Post*, *Hypebeast*, *Complex*, and *Riposte*. She has also contributed to documentaries such as *Brasilintime* with Mochilla; produced photo shoots for publications such as *Wax Poetics*; and worked on the Timeless Music Series. Joy enjoys traveling and eating, and especially traveling to eat. She grew up in Los Angeles and currently resides in Europe.